# The Complete
# Family Scrapbook

# AS THE WORLD TURNS

## The Complete Family Scrapbook

BY
JULIE
POLL

General Publishing Group  Los Angeles

Publisher: W. Quay Hays
Editor: Peter Hoffman
Art Director: Susan Anson
Assistant Art Director: Kurt Wahlner
Projects Manager: Trudihope Schlomowitz
Production Director: Nadeen Torio
Color and Pre-Press Manager: Bill Castillo
Color and Pre-Press Director: Gaston Moraga
Production Artist: Phillis Stacy
Production Assistants: Tom Archibeque, Alan Peak
Copy Editors: Dianne Woo, George Garrigues

© 1996 by Procter & Gamble Productions

As The World Turns is a registered trademark of Procter & Gamble Productions
licensed to General Publishing Group, Inc.

All rights reserved under International and Pan-American Copyright Conventions.
This book, or any parts thereof, may not be reproduced in any fashion whatsoever
without the prior written permission of the publisher:

For information:
General Publishing Group, Inc.
2701 Ocean Park Boulevard
Santa Monica, CA  90405


**Library of Congress Cataloging-in-Publication Data**


Poll, Julie
    As the world turns : the complete family scrapbook / Julie Poll.
        p.    cm.
    Includes index.
    ISBN 1-881649-91-1
    1. As the world turns (Television program)    I. Title.
        PN1992.77.A8P66  1996
            791.45'72--dc20                                                              96-1901
                                                                                          CIP


Printed in the USA by RR Donnelley & Sons Company
10 9 8 7 6 5 4 3 2 1


General Publishing Group
*Los Angeles*

# Table of Contents

INTRODUCTION: Helen Wagner . . . . . . . . . . . . . . . . . . . . . . . . . . . . . 7

ACKNOWLEDGMENTS . . . . . . . . . . . . . . . . . . . . . . . . . . . . . . . . . . . . 9

THE COMPLETE STORIES . . . . . . . . . . . . . . . . . . . . . . . . . . . . . . . . 11

   The Back Story . . . . . . . . . . . . . . . . . . . . . . . . . . . . . . . . . 12

   1956–1960 . . . . . . . . . . . . . . . . . . . . . . . . . . . . . . . . . . . . 15

   1961–1965 . . . . . . . . . . . . . . . . . . . . . . . . . . . . . . . . . . . . 21

   1966–1970 . . . . . . . . . . . . . . . . . . . . . . . . . . . . . . . . . . . . 32

   1971–1975 . . . . . . . . . . . . . . . . . . . . . . . . . . . . . . . . . . . . 40

   1976–1980 . . . . . . . . . . . . . . . . . . . . . . . . . . . . . . . . . . . . 49

   1981–1985 . . . . . . . . . . . . . . . . . . . . . . . . . . . . . . . . . . . . 79

   1986–1990 . . . . . . . . . . . . . . . . . . . . . . . . . . . . . . . . . . . . 120

   1991–1995 . . . . . . . . . . . . . . . . . . . . . . . . . . . . . . . . . . . . 178

THE FAMILY ALBUMS

   The Hugheses . . . . . . . . . . . . . . . . . . . . . . . . . . . . . . . . . . 202

   The Lowells and the Stewarts . . . . . . . . . . . . . . . . . . . . . . . . 205

   The Snyders . . . . . . . . . . . . . . . . . . . . . . . . . . . . . . . . . . . 208

   The Walshes . . . . . . . . . . . . . . . . . . . . . . . . . . . . . . . . . . . 211

LOVE STORIES

   Young Love, First Love . . . . . . . . . . . . . . . . . . . . . . . . . . . . 215

   Lisa In Love . . . . . . . . . . . . . . . . . . . . . . . . . . . . . . . . . . . 225

   Married Love . . . . . . . . . . . . . . . . . . . . . . . . . . . . . . . . . . 230

   Nancy and Chris: Until Death Do Us Part . . . . . . . . . . . . . . . 236

Notable Nuptials . . . . . . . . . . . . . . . . . . . . . . . . . . . . . . . . **237**

DASTARDLY DEEDS

John Dixon . . . . . . . . . . . . . . . . . . . . . . . . . . . . . . . . . . **243**

James Stenbeck . . . . . . . . . . . . . . . . . . . . . . . . . . . . . . . **244**

HAPPY ANNIVERSARY!

Cast Pictures Through the Years. . . . . . . . . . . . . . . . . . . . . **246**

The "As The World Turns" Family on the Uniqueness of the Show. . . . . . **250**

A Fond Goodbye . . . . . . . . . . . . . . . . . . . . . . . . . . . . . . **252**

BEHIND THE SCENES: THEN AND NOW . . . . . . . . . . . . . . . . . . . **253**

A Day in the Life of "As The World Turns" . . . . . . . . . . . . . . . . **254**

The People Behind "As The World Turns" . . . . . . . . . . . . . . . . **273**

STAR TURNS ON "WORLD TURNS" . . . . . . . . . . . . . . . . . . . . . . **278**

FANFARE . . . . . . . . . . . . . . . . . . . . . . . . . . . . . . . . . . . . . **284**

AND THE WINNER IS . . . . . . . . . . . . . . . . . . . . . . . . . . . . . . **289**

CAST LIST. . . . . . . . . . . . . . . . . . . . . . . . . . . . . . . . . . . . . **295**

SHOW CREDITS. . . . . . . . . . . . . . . . . . . . . . . . . . . . . . . . . . **303**

# *Introduction*

Once upon a time—magic words—Irna Phillips, writer, and Ted Corday, producer, put together the first half-hour entertainment on daytime television. They believed the best entertainment was storytelling, and the best of that was continuing stories about *people*. So, with the words, "Good morning, dear," spoken by Nancy Hughes to her husband Chris, on April 2, 1956, the world started turning for the Hugheses and the Lowells and four generations of their family and friends. I, Helen Wagner, the actress who spoke those words, have lived through the triumphs and tragedies of Nancy's loved ones for four decades, and viewers could always take comfort in the fact that no matter how many times the world turned, Nancy would always have a batch of cookies in the oven, a pot of coffee on the stove and free advice for everyone. The show has never forgotten its core characters, and Nancy is still, today, the beloved, no-nonsense matriarch of the Hughes clan.

As Nancy, I often had to be cooking, and, necessarily, I steadily improved my technique of peeling potatoes, stringing beans, dredging a roast or stirring a cake, while discussing life and times with whoever was there to drink coffee and talk. My most treasured friend besides "Chris"—Don MacLaughlin—was the prop man on the crew who supplied all the beautiful meat and clean vegetables that Nancy then prepared and popped into the proper pan. It came as a major revelation to me, Helen, that parties at my home seemed to become more and more work. After all, I didn't have property-man Herb Gordon or Eli Bergman there to buy and clean all that food; Helen had to buy it, haul it home, clean it, *then* step up and prepare it and plop it into the proper pan. It clearly brought home to me again the importance of every single person working on the show—technical crew, stage crew, office staff, makeup, hair and wardrobe people, as well as writers and actors!

I have thoroughly enjoyed living two lives. I haven't always approved of Nancy—she's very possessive—but then I guess I haven't always approved of Helen. And while the show is "The Thing," the side effects of fan reaction are very rewarding. In the cynical years of post-World Wars I and II and

the atom bomb, literary critics stretched themselves to outdo each other in deriding "soap operas" to the point at which Irna Phillips refused to give interviews or talk to the press. But she went right on telling her "people stories." Those of us playing in them enjoyed many of the jokes—Carol Burnett's, on our same network, were some of the funniest. We enjoyed them, shrugged and said with Mike Todd, "As long as they spell my name right."

We actors were always recognized and approached in the supermarkets, the automat or just walking down the street: "Please sign this paper for my mother (aunt, grandmother, cousin), who always watches your show." No one ever admitted to watching the show themselves. One would see recognition in a face at Sardi's restaurant or at the opera, but it was only a glance, no admission to being a fan. But for the most part, the audience scorned the critics' scorn and "As The World

Turns" skyrocketed to the top in popularity. A men's club in Indiana wrote asking for some way of knowing what happened on the show while they were traveling in Europe; they couldn't bear to miss the story. This was long before videotape.

Technology was advancing with lightning rapidity. We moved from heavy black-and-white two-man cameras with flip-and-focus lenses, to color cameras with zoom lenses and automatic focus. When we stretched to an hour, we became the last live show on the air to go to tape. At first there was one fan magazine, which gave Chris and Nancy best actor awards. We didn't find out about the honor, though, until weeks later when a fan sent us a clipping from the magazine. However, the industry was beginning to learn from fan interest that "soaps" were important. Fan magazines grew more numerous, and we were finally deemed worthy of public recognition and awards. Even the sophisticated public gave in and admitted they loved us. In the last decade, when I'd be doing my volunteer work at the Metropolitan Museum of Art, a day didn't pass that someone—young or old—came up and asked in an awed tone, "Aren't you Nancy Hughes?" One of the nicest things about that is the number of young people who speak. Most often, they say, "I've been watching you since I was five" or "I grew up with you, watching with my mother," then "grandmother," and now "*great* grandmother!" Forty years covers a lot of growing up.

I have loved being Nancy, and it has been a great privilege, particularly because I could leave the studio and change into Helen. I have been asked if I "take Nancy home"—my husband firmly answers, "No." He is a theatrical producer, so he knows more about the business than I do. That's one of the reasons my real pleasure is in being Mrs. Robert Willey.

I've been asked, too, about the changing face of America, its mores. How have we influenced it, if at all? I think we mirror people's lives, and as a reflection, we've changed as the reality changes. I deplore the raging sex and violence, but watching it and studying the resulting tragedy and broken lives—which are the stories we tell—hopefully seeing this will persuade the audience that irresponsibility and unbridled passion are wrong. Not because someone says they're wrong, but because *they do not work*. Irna said she never wrote villains or heroes, but people who behaved badly in some

situations and well in others; that it is impossible to legislate people to be good, so *show* the lovely results of doing right, or the horror of doing wrong, judged by that marvelous definition of ethics: "obedience to the unenforceable." I think the essence of the show can be expressed in this early dialogue:

CAROL: *"I've wondered sometimes if you don't get bored living in Oakdale. New York or on the Coast must be so much more exciting."*

SANDY: *"Excitement is one thing. Real feelings are another."*

As you leaf through this album, I hope you will enjoy the rich history of "As The World Turns" as the inhabitants of Oakdale continue to live out the philosophy of the show's creator, Irna Phillips:

*"As the world turns, we know the bleakness of winter, the promise of spring, the fullness of summer and the harvest of autumn. Follow those seasons with the Hughes, Lowell and Stewart families as they brave the elements in Oakdale, U.S.A."*

—Helen Wagner

# Acknowledgments

The challenge of writing a celebration spanning 40 years—four generations of a daily television drama—is both exhilarating and daunting. The task of amassing over 10,000 episodes of chronology, interviewing well over 100 people and sifting through hundreds of photographs and tens of thousands of facts that have kept "As The World Turns" turning, has required the invaluable help of scores of people who gave of their time and their energy with unfailing generosity and insight. First to Procter & Gamble Productions and the Columbia Broadcasting System without which there would be no "World Turns"—and no anniversary book! In particular my appreciation to Kenneth L. Fitts, Procter & Gamble executive in charge of production, for his invaluable guidance and historical perspective, and to Lucy Johnson, Senior VP of Daytime Programming and Special Projects at CBS, for her insight and support. To Janet Storm, director of program publicity, who opened up and dusted off the vaults of information that fill these pages, and to Rose Southworth, Susan Savage and Maria Ferrari of DMB&B and their staffs. To John Behrens at the CBS Archives, John Filo and Maggie DeVora at the CBS Photo Department and Robert Christie of the National Academy of Television Arts and Sciences for their time and their help.

None of this could have been written without the help of my friend and colleague, Fritz Brekeller, who served as research assistant, go-between, hand holder and master magician in collecting, analyzing and putting together enormous amounts of material with clarity and sensitivity, and researcher/writer John Kelly Genovese, whose vast knowledge of soap operas, and "As The World Turns" in particular, was an invaluable asset in putting together the early chronology of the show, and who contributed much insight and many hours to other areas of the book as well. To Laura Bernstein who cheerfully compiled reams of essential material. To Ed Rider, head of the P&G archives in Cincinnati and Jennifer Dakroub, who researched the early years from their files, and to my daughter Amy Poll, who gave up her holidays and weekends to help Mom through this project. My thanks to the people who helped put together the chronology: Zak Berman, Chip Capelli, Patrik Bass, Alex Verner Roalsvig, Alex Goerrs, Rodney Christopher, Tamara Pica, Kristen Powers and David W. White. To my transcriber Donna Hornak, whose fingers flew over hundreds of hours of interview tape and who was always a study of grace under pressure. To photographers E.J. Carr, for his magical "Behind the Scenes" shoot and more, and Victoria Arlak, for her invaluable contribution to this book.

My special appreciation to John Valente, executive producer, who opened the doors to the studio and lent his enthusiastic support to this project. I am also very grateful to Vince Liebhart, casting director of "ATWT," for his invaluable suggestions and "leads" to cast members past and present and to associate producer, Leela Pitenis, for always being ready, able and willing to share her vast knowledge of the show, and to Brett Hellman, David Ryan and Jef-Spenser Hira for their help. And to all the actors, producers, writers, directors and crew of "As The World Turns" past and present, who allowed me to invade their valuable time and their brains for hours on end. An additional personal thanks to Helen Wagner for the introduction and her husband Bob Willey for contributions above and beyond the call of duty. Much of the material for the chronology came from *Soap Opera Digest* and *Soap Opera Weekly*. My thanks to the editors-in-chief of both magazines, and most especially to Jason Bonderoff, Christine Champagne, Jody Reines and Caelie Haines, who walked me through it. Much thanks to General Publishing Group, Inc. To Quay Hays, who launched this project, and to my editor, Peter Hoffman, who stood beside me and held on tight during the long summer and winter months, and to Susan Anson, Kurt Wahlner, Sharon Hays and Joni Solomon. A very special thank you to Marnie Winston-McCauley, author and former writing colleague, whose insights and expertise inform every area of this book. And on a personal note…my other daughter Melissa Poll, who was always "there."

And finally, to the late Douglas Marland—mentor, friend, legend. It is to Doug that I owe my enduring love and respect for this medium and most particularly for "As The World Turns."

## CHAPTER ONE

The
Complete
Stories

# *The Back Story*

As the world turns, we know the bleakness of winter, the promise of spring, the fullness of summer and the harvest of autumn—the cycle of life is complete. What is true of the world, nature, is also true of man—he too has his cycle.

—Irna Phillips, creator of "As The World Turns"

---

It began on a farm in Gilman, Ohio, run by a simple man named Will ("Pa") Hughes. Pa didn't question or analyze life the way his children or grandchildren would do in later, more complicated times. To him, "Things are the way they are, and they ain't the way they ain't." Boys were raised to become responsible men who worked hard to provide for their families, and girls grew up to be homemakers. Alcohol was not a part of his family's routine—the Hugheses drank coffee for much of the day, and warm milk on the nights they couldn't sleep. That was pretty much how life was for Pa.

Pa and Ma Hughes raised three children—son Christopher and fraternal twins Edith and John. Christopher ("Chris"), by far the most responsible of the three, was sent to college with the understanding that he would in turn help educate his younger brother and sister, should they decide to seek a higher education. Instead, Chris met and married a schoolteacher from

Unconventional and freewheeling, Edie was Penny's favorite aunt until her affair with Jim Lowell alienated her from the family.

Penny heard her mother's anguished cry "Why did it have to be Susan?" over and over in her head, and she believed that Nancy loved her dead sister Susan more than her.

The Hughes family (Penny, Nancy, Don and Chris) gather in the living room after dinner.

Kansas named Nancy, and they moved to Oakdale, Illinois, where Chris went to law school and Nancy took a teaching job to support them.

Chris always felt some measure of guilt that he had started his own family at the expense of John's and Edith's education, but he needn't have blamed himself, because, as it turned out, neither sibling was the least bit interested in college. After Ma Hughes died, Edith followed Nancy and Chris to the Oakdale area. Determined to remain single, she lived a citified existence and kept her private life under wraps. She felt alienated by the close-knit, traditional nature of the Hughes family, yet she loved her father and brothers—although she found Nancy overly opinionated and hopelessly provin-

cial. Well-meaning though Nancy was, there was some measure of truth to Edith's assessment. Meanwhile, Pa struggled to maintain the family farm, while his hotheaded son John began drifting away, getting into frequent trouble with the law.

In time, Chris became a successful corporate lawyer with the firm Lowell, Barnes & Lowell. Nancy left teaching to devote her full time to their four children, Donald, Susan, Penny and Bob. Donald was aggressive and upwardly mobile, constantly hounding his parents to join the local country club, which they steadfastly refused to do. Sadly, the elder Hughes daughter, Susan, was killed in a freak accident while diving into a swimming pool during a violent thunderstorm. The tragedy brought out the rebellious side of Penny, an out-spoken but vulnerable teenager who found a kindred spirit in her Aunt Edith.

Naturally, Nancy was displeased when Penny bonded with her "Aunt Edie," whose single, freewheeling lifestyle did not sit well with Nancy. Chris usually defended Edith and indulged Penny, acting as a buffer between his strict wife and spirited teenage daughter and sister. Bob, the youngest of the Hugheses, was a cheerful, uncomplicated boy with a quick sense of humor.

The law firm Chris joined was the most respected in Oakdale, thanks to the sterling

Judge Lowell approved of his son Jim's marriage to the wealthy and eligible Claire English.

Teenage confidants and best friends Penny Hughes and Ellen Lowell spent many an afternoon baring their souls when they should have been doing their homework.

reputation of its commanding senior partner, Judge James T. Lowell. Although his style was smooth and diplomatic, one sensed that "the Judge" was very much the "iron hand in the velvet glove." His tastes, like his home, were classic and timeless. After dinner, he always enjoyed a glass of fine sherry and a few chapters of a favorite mystery novel. Judge Lowell loved his vivacious wife, Alice, very much, but his first love was his law firm—and he instilled that love in his impressionable and only child, James Jr. The Judge always addressed his son as "James," for he saw the boy as little more than a reflection of himself. But to the rest of Oakdale, James Lowell Jr. was just plain "Jim."

From the time he was a small boy, Jim Lowell lived according to his father's agenda. He became a lawyer and married Claire English, the product of a family even

wealthier than the Lowells. Jim had grown up with Claire and her brother, Steve, and it seemed perfectly natural to the Lowell and English families that Jim and Claire would get together—it was the thing to do.

Jim and Claire had a daughter, Ellen, and they tried to keep their loveless marriage together for her sake. But shortly after the death of his beloved mother, Jim left his family and began a secret affair with his junior partner's sister, Edith Hughes, a woman who, coincidentally, looked much like his mother. Claire wanted Jim to return home, more out of her blueblood sense of propriety than any semblance of true, mutual love. Ellen adored her father and was bewildered by his departure. She lived for the "father-daughter" days when he would take her downtown to the Sweet Shop for ice cream. Fortunately for Ellen, she found comfort in the loving, well-adjusted home of the Hughes family. Penny and Ellen were classmates and best friends, and they spent many an afternoon discussing their boyfriends and family problems.

# 1956-1960

The years 1956 to 1960 marked a painful coming of age for Ellen Lowell and her friends Donald, Penny and Bob Hughes. As they dealt with the pitfalls and disappointments of young love, they were also deeply affected by the actions and reactions of their elders. While Nancy and Chris prepared to celebrate their 19th wedding anniversary, Ellen struggled to come to terms with her own broken home.

The secret romance between Jim Lowell and Edith Hughes gradually became common knowledge to practically everyone in Oakdale. Nancy and Judge Lowell were particularly incensed by the scandalous affair, and badgered a reluctant Chris into asking Edith to leave town. When he did, Edith refused. Not only did she resent the intrusion of her brother and sister-in-law, but she was also more determined than ever to marry the man she loved!

Claire was equally adamant about holding on to Jim. He reluctantly returned home for Ellen's sake, but he refused to sleep with his wife. When Claire accidentally overdosed on sleeping pills, Jim was convinced that she had purposely downed the narcotics to keep him at her side. He also resented her for making herself so helpless that Ellen had to "mother" her own mother, taking on adult burdens inappropriate for a teenager. Claire rallied long enough to force a steely confrontation with Edith, but soon afterward, she lapsed into a clinical depression that also appeared to be suicidal. She was also inexplicably hostile when Ellen began to increasingly enjoy the company of her childhood buddy, Donald Hughes.

One person who was especially concerned for Claire's well-being was Dr. Doug Cassen, the Lowell family physician. Doug was in his early 40s and had never been married to anything but medicine. However, he found himself increasingly drawn to Claire and was offended by Jim's cavalier treatment of his wife. At Doug's urging, Claire sought the help of a prominent psychiatrist, who helped her realize the folly of her marriage to Jim. She also was able to understand why she disapproved of the closeness between Ellen and Donald—it reminded her of her early, deceptively comfortable courtship with Jim. Claire simply wanted Ellen to find love away from their tight family circle.

Completely revitalized after her therapy, Claire told

Donald Hughes dated his sister's best friend Ellen, but Ellen's mother Claire didn't approve.

Jim that she would grant him a divorce. When she related this to Judge Lowell, he reacted negatively, as he and Claire had always been very close, and he suffered a minor heart scare. The Judge later apologized to both Jim and Edith for his interference and even began calling his son "Jim" instead of James. Ellen was devastated by her parents' breakup and bitterly rejected her once beloved father. Before going on a fishing trip to Florida with Judge Lowell, Jim sadly told his daughter, "Some place, at some other time…we'll meet again." Jim and Judge Lowell shared a wonderful father-and-son vacation in Florida, and they came to truly know each other for the first time. Yet their newfound bond was tragically short-lived. While taking out a small fishing boat, Jim fell, hit his head and died.

Edith was so devastated at losing the man she hoped to marry, that she became more reclusive than ever. To make matters worse, once Penny learned the truth about her aunt and Jim, she rejected Edith as well. Nancy could not contain her relief!

Nancy was also very vocal in her disapproval when

When "Pa" came to live with Nancy and Chris, he and his daughter-in-law had their differences, but they soon formed a warm, loving relationship.

Nancy didn't approve of Donald's relationship with Janice Turner, and neither did Janice's mother. Janice married Carl Whipple, who later died. Then she and Donald were married briefly before her own untimely death.

Chris helped his misfit brother, John, get back on his feet. John had taken over the family farm in Gilman and married a woman named Marion. Chris was hurt by Nancy's condescending attitude toward his sister and brother but was nonetheless delighted when she allowed Pa to move in with them. Of course, Nancy and Pa had their differences—he frequently washed his hands in Nancy's kitchen sink and often told her to stop meddling in her family's affairs. She couldn't help but adore the plain-spoken old man, who kept an immaculate garden and made wonderful keepsakes for the family in his basement workshop. The two would talk for hours over coffee.

Jeff Baker joins his sweetheart Penny in the Hughes kitchen for coffee from Nancy's seemingly bottomless pot.

Nancy's coffee pot seemed bottomless indeed, for she and Pa certainly had plenty to talk about! Nancy was not happy when Donald, now a law student, became engaged to Janice Turner, a hard-working but uneducated waitress who was a few years older than Donald. Janice's widowed mother, Thelma, was also uncomfortable with the match, because she and Janice felt out of place in the Hugheses' world. Chris assured both mothers that Donald and Janice's relationship would run its course without their interference—and he was right. First, Donald became a popular fraternity man in college, enjoying a social life apart from Janice. Then he refused to marry her until he could support her on a lawyer's pay. Finally, when Janice turned to Edith as a friend and confidante, Donald disapproved because his aunt had helped wreck the Lowells' marriage. As much as he loved Janice, Donald also harbored feelings for Ellen and idolized her wealthy grandfather, Judge Lowell. Janice ultimately realized that she and Donald were destined to travel in different circles. She broke off their engagement and eventually married Carl Whipple, a gentlemanly bachelor some fifteen years older than she, who offered Janice the emotional and financial security she craved.

By contrast, Penny's new love interest had plenty of money but lacked security within himself. Jeff Baker was notorious in high school for his fast cars and glib attitude. Jeff was the only child of Dick and Grace Baker, Claire's country club acquaintances. The Bakers spoiled Jeff with material things and taught him how to conduct himself comfortably with adults, but they had little time

Nancy was thrilled when Penny dated Tom Pope. Everyone seemed to love him, except for Donald, who was jealous when Bobby turned to Tom instead of him for "brotherly advice."

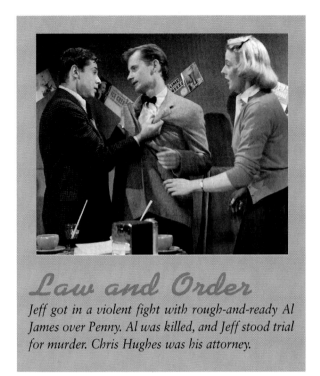

## *Law and Order*

*Jeff got in a violent fight with rough-and-ready Al James over Penny. Al was killed, and Jeff stood trial for murder. Chris Hughes was his attorney.*

to give him the nurturing and attention he needed. Nancy disapproved of Penny and Jeff's relationship, and Penny responded by accusing her mother of loving her deceased sister, Susan, more than her. Chris and Pa did not condone Penny's attitude toward her mother. However, they came around when Nancy's righteousness and intractability became unbearable for the entire family. Partly out of rebellion, Penny eloped with Jeff one night across the state line, but quickly had second thoughts and came home. At Nancy's insistence, the marriage was annulled.

Jeff's world fell apart when Penny rejected him. And he had to deal with an abrasive classmate named Al James, a scruffy blue-collar type who called Penny a tramp and taunted Jeff about being a spoiled rich kid. One day, Jeff and Al got into a violent scuffle that resulted in Al's death. Jeff was arrested for murder, and Chris agreed to defend him. It displeased Nancy to see Chris and Jeff forming a bond, and she was relieved when Penny began to date Tom Pope, a handsome new attorney with the Lowell firm, who was assisting Chris on Jeff's case. Jeff was cleared of the murder, but by this time Penny, still unsure of his emotional stability, had become engaged to Tom.

Most of the Hughes family adored Tom Pope—except for the social-climbing Donald, who was livid when he realized that Nancy and Chris loved this outsider like a son. Even Bob looked to him for brotherly advice. So

After Jim Lowell's accidental death, Claire married confirmed bachelor Doug Cassen. He was a more attentive husband than Jim had been and an excellent father to Ellen.

when Donald graduated from law school, he refused a job offer from Judge Lowell and went to work for Mitchell Dru, a rumpled, no-nonsense lawyer whom Chris highly respected. Mitch gave Donald invaluable training, but Donald was so brash and overly eager that he ended up arguing with a judge at his first trial! When Chris urged his son to listen to Mitch's coaching, Donald only grew more resentful and distant toward his father. Donald left Mitch's firm to join the District Attorney's office, but he took so many liberties with cases that the D.A. moved to disbar him. Fortunately, Chris was able to discredit a witness who helped put Donald in hot water, and they were once again able to enjoy a close father-son relationship. Donald eventually joined

Ellen fell deeply in love with married doctor Tim Cole, and they conceived a child, whom she named Jimmy to honor her late father. Adoption and bitter custody battles followed.

the Lowell firm, but greatly resented reporting to Tom Pope. He would take this attitude with several other attorney colleagues over the course of his working life.

Donald was becoming friendly with other young, single professionals in town, including Greg Williams, an ambitious reporter who nosed around the courthouse for stories, and Julie Spencer, a bright young attorney who was Mitchell Dru's ward and Tom Pope's good friend from law school. Judge Lowell never stopped hoping that Donald would someday marry his granddaughter, Ellen. Like Nancy, the Judge found it difficult to accept the fact that he could not always dictate his children's love lives. He was equally protective of his daughter-in-law, Claire, and disapproved when she married Doug Cassen so soon after Jim's death. It didn't take the Judge long, though, to realize that Doug was a far better husband to Claire than his own son had been, and was also a strong, responsible father figure to Ellen.

It was through Doug that Ellen met Dr. Tim Cole, a charming young research doctor new to Memorial Hospital. The two fell deeply in love, and at first he concealed the fact that he had a wife, Louise, back in Cincinnati. Ellen and Tim soon conceived a child. Wanting to keep the pregnancy a secret from everyone except the immediate family, Ellen left town and stayed in nearby Columbus with Doug's old friends, Dr. Joe Meadows and his wife, Anne. Ellen gave birth to a baby boy whom she named James (or "Jimmy"), after her father. While she was away, Tim's wife, Louise, arrived in Oakdale and was involved in an automobile accident, which temporarily bound her to a wheelchair. When she recovered, Louise initiated an alienation-of-affection suit against Tim. Confused and disillusioned, Ellen temporarily entrusted baby Jimmy to the care of Dr. and Mrs. Meadows. Ellen thought she could forget Tim when Jeff Baker fixed her up with dashing Burt Stanton. In time, Ellen and Burt became engaged, but when she admitted she had a child, he dropped her. With no recourse in sight, Ellen sadly contacted an adoption agency and gave up her little boy. Tragically, she was unaware that at the same time, realizing her marriage to Tim had long been over, Louise finally agreed to a divorce.

Tim had a close friend and confidant in Dr. George Frey, a cheerful research physician. Like Doug, George was in his early forties before he even thought about marriage, but he decided to take the plunge when he met and fell in love with Edith Hughes, who was working for Doug at the hospital. Edith was now on good terms not only with her own family, but also with Claire—

Tim Cole's embittered wife Louise sued for alienation of affection and was represented by the kindly Mitchell Dru. Dru later represented Ellen in her custody fight for Jimmy.

Doug Cassen's good friend, Dr. George Frey, seen here at the hospital with Ellen and Doug, married the flamboyant Edie Hughes after she recovered from the loss of her lover, Jim Lowell.

although she had not yet shaken the memory of Jim Lowell. With the help of family and friends, Edith was finally able to put Jim in the past and marry George. The newlyweds left Oakdale and moved to Seattle. Edith was replaced at the hospital by Laura March, a very attractive but aloof young woman. Because she was feeling old and neglected in her marriage, Claire became irrationally jealous of Doug's growing attentions to Laura. Actually, Doug was preoccupied, not by another woman, but by a new research project that consumed him several nights a week. Judge Lowell urged him to

When Tom Pope overheard Jeff declare his love for Penny, he nobly released her from their engagement.

spend more time at home with his wife.

Jeff's work also obsessed him when he joined the Baker family business after graduating from high school. He was intent on proving himself to his parents and to Penny, whom he hoped to remarry. One night, when he declared his love for her, Tom Pope overheard and nobly released Penny from their engagement. This time Penny and Jeff were married in a beautiful church

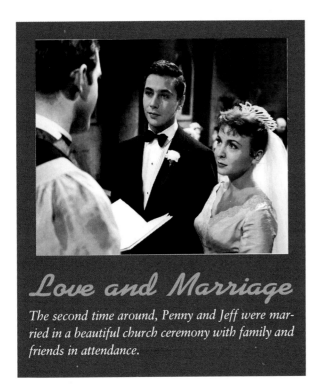

## Love and Marriage

The second time around, Penny and Jeff were married in a beautiful church ceremony with family and friends in attendance.

ceremony, surrounded by family and friends. Shortly afterward, Jeff revealed a previously hidden talent—he was a wonderful piano player! His mother, Grace, secretly hoped Jeff would make a living at music, because he was becoming an embarrassment at work. He fired Phil Banner, a valued employee, and concocted grandiose schemes that had no basis in reality. Dick had confidence in his son, but Grace didn't, and she worked with her right-hand man, Ed Richardson, to ensure that Jeff would be a mere figurehead in the business. Grace confided in Penny, hoping that she would convince Jeff to resign, but Penny refused to interfere. Jeff learned the truth when he overheard a conversation between Phil and Ed, and he began to drink. When he angrily confronted Grace, she also accused Penny of knowing all about the sham. Humiliated, Jeff left Oakdale and became a barfly in another town under the assumed name of Jack Bailey. In his absence, Penny discovered she was pregnant, but she later lost the baby during a severe bout with pneumonia. Holding herself partially responsible for Jeff's problems, Grace became ill and withdrawn.

Penny's brother, Bob, was having a different sort of romantic problem. Bob was in college and planning to go to medical school, but much of his time was taken up by his new girlfriend, pretty Lisa Miller. A feisty girl from Rockford, Illinois, Lisa used every trick at her disposal to get Bob to marry her, because, she reasoned, an aspiring doctor had a world of prosperity ahead of him.

Bob succumbed to her charms and the two were secretly married in Gary, Indiana. Lisa's doting parents, Alma and Henry Miller, were delighted that their darling Lisa was marrying into such a comfortable family. But Bob refused to ask his parents for financial assistance, and, knowing they would disapprove, he insisted to Lisa that the marriage be kept a secret. When she discovered she was pregnant, however, Lisa told Nancy the truth. Chris was so furious about this hasty marriage that he initially refused to help Bob and Lisa. It was Pa who persuaded Chris to let Bob and Lisa live in their home. To make ends meet, Bob worked part-time at a phar-

Lisa Miller was Bob Hughes' first love, and he fell hard. Lisa used every trick in the book to get Bob to pop the question, and the two were secretly married.

macy. He was delighted to win an internship at Memorial under Doug Cassen, who would become his mentor in medicine.

At this time, Doug made the painful discovery that Tim had leukemia, and he put aside his animosity toward the young doctor and told Ellen the truth. Determined to share Tim's final days, Ellen ignored Judge Lowell's disapproval and married the man who had fathered her child. Within weeks, Tim was dead. He was replaced at Memorial by Dr. David Stewart, a brilliant and ambitious research physician who had relocated from New York City with his wife, Betty, and two little boys, Dan and Paul. Doug was impressed with David and took him into his practice. Everyone who came in contact with the Stewarts socially could not help noticing that Betty's world revolved around her children—particularly her older boy, Dan.

# *1961-1965*

These were crucial years in the lives of the Hughes and Lowell families. The Hugheses suffered through a sudden death, celebrated a birth and had mixed emotions regarding three marriages. Their lives seemed almost routine, however, compared to the turmoil surrounding the tormented young Ellen Cole.

Still haunted by the memory of surrendering her infant son Jimmy for adoption, Ellen searched for any conceivable means of being with children. She was grateful, therefore, for the opportunity to baby-sit Dan and Paul, the toddler sons of Dr. David Stewart and his wife, Betty. One day, Ellen saw a picture of Dan taken when he was six months old. She was shocked. The boy was the spitting image of Jimmy! Ellen had always assumed that both Dan and Paul were the Stewarts' biological children, when in reality Betty had taken great pains to conceal the fact that Dan was adopted. The resemblance was too striking for Ellen not to follow through on her hunch. She engaged Dan in a game in which she was able to get his fingerprints and footprints, and then secretly flew to Columbus to compare them with Jimmy's.

Her suspicions proved heartbreakingly correct. Dan Stewart *was* the son she had given away. "I've found my son," she cried—and she was determined to get him back. Confronting David and Betty with her findings, Ellen informed them that she intended to get her son

Early ad copy for "career girl" Penny, trying hard to cope with the disappearance of her beloved husband, Jeff.

back, and she initiated a bitter custody suit against the couple. Betty was so upset that she almost left town with the boys, but David persuaded her to remain in Oakdale so they could openly fight Ellen.

The discovery had a staggering effect on everyone. Ellen's family was bitterly split—Claire sympathized with her daughter, while Ellen's stepfather Doug Cassen was supportive of the Stewarts. Matters worsened when Ellen named Doug and Judge Lowell as instrumental in forcing her to give up her child. Doug angrily denounced Ellen as a selfish liar, and Judge Lowell suffered a heart attack after having to testify against his own granddaughter. Even the Hughes family was affected. Donald still had feelings for Ellen and briefly left the Lowell firm to represent her. Although Ellen was not in love with Don, his actions so touched her that she promised to marry him if and when she won back her child.

But Ellen was not to get her wish. As was the custom at this time, the presiding judge ruled that the Stewarts could keep their adopted son. After getting over the initial shock, Ellen apologized to her family, as well as to David and Betty Stewart. Betty and the boys returned to New York City for a while to be near her parents, while David maintained his practice at Memorial alongside Doug. Ellen was also relieved when Donald let her off the hook regarding her promise to marry, since he knew she really didn't love him. At the same time, a recovering

When Ellen discovered that her son, now called Dan, had been adopted by David Stewart and his wife, she vowed that nothing would stop her from getting him back!

Using the name "Jack Bailey," Jeff found his niche as a piano player and songwriter in another town.

writer. Under the name Jack Bailey, he landed a gig at Joe's Place, a cozy bar in another town. His true identity was revealed, though, when his new friend, Meg Blaine, saw a newspaper article about him and learned that "Jack" was Jeff. When she confronted him with this information, Jeff swore her to secrecy. Soon after, Jeff came down with a serious case of pericarditis. As he recovered in a hospital, Meg stole into Oakdale with the intention of telling Grace and Dick Baker that their son was ill. While there, she overheard Penny and Greg make plans for a date.

Infused with new hope for a future with Jeff, Meg went home and encouraged him to write a hit song, which he did. He then wrote another, and for the first time in his life, he felt secure within himself. He even stopped drinking. Although he acknowledged Meg for her role in his rehabilitation, Jeff gently made it clear that she was just a friend—he would always be in love with Penny. Jeff returned to Oakdale just as Penny was about to proceed with the divorce. He pleaded with her to give him another chance, and after considerable soul-searching, Penny took him back. Jeff was obviously more mature and self-assured—even Nancy had to ad-

Judge Lowell reluctantly heeded Doug's advice to become a figurehead at the firm and promote Chris Hughes to senior partner.

While Ellen was going through her own public and private hell, her friend Penny also had plenty to worry about. She had no idea where Jeff was or what kind of romantic future she had to look forward to. She did find fulfillment as a feature writer for the local newspaper, but a life as a career woman did not sit well with her opinionated, conservative mother. To Chris's annoyance, Nancy tried to pressure Penny into divorcing Jeff. Nancy was, of course, delighted when both attorney Tom Pope and newspaper editor Greg Williams pursued her daughter. But Penny never stopped loving Jeff or hoping that he would find his true calling in life and come home to her.

Jeff, in fact, *had* found his niche as a piano player and song-

Nancy was far from pleased when Donald's former love, Janice, a widow with two daughters, returned to Oakdale. The youngest, Debbie, was a wild one, who managed to turn the Hughes household upside down, until Nancy put a stop to her late nights and constant lies.

Lisa knew just what to do to get what she wanted from her in-laws and her husband. But Nancy liked her spirit, and the two became lifelong friends.

mit that the brash but floundering young man had finally grown up.

Nancy was not easy to please when it came to her children's choices of mates. Her reaction was, at best, guarded when Donald's former love, Janice Whipple, returned to Oakdale a widow with two grown daughters, Alice and Debbie. Alice was a responsible girl who developed a harmless crush on Don, while Debbie was an insolent sexpot who smoked and ran with a fast crowd. When Janice attended Alice's college graduation in Arizona, Debbie stayed with the Hugheses and turned the staid household upside down with her incessant lying and late nights out. Exasperated, Nancy told Don he'd be making the biggest mistake of his life if he married Janice and inherited her family problems. Debbie overheard this confrontation and was quick to tell Janice that Nancy disliked her. But Don, intent on living his life as he saw fit, married Janice anyway.

Ironically, Nancy was considerably more tolerant of the daughter-in-law who *really* turned the Hughes family upside down. Self-involved, calculating Lisa Miller Hughes played the members of her new husband's family like pawns in a chess game. With great aplomb, Lisa manipulated Nancy into lecturing Bob about spending too much time at the hospital. Then she had the nerve to spread false rumors that Pa disliked her, and prevailed upon the old man to move back to the family farm with his other son, John! Fortunately for everyone, Pa remained in the family fold.

But this was mere child's play for the conniving shrew from Rockford. When Lisa was expecting a child, she immediately cried "difficult pregnancy" so Nancy would do her household chores for her. After Bob and Lisa's son, Thomas Christopher Hughes, was born, Lisa blithely made social plans with friends and breezed home on a whim to see her adoring parents, Alma and Henry Miller, leaving Nancy to shoulder most of the day-to-day duties of caring for the infant. Her immaturity notwithstanding, Lisa characteristically justified her actions by saying she was bored being a doctor's wife. At this point, Bob was putting in long hours at Memorial as an intern and, later, as a resident. He was too busy forging a career and spending every spare moment with his new son to be concerned about his wife's activities.

His older mentor, Doug Cassen, was finding himself in a similar situation. Doug had always been a caring, responsible stepfather to Ellen, but it was painfully obvious to Claire that he'd married too late in life. A relentless workaholic, he was always quick to leave a country club function to attend to the next emergency. So when Doug was promoted to Chief of Staff at Memorial, Claire could not share in his elation because she knew he would be absent from home more than ever. Taking matters into her own hands, Claire decided to enjoy a social life away from her husband, and soon found herself attracted to Bill Abbott, an acquaintance of her brother's in California who had come to Oakdale to set up an office for his construction company. One night Claire and Bill were kissing in a parked car when they were sideswiped by another car. Claire sustained injuries that resulted in a lingering back problem, but that was the least of her worries. Doug was hurt and embarrassed and demanded that Claire stop seeing Bill. Although she refused, Bill proved he had a conscience, and he told Claire he had no intention of destroying her

After Tim Cole's tragic death, Ellen was briefly engaged to Jim Norman, but Jim balked when she told him she was the mother of an illegitimate child, and the liaison didn't last.

marriage. He then left Oakdale and a lonely Claire to pine for him.

Claire became so withdrawn that she seemed not to care about or even notice Ellen's problems. Still bearing the emotional scars of losing her son a second time, Ellen went through a procession of loveless relationships, including a brief engagement to a humble young lawyer named Jim Norman, whom she delayed telling about her illegitimate child. She had all but lost hope of being reunited with little Dan when Betty Stewart suddenly died in New York City of double pneumonia. Ellen was unaware, of course, that Betty had extracted a deathbed promise from David that Dan would never know Ellen was his biological mother. Deluding herself that she could reclaim her now motherless child, Ellen told her painful story to Jim and almost persuaded him to marry her and become Dan's adoptive father. Concerned about Ellen's welfare, Doug convinced Jim that this would be a disastrous move. Jim then left town.

In contrast to Ellen's unstable life, Penny's marriage to Jeff seemed to be on solid ground. With his parents'

blessing, and thanks to his new love song appropriately entitled "Penny," Jeff swore off the family business and established himself in the recording industry. Although Penny and Jeff were disappointed when she couldn't conceive a child due to endometriosis, they were on the verge of adopting when tragedy struck. On their way to a family celebration, their car skidded on a wet road and hit a concrete support. Jeff was killed instantly, and Penny fell into a long coma. When she regained consciousness, she suffered from amnesia.

It was while she was in this state that Penny would make a revealing discovery—her sister-in-law Lisa was having an affair with a slick shoe tycoon named Bruce Elliot. Dazzled by Bruce's worldly ways, Lisa soon fell for him and lost interest in Bob. She confided in a few people about her attraction to Bruce, namely her incredulous mother, Alma, and Linda Elliot, Bruce's sister and Lisa's closest friend. Just as Lisa felt confident about having a future with Bruce, she became pregnant again—by Bob. But to her selfish relief, she miscarried, prompting her to tell Bob she no longer loved him and wanted a divorce, which Bob granted. Lisa and Bruce went public with their relationship and even planned to marry, but Bruce was becoming increasingly embarrassed by Lisa's lack of sophistication. For all her pretense and bravado, Lisa was just a naive small-town girl, and that wasn't good enough for the wily Bruce. He eventually broke off the relationship.

Lisa was devastated. To save face, she told everyone she had refused to marry Bruce. Soon afterward, she was thrown together with Bob when Tom became seriously ill. After all her complaints and machinations, Lisa realized she loved Bob, but by this point he was fed up and bitterly refused her pleas for a reconciliation. Bob was now romantically involved with Sylvia Hill, a lovely young nurse bravely coping with the rare and fatal disease lupus. He was also enjoying the social life of a young doctor, as he and Sylvia frequently double-dated with his fellow resident Chuck Ryan and nurse Mary Mitchell, Sylvia's close friend. But Chuck soon left Oakdale to accept another position, and Sylvia went home to Michigan so she could have the support of her family during her battle with lupus. Fortunately, Bob had the moral support of the somewhat older David Stewart, who was to be Bob's closest friend and unswerving champion for many years. David was always quick to defend Bob to Doug Cassen, who believed Bob was a potentially fine doctor but criticized him for becoming too emotionally involved with his patients. Indeed, in years to come, he would become affectionately known as "Dr. Bob."

Doug had a sterling reputation as a physician, and when Mitchell Dru's young secretary, Carol Rice, mentioned that her father was having medical problems, Dru recommended Doug without reservation. Rice consulted Doug, who diagnosed him as having a duodenal ulcer. Meanwhile, on the home front, Claire was clinically depressed to the point where Doug, as much as he loved her, feared that divorce might be their only solution. When he voiced this to Claire, she mistakenly assumed he was in love with another woman and overdosed on sleeping pills. Bob was with Doug when they found her and, with Bob's help, Doug saved her life, unaware that during this family emergency, Edna Rice was frantically trying to reach Doug about a complication in her husband's condition. According to the answering service, the doctor was not available. By the time Doug received the message hours later, his patient had died. Shocked and aggrieved, Edna's children persuaded her to sue Doug for malpractice.

As sensitive as the situation was, it could have been resolved more quickly had it not been for the Lowells' obsession with their social standing. Desperate to salvage Claire's reputation and Doug's career at the same time, Judge Lowell concocted a false alibi that he had had a minor heart attack that night and that Doug had saved his life. Doug reluctantly told this story to his friend and lawyer, Chris Hughes, and swore Bob to secrecy about Claire's attempted suicide. As the malpractice trial progressed, Chris became increasingly suspicious of the situation, and Doug and Bob became more and more uncomfortable with their roles in the deception. Claire remained withdrawn for quite a while, then finally summoned the fortitude to walk into the courtroom and tell the truth. Doug was cleared and had his wife and his position at the hospital back.

Unfortunately, Doug again had reason to worry

Alma Miller adored her daughter, but she never hesitated to give her a piece of her mind when she thought Lisa was stepping out of bounds.

about his stepdaughter, Ellen. Since Betty Stewart's death, Ellen had become obsessed with winning back her son to the point where she shamelessly pursued a romantic interest in David, even though David was not interested. While Dan and Paul were being cared for by Betty's parents in New York City, David threw himself into his work. He became an irritable wreck, popping Benzedrine to get him through the day, until one night Ellen found him asleep in his office with a lit cigarette in his hand. Ellen reported this to Doug, who threatened to fire his friend and associate if he didn't take better care of himself. Sobered by Doug's warning, David cleaned up his act and brought Dan and Paul back to Oakdale.

Donald Hughes also made his stepdaughter Debbie clean up *her* act after she was caught illegally driving her boyfriend's car. His solution was to send the insufferable teenager away to a regimented school. He then accused Nancy, in front of the entire family, of ostracizing him and Janice. Chris pleaded with Nancy to make amends so they wouldn't lose their son, but Nancy was blatantly halfhearted in her attempts to smooth matters over. Disgusted by his mother's treatment, Donald left Oakdale with Janice to take a position with a firm in Texas.

Penny, however, remained in the family fold—if not mentally, at least physically. One night, during a fierce thunderstorm, she flashed back to the night of the accident. It was the catalyst for her to heal and mourn her beloved Jeff. Gradually, her memory began to return with the help of David Stewart, who had become a close friend. For a split second, Ellen worried whether her best friend would become her son's next mother figure, but a new man in Penny's life proved Ellen's fears unfounded. On one of her frequent walks to the park, Penny met a cynical, enigmatic young man who was having difficulty finding a direction in life. He was a more mature, mysterious version of Jeff. As Penny began to have intimate conversations with him, his story began to unfold

## Medical Matters

*Lisa wanted Bob back, but Bob wasn't interested. He was romantically involved with Sylvia Hill, a young nurse who was bravely coping with the rare and often fatal disease, lupus.*

and eventually touched many lives in Oakdale. His name was Neil Wade.

Neil held a dead-end job as a night clerk in a seedy hotel, but his demeanor and vocabulary convinced Penny that he was an educated man. He had a widowed mother in New York City, Judith, from whom he'd been estranged for several years, until Penny convinced him to re-establish contact. Judith was thrilled to be reunited with her son. Their separation had not been caused by a conflict between them, but rather by one *within* Neil. Unbeknownst to Penny, Neil was a doctor who had left the profession after he couldn't save the life of his dying father. When Neil returned to New York City, Judith talked her longtime friend Dr. Jerry Stevens into coaxing Neil back into medicine by employing him at his clinic. But Neil's New York career proved short-lived when he felt enormous guilt over a patient's death, even though he'd done all he could do. He returned to Oakdale to pursue a relationship with Penny, keeping his medical background a secret.

Penny's patience with Neil was wearing thin. Once again she was stuck in the position of helping a floundering man find himself. Chris was aware of her frustration and encouraged her to date other men, but Penny

sensed something substantive about Neil. She got the evidence she needed when she and Neil were having dinner at the Hughes home and Pa choked on a piece of meat. With swiftness and authority, Neil performed an emergency tracheotomy on Penny's grandfather. Penny recognized this as the work of a professional, and Neil confirmed her suspicion that he was, indeed, a doctor.

Thanks to her reunion with her son, Judith became totally enmeshed in Neil's life and obsessed with forcing him back into medicine. This irked Jerry Stevens, who was in love with Judith and believed they could have a future together if she would just let her son find his own path in life. But Judith was undaunted, and she admitted to Jerry that she had a potential ally in Oakdale who might help Neil realize his potential. Years ago, she had worked at Memorial and shared a lonely New Year's Eve with an industrious young resident. They had one night of passion and never saw each other again. Finding herself pregnant, Judith married Frank Wade. To this day, her onetime lover had no idea of her whereabouts, or that he had a son.

The man's name was Doug Cassen.

Judith came to Oakdale and confronted Doug with the revelation that Neil was his son. She begged him to help Neil become the great doctor she knew he could be. Doug initially believed he shouldn't interfere, but he soon found himself obsessed with becoming part of his son's life. Having grown up in an orphanage, Doug had always felt the nagging void of childlessness. Ellen had managed to fill that void until he was faced with the knowledge that he had a flesh-and-blood son who shared the profession he so loved. Without revealing that he was Neil's father, Doug allied himself with Penny to mold Neil into a first-rate physician. These actions baffled Doug's colleagues and family. Just as David was ready to secure a position for Bob at Memorial, Doug went over his head and offered it to Neil. Bob was deeply hurt. He had looked up to Doug for a long time. When Claire and David angrily told him they sympathized with Bob, Doug revealed to them that Neil was his son.

Bob found it difficult to rationalize Doug's slight, but he believed it might have been due to his inordinate interest in a patient. Helene Suker was a vivacious drama student whose father, the gentlemanly Dr. Al Suker, was a well-loved doctor at Memorial. One day, Helene was rushed to emergency after a bad fall backstage at the university theater. She sustained spinal injuries that Al discovered would render her paralyzed for life. Al's wife,

Martha, believed Helene should know the truth, but Al didn't want to dampen his daughter's enthusiasm for acting and he kept it a secret. In time, Martha leveled with her daughter, who was devastated by her father's dishonesty. Bob encouraged Helene to forgive her father and made her physical and emotional well-being his project. Doug and Neil felt Helene would benefit more from psychiatric help than from Bob's personal attentions, but Al was so delighted with Helene's uplifted spirits that he took Bob into his practice. Sadly, soon afterward, Helene developed a kidney ailment and died.

Bob's home life at this time was as thankless as his romantic prospects at Memorial. Lisa had so poisoned Tom's mind against him that the boy began beating up on "father" dolls and destroying the gifts Bob gave him. Lisa ran away from Oakdale with Tom, and to add to the insult, Nancy blamed Bob! Much to Bob's dismay, Nancy felt sorry for Lisa and saw some potential in her spitfire of an ex–daughter-in-law. Their mutual fondness for each other would continue for years to come. Nancy believed Bob was too involved with his work to be an attentive father to Tom, and was angry with him for refusing to take Lisa back. Then Bob learned Lisa had stashed Tom in a military school in Los Angeles before disappearing once again for parts unknown. Over the objections of Lisa's parents, Chris and Bob brought Tom back to Oakdale. The Hugheses' hearts went out to this lonely, alienated little boy, even though he treated them like strangers. They knew it wasn't Tommy's fault. He was a child of divorce, and Lisa had convinced him Bob's family had no use for him.

With Ellen's help, Tom soon warmed up to Bob and the other Hugheses. Through her work at a kindergarten and a settlement house, Ellen had become remarkably adept at getting through to children. She was understandably hurt, therefore, when Penny accused her of becoming too attached to Tom to compensate for the loss of Dan. If anyone had a neurotic attachment to children, however, it was David Stewart's new housekeeper, Franny Brennan. From day one, Franny set herself up as a mother figure to Dan and Paul, harboring a twisted yearning to marry David and take over his family. David kept Franny on because the boys liked her, but he constantly had to remind her that she was not the mother of his household.

Penny and Neil, who were David's neighbors in his apartment building, also sensed Franny's agenda. Although still unsure whether she was in love with Neil, Penny married him and was delighted when he became Doug's protégé in cardiology. While Judith was finally able to let go of Neil, marry Jerry and return to New York City, Doug's all-consuming interest in his newfound son left Claire once again feeling neglected. The situation came to a head when Judge Lowell was admitted to Memorial for tests. Neil was taking the Judge's blood pressure when the old man suffered a serious heart attack. Thinking the Judge was dead, Neil pan-

Bob and Lisa's divorce put Tommy in the middle, and Nancy was quick to criticize Bob for spending too much time at the hospital and not enough time with his son.

icked and ran. Judge Lowell recovered, but this was the last straw for Claire. Her beloved father-in-law had almost died, thanks to an incompetent and spineless doctor in whom her husband had placed blind trust. Claire threatened to leave Doug if he ever saw Neil again, and Neil, blaming Penny for pushing him into medicine, initiated divorce proceedings. But Doug couldn't stay away and he lent Neil money to open his own business—the Wade Book Shop.

At this point, Nancy and Chris had Pa, Penny, Bob and Tom living under their roof. Then Judge Lowell brought them a reminder that their family was not quite together. Through fellow attorneys he had learned that Donald's wife, Janice, had died several months earlier in

Neil Wade befriended the mysterious Amanda Holmes and gave her a job at the Wade bookstore. Amanda had been adopted and both she and her natural mother, Sara Fuller, became romantically interested in Donald Hughes.

Texas. Saddened that Donald hadn't shared this loss with his family, Chris sent him a letter, which Donald tore up. He could not bring himself to forgive Nancy for breaking up his youthful romance with Janice, and then rudely dismissing their brief marriage. Don ultimately decided to return to Oakdale in order to put the memories of Janice behind him, but he avoided Nancy and Chris until Judge Lowell strongly urged him to reopen the door with his mother. He did so, albeit as coolly and begrudgingly as Nancy had treated Janice and their union.

Judge Lowell was delighted when Donald began to rekindle his old flame with Ellen. At the same time David was beginning to see Ellen as a mature, sensitive young woman. When Dan became seriously ill with encephalitis, the illness he had had as a child, Ellen kept vigil by his bedside, and in his delirium Dan called her "Mother." David was touched by Ellen's willingness to show concern for Dan without demanding that he be told she was his real mother. But as fate would have it, Franny discovered part of an old letter from Betty referring to Dan as an adoptee.

Back in the Hughes household, Bob received word from the military school that Lisa had arrived looking for Tom. Bob flew out to meet her and found his ex-wife

nearly catatonic. Lisa had been kidnapped by two men in Los Angeles who repeatedly raped her before finally dumping her in San Antonio. She had sought shelter at a farm and made her way back to Los Angeles to reclaim Tom at military school, only to discover he was no longer there. Lisa's mental state was so fragile that she had to be briefly institutionalized in Chicago. Bob offered to remarry her for Tom's sake, but Lisa refused, knowing that he really didn't love her, that his heart belonged to Sylvia Hill, who had since returned to Oakdale with her lupus in remission. By the time Bob and Sylvia became engaged, however, Lisa was cured and back to her old feisty self. She railed at Sylvia for splitting up her family and told her she was still in love with Bob. Just as Lisa hoped, Sylvia felt guilty over the effect of this triangle on Tom and broke off her engagement to Bob. Sylvia later married Al Suker, now divorced from Martha, and they left Oakdale together. As for Lisa, she went to work part-time for Neil at the bookstore, and he became her sounding board and confidant.

The friendship between Lisa and Neil did not sit well with Penny, who had never forgiven Lisa for hurting Bob. Penny at first resisted Neil's divorce action, but then decided not to fight it and allowed Chris to legally represent her. Chris gave Doug fair warning that as

Penny's divorce attorney, he might need to use the fact that Doug pushed Neil into medicine because he was Neil's father. So at long last Doug told Neil the truth, in hopes that he would stop blaming Penny for forcing him to return to medicine. Upset over this revelation, Neil ordered Doug out of his life and reconciled with Penny, but soon afterward, he came down with a mysterious blindness.

To help him in the store, Neil hired a quiet, studious teenage girl who said her name was Jennifer Roberts. Neil gradually helped the girl open up, and she revealed her disillusion upon recently discovering that she had been adopted. When Neil related this to David in a casual conversation, David figured out that Jennifer was really Amanda Holmes, the estranged daughter of his diabetic patient Bill Holmes and his wife, Ann. Amanda sought help from Donald in investigating her natural background, which turned out to have an ironic twist. Ann told Donald in confidence that although she herself was Amanda's adoptive mother, Bill Holmes had in fact fathered Amanda with another woman. That woman turned out to be Sara Fuller, a flirtatious and independent fashion designer who had befriended Nancy when they were both patients at Memorial Hospital. Nancy was there for a hysterectomy, while Sara was admitted for headaches and dizziness. While Ann and Bill contemplated telling Amanda her biological mother's identity, Amanda came face to face with Sara while visiting Nancy's and was immediately impressed by her.

At the same time that Donald was being drawn deeper into Amanda's situation, his love life began to look promising when Ellen finally accepted his marriage proposal. But a short time later, Ellen received another offer of marriage—from David! She contemplated the decision for weeks and accepted David's proposal with the promise that she would not reveal she was Dan's mother. Both Ellen and David were disappointed when Paul was much happier about the impending marriage than Dan. Franny seized the moment to play head games with Dan, asking him how he felt about being someone else's son. She then recalled Ellen's frequent visits to Dan during his illness and deduced that they were, in fact, mother and son. Growing more deranged by the minute, Franny began corresponding with David's mother-in-law, Mary, who had shared Betty's hatred of Ellen. When David discovered Franny and Mary's alliance, he was livid! Claire sensed that a potentially dangerous situation was brewing and urged Ellen to dismiss Franny as soon as she and David were married.

By now, Dan and Paul had grown into teenagers with markedly different personalities. While Paul was cheerful and uncomplicated, Dan was an aspiring doctor who showed signs of cold ambition. That tendency was encouraged by his girlfriend Susan Burke, and together they dreamed of becoming a wealthy husband-and-wife team of research doctors. David worried that Dan and Susan were too close, and he cautioned Dan about becoming romantically entangled at such a young age if he wanted to become a doctor.

On the Hughes family front, Lisa was having problems of her own. She decided to move to Chicago, where she became engaged to John Eldridge, a successful attorney from a wealthy Lake Forest family. She returned to Oakdale, however, following the death of her father, Henry. Nancy and Alma tried to reconcile Bob and Lisa, but Lisa decided to marry John in secret. She sued Bob

Dan Stewart married ambitious research doctor Susan Burke. He soon fell in love, though, with Liz Talbot, who would marry his brother Paul.

for custody of Tom, whom she intended to relocate to Chicago. Lisa was granted custody but waited until Tom reached Chicago to tell him that she'd married John. Tom turned around and called Bob to come and get him, which he did. Lisa followed them to Oakdale and showed up at the Hughes house demanding Tom. Penny denounced her as a rotten wife and mother and ordered her out of the house!

# *Our Private World*

The first and only nighttime spinoff from a daytime soap, "Our Private World" followed feisty and much-loved Lisa Miller Hughes as she tried her luck with life and love in the Windy City. The show, which represented a unique innovation in television programming, premiered on the CBS television network on May 5, 1965, and ran until September 10, 1965.

*On Air:*
> Wednesdays: 9:30–10:00 p.m., EST
> Fridays: 9:00–9:30 p.m., EST

*Format:*
> Dramatic series based on a young divorcee's attempt to make a new life for herself in Chicago, and how tangled emotions and interwoven problems of her newfound friends directly affect her own life.

*Origination:* New York (tape)

*Cast:*

| | |
|---|---|
| Lisa Hughes | Eileen Fulton |
| Helen Eldridge | Geraldine Fitzgerald |
| John Eldridge | Nicolas Coster |
| Eve Eldridge | Julienne Marie |
| Thomas Eldridge | Sam Groom |
| Brad Robinson | Robert Drivas |
| Dr. Tony Larson | David O'Brian |
| Sandy Larson | Sandy Smith |
| Franny Martin | Pamela Murphy |

*With special guest appearances by "As The World Turns" regulars...*

| | |
|---|---|
| Pa Hughes | Santos Ortega |
| Tom Hughes | Frankie Michaels |
| Donald Hughes | Peter Brandon |
| Sylvia Hill | Millette Alexander |
| *Created by:* | Irna Phillips and William J. Bell |
| *Written by:* | Robert J. Shaw |
| *Producer:* | Allen Potter |
| *Director:* | Tom Donovan |
| *Scenic Designer:* | John Ward |
| *Musical Director:* | Wladimir Selinsky |

*Sponsor and Agency:* The Procter & Gamble Company, represented by Young & Rubicam, Inc.

## "OUR PRIVATE WORLD": THE CHARACTERS

The life of Lisa Miller Hughes reached a crossroads when her son, Tom, was seven years old. At that time, Tom was living with his father, Bob Hughes, who had no intention of remarrying Lisa. In fact, he planned to marry nurse Sylvia Hill.

Dejected by the turn her life had taken in Oakdale, Lisa boarded a train for Chicago. She symbolically dropped her wedding ring in an ashtray and arrived in the Windy City to begin a new life. Lisa took up residence at a comfortable boarding house run by an elderly widow named Mary Shaw and landed a job in the admitting office of University Hospital. It was there that Lisa met Dr. Tony Larson, a handsome young resident with an eye for the ladies, and his fanatically jealous wife, nurse Sandy Larson. Lisa soon moved to an apartment across the hall from this unhappy couple and became enmeshed not only in their lives, but also in the lives of the wealthy Eldridges and upper-middle-class Robinsons, who lived in nearby Lake Forest.

The widow of a prominent attorney, Helen Eldridge enjoyed her social position as a grande dame. Yet her first priority was her family. John, her eldest, was an attorney with Eldridge & Eldridge. Charming and assertive, John moved back to the family home after the untimely death of his wife, but hoped to marry again. John was delighted that his younger brother, Thomas, was a part of the family law firm, although Thomas was nagged by a lingering desire to become a doctor.

Helen also had 19-year-old twin daughters, Eve and Lenore. She lavished special attention on Lenore, who was away in an institution, leaving the neurotic, rebellious Eve to resent her mother's apparent preference for her twin. After Eve was thrown out of college, she planned to marry her longtime sweetheart, Brad Robinson, a well-adjusted architectural student at Northwestern University. Brad was the only child of Dick and Ethel Robinson, a happy couple with solid values. Dick owned a large architectural firm, the Robinson Corporation, and was thrilled Brad planned to become a part of it once he graduated. Although his childhood friend, Franny Martin, made no secret of her affection for him, Brad was deeply in love with Eve.

## "OUR PRIVATE WORLD": THE STORY

One day, Lisa admitted Eve into the hospital with a mild concussion and immediately took a liking to this unhappy and complex young woman. When Eve attempted suicide in Lisa's apartment, Lisa quickly summoned her physician neighbor, Tony Larson, who recognized that Eve was just crying out for attention. Thomas Eldridge held his mother, Helen, responsible for Eve's fragile state and was drawn to Lisa through their mutual concern for Eve. John Eldridge took a firmer stance and insisted Eve straighten out and come home. He, too, was attracted to this newcomer who had taken his sister under her wing.

Brad came to share John's opinion that Eve was selfish and immature and began keeping company with Franny. Eve poured on the melodrama, though, and convinced Brad of her undying love. The two were married in a lavish ceremony that ended when Eve bolted from the reception. She later told Brad that while she was willing to make a go of the marriage, she was deathly afraid of commitment and feared she might someday run out on him. Brad was so blindly in love that he accepted Eve's terms, and the two were finally wed. They did not, however, consummate the marriage.

As Eve sorted out the fears that haunted her, she found a willing confidant in Tony Larson, who dreamed of having a large medical practice in wealthy Lake Forest and saw this attractive, well-connected young lady as an entrée to a bevy of high-powered patients. He saw even more dollar signs when Eve's father-in-law, Dick Robinson, became his cardiac patient and offered to set him up in private practice. Sandy worried that Tony was letting his sudden good fortune go to his head and wanted him to come down to earth so that they could start a family. Instead, Tony wove his way into the rich Lake Forest fabric, playing psychiatrist to Eve with Svengali-like aplomb. His influence was not entirely negative, as he persuaded Helen to apologize to Eve for favoring her sister. Both Brad and Sandy were uncomfortable with Tony and Eve's new "friendship."

Lisa's sudden appearance in the Eldridge family's lives prompted Helen to wonder about this enigmatic young woman. The newcomer obviously had had a positive effect on Helen's daughter and was being pursued by both of her sons, but Lisa remained evasive about her past. She carried around a picture of a little boy whom she claimed was her nephew—but, unbeknownst to everyone except Lisa, it was really her son, Tom. Lisa's lie was compounded when her ex–brother-in-law, Donald Hughes, showed up unexpectedly to convey Bob's threat of a custody suit. Feeling cornered, Lisa unconvincingly introduced Donald to her friends as the father of her nephew. The truth about Lisa finally surfaced when Sylvia Hill, who was an old friend of Sandy Larson's, visited Sandy and told her Lisa had been married to Bob Hughes, and they had a son, Tom. The deception finally over, Lisa chose John over Thomas, and the two made plans to marry.

Strengthened by her emotional connection to Tony, Eve boldly asked Brad for an annulment. Brad bitterly refused to free her despite Lisa's advice to do so. It was then that Eve and Tony finally admitted their mutual love, and Tony walked out on Sandy with the intention of obtaining a Mexican divorce. Shortly thereafter, Tony was found slumped over his desk, unconscious from a blow to the head. He died, and Brad was arrested for his murder.

Fortunately for Brad, Sandy confessed to the crime and began a short prison term made more tolerable by the news that she was going to have Tony's baby. Brad subsequently agreed to annul his marriage to Eve, who then mended fences with Helen and planned to become a nurse. Thomas, embittered by Lisa and John's engagement, left Chicago to pursue his dream of becoming a doctor elsewhere. The road to Lisa's happiness with John was now clear, and she made plans to return to Oakdale.

# 1966-1970

For the Hughes and Lowell families, 1966 to 1970 were tumultuous years of pain, hardship and triumph. Several Oakdale citizens fell victim to sudden and violent deaths, and young people struggled to find themselves amid family skeletons and against the backdrop of the turbulent 1960s.

Heeding Claire's advice, Ellen informed Franny Brennan that her services would no longer be needed once Ellen became Mrs. David Stewart. Franny responded with a vicious threat—she would tell Dan that Ellen was his mother. Desperate, Ellen grabbed a statue and hit Franny over the head with it, killing her. Ellen confessed to the murder without giving any reason for her actions. This tragedy resulted in a variety of reactions among the Stewart family: David was baffled and Paul was supportive and sympathetic, but Dan vowed to disown his family if David were ever to marry that murderess!

In prison, Ellen met an attractive but confused young woman named Sandy McGuire. The two formed a close, if not unlikely, friendship—Ellen was from the town's wealthiest family, while Sandy came from a working-class background. Sandy was incarcerated for unwittingly driving the getaway car for her husband, a slick thief named Roy McGuire. It was in prison that Sandy gave birth to a son, with Ellen serving as godmother. Ellen persuaded Sandy to name the boy Jimmy, the name she had given to Dan before he was adopted.

Meanwhile, another adoptee was to learn the ironic truth of her heritage. Bill Holmes, on his deathbed, admitted to his adopted daughter, Amanda, that Sara Fuller was her real mother. Amanda was at peace with this knowledge but was held back from revealing it when she and Sara found themselves in fierce competition for Donald Hughes's affections. Sara tried to make Donald believe she was selling out her interest in her dress shop so she could be a traditional wife to him. Nancy was so won over by the charming Sara, she even went to work in the shop part-time—a first for Nancy. This did not sit well with Pa Hughes, who was accustomed to Nancy's keeping the household running efficiently. Nancy also infuriated Chris when she interfered in Donald's life by trying to push him into marrying Sara.

Donald, however, was wary at the idea of marriage.

He was still smarting from Ellen's rejection, even though he was working on her case as head of the Lowell firm's new criminal law division. In time Sara's feminine wiles ultimately won out, and the two planned to marry, much to Nancy's delight. When Don told Amanda the news of his impending marriage, Amanda confided to her employer and friend, Neil Wade, about the details of her birth.

Neil was a well-loved character in Oakdale, dispensing advice and wisdom from his cozy bookstore. Putting his disastrous medical career safely behind him, Neil became so successful at his retail venture that he repaid Doug's loan and eventually accepted him as his father. Unfortunately, he was still plagued by recurring bouts of blindness. Neil intended to stay in Oakdale, although Penny persuaded him to purchase another store in New York City. Having spent a lot of time in the city because of Jeff's recording contacts, she decided she liked the culture and sophistication the Big Apple had to offer.

Doug was relieved to have a renewed relationship with his son, and Claire was ecstatic over this happy development. Doug took on an assistant, the suave young Dr. Michael Shea. One of Doug's patients was Ann Holmes's friend Joan Rogers, who had inexplicable physical problems. Joan and her husband, Ted, had no children but enjoyed a loving, vibrant marriage. Naturally, Doug was saddened when he operated on Joan and discovered she had a malignant tumor. As was his practice, Doug decided not to tell her that her sorry fate was sealed. But this time the decision proved tragic. Joan died, and Doug was forced to tell Ted the truth. Insane with grief, Ted gave Doug a violent shove. Doug hit his head, suffered a concussion and soon died. Not long afterward, Neil died of an embolism. History had cruelly repeated itself in Penny's life—she had buried two husbands just when they'd finally discovered their niche in life.

Struggling to put her life back together, Penny was dumbfounded by Ellen's confession to killing Franny Brennan. Even Dick Martin—the diamond-in-the-rough prosecutor—investigated the case in hopes of exonerating Ellen. David finally figured out that Franny had blackmailed Ellen about Dan, and persuaded Chris and Donald to reopen the case. Thanks to Judge Lowell's influence, the lawyers secured a closed-door session with the governor and confided to him about Dan's parentage. The governor obtained a parole for Ellen and she was released. At long last, Ellen and David were married in a lavish ceremony.

Yet the Oakdale court calendar was to remain heavy for quite some time. On Amanda's 22nd birthday, the Lowell firm presented her with a letter from Bill Holmes confirming that Sara and Amanda were mother and daughter. Out for revenge over her mother's plans to marry the man she loved, Amanda threatened to show Donald the letter unless Sara broke off the engagement. While

Chris defended Amanda Holmes against a charge of murdering her mother. Nancy, a close friend of the deceased, was so infuriated that she ordered Chris to sleep in another room!

chasing Amanda through her apartment building trying to retrieve the letter, Sara took a fatal fall down a flight of stairs.

The ensuing trial drove Nancy and Chris closer to separation than they had ever been in their married lives! Chris took on Amanda's defense, much to the horror of Nancy, who was stubbornly convinced that the girl had murdered Sara in cold blood. When Nancy gave damaging testimony against Amanda, Chris subjected her to a blistering cross-examination. Nancy responded by moving into a separate bedroom. Donald, usually at odds with his mother, was for once in agreement with Nancy that Amanda was guilty. The Hughes family fences were mended when Amanda was found innocent and matured into a likable, well-adjusted woman. She dated Donald for a while at a later time, but left Oakdale once she realized that he would never really love her.

Donald certainly seemed to be the confirmed bachelor as well as a rebel in the workplace. Long an admirer of Judge Lowell, he was nonetheless angry when the Judge brought Dick Martin into the criminal law division over his head. Don crassly accused the Judge of using this plum position to buy Ellen's freedom through

Dick. When Chris rebuked his son for forcing this confrontation, Donald agreed to play along with Dick's appointment. Secretly, however, he aimed to force his new rival to resign. Dick confided to his father, retired policeman Otto Martin, that he was happy to be in the Lowell firm so he could be closer to Claire, whom he fancied. But Claire was being courted by the charming Michael Shea, who had taken over Doug's practice after his death and intended to win Doug's wealthy widow as well.

Michael Shea was a complex and potentially dangerous man. While his public persona was charming, underneath lay a dark and evil disposition. Raised by an impoverished grandmother whom he adored, Michael resented doctors like Bob Hughes and David Stewart, perceiving them as being overly privileged and well connected. He was also a womanizer, having broken many hearts while building his medical career in various midwestern cities. Now that he was in Oakdale, Michael saw Memorial as a means of becoming a big fish in a small pond, and he considered Claire his ideal ticket to the high-powered country club life he craved. Though still attractive and poised, she was quite a bit older than Michael and extremely lonely after Doug's death. However, as Claire found herself attracted to Michael, she became increasingly insecure over their age difference. She began using wrinkle removers and wearing short skirts, prompting Judge Lowell to remark, "Going to the beach, Claire?"

Ellen worried about her mother's preoccupation with this new doctor, but she finally had a full life of her own—she and David were expecting a child. She continued her friendship with Sandy McGuire, who was now out of prison, and helped Sandy readjust to civilian life. Ellen introduced her to the most eligible of men—Bob Hughes! For a long time, Bob had been preoccupied with Tom, who was fast becoming a rebellious teenager.

## Love and Marriage

*It had been a long haul for David Stewart and Ellen Lowell. David and his first wife unwittingly adopted Ellen's illegitimate child. After a bitter custody battle, the two fell in love. As they were about to marry, Ellen accidentally killed a housekeeper who had discovered the secret of her child's identity. Upon her release from prison, these two lovers finally got to say "I do."*

In fact, the boy felt totally alone and alienated, shuttling between the Hughes household and the Eldridges in Chicago. When Bob began a serious relationship with Sandy, Tom refused to accept her. Soon afterward, Lisa, having received a hefty divorce settlement from Eldridge, returned from Chicago and dreamed of a future with Bob.

Nancy even told Sandy point-blank that she would always think of Lisa as her daughter-in-law. Opposition to Bob and Sandy also came from Roy, Sandy's ex, who had been released from prison and wanted to go straight in hopes of winning her back. But Sandy's parents, good-natured dreamer Carl Wilson and his dour wife, Martha, thought Bob was good for Sandy, and they were happy when the two were married.

At first Roy's plan to reform was strictly a means to win Sandy back and then return to a life of crime, but he managed to become a good citizen despite himself. When Dr. Bellows, an African-American prison physician, encouraged Roy to go into medicine, Roy answered the call. After he realized that he'd lost Sandy for good, Roy found a friend and confidante in Penny, who had taken over Neil's bookstore after his death. Penny began to play an integral role in the lives of Sandy, Roy and their little boy Jimmy, with whom Penny became increasingly obsessed. Bob and Sandy considered leaving Oakdale for a small town in Vermont, where Bob planned to take over a modest medical practice. However, during a visit there, the medical office burned down and Sandy sustained serious facial burns. She recovered from her wounds but became clinically depressed to the point where Bob had to place her in a sanitarium.

This development left the door open for Penny to take care of Jimmy. Martha and Carl Wilson wanted temporary custody of the boy, while Roy believed he would be better off with his new stepfather, Bob. Desperate to fill the void of children in her life, Penny persuaded Roy to marry her, and a judge awarded them custody. This placed Bob and Penny at odds, as Bob was angered to see his sister replace Sandy in the little boy's life. Penny's longtime friendship with Ellen also suffered a rift, because Ellen remained more supportive of her new friend, Sandy, than of her old pal. In the meantime, Sandy became emotionally fit, had plastic surgery and returned to Oakdale stronger and more assertive than she'd ever been. She was angry that Penny had tried to keep Jimmy from her and that Jimmy was now calling Penny "Mommy." Realizing the folly of the situation, Roy stepped in and insisted Jimmy be returned to his mother. Now that Jimmy was gone, Penny and Roy decided they didn't have a future together. Because they'd never consummated their marriage, they were able to obtain an annulment, and Penny left Oakdale for New York City, where she'd longed to live for some time.

Whereas Penny was able to resolve her problems, Ellen was in for a new series of concerns. She and David had a baby girl, Carol Ann, but Ellen angered David by being more concerned with the problems of her son Dan than with her new baby girl. Fellow intern Susan Burke continued to work her charms on the aspiring young medic, flaunting the credentials of her successful father, Dr. Fred Burke. She persuaded Dan to abandon research in favor of surgery, which she believed would be a more glamorous and lucrative field for him. Dan and Susan were secretly married, but Dan continued to live at home with David and Ellen while carrying on a secret life in Susan's apartment. They were soon faced with the first hurdle in their relationship—Susan discovered that she was pregnant. Dan was ecstatic, but Susan was far from happy because a baby did not fit into her plans for a successful career. To her relief, she miscarried. The tragedy brought Dan and Susan's marriage out into the open, and David angrily threw Dan out of the house. Dan and Susan moved to a small apartment near the hospital.

As Ellen and David dealt with Dan's situation, they were also dismayed to see that Claire and Michael were becoming close. So was Dick Martin, who confided to Judge Lowell that he was interested in Claire. The Judge urged Martin to "plead his case" with Claire, as he was not at all comfortable with the suave doctor who was courting his daughter-in-law. Secretly, Judge Lowell investigated Shea and discovered he'd left Indianapolis because he was named as co-respondent in a married woman's divorce case. The mess resulted in the suicide of the woman's daughter. What Judge Lowell and most of Oakdale didn't yet know was that Michael was already two-timing Claire with Lisa!

Discouraged by Bob's marriage to Sandy, Lisa found fellow schemer Michael Shea exciting, and the feeling was definitely mutual. Sexual sparks notwithstanding, Michael was first and foremost an opportunist, and he talked Claire into eloping with him to California. When the happy couple returned, Claire's family was upset, not only by the news of her hasty marriage, but also by her increasingly heavy drinking. Michael prided himself on knowing the proper aperitif and digestif for every occasion, and Claire was trying to keep up with him. She was clearly out of her element, though, and was developing a problem with alcohol. Bored and repulsed by Claire, Michael resumed his affair with Lisa, and Claire began drinking more heavily as a result of her husband's neglect. She even let it slip to him during a bender that Dan was Ellen's illegitimate son!

Claire was also furious with Michael for the political games he was playing at Memorial. Michael was in competition with Bob for the position of Chief of Staff, and he wanted this prestigious appointment at any cost. His golden moment came when Bob saved the life of a young patient named Diane Steiner by administering a transfusion against her parents' wishes. The Steiners initiated a suit against the hospital, then decided to back down provided Bob resign from Memorial, which he did. Michael was then appointed Chief of Staff, only to learn some unwelcome news from Lisa—she was pregnant with his child! Desperate to give the child a name and a better home life than she had given Tom, Lisa begged Michael to divorce Claire and marry her, but he callously refused. Lisa soon developed serious cold symptoms which turned into staph pneumonia. During her illness, she gave birth prematurely to a baby boy. She named him Charles—Chuckie for short. This shocking development led Lisa's acquaintances to wonder aloud who the boy's father was. To Michael's delight, many people at Memorial mistakenly assumed that it was Bob.

But Michael Shea's world was about to slowly un-

Sandy McGuire's crooked husband Roy wanted her back, but Ellen had introduced her to Oakdale's most eligible bachelor, Bob Hughes, and the two eventually were married.

ravel. Lisa confronted Claire with the news that she'd given birth to Michael's child and begged her to divorce him, but she refused. Then the Steiners returned to Memorial, this time for the hospitalization of Mr. Steiner's elderly mother. Michael was struck by the woman's resemblance to his beloved grandmother and ran in panic when he was supposed to administer a hypodermic needle. As a result of his actions, Mrs. Steiner died. Later that night, Michael was arrested for drunk driving. Claire realized that in some strange way she still loved

Michael, so she persuaded a reluctant Chris to represent him. Michael was ordered not to practice medicine for six months and to sign an affidavit acknowledging that he was the father of Lisa's son, Charles. When Lisa gave the letter to Claire, it was finally too much for the unhappy Mrs. Shea. Claire ordered Michael out of the house and divorced him. In the process, she formed a bond with Lisa, who now realized how deeply she herself hated Michael after all the damage he had caused.

Encouraged by David to fight his ouster, Bob returned to Memorial. One day at David's invitation, he was attending a laboratory experiment that resulted in an explosion! Bob was temporarily blinded, causing David to feel guilty and Sandy to run away, unable to cope. That was the last straw for Bob, and he obtained a divorce on grounds of desertion. With his professional and personal life in turmoil, Bob lacked sufficient time to spend with Tom, who was also becoming more and more confused by his mother's erratic behavior.

The tawdry situation with Michael left Lisa with a need to be surrounded by family. Her mother, Alma, moved in with her, and Tom was becoming a more attentive son. Because Lisa was only four months pregnant when she delivered Chuckie, Tom never noticed her condition. Desperate to keep Tom's love, Lisa passed Chuckie off as the child of an old friend who was ill. But Tom soon saw through his mother's story, denounced her as a liar and wrote her off. Alma was delighted when her daughter started keeping company with Dick Martin, while Judge Lowell still hoped that Claire would become involved with the upstanding lawyer.

But Michael was not through with Claire, as her prestigious connections with Memorial were key to his reinstatement. When

Judge Lowell confronted Michael about his past in Indianapolis, Michael admitted it to Claire in order to release the Judge's hold over him. Claire was taken by his honesty and agreed to remarry him, until she overheard him tell his lawyer that he was only marrying her to get back into Memorial. Claire went into a drunken stupor and stabbed Michael with a letter opener. Bob and Tom found them on Claire's living-room floor, a drunken Claire muttering, "I killed him." Michael recovered and cleared his wife by lying, saying that he'd been trying to prevent Claire from stabbing herself. He approached David and threatened to reveal that Claire stabbed him unless David helped reinstate him at Memorial. With clenched teeth, David buckled under Michael's pressure in order to salvage his family's reputation.

Tom's inadvertent role in this discovery brought his bitterness and alienation to the fore. He seized the opportunity to incriminate Claire, whom he considered a key player among the dreaded "establishment." In fact, during this period, Tom was as much a stranger to himself as he was to his family and friends. He was obnoxious to his grandparents, Nancy and Chris, who shared Lisa's conviction that Bob had become neglectful of his son. Donald was the only one in the family who was able to develop a good rapport with Tom. In one conversation, Tom complained to his uncle that being prepared for adulthood was like being "a Boy Scout...a straight arrow going nowhere." Don correctly sensed that Tom was going nowhere but downward, thanks to his long-haired college roommate, Hank Barton. Hank was a criminal who was getting Tom hooked on speed, and he enlisted Tom's help in robbing Hank's father's pharmacy. Bob also became concerned about Tom's attitude and warned him he'd cut off his

Susan Stewart must have noticed her husband's attraction to Liz Talbot early on, because she was quick to fix her up with her brother-in-law Paul.

financial support unless he took Lisa back into his life. Tom begrudgingly heeded his father's advice, acting little more than cordially to his mother.

While the Hugheses were plagued by Tom's teenage crises, they were comforted by a new presence, a soft-spoken, intelligent young British woman named Elizabeth Talbot. Penny had stayed with the Talbot family in England and had invited Liz to come to Oakdale and stay with Nancy and Chris. Liz found new friends in Dan and Susan Stewart, and Susan was quick to play matchmaker between Liz and her brother-in-law, Paul. During Dan and Susan's early years together, Paul had flirted with a career in professional football before answering the call of the Vietnam War. He wasn't there long when he sustained an arm wound in action and was discharged. When Paul returned to Oakdale, it was to become a doctor, but not a high-priced physician like Dan. He instead opened a modest practice in a neighborhood where he could reach poor and working-class patients. Paul enjoyed spending his free time chatting with Liz at the bookstore where she worked. He had no idea that his brother, Dan, was also developing feelings for the lovely Britisher.

Meanwhile, Dan was becoming more and more miserable, both at home and at work. When he amassed evidence that Michael was giving faulty diagnoses, he received no support whatsoever from Susan. A skilled politician, Susan advised Dan to swallow his pride and curry favor with Michael in the interest of getting ahead—but Dan refused to let the matter drop. He confronted Michael, who responded by doing what Franny Brennan had threatened to do some years before: He cruelly told Dan that he was the illegitimate son of his stepmother and the late Tim Cole!

Ellen, though, had already given up on the idea of telling Dan this painful truth. She and David now had a second child together, Dawn, and Ellen had sadly acknowledged that her stepson Paul liked and accepted her far more than Dan did. Around this time, Ellen was suddenly incapacitated by a perforated ulcer. Because a flu epidemic had swept through the hospital, Dan was the only surgeon available to save her life. After performing a brilliant operation, Dan sat by her bedside as she slept under the anesthetic. As he held her hand, he looked down at her and said, "I did my best, Mother." Dan angrily confronted David with the painful question: "Is Dr. Shea a liar...or are you?" David tearfully told Dan the entire story of his background, including Ellen and Tim Cole's relationship, the ensuing custody battle and Betty

Stewart's death. After she recovered, Dan went to Ellen and told her he was proud to be her son. As he dealt with accepting this incredible story, Dan found himself confiding it not to his wife Susan, but to Liz, who was a refreshing departure from Susan's callous and single-minded ambition. Before long Liz and Dan realized they'd fallen in love.

The Hugheses and the Stewarts were greatly relieved when Bob had a successful corneal transplant, curing his blindness once and for all. Sandy returned soon thereafter, once again exuding confidence, only to learn that Bob had divorced her. During her absence, Sandy had launched a promising modeling career in New York City under the guidance of an influential new admirer, Peter Kane. Still attracted to each other, Bob and Sandy planned to remarry, but Bob had a change of heart when he discovered he would have to take a backseat to Sandy's career. Then Sandy's mother, Martha, developed a heart condition. She was treated by Dr. John Dixon, a young resident who had roomed with Dan. John appeared quiet and unassuming, revealing very little of his character to his coworkers. Both David and Michael knew that John was a brilliant, industrious young man and they approached him about joining their respective practices. John accepted Michael's offer and became his protégé—in every respect. It soon became clear to everyone at Memorial that John shared Michael's jealousy of Dan and Bob, who he mistakenly thought had had the world handed to them on a silver bedpan. Indeed, Michael Shea helped to create the monster that was John.

As his parents sorted out their convoluted love lives, Tom was bedeviled by demons of his own. His grades were so bad that he confided to Chris that he was about to join the Army. Chris tried to reach out to his grandson, but the boy went to Vietnam and ended up recovering from self-inflicted injuries at Great Lakes Hospital. When he returned to Oakdale, Tom resumed his dependency on his old college roommate, Hank, for dubious companionship and drugs. One night, when Tom was high, Hank put him up to breaking into Michael Shea's office for narcotics. Michael caught Tom and extracted a written confession, which he used to blackmail Lisa into marrying him. After losing Claire, Michael had become obsessed with having Chuckie know him as his father, and he wanted the boy all to himself. He was, however, already tired of Lisa and was now carrying on with Karen Adams, a sympathetic but impressionable young nurse.

Shortly after Lisa and Michael married, Lisa left Chuckie in her car during an errand and the boy pressed the accelerator. Chuckie was unhurt, but Michael, as usual, capitalized on the situation. He devised a series of near mishaps designed to make Lisa seem an unfit mother so he could divorce her and sue for Chuckie's custody. Then Tom foolishly tried to rob Michael's office again, prompting the devious doctor to attempt to blackmail Lisa into handing over his son. But it was not to be. Michael was shot and killed, and Tom was seen leaving the scene mumbling, "He got what he deserved." Tom went to trial, while Lisa disappeared with Chuckie. Trying to protect Lisa, who he secretly suspected was the murderer, Tom made no effort to help himself. Karen Adams was also a suspect, since she'd been late for her nursing shift the night Michael was murdered, but the evidence against Tom was overwhelming. The one bright spot in Tom's life was Carol Deming, a sweet, uncomplicated girl he'd recently met. Carol was convinced of Tom's innocence and stuck by him despite the misgivings of her psychiatrist father.

As Tom took the witness stand, Lisa returned to Oakdale and rushed into the courtroom, only to collapse and awaken with amnesia, giving her name as Mrs. Robert Hughes. Tom was convicted of the murder.

While Bob tried desperately to help Tom, he was also preoccupied with a mysterious terminally ill patient named Miss Thompson. One day she entrusted Bob to represent her in some banking transactions and he noticed that the bank listed her name as Helen Pearce. When Bob questioned his patient, she remained secretive until he happened to mention that his son, Tom, had been convicted of Michael Shea's murder. Much to Bob's shock, Miss Thompson told him that she was the killer! She was the woman from Michael's past whose daughter had committed suicide. To prove her guilt, Miss Thompson gave Bob one detail of her crime—Michael was fixing her a very dry Rob Roy on the night she shot him. Then she died, leaving Bob with a story but no witnesses. Frantically, Bob investigated Miss Thompson but turned up nothing solid until he discussed the situation with Claire and Judge Lowell. Claire recalled Michael taunting her about an old girlfriend named Marcia Campbell who'd introduced him to the very dry Rob Roy. Further investigation corroborated the woman's true identity and Tom was freed. Soon afterward, Lisa regained her memory but was disappointed to find that she was no longer married to Bob.

Even though Claire stopped drinking after Michael's death, she was still extremely lonely. She also harbored an intense dislike for Dan—she had never forgiven him for treating Ellen so shabbily. Therefore, when Ellen mentioned to her mother that Dan seemed distant in his marriage to Susan, Claire immediately suspected that he was seeing another woman. Dan did eventually ask Susan for a divorce, but she refused. Ellen interfered, advising her daughter-in-law to become more of a traditional wife and to consider having a child. Susan heeded her advice and seduced Dan. When she discovered she was pregnant, Susan told Dan that thanks to Ellen's advice, she was ready to be a mother. His life now a shambles, Dan disowned Ellen for sticking her nose into his dead-end marriage! Steely-eyed, he told her, "You're not my mother."

Plagued by indecision, Liz tried to put off the romantic overtures of both Dan and Paul. The latter had no clue of Dan and Liz's relationship, even when he accidentally picked up a phone call from Liz's gynecologist. Guessing correctly that Liz was pregnant by another man, Paul nobly proposed and insisted that he never had to know the father's identity. By this time, Susan was unknowingly treating Liz like a confidante, pouring out her heart and soul about her latest tricks to keep her husband under her thumb. Liz was so guilt-ridden that she married Paul—in name only. She consulted Dr. Deming for psychiatric sessions and admitted to him that Dan was her child's father. Dan was so torn apart by Liz and Paul's marriage that he had a violent fight with Susan, during which she fell down a flight of stairs, miscarrying their child. Susan developed a back problem that confined her to a wheelchair, and she milked this for every drop of melodrama in order to keep Dan. Soon Susan was able to walk, but she concealed this fact until Liz accidentally saw that her "friend" was ambulatory. With the aplomb of the great drama queens of stage history, Susan rose from her wheelchair in front of Dan and his family.

As frustrated as Dan was that Liz had married Paul, he loved the young man he had always considered his brother and decided to come clean about his background. Paul replied that he'd known for some time. He had found a letter Ellen had written to Claire, referring to Dan as her natural son. Paul's admission brought the Stewart family closer, as did the birth of Liz's daughter, Betsy. Liz, however, suffered from such acute postpartum depression that Paul brought her supportive older brother, Ronnie Talbot, to Oakdale to cheer her up. Ronnie privately reminded Liz that he recalled a letter she'd written to their family in which she mentioned a special man named Dan. When he guessed that Dan had fathered Betsy, Liz confirmed his suspicions. Eventually, Paul and Liz consummated their marriage.

In the wake of Michael Shea's death, John Dixon became his heir apparent in machinations and deception—albeit with a smoother, more covert style. The only person he revealed himself to was Susan, his new pal and sounding board, who saw him as the male version of herself. Susan encouraged John's growing attraction to Sandy, reminding him that the lovely model would make a wonderful trophy wife for his advancing career. John proposed marriage to Sandy, but she'd already planned to marry Peter Kane in New York City. Susan also prevailed upon John to snoop on Dan in the interest of discovering if he was having an affair. John didn't need to work very hard on this assignment; one day, he overheard Liz and Ronnie discuss the fact that Dan and Liz had had an affair. Susan confronted Dan and warned him that if he ever divorced her, she would countersue and name Liz as co-respondent. John was ambivalent about the outcome of this romantic merry-go-round, as he was beginning to look upon Susan as more than a buddy.

With Sandy safely out of Bob's life, Lisa saw Tom as the ideal means to cement a new bond with her ex. Tom had became closer than ever to the Hughes family and had begun working at Paul's clinic, where he met a mysterious young patient named Meredith Harcourt. Weakened by an indeterminate illness, Meredith told Tom she had been evicted from her apartment. Tom felt sorry for the girl and let her move in with him, but he found it difficult to explain this situation to his girlfriend, Carol. Dr. Deming made it clear that he didn't approve of Tom as a mate for his daughter and urged her to move to another city, where he had accepted a new position. Carol chose to remain in Oakdale and build a relationship with Tom.

To the consternation of both Lisa and Nancy, Tom was becoming infatuated with Meredith. Something in the girl's demeanor led Nancy to believe she was not as down-and-out as she claimed—as a matter of fact, she seemed almost chic. To ingratiate herself with the family matriarch, Meredith gave Nancy a piece of "costume jewelry." When Nancy had the piece repaired, the jeweler estimated its worth at $2,000! This confirmed Nancy's suspicions at a time when she had zero tolerance for jet-setters. She was already upset that Chris had become corporate counsel for Simon Gilbey, a charismatic, demanding millionaire with holdings all over the world.

Nancy could relate much better to her best friend Claire, who had been born with money but was unaffected by it. After three marriages, Claire was finding a new peace in her life. She was especially inspired by the song "People," as it was comforting for her to remind herself that "people who need people are the luckiest people in the world."

When Edie Hughes Frey took ill in Seattle and called Claire and Ellen to her bedside, both women found it in their hearts to forgive her for her role in the destruction of Jim and Claire's marriage. Fortunately, Edie recovered from her illness and the only issue that remained unresolved for Claire was her lingering dislike

When Bob and Sandy split up, Lisa tried to win back Bob by using son Tom as a buffer.

for Dan. Wanting to make his family whole, Dan pleaded with Claire to accept him as her grandson, but she continued to turn him away. After one confrontation, Claire finally realized that she blamed herself for the years Ellen had lost with Dan, and she ran after him. Tragically, she was hit by a car and lived just long enough to apologize to her grandson.

The profound loss of Claire Cassen redefined the Stewart family. Judge Lowell, who had always liked Dan, persuaded him to tell Susan he was Ellen's son. Dan was also pleasantly surprised to learn that Claire had included him in her will. With Judge Lowell now alone in Claire's classically elegant house, Ellen and David and their growing children, Carol Ann and Dawn, moved in to give Claire's home, and her beloved father-in-law, a welcome infusion of new life.

# *1971-1975*

This period established the complex, self-destructive Dr. John Dixon as a major catalyst in the lives of the Hughes and Stewart families.

After Sandy married Peter Kane in New York City, John had reason to hope for an exciting relationship with Susan Stewart, his female counterpart in scheming. Susan briefly dated John to make Dan jealous, but John soon realized Susan was using him, and he made it clear he would not be a pawn in her game. Meanwhile, Dan was so miserable with Susan that he was becoming sarcastic, hard-drinking and downright offensive. His behavior was almost justifiable, since Susan was blackmailing him into staying married to her by threatening to tell Betsy that Dan was her real father. Dan finally confided this to an understanding Judge Lowell, who quickly recognized Betsy's resemblance to Ellen and realized that she was, indeed, Dan's daughter.

At this time, Betsy's mother Liz once again found herself pregnant, this time by her husband, Paul, Dan's brother. A jealous Susan bitterly confronted Liz with the unfounded accusation that she was still carrying on with Dan. Liz became so distraught that she miscarried and had a nervous breakdown, forcing Paul to institutionalize her. It was at this point that Paul's "good guy" image began to fade, as he realized that he resented Betsy because she wasn't his daughter and hated the "unknown" man who'd fathered her. Ironically, he entrusted Dan and Susan with Betsy's care while Liz was recovering in the sanitarium. The experience brought out a more human side in Susan, because she truly felt guilty for having caused Liz's miscarriage. In time, Liz recovered from her emotional breakdown and resolved to divorce Paul and marry Dan. She was not to carry out her plan, however, because Susan seduced Dan in one of his weaker moments and became pregnant!

During this trying time, Liz told one other person about her involvement with Dan—her dear friend, Penny. Penny had returned from New York City to find Ellen obsessed with saving Dan and Susan's marriage. She was now placed in the awkward position of knowing Liz's secret, and found herself disliking Dan intensely for his callous treatment of both Susan and Liz. This scenario ultimately led Penny to leave the incestuous atmosphere of Oakdale and move to England, where she married a professional race car driver, Anton Cunningham.

The Hughes family was under tremendous strain, due in large part to business tycoon Simon Gilbey and Meredith Harcourt. Nancy's suspicions were indeed correct that Meredith was not the poor waif she represented herself to be. She was, in fact, Simon's ward! Meredith had come to Oakdale to escape Simon's strict control, only to find that the millionaire had also found his way to the city. Simon was the classic "Type A" personality, constantly working and making impossible demands on everyone around him. This behavior resulted in a heart attack, and Bob and David gave him an ultimatum: slow down or die. Simon believed he'd finally found balance and purpose in his life when he fell in love with a most exciting Oakdale resident—Lisa! He proposed, and Lisa almost accepted in order to use his money to recoup a loss from a bad investment. But when Tom and Simon formed an intense dislike for each other, Lisa couldn't bring herself to take the step.

Nancy also disliked Simon, and with good reason. Chris was his lawyer, and Simon overworked and bullied him so mercilessly that Chris suffered an apparent heart attack. Donald rushed home from his new job in California to be at his father's side—but, ever the troublemaker, Donald ended up making the situation worse. He criticized Bob and David for being overly cautious in diagnosing his father's illness and pressed Dan to perform an elaborate, experimental surgical procedure on Chris. Chris agreed with Bob that the surgery was unnecessary and he soon recovered. It turned out that Chris had an abdominal obstruction that had affected his heart. Donald went back to California to wrap up his business affairs and soon returned to Oakdale and the family firm. As for Meredith, she left Oakdale with Simon—not as his ward, but as his new love interest!

Lisa was a tremendous source of support to the Hughes family during Chris's illness, but Bob managed to elude her attempts to win back his affections. In addition to worrying about his father, Bob had to deal with the impending death of his longtime friend, Chuck Ryan. Years earlier, Chuck had left Oakdale for nearby Centerville, where he became romantically involved with two sisters, Kim and Jennifer Sullivan. He married

Simon Gilbey was a powerful millionaire who was quite taken with Lisa. Gilbey was Chris Hughes's client and he was so demanding that he caused Chris to suffer a heart attack! Eventually, Gilbey became romantically involved with his one-time ward, Meredith Harcourt.

Jennifer and they had two children, Barbara and Rick. Now Chuck was terminally ill and he secured Bob's promise to look after his family when he was gone. Chuck's death was particularly devastating to Rick, a new intern at Memorial, who idolized his father and resented Bob for withholding the knowledge of his illness from him.

At the same time, David stepped down from an administrative position to devote full time to his new specialty, research. He recommended to the board that Bob replace him, but John Dixon waged a high-profile campaign to secure the post for himself. To Bob's disgust, John won the appointment with support from both Susan and Rick. Rick shared John's resentment of Bob, and

Susan backed John reluctantly when he threatened to tell Paul about Liz and Dan's affair. But this was the least of Susan's problems—Betsy fell from a monkey-bar apparatus while under her care and was severely injured. A blood donation from Dan saved her life. When Betsy remained more attached to Dan and Susan than to Liz and Paul, Liz became so weary of the situation that she told Paul she never really loved him, and they divorced. Paul later died of a brain tumor, never knowing that his wife and his brother had conceived a child and were very much in love.

As the poignant story of the Stewart brothers ended, the Hughes brothers became embroiled in their own romantic triangle when the widowed Jennifer Ryan took a nursing position at Memorial. Nancy fervently hoped that Donald and Jennifer would get together so that Bob would finally look in Lisa's direction, but contrary to Nancy's hopes, Bob and Jennifer were soon very much enamored of each other. So Donald did the unthinkable—he took up with Lisa, the ex–sister-in-law he once claimed he couldn't stand! It was a colorful match, to say the least, as both were headstrong, volatile and a bit immature. Donald even became buddies with Lisa's young son, Chuckie, but he resolved to remain unattached. When Lisa began experiencing pregnancy symptoms, she panicked because she didn't want Don to think she was attempting to trap him into marriage. She went to Memorial for an abortion, only to have her surgeon, Dr. Eric Lonsberry, tell her that the pregnancy was false! What she had was an ovarian cyst. As luck would have it, Rick was present during Lisa's ordeal and rushed to tell his mother, Jennifer, a lie—that Lisa believed Bob to be the father of her baby. But Jennifer didn't let her son's lies keep her from making plans to marry Bob.

Tom delighted his family when he decided to become an attorney. Having grown up as a child of divorce, Tom saw the legal profession as an ideal vehicle to wipe divorce off the planet. It was therefore not surprising that as he matured, he became cautious and even a bit cynical about romance. He was briefly pursued by his stepsister-to-be, Barbara Ryan, who was an art student and aspiring fashion designer with an assertive and flirtatious personality. But once she realized Tom preferred his law studies to her company, Barbara briefly dated John before moving to New York City. Tom turned his attentions back to Carol Deming, an uncomplicated girl who was steadfast in her affection for him, and he decided that he'd found the person he wanted to

## Love and Marriage

*When Tom Hughes was ready to settle down, he married sweet, uncomplicated Carol Deming in a beautiful church ceremony. The Hughes family was very pleased.*

spend the rest of his life with. Tom and Carol were married in a beautiful church ceremony.

Shortly thereafter, Bob and Jennifer were also married. This did not come as thrilling news to Nancy, who didn't like the idea of inheriting a problematical stepfamily. Indeed, Rick was so vehemently opposed to the union that he refused to attend the wedding! But Jennifer continued to defend her son, even as he became a bigger thorn in Bob's side at Memorial. He shamelessly stole patients from Bob and David and made unilateral, near-fatal diagnoses. Feeling he had no choice, Bob reported Rick to the hospital board. John jumped in, publicly accusing Bob of carrying on a vendetta against Rick, while privately warning the insolent young medic to shape up.

Soon John began to look in the direction of Jennifer's widowed sister Kim Reynolds, a tall, beautiful brunette who had once been a professional lounge singer. Kim dated John and found him to be charming, although she couldn't help but be attracted to her handsome, upstanding brother-in-law, Bob. Half hoping that she could win Bob for herself, Kim warned Jennifer she would lose him if she continued to defer to her son at her husband's expense.

As the Hughes family celebrated two weddings, the Stewarts rejoiced at the birth of Emily, Dan and Susan's daughter. Ambivalent about assuming motherly duties, Susan soon returned to research medicine, leaving Emmy in the care of a baby nurse, Peggy Reagan, who developed a crush on Dan. But the catalyst for ending Dan and Susan's marriage turned out to be Susan's new boss, Dr. Bruce Baxter, a vain, self-involved workaholic. Certain that she'd finally met her ideal mate in Bruce, Susan finally granted Dan a divorce and married Bruce. Bruce, however, had zero tolerance for children and was not happy about the prospect of having Emily live with them, so Susan agreed to let Dan have temporary custody. The newlyweds were all set to move to the Boston area until Bruce admitted he'd undergone a vasectomy several years earlier. Realizing they had no real future, Susan annulled the marriage and Bruce left Oakdale alone.

Divorcing Susan would have been a happy experience for Dan had not a few other tragedies occurred. On the same day, Dan performed emergency gall bladder surgery on Kim and on Maria Marino, whose husband, Tony, worked at the Lowell firm. Although Kim recovered, Maria mysteriously died after the operation, leaving her policeman brother, Joe Fernando, so distraught that he shot Dan in his operating arm. Despite this physical and professional setback, Dan at long last married his beloved Liz—but sadly, the union was to be short-lived. After a visit with Emily, a bitter Susan forced a confrontation with Liz. Susan accidentally left the safety gate open, and after she left, Liz looked up and saw Betsy teetering at the top of the stairs. She hurried to secure the gate—only to fall *up* the stairs in a bizarre accident and rupture her liver. On her deathbed, Liz revealed that Dan was Betsy's father. Dan was so shattered that he became self-destructive, mixing alcohol with pills. But he soon realized that he needed to be a responsible parent to his daughters, and the family moved to England to heal.

Paul's private medical practice was assumed by Dr. Wally Matthews, a soft-spoken physician who was also a Doctor of Divinity. He immediately attracted the attention of Lisa, who considered him to be one of the gentlest men she had ever known. Many people in Oakdale sought his counsel, including a young medical student named Peter Burton, whose adoptive mother, Grace, was a friend of Nancy's. Peter consulted Wally about helping him learn about his origins—and in an ironic twist, Wally discovered from a former colleague that Peter was his son! Wally's wife had died shortly after giving birth to Peter, leaving him so grief-stricken and lost that he gave the boy up for adoption. At this time, Lisa and Don had become engaged, but Don was irked when she kept putting off setting a date because of her feelings for Wally. Sensing that Wally was holding something back from his past, Don asked Tom to investigate the mysterious minister. When Tom refused and Chris supported his grandson's position, Don realized there was one too many Hugheses in the firm and he returned to California in a huff. Soon afterward, Wally told Peter the truth about their relationship and Peter left town with his new wife Marian. When Lisa realized she wanted more excitement than Wally could offer her, he also departed Oakdale.

Another biological family was reunited when Amy, Penny's adopted Eurasian daughter, arrived from England after a disagreement with Penny's husband, Anton. A well-spoken, intelligent young lady, Amy was welcomed warmly by the Hugheses but felt like an outcast with most of the Americans her age. Tom discovered that Amy's grandmother, Mrs. Parsons, was, by coincidence, a resident of Oakdale and a patient of Rick's. Mrs. Parsons and her husband were overjoyed to find their granddaughter; however, uncomfortable in her new surroundings, Amy soon returned to Penny and Anton in England.

Not every Oakdale teenager was a joy to have

The Sullivan sisters, Jennifer and Kim, both fell for Bob Hughes, but Jennifer married him first.

around. Carol Ann Stewart turned a not-so-sweet 16 and decided to call herself "Annie." She went out of her way to be obnoxious and began riding motorcycles with her older boyfriend, a fast-living loser named Richard Taylor. Ellen was intolerant of Annie's bad behavior and set stringent limits—she was determined that her daughter not repeat her own mistake with Tim Cole! David occasionally came down on his daughter as well, but he warned Ellen that Annie might get worse if they didn't let up on the reins a bit. Ellen was hopeful when Dr. Bill Jenkins, Dan's straight-arrow protégé, took an interest in Annie, but the girl only used Bill to secure his secrecy when she was admitted to the emergency room after a motorcycle accident with Richard. Annie managed to maintain her virginity in the relationship, and Richard became so frustrated that he made certain that they got "lost" during one of their motorcycle jaunts. He hoped to make the proverbial score, but Annie outsmarted him and called David to come get her, while Richard rode off in a cloud of dust in search of new conquests.

While David had his own family problems to contend with, he was also worried about his friend Bob's troubled marriage to Jennifer. Rick's performance at Memorial worsened to the point where Bob was forced to place him on probation. Furious, Jennifer then moved out of the house, and Nancy further aggravated the situation by telling Jennifer that she'd foreseen this development all along. David advised Bob that although he was right to discipline Rick, he should ease up on the boy for the sake of his marriage. But Bob was not willing to give his incompetent stepson any leeway.

Watching all this from the sidelines was the scheming John Dixon, who was plotting to marry into this troubled but financially comfortable family. In John's eyes, Kim would be the ideal "doctor's wife"—she was

Separated from his wife Jennifer, Bob thought he accidentally ran into Kim in Florida. But Kim had planned to be there, and when he saw her singing "Can't Help Lovin' Dat Man" in the hotel lounge, he was smitten, and the two shared a night of forbidden passion.

wealthy, attractive and poised. But when John proposed marriage, Kim was noncommittal. Like Nancy, she had expected trouble in her sister's marriage to Bob and she wanted to see what would happen. As fate would have it, Bob was attending a medical convention in Palm Beach, Florida, when he walked into a posh lounge and saw Kim singing "Can't Help Lovin' Dat Man" to the piano accompaniment of Bobby Short! Bob was mesmerized at the sight of his ravishing sister-in-law seduc-

tively putting across a torch song. The two made love—only to return to Oakdale and the news that Jennifer was pregnant!

The lives of Bob, Jennifer, Kim and John were to become even more tortuous and complicated! Bob and Jennifer reconciled for the sake of their child, but Jennifer remained hostile to Nancy despite her mother-in-law's sincere efforts to bury the hatchet. She was also disturbed by Kim's new friendship with Bob's overly friendly ex, Lisa. Kim needed all the friends she could get—she was pregnant with Bob's child, too! Bob suspected that he was the father, but Kim stubbornly refused to confirm his suspicions and resolved to raise the child herself as an independent, unmarried woman. Yet when Kim admitted to John that she was pregnant but didn't reveal the father's identity, John seized the chance to use the "give the baby a name" argument and persuaded Kim to elope with him to Las Vegas. John then conveniently learned that Bob and Kim had been in Palm Beach at the same time, and put two and two together. Meanwhile, Rick was driving such a deep wedge between Bob and Jennifer that Jennifer was ready to leave her husband. One day, the two argued on a street corner, and Jennifer turned and ran into the path of a speeding car. Bob pushed her out of the way and was himself struck by the car. Under anesthesia, Bob told Jennifer that he was the father of Kim's child.

As Bob struggled with his love life, Lisa took over the Wade Book Shop and was soon enchanted by two newcomers in town. Grant Colman was a distinguished but brusque attorney from San Francisco, who accepted a position at the Lowell firm on the condition that the firm be renamed Lowell, Hughes & Colman. Grant was attracted to Lisa and they began to date, but he was disturbed to see that she was also becoming friendly with a younger man who was renting the apartment behind the bookstore—a hard-edged, blue-collar sort named Jay Stallings. Because he had a chip on his shoulder and was secretive about his past, both Tom and Grant found Jay a suspicious character. So when Jay was falsely implicated in a local lumberyard fire, Grant investigated and learned Jay had set fire to his family home in Salt Lake City.

When Lisa confronted Jay with Grant's findings, Jay assured her the fire was an accident. He explained that he'd fled the house, certain that his mother and stepfather would think he started the fire on purpose. His mother had since died and therefore wasn't able to corroborate the story. Grant grew even more distrustful of Jay when Lisa was struck by an unseen assailant and Grant discovered that someone had tampered with the brakes in her car. Jay finally figured out that he himself was the target, and the culprit was his stepfather, Gil Stallings, who was after Jay's sizable inheritance. Gil held Lisa hostage and set fire to the bookstore, but Grant cornered him. While trying to escape, Gil was fatally run over by a truck.

Determined to forge a respectable reputation for himself, Jay used his inheritance to buy a local construction company. His chief motivation was to win Lisa's love, but when Lisa convinced him that her heart belonged to Grant, Jay found friendship with Lisa's daughter-in-law, Carol. It was evident by now that Tom and Carol had married too young. Tom was so busy building his law career that he had little time for his wife. To further complicate matters, Carol discovered she couldn't have children.

Tom and Carol's marriage was disintegrating, but Bob and Jennifer reconciled in time for the birth of their daughter. They named her Frances, "Frannie" for short, after Jennifer and Kim's mother. After Frannie was born, Jennifer began to spend more time building her nursing career, to the consternation of Bob, who wanted a traditional, "stay-at-home" wife, a sentiment seconded by Nancy. With Jennifer absent much of the time, Carol formed an obsessive bond with little Frannie. Tom, meanwhile, was attracted to his first legal client, a sultry, mysterious young woman named Natalie Bannon. Natalie was charged with grand larceny, but she was cleared when Tom proved that her ex-boyfriend was the culprit. Tom was tragically unaware that this was only a particle of the tangled web that was Natalie's life, and fell hopelessly in love with her. As a result, the idealistic young lawyer who hated divorce became another statistic as he divorced Carol amicably, if not hastily.

John's machinations were holding his marriage to Kim together. During a snowstorm, Kim developed complications in her pregnancy and was rushed into surgery. When she awoke, John told her she'd lost a baby girl. As Kim recovered, she tried halfheartedly to make a go of her marriage but assiduously continued to avoid consummating it. She pleaded with John for a divorce, but he responded by threatening to tell Jennifer about Bob and Kim's liaison, not realizing, of course, that Jennifer already knew. John knew that Kim was a good career wife—she was already a big hit with his high-placed society cronies Marsha and George Davison. So at first John was willing to live with a sexless marriage. He

When he took over the apartment behind the Wade bookstore, hard-edged Jay Stallings had a chip on his shoulder and a secret in his past. Grant and Tom found him suspicious. Lisa found him very attractive.

Although married to the lovely Carol Deming, Tom found himself falling for the charms of his very first legal client, seductive Natalie Bannon.

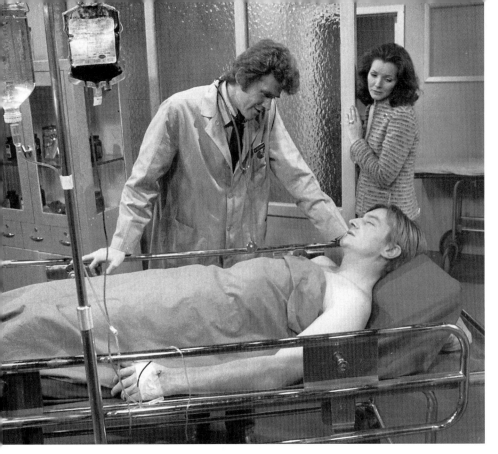

After a bitter fight, Kim asked John for a divorce and tried to leave. When John followed, he fell down a flight of stairs, becoming temporarily paralyzed. He was operated on by his rival for Kim's affections, Dan Stewart.

made a few passes at Susan, his buddy and compatriot in hospital gossip, but Susan was already torn between a new boyfriend, industrial engineer Mark Galloway, and Dan, who had returned from England with Betsy and Emily.

Unable to stand the tension any longer, John forced himself on Kim. With no legal recourse, since marital rape was not yet a crime, Kim quickly told Bob what John had done. Bob was sympathetic but told Kim it was not appropriate to tell Jennifer because she was tragically dying from a rare disease of the central nervous system. A devastated Kim told John about Jennifer's illness at a time when he and Bob were in contention for the Chief of Staff position, in hopes that John would have compassion and back down. John was coldly immovable, but Bob decided to take himself out of the running. Greatly relieved when Jennifer went into remission and Rick finally left Oakdale to "find himself," Bob soon lost Jennifer in a fatal car accident.

The situation between John and Kim had grown so intolerable that one day Kim ran out of their apartment to escape his wrath. John followed, fell down a flight of stairs and was seriously injured. Dan successfully operated on John. As a result, John was confined to a wheel-

chair and in need of his wife's constant care. Because of this accident, the pathetic side of John's character emerged. His parents offered to come from Florida to visit him, but he refused; to him, they were simple blue-collar people and he was ashamed of them. However, his influential "friends," the Davisons, dropped out of sight. All John had was Kim, and he was determined to hold on to her! He prolonged his recovery to keep her at his side, confiding only in Dan.

John's admission was to prove potentially self-defeating, as Dan and Kim were starting to form a close friendship. Kim was Dan's confidante when Susan threatened to press charges against him for having taken their daughter out of the country for an extended period of time. Susan sued for custody of Emily, which angered David, who was now her supervisor at the hospital's Antibody Research Laboratory. Dan, however, reluctantly returned Emmy to Susan, much to the disappointment of Susan's boyfriend Mark, who had about as much empathy for children as Susan's other ex, Bruce Baxter, did. While Susan and Mark were arguing,

When Susan was declared an unfit mother, Dan, a caring father who adored his daughters Betsy and Emily, was happy to have his family together again.

Emmy disappeared, only to turn up in the back of a truck! Dan then sought full custody, and Susan reacted by threatening to tell Betsy that her "Uncle Dan" was really her father! Susan's intentions were quashed by the two people she had counted on most—Mark and her mother, Julia Burke. Mark testified that Susan was an unfit mother, and Julia was so horrified by her daughter's wrath that she recommended that Dan have custody of Emily. A caring father, Dan was thrilled to have his daughter back. Dan professed his love to Kim and confided to her that he was Betsy's father. This admission helped to cement their relationship and Kim quickly bonded with Betsy.

After losing custody of her daughter, Susan's karma with John grew more pronounced as she, too, sank to emotional depths, becoming a bar-hopping drunk. In her nocturnal travels, she found a soulmate and bedmate in Jay Stallings. Jay was in love with Carol, who was working for him at his construction company, but she was an "old-fashioned girl" who was not about to give in quickly to Jay's raw sexuality. Carol and Jay eventually married in a quiet ceremony in another town, while Jay and Susan continued their torrid affair.

Susan and Dan reunited, if only temporarily, when Emily developed bacterial meningitis and almost died. Susan had been on a bender that night, and when Kim found her passed out in her apartment, she threw her into the shower and then brought her to the hospital. Susan and Dan kept vigil and comforted each other while their daughter fought for her life in intensive care. Happily, Emily recovered.

It was at this time that John and Susan discovered that Dan and Kim were in love. Finally recovered from his injuries, John used Susan's alcoholism to play on Kim's guilt and keep her from Dan. Kim finally got fed up with her devious husband and made plans to go to Nevada for a quick divorce. But before leaving she was injured in a tornado that hit Centerville and suffered a concussion. When she regained consciousness, Kim had no memory of Dan! Meanwhile, John found a letter Kim had written to Dan and set fire to it. Then he eagerly took Kim home and kept her all to himself, refusing to allow friends such as Bob and Lisa to see her. He also tried to discourage the efforts of her psychiatrist to hypnotize her. Fortunately Kim made progress, and as her memory returned, she resumed her relationship with Dan.

Lisa desperately needed Kim's friendship at this time, because her romance with Grant was becoming a farce! Grant's unstable, neurotic ex-wife, Joyce, had come to Oakdale in hopes of winning him back and she was wreaking havoc on Lisa's relationship with Grant. As a way of weaving her way into the convoluted Oakdale fabric and becoming part of Grant's new world, Joyce took a job as a file clerk at Memorial. One night, Joyce accidentally ran over and killed a drunk, and she called Grant and begged him for his legal help. Both Grant and Dick Martin, who was now in the District Attorney's office, were baffled by Joyce's erratic behavior and conflicting accounts of the incident. Grant later discovered that the deceased pedestrian, a tennis bum named Gregory Paget, had carried on with Joyce throughout her marriage to Grant in San Francisco! Joyce was acquitted when the police proved she'd killed Paget accidentally, and Lisa and Grant finally married despite Joyce's machinations.

Lisa soon learned she was pregnant, but she lost the baby as the pressures from Grant's neurotic ex began to mount. Joyce told Grant that after their separation she found herself pregnant with his baby boy, whom she'd given up for adoption. Investigating Joyce's story, Lisa and Grant discovered she was telling the truth. The boy was named Teddy and he was adopted by a working-class couple, Mary and Brian Ellison, in Laramie, Wyoming. Deluding herself that she, Grant and Teddy could become a family, Joyce initiated a custody suit

He had helped her through her troubled marriage to John Dixon, and now Kim was at Dan's side when Susan threatened to press charges against him for taking their daughter Emily out of the country. By this time, Kim and Dan were very much in love.

against the Ellisons. Although Grant formed an attachment to the boy, he assured Mary and Brian that he would fight Joyce's attempts to take him from them. But Grant soon found himself with an uphill battle on his hands—his signature had been forged on Teddy's transfer papers, rendering the adoption invalid!

Joyce was not the only woman in Oakdale who had a bundle of secrets. Her new pal and neighbor, Natalie Bannon, was withholding some facts of her own. Bob had been treating Natalie for Wilson's disease, a potentially fatal ailment, and he had waited months before Natalie allowed him to reveal her illness to Tom. This revelation only strengthened Tom's resolve to make a life with this seemingly fragile young woman, and he proposed to her. Lisa did her best to accept her, even hiring Natalie to work at the bookstore, but Lisa was put off by Natalie's mysterious behavior. One day, in front of Carol, a customer at the bookstore recognized Natalie as Mrs. Ralph Porter from Kilbourn, Pennsylvania. At the same time, Natalie made the discovery that Jay and Susan were having an affair. Natalie and Jay had a past, and when Natalie confronted Jay with what she knew, Jay threatened to tell Tom that she was withholding her married name. Natalie finally told Tom that she had once been married to Ralph Porter and that he was a drug addict. What she did not reveal was that she'd carried on an affair with Ralph's married brother, Luke, who had recently arrived in Oakdale! Swept away by Natalie's "Little Miss Innocent" act, Tom married her anyway.

As the Hughes family wrestled with their mixed reactions to Tom and Natalie's relationship, they were surprised by the return of Bob's ex-wife, Sandy. Sandy had divorced Peter Kane and married Norman Garrison, an abrasive, shady businessman. Due largely to Norman's vicious temper and frequent financial problems, the marriage was a disaster. Sandy admitted to Bob that she was back in Oakdale because she was afraid of Norman, who followed her in hot pursuit. Angered that Bob and Sandy were still on friendly terms, Norman confronted Bob and accused him of having an affair with Sandy, only to suffer a heart attack during the argument! While he convalesced at Memorial, Norman was paid an unexpected and unwelcome visit by his girlfriend Tina Cornell, a crass, gum-chewing low-life. When Tina demanded that Norman support her in high style and dump Sandy, Norman suddenly died. Tina fled the scene, leaving the attending nurses to mistakenly believe that it was Bob who had forced the fatal argument. As usual, John jumped into the fray and fueled the fire against Bob.

As chaotic as this period was for the Hughes family, they rejoiced in yet another marriage, which was sure to be on solid ground. Pa Hughes married his longtime ladyfriend, Irma Kopecki, and left Nancy and Chris's home to set up housekeeping with his new bride. Nancy missed Pa, whom she had lovingly chided through the years for washing his hands in her kitchen sink. Now she and Chris were left alone to worry about the constantly changing love lives of Donald, Bob and their grandson, Tom.

## Troubled Triangle

*When Grant's ex-wife Joyce came to Oakdale, she did everything she could to come between him and Lisa. Joyce revealed that Grant had a son he never knew about, as she had put him up for adoption right after he was born.*

# 1976-1980

It was 1976 in Oakdale, and as "As The World Turns" celebrated its 20th anniversary, the beautiful Kim Dixon, having regained her memory, knew it was time to end her marriage to John. John didn't know how he could live without her, but Kim loved Dan and had to let him know. Kim left several messages on Dan's machine. Growing impatient, she hurried over to his house. As fate would have it, it was Susan, not Dan, who greeted Kim. Dan was preparing to leave on a medical mission and was getting Emily and Betsy settled in at David and Ellen's. Emily had forgotten her clothes and Susan had offered to get them. At Dan's place, she heard Kim's messages on the machine. Susan knew full well that if Dan learned Kim had regained her memory, Susan wouldn't stand a chance of getting him back, so she snatched the tapes and stuffed them into her purse. When Kim arrived, Susan lied and told Kim that Dan had received her messages but was on his way to South America. Kim was devastated and Susan tried to play on her feelings by making her feel guilty—how could Kim possibly leave John after all he had done for her?

Needing a new direction in her life, Kim took a job as a receptionist at Lowell, Hughes & Colman. John, meanwhile, was trying to get on with his life, too, and he started to date an impressionable young nurse named Pat Holland. Soon afterward, Kim learned she was pregnant with John's child! Despite John's pleas to reconcile for the sake of their unborn child, Kim went ahead and got a divorce. John drowned his sorrows in alcohol. The problem did not go unnoticed at the hospital. Kim was sympathetic; she didn't want John to ruin his life over their divorce, so she swallowed her pride and asked Susan, who was a friend of John's and had drinking problems of her own, to help. Susan didn't want to get involved because she'd told John about the stolen tapes and was afraid he might blurt something out. She asked another doctor to investigate instead, and it was confirmed that John had indeed been drinking on duty. A broken man, John suffered a mental breakdown and Susan was in a constant state of fear that he would blow the whistle about the tapes.

When Dan returned from South America, he found no messages from Kim, so he thought she no longer loved him and he made no effort to contact her. Instead, he became interested in Valerie Conway, the jet-setting sister of Kim's deceased husband, Jason Reynolds. Valerie literally crashed into town while piloting her plane and ended up in the ER as a patient of Dan's. Valerie resented Kim for having supported Jason's attempts to interfere in her love life, and so there was no love lost between the two women. When Valerie heard that Dan had been involved with Kim, she was doubly determined to win him, even though she had her eye on Bob Hughes as well.

Susan could not accept losing Dan to Valerie. She told John the only way to get Valerie out of Dan's life was to tell him about the tapes. John still had hopes of winning Kim back and begged Susan not to tell. Susan had also confided in Kevin Thompson, a handsome, perceptive young man who was very interested in her but was also a friend of Valerie's. Not wanting to see Valerie hurt, Kevin told Susan that if she didn't tell Dan about the tapes, he would. Knowing she had no choice, Susan went to Kim. After learning the truth, Kim was in shock and told Susan she planned to tell Dan the whole story. Pained by the realization that Dan would never forgive her, Susan "fell off the wagon" and bought a bottle of scotch. Meanwhile, Kim had second thoughts about telling Dan when he began to see Valerie, who by this time had decided to let bygones be bygones with Kim. Dan found out about the tapes anyway, gently broke things off with Val and was reunited with Kim. Around this time Kim had a baby boy whom she named Andrew.

As Kim welcomed her son into the world, Mary Ellison was in grave danger of losing hers, because Teddy's natural mother, Joyce Colman, was suing for custody. Grant didn't want his son anywhere near his unstable ex-wife and, to make matters worse, the custody fight was wreaking havoc on his marriage to Lisa, who had had it up to her ears with Joyce! Because of Dan's adoption, Joyce found a temporary ally in Ellen, but as Nancy pointed out, Ellen had to give her son away; Joyce did not. Nancy was sure Joyce was using Teddy to get Grant back into her life and her bed. At the hearing, under questioning by her attorney, Dick Martin, Joyce related how her doctor had badgered her into giving up her child by administering drugs to increase her anxiety and telling her how hard it would be for a beautiful, single woman like herself to raise a child. Mary came in from Laramie to attend the hearing and Dick did his best to discredit her. The judge, however, maintaining that the bond between loving adoptive parents and their child should not be destroyed, awarded custody to Mary and her husband, Brian. After the hearing, a distraught Joyce crashed her car and ended up in the hospital. Much to Lisa's dismay, Grant was very concerned about his ex-wife's suicide attempt. Lisa angrily told him she never wanted to hear Joyce's name again! In the hospital, Joyce seemed to have given up on life, and Bob asked Grant to visit her. When Lisa found out, she filed for divorce and Grant moved into the Lawyer's Club. Meanwhile, Joyce had begun to rely heavily on the sympathetic Dr. Bob. When Brian Ellison was killed in a construction accident, Mary moved to Oakdale with Teddy to find a job with Grant's help. Although Lisa liked the young widow and enjoyed getting to know her, she knew Joyce would never be able to leave Mary and Teddy alone.

Grant tried in vain to get Lisa out of his mind. One night, he drowned his sorrows in drink. Forgetting that he was staying at the Lawyer's Club, he took a taxi home. When Lisa found Grant half asleep in their bed, they fell into a passionate embrace, and the Colmans' marriage was back on track. It didn't take long, though, for Lisa to get upset by her husband's late hours at the office, and she swore she could understand why Joyce took a lover when she was married to Grant. Meanwhile, Joyce found the perfect weapon to use against the two men she felt had wronged her—Grant and Bob—and that man was Donald Hughes. Donald had just returned to Oakdale from Los Angeles and gone to work at Lowell, Hughes & Colman. Grant remembered all too well that Donald almost married Lisa. Since Donald and Grant were both criminal lawyers, Joyce wasted no time in playing on Donald's strong competitive streak. Donald soon became antagonistic toward Grant and, per Joyce's plan he was so enthralled by her that he couldn't see her flaws. When Bob tried to get Joyce to stop using his brother, Joyce lashed out and accused Bob of leading her on when she was in the hospital—and nobody made a fool out of her!

That wasn't the only trouble Bob was having at Memorial, and Nancy was becoming increasingly worried about her son. Bob had received an official reprimand from the board over the death of Norman Garrison, which was orchestrated by the devious Dr. Dixon to bring down his rival by charging him with malpractice. Bob remembered picking up the phone in Garrison's room. Hearing a woman's voice on the other end, he thought she might hold a clue as to how Garrison had died. The woman was Tina Richards, but John had gotten to her first and found out that she and Garrison were to be secretly married. It was, in fact, Tina who argued with Garrison the day he died. John knew this but withheld the information in order to implicate his nemesis, Bob. Then Tina arrived in Oakdale to hit up Sandy (Norman's widow) for the money Garrison owed her! Sandy was so shocked to see her that she didn't realize this was the "mystery woman" Bob had been searching for. Tina was brought before the hospital board and disclosed in great detail what had happened in Norman Garrison's room the day he died. She added that John Dixon had all this information a month ago. Bob received an official apology from the board, then went downstairs to the hospital chapel and said quietly, "Thank you, Jennifer." Practically everyone at Memorial sent up a hue and cry for John to be fired, but the fair-minded Bob said John was too good a doctor to be let go. He did lose his position as chief of medicine, which was offered to Bob, who turned it down. He didn't want to gain because of someone else's loss. Meanwhile, John moved into the same apartment house as Mary Ellison and the two formed an abiding friendship the likes of which John had never known.

Someone was causing havoc in Bob's son Tom's marriage and that someone was Jay Stallings. Jay was married to Tom's ex-wife Carol but was attracted to Tom's present wife, Natalie. While Carol was sweet-natured, Jay had an edge. Jay loved Carol very much, but he recognized that he and Natalie were two of a kind. They both wanted more out of life than a mundane small-town existence—much more. Natalie decided to have Carol and Jay over for dinner one night, and it was a disaster—the roast was overcooked, the vegetables were undercooked, everything that could possibly go wrong, did. Jay tried to calm Natalie down, but Natalie felt so nervous around him that she burst into tears and left the room. Neither Natalie nor Jay wanted to jeopardize their marriages. They were constantly being thrown together, though, and Lisa was getting suspicious. She wasn't the only one. Tom noticed how uncomfortable Natalie was whenever she was around Jay. Nat covered it up by telling Tom she was sure Jay had designs on her. In response, Jay told Tom that Nat was reading him all wrong, and Tom bought the story. The attraction grew, and when they found themselves alone, Jay took Natalie in his arms and kissed her passionately. Natalie did not resist.

At the bookstore, Lisa overheard a customer talking to Natalie. The customer knew her from Kilborn and had hoped never to lay eyes on her again! He also hoped she'd gotten the punishment she deserved for the misery she'd inflicted on others. Lisa's interest was piqued, and out of concern for her son, she asked Dick Martin to run a check on Natalie. Dick discovered that Natalie had lied about her past. Her husband didn't die from a drug overdose as she had claimed, but committed suicide after he found out Natalie was having an affair with his married brother. Kilborn was a small town and Natalie had shaken it up but good! Lisa turned to Bob for advice. Bob summoned Natalie to his office and told her that honesty was very important in a marriage. Everyone made mistakes—Tom would understand.

As Bob predicted, Tom forgave Nat her past; however, he couldn't condone the fact that she told him only because his parents forced her to, and he stormed out. Distraught, Natalie turned to Jay. After Tom had a chance to think it over, he decided to forgive Natalie again until he inadvertently overheard a phone conversation between her and Jay. Apparently, Nat left her wallet on Jay's couch the night before. There were some things Tom couldn't forgive, and infidelity was one of them. In his mind, the marriage was over. Tom's temper got the better of him and he was about to strangle Jay when the secretary's screams brought him to his senses. Jay begged Tom not to tell Carol about his one-night stand with Natalie—it would kill her. Because Tom still cared for his ex-wife, he honored the request. Carol was puzzled by the hatred between Jay and Tom, and even though Jay tried to hide the truth, Carol knew something was up. Because he felt guilty about Natalie and would do anything to make Carol happy, Jay finally agreed to adopt a baby. Natalie went back to Kilborn, but Jay was very much on her mind and she started making phone calls to him and hanging up. When Tom went to Kilborn to warn her to stop calling, Natalie accused him of still being in love with Carol and not wanting to see her hurt. Natalie decided to return to Oakdale and, using the threat of going to Carol and revealing everything, she blackmailed Jay into getting

her a cushy, high-paying job at a construction company. Lisa continued to worry about Carol and wanted to tell her about Jay and Natalie's one-night stand, but Bob advised against it. When Carol was contacted by the adoption agency, she was on cloud nine until she found

Joyce Colman found the perfect weapon to use against Grant Colman and Bob Hughes, the two men she felt had wronged her. He was Bob's brother, Donald, and he was quickly charmed.

out it might take two years to adopt. Carol was heartbroken, but Jay seemed relieved.

Now that she'd lost Tom for good, Natalie was determined to get Jay back in her life, and she told him her body ached for his. As far as Jay was concerned, they'd had a one-night stand and that was the end of it, yet he continued to be tormented and tempted by thoughts of Natalie. One night, while Carol was visiting her father in New York, Jay found himself at Natalie's door, in her arms and in her bed. Oh, how he wished Carol had come back from New York one night sooner! Jay was determined not to let this be more than another

Bob Hughes's nemesis, John Dixon, had gotten him in hot water with the hospital board over the questionable death of Norman Garrison, and Nancy was worried about her son's reputation and future.

Ellen was sure her daughter was making a terrible mistake. David realized Dee was no longer a little girl and had to make her own decisions. One night, out driving in a heavy rainstorm, Dee swerved to avoid hitting a dog and struck a barricade, sending it flying into the air. It was not until the next morning, when Annie showed her the paper, that Dee found out the barricade had hit a car and put the driver in the hospital. Dee rushed to Memorial, where her brother, Dan, was taking care of the injured young man. His name was Beau Spencer. Dee kept a vigil at his bed, waiting to see if he would live or die. To Dee's great relief, he recovered, and although he didn't blame her for the accident, he ignored her overtures of friendship. Dee liked him anyway. He gave her a new meaning in life, and she registered at college—the same college Beau would be attending for graduate school.

When Annie met Beau, she had the opposite reaction from her sister's. She found him self-centered and cocky and thought Dee could do much better. Beau was definitely attracted to a Stewart, but it wasn't Dee, it was Annie. Annie sensed this and was afraid her sister would be hurt. Dee didn't make it any easier by wanting her two favorite people, Annie and Beau, to get along. Annie was determined to stay out of Beau's way and she shared her fears with her good friend Tom. Tom had an idea: If he told Beau that Tom and Annie were dating, maybe Beau would leave her alone. The plan didn't work, and one night Beau kissed Annie. He promised her they'd just be friends. Annie hoped he meant it, but she confessed to Tom that if it weren't for Dee, she might be pursuing Beau, too. When Beau figured out that Annie and Tom were just friends, he launched an all-out effort to win her. Ever since Beau kissed her, Annie realized she had deep feelings for him, but knowing how much Dee cared for him, and unwilling to hurt her little sister, Annie decided to transfer to another college, even though Beau told her the only reason he was hanging around Dee was so he could be near Annie.

one-night stand, but Natalie had other ideas. She planted the seed in Jay's ear that Tom was still in love with Carol, and although he would never admit it, Jay was jealous. Natalie and Jay embarked on a full-fledged affair and Jay was racked with guilt. When Jay's and Carol's names were moved up on the adoption list, Tom wondered if he should tell Carol about Natalie and Jay, or let them bring a child into their mockery of a marriage. Finally, Natalie confessed to Lisa about the affair and told her she would rather have Carol find out the truth from Lisa. Lisa had no choice. Carol was devastated and threw Jay out. Jay appealed to Bob to help him win Carol back, for he knew Bob was fair and nonjudgmental. Bob believed Jay's story once again and promised to help. As for Natalie, she wanted Jay back in the worst way! Jay still loved Carol, though, and he wanted nothing more to do with Nat.

Over at the Stewart residence, Dee announced to her parents that she had decided not to go to college.

Beau felt comfortable enough with Ellen to confide in her about his parents, Ron and Jane Spencer, who were wealthy but had a troubled marriage. Coincidentally, Dick Martin was the Spencers' attorney, and he learned from Judge Lowell that Ron Spencer was the accused party in a paternity suit the Judge had presided over years ago, and he had lost. Out of concern for his great-granddaughter, the Judge ordered a background check on Beau.

Sadly in this 20th year, Oakdale lost one of its most beloved citizens, Grandpa Hughes. His eulogy was given by a third-generation Hughes, his grandson Bob. Grandpa will be missed.

## EULOGY FOR GRANDPA HUGHES
## JUNE 4, 1976

*Thank you for being with us today. Pa would have liked this rain, and what it would do for all growing things. He loved birth, growth, maturing. This would be his kind of day—and perhaps it is. Because here we are, too—his friends, his neighbors, his pastor and three generations of the family whom he loved so much together. He would love the fact of Mom cooking this morning, so that people could eat later on—if they wanted to stay together a little longer and talk a little longer. We loved him, and he loved us. That love will always be with us, because we each carry some living memory of him, and that will go on as long as we go on. We Hugheses all shared for many years my grandfather's blessing of having such a good man live among us. Grandpa had a sweetness and a tolerance. He believed there was good in everyone. When we were kids we used to say, "Now, Grandpa, not everybody's good." And he'd say, "Oh, yes—it's there—but in some people it just never had a chance to grow." He never tried to tell you what to do, but he had a way of leading you to what was right, and what was the truth. Sometimes—sometimes we didn't take his hand when he offered to lead us, and that's when we got into trouble. In the last year of his life, he married a lovely woman. She's with her family today. She needs them just as we need each other here. Grandpa has a great-granddaughter who is only two and a half. She's home. She may not understand our sadness, but she will share the memories of Pa through all of us, and someday pass some of them on to her children—and so on and on part of his spirit will always be with us. It's stopped raining. As much as he loved the rain, Pa loved the sun that came after the rain. Pa loved life. Pa loved God. He's with Him.*

# 1 9 7 7

In the winter of 1977, a terrible accident rocked Oakdale. An entire wall of scaffolding collapsed at a construction site, burying Annie Stewart and Jay Stallings in the rubble. Jay was crushed trying to save Annie's life. Annie sustained a hairline fracture, while Jay was in serious condition with broken bones and internal bleeding. Bob Hughes was in charge of the case. While waiting for news of Annie, Beau confided to Tom that he felt responsible for her accident. He had just given Annie an ultimatum: either she tell Dee about her feelings for him, or he would. Beau was sure that was why she didn't hear Jay's warning.

Dee had just finished telling Joyce Colman how much she loved Beau when she overheard him telling a still-unconscious Annie how much he loved her. Beau told Annie that neither of them wanted to hurt Dee, but he knew he wouldn't be able to keep his feelings to himself much longer. A heartbroken Dee decided not to tell anyone what she overheard. When Annie regained consciousness, she confided in Tom that although she loved Beau deeply, she couldn't be with him because of Dee. Beau tried hard to convince Annie that denying their love was wrong, but Annie said she would rather hurt herself than hurt her younger sister, and she didn't think they should see each other anymore. However, Dee proved equally selfless and freed Beau and Annie to pursue a relationship, and the two became engaged. Nevertheless, Dee still pined for Beau and finally grew so despondent that she told her father about the whole heartbreaking triangle. David was angry that Beau had played his two daughters against each other. He begged Annie not to keep seeing this young man, whom he considered unprincipled and selfish. In time, David came to realize Beau truly loved Annie, although he was still not completely sold on his son-in-law-to-be. The main problem Annie and Beau now faced was Beau's mounting debt. He had grown up privileged but was now enjoying his champagne tastes on a beer budget. Annie helped him get back on his feet by landing him a clerk job at Lowell, Hughes & Colman. Then Beau's mother, powerful businesswoman Jane Spencer, owner of the prestigious Spencer Hotel, came to town and offered Annie and Beau financial support. Beau was adamant about his mother not getting involved in their lives, and with Annie's approval he turned down her offer. Then Annie learned the real reason Jane was in town. Beau's father had left her, and Jane didn't want to tell Beau, because there'd been a long-standing feud between father and son.

Although Annie recovered fully from the accident, Jay's injuries took longer to heal. It was Tom who comforted a tormented Carol as she waited for word of her husband, while Natalie was left to seek advice from her new pal and fellow schemer, Joyce Colman, on how to win Jay back. The devious Joyce told Nat that Bob probably lied to Jay when he said he would help Jay work things out with Carol. After all, wouldn't Bob be on Carol and Tom's side? A desperate Natalie clung to Joyce's words. When Natalie finally did see Jay in the hospital, he made it clear that the only woman he wanted was Carol. Natalie warned him that he'd end up alone because Carol was seeing Tom again. But things had already begun to turn in Jay's favor. Because of his heroism in saving Annie's life, a great many people began to see him in a different light, and Carol was one of them. Not only did she visit him frequently at the hospital, but she gave of her time to help out at Stallings Construction as well. The fact that her hostility had subsided gave Jay hope that he and Carol could get back together. But even though she no longer hated him, she didn't love him either, and as soon as he was well enough, Carol planned to file for divorce.

Meanwhile, Natalie hadn't stopped scheming to get Jay back. She knew the only thing he loved more than sex was money, and because she worked at another construction company—a job she had blackmailed Jay into getting for her—she was able to wrangle the rights to Valerie's sprawling farmland and dangle them in front of Jay. She told him that if he wanted the Conway farm, she wouldn't breathe a word to her boss. Jay played it cool, but he was very tempted and decided to talk to Valerie. An ecstatic Nat thought she'd scored big until she found out Jay wanted the farmhouse because he thought it would be a perfect place for him and Carol. Jay finally came clean about his affair with Natalie. He told Carol that being with Natalie only made him love Carol more and begged her for a second chance. Touched by his honesty, Carol agreed to try again. Willing to do anything to make his wife happy, Jay urged Carol to get the ball rolling at the adoption agency. But all was not bliss, because at the same time, Natalie found out she was pregnant. Nat asked Jay for money to pay for an abortion. Jay was against the abortion, but now that things were back on track between him and Carol, he was afraid to tell her about the baby. He turned to Kim for advice. Kim told him to be honest about the baby and assure Carol that he loved her, not Nat. It worked, and

Carol even decided she wanted to adopt the baby. Jay offered to set Natalie up in her own real estate firm if she agreed, and money-hungry Nat said yes. Carol was on cloud nine! She suggested they go to Chris Hughes and have a legal document drawn up so everything would be aboveboard. Chris told Natalie that Jay's name would have to appear on the birth certificate. Nat didn't know if Jay would agree. Then the plan hit another snag. Natalie wanted to go out of town to have the baby. The adoption agency claimed that such secrecy could backfire years later when the child discovered the truth. He or she could hold it against Carol and run to Natalie, so it was best to keep the adoption out in the open. Carol agreed, but Natalie told Jay that to bring everything out in the open would cause her severe emotional anguish. However, $10,000 just might ease the pain.

At the same time, Joyce had been giving her friend Natalie an earful about how Grant and Lisa wanted to break up Joyce and Donald. As for Don, he was making every effort to make the relationship work. He approached Grant at Lowell, Hughes & Colman, where they both worked, and told him he'd like to bury the hatchet and be friends. Grant agreed and they shook hands on it. Meanwhile, Lisa decided to play matchmaker and fix up Mary and Don, so she invited Donald to dinner but forgot to tell him about Mary. When Don saw Mary he realized Joyce was right about Lisa and Grant wanting to break them up, and he ripped into Grant and stormed out of the house. Grant was sure Lisa's blunder had cost him his newly cordial relationship with Don. Joyce cornered Mary at the hospital and told her in no uncertain terms, "Hands off my man!" She decided it was time to put pressure on Donald and get him to make a commitment. When she told him she loved him, he replied that he was still "finding himself" and wasn't ready to settle down. Joyce showed Donald the door and told him to come back when he was more sure of his feelings. Until then, she wanted nothing to do with him! Fortunately for Donald, Chris Hughes offered him a position working for a big client whose home office was in Switzerland. With nothing to keep him in Oakdale now, Donald was thrilled. Joyce heard about the Switzerland move and announced to Chris that she might be leaving Oakdale, too. Natalie came up with the perfect plan! She suggested that Joyce empty her apartment to make it look as if she had left town. Natalie would call Donald and pretend to be worried about her, hoping Donald would realize what he "almost" lost.

The plan worked like a charm. Joyce let Donald stew for a couple of days and then made a surprise appearance at the Hughes home. The next day Donald proposed.

Even though she was married to Grant, Lisa kept going back to Bob, and she was determined to break free of Grant so that she could pursue Bob once again.

Maybe now, Joyce could do something for Nat in return. But knowing how the Hugheses felt about Natalie, the calculating Joyce wanted to end the friendship. When Joyce discovered she was pregnant, the Hughes clan had no choice but to accept her. And so Nancy was once again in a position to bemoan Donald's choice of a spouse. Chris, however, reminded her to keep her disapproval to herself or they might lose their son again. Donald was summoned to Switzerland on business and because of Joyce's pregnancy her doctor advised her not to go. Donald offered to cancel the trip, but seeing the dollar signs this account would bring in, Joyce urged him to go. While Donald was gone, Joyce went to stay with Nancy and Chris, and she did everything in her power to forge a bond with Nancy. Unfortunately, marriage and pregnancy had not changed Joyce's devious ways. She told Sandy in the strictest confidence that Bob was still in love with her. In truth, Joyce was still in love with Bob and wanted to spread this rumor as revenge for his rejection of her.

Lisa was also interested in her ex-husband Bob, even though her mother, Alma, warned her that she would be making a serious mistake if she didn't value Grant as the loving husband he was. Lisa told her mother that she did value Grant, but Bob would always hold a special place in her heart.

It was Grant's turn to play matchmaker and he asked Lisa to invite Bob and Val for dinner. The only reason Lisa agreed was because she saw it as an opportunity to renew her intimacy with Bob. Lisa was determined to get him away from Valerie, even though it was clear that Bob and Val were enjoying each other's company very much. Not one to be daunted by the competition, Lisa determined to break free of Grant so that she could pursue her first husband. But Grant loved her too much to let her go.

Even though Valerie was seeing Bob, she was still pining for Dan and she blamed Susan Stewart for ruining that relationship. If Susan hadn't opened her big mouth about taking the tapes, Valerie would be Mrs. Dan Stewart. Val was sure Susan had told Dan only to keep him away from Val. Susan thought Val should blame her ex-sister-in-law Kim, who knew Susan was on the verge of cracking and simply waited for her to spill the beans. Now Kim had gotten everything she wanted without tainting her "angelic" image. Val didn't want to believe this, but after all, Kim did shaft her once before, with Valerie's first love, Cliff. Val told Kim what Susan had said and accused Kim of lying when she said it was over between her and Dan. Kim tried to convince her she said that because she didn't want to ruin Val's happiness, but Val wasn't buying it. As far as she was concerned their friendship was over and she never wanted to see Kim again! What Valerie didn't realize was that there was more to the story behind her estrangement from Kim than she knew. Kim confided to Lisa that one night when her late husband, Jason, was out of town, Cliff had tried to rape her. In order to protect Valerie, Kim and Jason paid him off to leave town. Valerie's heart was broken and she blamed Kim. Lisa inadvertently let the story slip to Val, but Val refused to believe it and she vowed to get back at Kim. She'd marry a respectable doctor, too—Dr. Bob!

As for Susan, she was turning more and more to the bottle for solace. Although she remembered what her alcoholism had done to her life in the past, Susan couldn't help herself. One night Kevin found her having a drunken fight with the desk clerk at the Spencer Hotel. He took her home and stayed with her until she fell asleep. Even though a romance was blossoming between Kevin and Sandy, Kevin still cared for Susan very much. But Susan's drinking was out of control and she refused to admit it. She even managed to get herself arrested for insulting an officer and Grant had to bail her out. The incident hit the papers and Kim was worried about how this latest development would affect Emily. Susan was subsequently fired when the acting chief of staff at Memorial, Jim Strasfield, noticed her alcohol problem and shoddy work. At the board hearing, Susan showed up drunk and accused Jim of carrying on a vendetta against her because his wife was an alcoholic and had drunk herself to death. At the end of her diatribe Susan collapsed, and Kevin came to the rescue. He offered her his cabin to recuperate in. Susan accepted, and she didn't touch a drop while she was there. But when she returned home, Susan ended up hitting the bottle once again. Things got so bad that she was arrested on a drunk and disorderly charge and ended up in jail. Susan didn't contact anyone, and Kevin thought it was because she was trying to teach herself a lesson by spending the night in jail, so he asked Grant not to post bail. When Kevin arrived the next day, Susan was furious at him for letting her spend the night in jail! That didn't last for long, though, and soon Susan was wearing Kevin's ring and trying very hard to get her life together. Susan eventually decided to break off her engagement to Kevin because she didn't think the relationship was a healthy one. She borrowed some money from David and left town, leaving behind a note and Kevin's ring. Kevin was shocked! The note said that she would be gone for two weeks, and when she came back, she didn't think they should see each other anymore. A hurt Kevin was sure that Susan was bent on a path that would ruin their lives forever. He went to Sandy and told her his relationship with Susan was over, and Sandy took him at his word.

Susan was busy destroying other lives besides her own. Just as Kim and Dan were reunited, Susan, in a drunken fit, blurted out to Kim that she wasn't the only one to keep Kim and Dan apart—John knew about those tapes all along! Kim confronted John and told him if he wanted to see Andrew, there would be no more dropping by; it would be by appointment only! Afraid Kim and Dan would keep him from Andrew, John was desperate for a plan. He and Kim

## Love and Marriage

*He had to free himself from the manipulative Susan Stewart, and she had to free herself from the devious John Dixon, so it was a happy day when family and friends gathered to see Kim Dixon and Dan Stewart say "I do." Dan's "pre-wedding" toast to his bride went like this: "To you. Your love is a joy to me that has no equal. I pledge to you all the life, the hope and the love that is mine to give. To Kim."*

had never bothered with a custody agreement, so, according to the law, whoever had possession of the child had a legal right to him. All John had to do was take his son, and Andrew would be legally his. When Kim announced she was having a legal custody agreement drawn up, John knew he had to act fast, and he needed help. He turned to nurse Pat Holland, who had always been infatuated with him, and persuaded her to look after Andrew in a house he had rented just outside of Oakdale. While Kim and Dan were busy making wedding plans, John carried out his own plan. One afternoon, when Kim's good friend Carol Stallings was looking after Andrew in the park, Pat showed up and pretended to cut herself. Kind-hearted Carol went to her aid, and John snuck up and swiped Andrew, leaving a fake note from a woman saying she took the child because she desperately wanted a baby and couldn't have one of her own.

It hurt John to see Kim in so much pain, but he couldn't let Dan Stewart raise his son! John had Pat type a note saying that the child was fine and well cared for, and he enclosed a photo. Grant told Kim the note might provide a clue for the police. John was not happy to hear that. The crib in the photo did give the police a lead, but to John's relief, they were looking for a woman. Dan began to notice John's strange behavior whenever the photo was mentioned and caught him in some lies as to his whereabouts at the time Andrew was snatched. Suspecting it was John who had taken Andrew, Dan began to follow him, and John unknowingly led him to the house where he was keeping the boy. Dan contacted the authorities, but they told him that since a custody agreement was never drawn up, legally John had done nothing wrong. As long as Andy was in John's house, Kim couldn't get him, and they couldn't arrest John for kidnapping, because all he did was bring his son to his

house. If John brought him out of the house, that would be a different story. When John found out that Kim knew he had Andy, he told her she'd never get him back. A distraught Kim begged Dan to rescue her baby! Dan showed up at John's house, and a frightened Pat offered no resistance when he took Andrew. When John arrived, he and Pat tried to follow Dan. In his anger, John became irrational. He opened the glove compartment, took out a revolver and told her one way or another, he was going to get Dan Stewart! Pat tried to persuade John not to use the weapon. He tossed it back into the glove compartment and it went off, hitting John in the chest. When he was brought to Memorial, John told the police that Dan had shot him, and Pat corroborated the story. Minutes later, Dan was arrested for kidnapping and attempted murder.

Kim knew in her heart that Dan didn't shoot John, and she prayed that the jury would find him innocent. Dick Martin was called back to the D.A.'s office to prosecute. Dick didn't want this assignment, but Grant convinced him that they were really on the same side because they both wanted to find the truth, Grant for Dan, and Dick for the people. To secure her testimony John asked Pat to marry him, and she said yes.

The case for the defense took a turn for the better when John made a fatal error in judgment. He told Kim and Dan that he would change his testimony if they gave him full custody of Andrew. Grant brought this out during his questioning of Dan, and this turn of events shed new light on the case. John denied making the offer and, when pushed further, he lost control and began making allegations about Dan that placed his emotional stability in question. At the end of his tirade, Pat, unable to stand his lies any longer, blurted out the truth. In her haste to escape John's almost certain wrath, Pat ran from the courtroom and took a bad fall down a flight of stairs. Minutes later, she lost consciousness and died. John looked at his wife's lifeless body and in a rare moment of humanity said, "I think you're the only one who ever loved me." No longer star-crossed lovers, Kim and Dan were finally wed. It was a happy day!

# 1 9 7 8

When Beau Spencer failed his bar exam, his overbearing mother, Jane, thought it was high time to call off his wedding to Annie Stewart, which was only days away. How could he possibly support Annie on the meager salary he was making as a law clerk at Lowell, Hughes & Colman? Nothing was going to keep Beau from marrying Annie, though, and the wedding went off as planned. Jane offered the newlyweds the old Spencer house, but Annie was sure this was a ploy on her mother-in-law's part to gain control over their lives and she persuaded Beau to move into an apartment of their own. However, the apartment was beyond their means, and Beau was forced to turn to his mother for a loan. Mother was more than willing. Jane Spencer's antipathy toward Annie stemmed from the fact that although she was a Stewart, Annie was not the country club type. So Jane threw them "the party of the year" at the country club, of course, and gave them the gift of a membership to boot. Beau was right at home in this setting, but Annie wasn't, and she decided it was time to go back to med school.

Meanwhile, Jane hired Chris Hughes to handle her divorce. She was dating her high school sweetheart, Dick Martin, but he was intimidated by her money and she was secretly hoping her ex-husband would contest. He didn't, and then Dick Martin stopped seeing her, so all Jane had left was Beau. Annie, beware!

It didn't take long for Jane to put her plan into action. First she wooed Beau back to a junior management position with the Spencer Hotel. Annie was on to her, but Beau was not, and the situation began to cause friction between them. The pressure built as Beau continued to work at the hotel, clerk for the law firm and study for the bar. Jane laid it on Annie that Beau was only becoming a lawyer to make her happy. Beau failed the bar a second time. He was devastated. Conversely, Jane was thrilled, and she offered him full management of the Spencer so that he could support his wife in proper style. Beau had finally caught on to his mother's schemes, but he swallowed his pride and accepted her offer. He made his mother promise never to tell that he had only done this to support Annie.

Around this time, a mysterious young stranger entered the Spencers' lives. One day, as Kim was placing flowers on her sister Jennifer's grave, a young woman came up to her claiming to be Jennifer's daughter. Kim was shocked! Jen had never told her she had another daughter. She was 18 years old and said her name was Melinda Gray. Then she showed Kim a locket with a picture of Jennifer as a young girl. Melinda said her adoptive father gave her the locket just before he died. The girl seemed sweet and honest, but Kim wasn't sure, so she went to the Reverend Booth in an attempt to calm her inner turmoil. The Reverend told Kim that before Jennifer married Bob, she told him the story of the daughter she'd given up for adoption. She was never able to forgive herself, and no else knew about the child. Because the Reverend knew about the locket, Kim was certain that Melinda was, indeed, Jennifer's daughter. She was also quite the social climber. Melinda was soon hired as Jane Spencer's girl Friday and hoped this would be her first step on the ladder to wealth and power. She was very attracted to Beau and had been observing the battle royal among mother, son and daughter-in-law with great interest. While Annie was busy at med school, Melinda was ready, willing and able to help Beau in any way she could.

Beau and Annie were fighting frequently, and the truth eventually came out about his quitting law to support her. This was not what Annie had wanted, and she turned to her family for help. David and Judge Lowell agreed to lend Beau and Annie money so that Beau could pursue his law career. When Jane got wind of this, she threatened to sell the hotel if Beau quit working there. Beau gave in. He threw himself into his work, and Jane threw Beau and Melinda together whenever she could. Melinda fit Jane's country club image much more than Annie did. Soon, to Jane's delight, Beau's attitude toward Annie changed. He no longer supported her dream of becoming a doctor and resented that because of her studies she couldn't be the proper corporate wife. Caught in the middle of trying to please her husband and pass her courses, Annie fell further and further behind. Dr. Jeff Ward, one of her resident doctors, took note. Tensions finally exploded, and one night Beau stormed out. Torn between marriage and work, Annie knew she couldn't have both. Aware of what was going on, Melinda was quick to make her move, and she left one of her slips in the closet for Annie to see.

Joyce Colman Hughes was accustomed to a very nice lifestyle and wanted nothing less than to run with Jane Spencer's wealthy crowd. Don loved his spoiled wife so much that he bought them an expensive house that was way out of their price range. This left them with no money to join the country club. Joyce begged Don to go to Chris, who didn't even believe in country clubs, and ask for a raise. Joyce managed to convince her husband that the reason he didn't get a raise at the law firm was because her ex-husband Grant resented him for

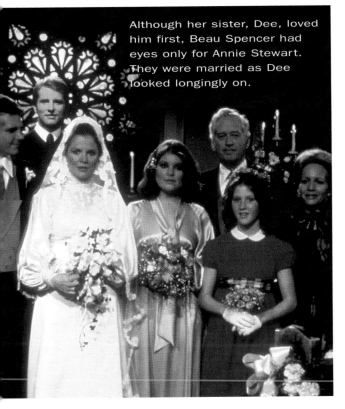

Although her sister, Dee, loved him first, Beau Spencer had eyes only for Annie Stewart. They were married as Dee looked longingly on.

marrying her. Don agreed to confront Grant and got his raise, but Joyce was still unhappy, and Don began to see the light about his greedy wife. Restless with her life, Joyce had a one-night stand with one of Valerie's jet-setting cronies, Ralph Mitchell, who was also one of Donald's clients. She decided to stay in town while Don went to Switzerland on business. An observant Nancy took note. Soon after, Joyce discovered she was pregnant. The baby was Ralph's, but Ralph was not about to marry her, so Joyce reluctantly told Don they were expecting, and she vowed to get revenge on Ralph for turning her down.

Everyone was delighted about the baby except for Nancy, who suspected the truth about the baby's parentage. Ralph was planning to tell Don everything and pull

out of their business dealings when the car they were driving in crashed. Ralph saved Don's life by pulling him out of the flaming wreck; then he quietly left town for a while. Later, Joyce fell down the stairs and miscarried. Don blamed himself, and Joyce knew deep down that his guilt would keep their marriage intact. After losing the child, Joyce longed to see her son, Teddy, who knew he was adopted but had no idea that Joyce was his natural mother. Teddy's adoptive mother, Mary Ellison, refused Joyce's request. Mary didn't trust Joyce, and for good reason. Mary worked for Don as his secretary, and he noticed she wasn't looking well. Soon afterward, she was hospitalized with hepatitis, and Teddy went to stay with Joyce and Don. When Mary recovered, the scheming Joyce said it would kill Don if the boy left. Since Joyce had lost "their" child, Teddy was the only person who could make Don smile. Mary adored Don and couldn't refuse him anything, so she agreed that Teddy could stay for a while.

Joyce's nemesis, Lisa, asked Grant for a separation, because she believed she was still in love with Bob. But Bob was still drawn to the enticing Valerie Conway. During his separation from Lisa, Grant had also become interested in Valerie, and Valerie didn't hesitate to drop hints to the unsuspecting Lisa that if she weren't careful, someone just might steal Grant away, and that someone might be Valerie. Lisa found this very amusing, but when Bob rejected her, she realized she had to work fast to win Grant back or she'd lose them both. Unfortunately for Lisa, Grant had decided he wanted a divorce. Lisa was crushed! She had to find a way to win him back! She begged for a second chance and got it, at which point she decided to make friends with Valerie and play matchmaker with her and Bob. Lisa confided in Alma that Grant seemed distracted and Lisa was determined to find out why. It didn't take Lisa long to figure out the distraction was Valerie. Grant was too moral to leave Lisa, and Valerie didn't want to cause him any more pain, so she turned to the intense, volatile Dr. Alex Keith for comfort. They had a lot in common because Alex was also in love with someone who was married—Kim.

Around this time, Valerie's sleazy ex-husband, Nick Conway, arrived in town low on funds and looking for a piece of Valerie's farm. Valerie refused and told him he'd have to talk to her lawyer, Grant Colman. Nick promptly filed a lawsuit against her. Lisa plotted to get Nick back into Valerie's life and succeeded in getting him to drop the lawsuit, which led Valerie to wonder what her ex-husband was up to. Valerie devised a plan to make Grant want her. It worked, and Grant asked Lisa for a divorce. But Lisa was not one to be outsmarted. She feigned illness and told Grant she'd deal with the divorce when she was better. Then she told Valerie she knew Grant was seeing another woman and she couldn't take it anymore—she was going to kill herself! If Valerie didn't believe her, Lisa said, she could come to the apartment tomorrow at a specified time. When Valerie arrived, no one was there. At the same time, Lisa miraculously appeared at Valerie's farm! To Valerie's dismay, Grant refused to see this staged suicide as one of Lisa's ploys, and Val turned to Nick for comfort, unaware that all he wanted was her money. Believing that Nick had changed, Valerie agreed to remarry him, while Grant suspected that all was not forgiven with Lisa. He was right.

Tired of waiting for her lover, Nick Conway, in New York, gum-chewing lowlife Tina Cornell arrived in Oakdale. Unaware that Lisa was on to them, Nick told Tina to sit tight; Valerie had signed over half the farm to him, and soon he and Tina would have enough money to get married. But Nick wanted to go further—he wanted to kill his ex-wife. That was too much for Tina. She confided in Lisa, and despite the fact that they were rivals, Lisa decided to warn Valerie. Valerie, however, thought it was another of Lisa's tricks. When Tina arrived at the farm, she spotted Nick about to drop a bale of hay on the unsuspecting Valerie. Shouting a warning, Tina pushed Val out of the way just as the hay fell, and a stunned Nick fell to the ground and was instantly killed. Valerie was in shock while Tina lay injured under the bale of hay. After the accident, Tina developed a severe case of agoraphobia and Lisa asked her to move in with her and Grant to recuperate. Nick had left all his worldly goods to Tina, but she decided to turn everything over to Valerie. After

## Law and Order

*Bob was taken with the beautiful Karen Peters and was convinced that she was trying to clear her father's name of illegal business dealings. Unfortunately for Bob, it turned out that Karen was a co-conspirator with her father, and she went to jail for her white-collar crimes.*

all, it was rightfully hers. Maybe now the town of Oakdale would forgive her for her involvement with the treacherous Nick Conway.

Bob Hughes had been lonely since Valerie rejected him. He couldn't stop thinking about the pretty woman who gave Frannie a Christmas star at the store. Suddenly, there she was in the emergency room, the victim of a car crash. She claimed her name was Karen Parker, but as she became closer to Bob, she revealed that she was really Karen Peters and she'd run away with a file that would clear her father of illegal business dealings. She had no idea what was in the file, but a lot of people wanted it, including her fiancé, Walter Vested, who was the D.A. in her hometown of Winterbrook. Walter managed to find Karen in Oakdale and tried to enlist Bob's help in turning over the papers because they would expose Walter as well. Bob was on to him and refused. Shortly after, Karen's hotel room was ransacked, and she left town, frightened. Walter wanted to find her before the thugs did and saw Bob as a way to get to her. He ordered the thugs to scare Bob, and when Karen heard about this, she offered to turn over the infamous file. Bob went to Karen to warn her that Walter was in on the illegal dealings, only to have Walter arrive and pull a gun on them. In the fight that followed, Walter was killed, but Bob soon discovered that Karen's father, Judge Peters, was just as corrupt as Walter. In fact, they had both been involved in a crime syndicate. Bob felt he owed it to Karen to tell her before she read it in the papers.

Then John Dixon got in on the act. Bob had kept him from getting reinstated at Memorial, and John was determined to get him back for it through Karen. John filled Karen in on how Judge Peters had paid for his medical schooling and how much John admired the man. Karen agreed that she should fight the charges against her father and John vowed to help her every step of the way. Bob was sure the legal battle was a lost cause and Karen's father was, indeed, corrupt. He warned her that John was using her to get to him, but Karen dismissed this—John Dixon was her friend. As luck would have it, both Bob and John were duped. It was soon revealed that Karen was a co-conspirator in the syndicate! Karen went to jail for her crimes.

When Bob's ex-wife, Sandy, heard that Kevin Thompson had been in a minor car accident, she rushed to his side, proclaimed her love and told him yes, she would marry him. Kevin swore she was the only woman in his life and Sandy prayed this was true. The honeymoon was wonderful. Coming home was not. The specter of Susan Stewart was everywhere. All Sandy had to do was look into Kevin's eyes and know that he still held a torch for Susan. To forget his past love, Kevin threw himself into a whirlwind of activity, but this only separated him further from Sandy, who feared the marriage would not survive his infatuation with Susan Stewart. When Sandy couldn't take it anymore and left town for a few days, Kevin showed up at Susan's drunk. She urged him not to ruin things with his wife. Sandy, however, thought Susan still had some kind of hold on her husband. Kevin tried hard to please his wife, but the fights continued, until one night, on the way home from a party, he asked if she wanted a divorce. She said she did. At that very moment, their car swerved out of control and hit a truck. Sandy was seriously hurt and Kevin was racked with guilt. The months she spent in the hospital left Sandy with nothing to do but think, and she decided to give her marriage another try. But Kevin was off on an alcoholic binge that landed him in the ward of a New York hospital. Sandy was relieved to find him and brought him back to Oakdale, only to encounter a woman with an even more dubious reputation than Susan's. She was Ginny Hopkins, a prostitute, and she was in love with Kevin. Ginny was arrested with stolen goods, among them Kevin's watch. Kevin ultimately hit rock-bottom when he crashed his car while on a business trip that turned into a drunken spree. His liver was so diseased from all the drinking that doctors couldn't stop the bleeding, and he died.

At this time, Susan Stewart was trying hard to stem her own desire to drink. She knew that work was the answer, and she swore if she were reinstated at Memorial, she'd never touch another drop. Susan was thrilled when David Stewart informed her that the board had approved her return. Back on the job, Susan worked hard to give a terminally ill patient, Mark Lewis, a reason to keep living. Mark was inspired by Susan's fight against the bottle and strived to battle his illness with the same courage. Dr. Alex Keith took note and was grateful. Alex had been in love with Mark's mother, but she died tragically in a plane crash on her way home from a vacation where she was to tell her husband of her affair with Alex. Mark was all Alex had left of her. Susan soon became frazzled helping Mark through this critical time and was in danger of returning to the bottle. David blasted Alex for using her to help Mark—he should have been helping her in her own battle. Finally, Mark was released from the hospital and returned home, but he died soon after. Alex confided in Susan that Kim reminded him of Mark's mother and he thought he was falling in love with her. Alex proclaimed his love to Kim and told her he hoped someday she would return his feelings. Dan became wildly jealous! However, at a medical convention in Washington, D.C., Dan was sorely tempted by the seductive Susan. It went no further than a kiss. Susan aroused him sexually, but Dan was very much in love with his wife! Seeing how much Kim and Dan loved each other, Alex stopped pursuing her and they remained good friends. Susan, on the other hand, wasted no time in telling Kim about D.C. Kim wasn't fazed one bit. Did Susan really think Dan would choose her over Kim?

It was at this time that John held another club over Dan's and Kim's heads: He threatened to tell Betsy that Dan was her real father, not her uncle, as she had been led to believe. She was a young lady of 14 now, and Dan realized she had a right to know. This shocking discovery upset Betsy enormously! She became troubled and withdrawn, and to Kim's and Dan's dismay, she ran away from home. She was discovered unconscious in a snowbank and brought to Memorial. Although Betsy recovered, it was soon learned that she was suffering from hysterical deafness. Once she could finally hear again, Betsy was ready to accept her father's love.

Meanwhile, Jay Stallings's construction company was in the red and Jay was convinced his former foreman Pete Larsen was to blame. Natalie Hughes, who was carrying Jay's baby, was also short of cash due to her failing company, and she went to Jay for a loan. Jay turned her down flat, and she vowed to make him pay! When he went out of town on business, Natalie went to Carol. Carol didn't want to upset Natalie because of the baby, so she gave her the money. Cash in hand, Natalie packed her bags and left town. Carol was devastated because they lost the baby. Jay was devastated because they lost the money. No one was happier to see this couple in trouble than Melinda Gray, who was as attracted to Jay's body as she had been to Beau Spencer's wealth.

After a careful review of his books, Jay found that, as he expected, Pete Larsen was responsible for his losses. They had a violent fight and Pete finally agreed to pay him back. After the fight, Jay was shaken and needed to talk, so he went to Melinda's place. Later, on his way home, Jay heard on the radio that Pete Larsen had been killed. He needed an alibi, and bad, because Carol must never know where he was. Jay was questioned and released on bail until an elderly neighbor came forward, described the fight and identified Jay as the guilty party. Jay wasted no time in getting Tom Hughes to represent him. He told Tom everything except the part about Melinda. Instead, he said he had driven around after the fight and then went to a bar. Tom sensed something fishy about Jay's story. Jay hedged and told Tom he was with some woman he'd picked up at the bar and he didn't want Carol to know. It was Melinda who spilled the beans to Tom, but she swore that she and Jay had only talked. Tom wanted to use this information at the trial. Jay refused, saying he still didn't want Carol to know. On the stand and under oath, Jay came clean about where he was, but Melinda changed the story! When she took the stand, she claimed Jay forced his way into her apartment and tried to force himself on her. Jay was acquitted by the jury, but not by his wife! It seemed as if everyone in Oakdale, except Tom, believed Melinda. Melinda eventually confessed the truth, but that didn't stop Carol from filing for divorce.

One day, out of the blue, a letter arrived from Natalie. She'd had a baby girl! Carol took it to Chris Hughes, who was handling the adoption. Because he still loved her, Jay promised to help Carol find Natalie and the baby. Not knowing of the split between them, Natalie deposited little Amy on Carol and Jay's doorstep and disappeared. Carol was thrilled! Jay was not. He couldn't support himself, much less a baby, and he wanted to give it up for adoption. Carol wouldn't hear of it. She even went so far as to stop divorce proceedings. She was not going to lose this child! Carol suggested that Jay contact Hank Robinson, a big builder in the area, and ask for a job. Hank was sweet on Carol, but years ago Jay had stolen Hank's girlfriend Linda, and Hank swore he'd get him for it someday. Now he would pay Jay back by stealing Carol. It didn't take Jay long to regress back

to his old egomaniacal, cocky self, and even though he did good work, Hank was still determined to even the score. When he heard Jay talking to John Dixon about the new cardiac unit at Memorial, he was sure Jay was trying to steal business away. Jay accidentally started a fire in Melinda's apartment building, and John became an unlikely hero by saving Melinda, Mary Ellison and Mary's adopted son, Teddy. After John was brought to Memorial with serious injuries, surgery was recommended. The doctor on call was Dan Stewart, so Dan

Always the troublemaker where Kim was concerned, John threatened to mar her happiness with Dan by telling Betsy that Dan was her real father, and not her uncle as she had been led to believe. Betsy was now a young lady of 14, and Dan realized she had a right to know. The shocking discovery led to a bout of hysterical deafness and it was some time before Betsy was able to accept her real father's love.

had no choice but to operate on his rival for Kim's affections. John developed a blood clot in his lung, and Dan feared he might not make it. Despite their history, Kim prayed for his recovery—he was, after all, the father of their child.

The recovering John was attracted to Mary Ellison, and when he asked to see her, the kind Mary could not refuse. As John's health improved, he claimed Mary was the reason. At this time John had written a book that he hoped would help get him reinstated at Memorial. Mary gave the manuscript to Alex, who was impressed. By now, Mary wanted nothing more than to free herself from her involvement with John, but he didn't make it easy. He wanted a deeper relationship than the one they had. Mary admitted to John that she had been warned

about him. John immediately suspected that it was Dan and concocted a plan to hurt his reputation at the hospital. Soon afterward, Mary learned that John was telling everyone they were living together. That was the last straw, and she broke off contact with him.

And elsewhere in the hospital, those old rivals were at it again! Bob Hughes was still blocking John's reinstatement to Memorial. But John saw an "in" with Jane Spencer. Jane was an influential member of the hospital board, and John had something on her—something big. The ubiquitous John managed to get a copy of Beau's birth certificate, which proved that Jane was not Beau's real mother. Jane agreed to get John reinstated at the hospital—she had no choice.

As the year drew to a close, Bob's stepdaughter, Barbara Ryan, arrived in Oakdale. She had been an art student in New York and was fleeing a failed romance with Dr. Steven Farrell. Unable to live without her, Steven followed her to Oakdale and got a job in the cardiology department at Memorial, and the couple rekindled their romance. But Steven had a secret past, one he could not share with the woman he loved. The year ended on a sad note when, on the night Nancy Hughes was to give an engagement party for the happy couple, Steven skipped town, leaving Barbara to nurse a broken heart.

# 1 9 7 9

Melinda Gray was a curious young woman. She wanted to know what John Dixon had on Jane Spencer. Why would Jane get John reinstated at the hospital when she didn't even like him? Melinda offered to help John type his book. While she was at his home, she spied on John as he opened his safe. When John was gone, the observant Melinda found the combination and opened the safe. There it was, plain as day: Beau Spencer's birth certificate. His mother was one Rose Lang. Melinda went straight to Jane and dropped a bombshell: She was pregnant with Beau's child. If Jane didn't help her win Beau now, she'd tell him who his real mother was. Again, Jane had no choice but to comply. Melinda told her half-sister Barbara and her aunt Kim about her pregnancy, and the family rallied around. Then she told Annie, who confronted Beau. She had given up her dream of becoming a doctor to be the wife Beau wanted, and this was her reward? As far as Annie was concerned, the marriage was over. With Melinda's threat hanging over her head, Jane worked on Beau to marry the mother of his unborn child, and he did. Melinda finally had the social status she craved, but Beau was still in love with Annie. To add to Melinda's troubles, John Dixon vowed to pay her back for using him to get the information on Beau. He'd see to it that her days as Beau's wife were numbered. When Melinda lost the baby, she was sure she'd lose Beau, too, but Beau was sympathetic. Enter John Dixon with his ammunition. He had found out that several years ago, Melinda had been named co-respondent in a very messy divorce. Let the blackmail begin.

John believed he had found a way to use Melinda when he learned that Memorial could not afford to back two cardiac units, so it was either John's unit or Bob's. Better still, they could combine! Not about to share his glory with the eminent Dr. Bob, John sprang into action. He asked Melinda to spy on Bob while she baby-sat for Frannie. Melinda had done a lot of underhanded things in her day, but she didn't want to hurt Bob, so she told Kim about John's plan. Kim threatened to have John thrown out of Memorial yet again if he didn't drop this devious scheme, and John backed off. Bob praised Melinda for her courage in coming forward and in admitting her past mistakes. He told her that she had inherited her late mother Jennifer's beauty and grace. Melinda came clean with Beau as well, but he couldn't find it in his heart to forgive her. He told his mother that

Melinda had confessed everything. Jane thought Beau was talking about the adoption, and she apologized for never having told him. Beau was shocked. Jane had revealed her precious secret for nothing! Beau told his mother he never wanted to see her again. Beau and Melinda divorced. Determined to get the true story of his birth from his father, Beau left Oakdale.

Meanwhile, Annie was moving on with her life. She got her own apartment, which she shared with Barbara, and she started seeing Jeff Ward. The new hospital administrator, Doug Campbell, liked Annie, too, and although she was very attracted to him, he was a married man and Annie didn't want to get involved. Doug vowed to resolve the situation with his absent wife. Jeff confided in Susan Stewart that he once loved a woman who had dropped out of med school to marry a successful doctor and he'd heard the marriage was now on the rocks. The woman in question was Marcia Campbell, Doug's wife! She'd been in Greece for a year with their three-year-old son. Doug wanted to have separation papers drawn up and sent to her, but Marcia saved him the trouble by returning to Oakdale. She liked the prestige that went along with being a hospital administrator's wife, and she was not going to give up without a fight. Jeff wondered how she would react to seeing him after all those years. Deep down, Jeff was afraid Doug would steal Annie the same way he stole Marcia. He need not have worried. Doug loved his young son, and because of him, he decided to give his marriage another try. Annie tried hard to focus on Jeff, but her thoughts kept going back to Doug, and Marcia began to suspect there was another woman. If Doug could play around, so could she! She turned to Jeff, but he didn't respond. Jeff had his eye on becoming chief of surgery. When Doug turned him down, Jeff was sure it was because of Marcia and Annie. Never at a loss for schemes, John Dixon thought Jeff should try another approach—Marcia. In the short time she'd been back, Marcia had more than a few board members in the palm of her hand. Because she still wanted him, Marcia told Jeff she'd do what she could. Driving home from the hospital one night, Doug told Annie he was going to file for divorce. Getting out of the car, Annie unknowingly dropped a scarf with her initials on it. Marcia found it and put two and two together. It didn't help that she'd seen Doug and Annie kissing. If Doug asked for a divorce, Marcia threatened to ruin Annie's reputation. Jeff got chief of surgery, but he refused to testify for Marcia against Annie and Doug. Marcia was livid! She

## Love and Marriage

*Kim's jet-setting ex-sister-in-law, Valerie Conway, had her eye on Dr. Bob and Grant when she first came to town. She almost remarried ex-husband Nick, who tried to kill her for her money. But it was Dr. Alex Keith who finally captured this lovely lady's heart, and they were married on Valerie's farm.*

went to Ellen and told her that her daughter was having an affair with a married man. That was it for Doug, and he packed his bags. Marcia tried to stop him from leaving, but she'd had too much to drink. She fell down a flight of stairs and was rushed into surgery.

Valerie, in the meantime, began to come out of her shell and, at Bob's urging, she returned to her job as a nurse's aide at Memorial. After her brush with death at the hands of her ex-husband, whom she was about to remarry, Valerie vowed never to be touched by anyone again! That was before she met Kate, a silent child who stirred deep memories in Val. Kate had injured her leg and refused to go to physical therapy because she knew that when she got better, she would be sent to a foster home. Alex told Val that the hospital was having trouble placing Kate, which meant she'd have to go to an institution. Valerie couldn't let that happen. She asked Kate's social worker if she could be Kate's foster mother. Valerie was granted a six-week trial. Valerie was determined to get Kate to speak again, and Alex was touched by her love for the girl. Although she was attracted to Alex, Valerie was determined to stick to her vow: After Nick, no more men! Valerie gave Kate a birthday party at the farm and invited Alex and Betsy. The two girls had a lot in common. Kate's mother left her at an orphanage when she was three, and Betsy's mother, Liz Talbot, died when Betsy was very young. When Valerie brought out the birthday cake, Kate ran out of the room, and Valerie was afraid that Kate would never open up to her. When Kate returned and saw Valerie's tears, she said her first words: "Don't cry, Valerie." Valerie was overjoyed! Kate made the decision to stay. As for Alex, he wasn't content to stay just friends, and Val wasn't ready to go any further. One afternoon, as Kate watched in horror, Valerie fell off her horse and was rushed to surgery. Valerie had a rare blood type and needed a transfusion to survive. Luckily for Valerie, Kate had the same blood type. Unfortunately, Kate had run away, fearing she was the cause of the accident. Kim and Betsy found her, and Kate's blood saved Val's life. With Valerie on the road to recovery, Alex told her he must leave soon for a job in Ann Arbor. Realizing how much she loved him, Valerie begged him to stay. Alex proposed. This time Val accepted, and they were married on the Conway farm.

While Valerie and Alex were blissfully happy, Lisa and Grant were not. Tina was convalescing at their home and claimed that her agoraphobia was getting worse. It wasn't her illness that was keeping Tina at the Colmans' home, however; it was her infatuation with Grant! When Lisa came home early one day and discovered Tina had been out, she realized she was faking her agoraphobia. Lisa ordered her to leave. Grant was appalled by Lisa's cruelty. Tina retaliated by telling Grant about Lisa's faked suicide and an angry Grant moved back into the Lawyers Club. Tina then landed a secretarial job at Lowell, Hughes & Colman, and one night while working late, she offered to massage Grant's tired neck. The massage led to a kiss, and Grant suddenly realized Lisa had been right about Tina. He'd had it with scheming women and told Lisa it was over for them as well. Lisa was distraught and vowed she would not make it easy for Grant.

Then Lisa disappeared. She was driving in a heavy rainstorm out in the country when her car stalled. Fortunately, she was near the Willows, a charming country inn. Bennett Hadley, the handsome owner, took her in and convinced her to spend the night. She had developed a bad cold, and Bennett asked his doctor, Henry Bickford, to examine her, and his housekeeper, Hester Pierce, to help take care of her. Privately, Hester wondered aloud to Bennett if Lisa reminded him of anyone. Bennett didn't think so. Meanwhile, a curious Lisa heard noises upstairs and decided to investigate. What she found was a beautifully appointed room with a portrait of a woman who looked very much like her. It was Bennett's wife, Ruth. She had left him two years ago, and he still loved her very much. Bennett told Lisa that he was a writer but had given it up to run the Willows. He thought country life would be good for his marriage, only his wife ran off with another man. Lisa thought he should go back to writing and make contact with the world. Hester confided in Lisa that it was Hester's brother, Martin, who stole Ruth away from Bennett, but she always thought Ruth had instead used Martin to get out of her boring marriage.

Back in Oakdale, Grant enlisted the help of Carol Stallings and Sandy Thompson to help him find Lisa. When Grant arrived at the Willows, he told Lisa he was worried when neither he nor Lisa's friends or family had heard from her. Lisa couldn't believe it—Bennett had lied about sending the postcards she had given him! Lisa returned to Oakdale. Bennett, however, was never far from her thoughts. Likewise, he missed her, so he closed the inn and headed for Oakdale. Hester was not pleased. When Bennett arrived and declared his love for Lisa, Grant was jealous. Lisa delighted in being fought over but was not happy when both Grant and Tom warned her that something about Bennett did not sit right. Grant located a woman in New York who had had an antique business with Ben's wife. She claimed that Ben took Ruth to the inn to keep her away from other men, and this woman was glad when Ruth left him. Lisa was furious with Grant for checking up on Bennett, and she said yes to Bennett's proposal. But Grant refused to give her a quickie divorce. Soon afterward, someone tampered with Grant's brakes. When Tom talked Grant into implicating Bennett, Lisa jumped in and gave him an alibi. Then Grant was attacked at his office, and after that, Ralph Mitchell saved him from being crushed by an elevator. Something was going on, and Grant insisted that the police run a check on Bennett. Lisa was concerned about Grant but irritated that he kept blaming the "accidents" on Bennett.

Bennett returned to the Willows, and Lisa went with him. Hester was thrilled to see Bennett but not Lisa. Then Bennett lied to Lisa again, this time about a necklace he gave her that had belonged to Ruth. Lisa later found Ruth's portrait slashed and Hester's letter opener nearby. She wanted Hester dismissed! Hester warned Bennett not to let Lisa end up like Ruth. Grant began to suspect Bennett of killing both Ruth and Martin. But Martin wasn't dead; he was languishing in a sanatorium. In this macabre course of events, Dr. Henry Bickford was mysteriously murdered. When Tom came to the Willows to check up on his mother, he was almost done in by someone brandishing a shovel. Soon after, Kim arrived to help Lisa plan her wedding. While rummaging in a closet, they found an old garment bag filled with dresses. Lisa tried one on, and it was a perfect fit! When Bennett saw her in the dress, he threatened to tear it off her because she looked so much like Ruth. Hester saw her and fainted. Kim also found a page torn from Ruth's diary describing how Bennett had locked her up in her room and detailing her planned escape with Martin. Bennett warned Hester never to tell Lisa about Ruth's final days. One night Lisa heard Bennett muttering in his sleep, "Ruth...I'm so sorry...I never meant to...Ruth." And over at the sanatorium, Martin kept muttering, "Bennett, cellar, shovel."

Tom was worried that his mother was cutting off all her ties to Oakdale. Still, Lisa happily continued to prepare for her wedding day. The wedding gifts began to arrive. Lisa excitedly opened them, only to find a box containing a burial shroud that reeked of Ruth's perfume! Lisa believed Ruth was still alive and had sent it.

Bennett knew otherwise, and Hester was fired for the loathsome deed. The wedding would be held as planned. Ben arranged for a honeymoon in Jamaica. Hester warned Tom and Kim to get Lisa away before the wedding, or they might never see her again. On the night of her engagement party, Lisa got a call from "Ruth" to meet her at the Willows at 9 p.m. At the party Bennett had a jealous fit when he saw Lisa dancing with Bob, and he stormed out. Lisa was about to go after him when she saw that it was almost nine. Arriving at the Willows, Lisa heard someone moaning. She found a secret passageway to a sealed-off bedroom, and when she entered, she saw a hand moving at the foot of the bed! It was Hester. She had blood on her fingers and dress, and a letter opener lay nearby. Weakly, Hester told Lisa that it was Bennett who had hurt her, because she knew his secret: Bennett killed Ruth in one of his jealous rages. Suddenly, Lisa heard Bennett coming up the stairs, and she fled through the secret passageway, only to find herself in the cellar. Stumbling over loose bricks, she came upon the half-mummified remains of Ruth Hadley. Then Bennett appeared with blood on his hands, holding a poker. Lisa ran for the stairs. Bennett followed, only to lose his balance and fall. Frantically looking for a key to unlock the door, Lisa came face-to-face with Hester, letter opener in hand. Hester reminded her that she had warned her to leave before it was too late. Then she told Lisa she must kill her. Thinking quickly, Lisa yelled "Ruth!" and Hester dropped the letter opener. Tom and Bob were pounding on the door, and Hester fled up the stairs and escaped. It was Hester, not Bennett, who had killed Ruth Hadley. Bennett said he had suspected this for some time, ever since Kim found the diary page that said Bennett had locked Ruth in her room, when the only one who could have done that was Hester.

After Bennett recovered from his fall and he and Lisa had a chance to talk things over, they decided that after all they'd been through, they couldn't be together. Lisa gave him back his engagement ring, and Bennett promised to keep it as a constant reminder of what his jealous rages cost him. As a final gift, Bennett gave Lisa his finished novel. The last paragraph of the last page read: "And so it was Lisa who finally taught me what love and loving are all about. Like her laughter, she'll always be in my memory, and whatever I do that's worthwhile in my lifetime, it will be because...she loved me once."

While Lisa Miller Hughes Colman (almost Hadley) was embroiled with Bennett, her ex-husband, Bob

Hughes, was once again a lonely man—that is, until he met a beautiful friend of Penny's named Dana McFarland. Penny had told Dana to be sure to look up her family if she was ever in Oakdale. Dana was a principal dancer in a major ballet company, but she gave it up for marriage. After several separations she had come to the conclusion that her marriage was over. Her husband, Ian McFarland, a famous composer and conductor, did not agree, and he sent his manager to bring Dana back to New York. Ian had no intention of losing her, especially to Bob Hughes! He told Dana he couldn't write his rock opera unless she was by his side. But Dana had given up her own career for Ian, and the more successful he became, the less she saw of him. She had no intention of wasting any more of her life. Ian was not one to give up, though, and Dana had to go to Grant for a restraining order. Meanwhile, Bob was concerned that he might lose her because of her love for the dance, and Dana assured him he had nothing to worry about. Finally, Ian agreed to leave Oakdale after he fulfilled his obligation to conduct a benefit concert. In the middle of the concert, Ian collapsed in pain. It was his heart, and although he recovered, Ian remained despondent. His spirits lifted when he was asked to

Mary Ellison, adoptive mother of Joyce Colman's son, Teddy, and Ralph Mitchell had an on-again, off-again romance. Mary agreed to be Ralph's wife, but realizing that Mary would always love Donald more, he released her from her promise, and she married Don.

compose the score for a new ballet, and the choreographer wanted Dana in the lead. Bob and Dana had already announced to the Hughes family that they would marry on Valentine's Day, so Dana said no to the ballet without mentioning anything to Bob. Once Bob found out, he selflessly urged her to do it, because he understood how much she loved to dance. He had learned from his failed marriages that it was futile and unfair to try to restrain a woman from her career.

At this time, Bob's son, Tom, was starting to date

Barbara Ryan. He had also gotten his first public aid case, defending a woman by the name of Sheila Winston, an enigmatic and attractive drifter who was accused of stealing jewelry from Valerie. Sheila insisted she was innocent, even though she was seen skulking around Kate's room the day of Valerie and Alex's wedding. Sheila thought Tom didn't like her, and Tom confessed to Barbara that Sheila reminded him of his ex-wife, Natalie. As Barbara struggled over whether or not to invite Tom to spend the night, she was concerned that he had not really gotten over Natalie. It was clear that Tom had grown fond of Sheila and had transferred his feelings for his ex-wife to this new woman. After the charges against Sheila were dropped, Tom helped her get a job at his mother's bookstore so she could stay in town. When Barbara saw them together, she knew her worst fears had come to pass.

Tom's uncle, Don Hughes, was mourning the loss of what he thought was his and Joyce's baby. Ralph couldn't bear to see his old friend suffer, and he told Joyce that Don must know the truth, that the baby was really Ralph's. Joyce was so desperate to stop Ralph that she planned to kill him, but her plan backfired. Instead of shooting Ralph, she shot Don, paralyzing him. The police believed Joyce's story about a prowler, and she was cleared, but she worried that Ralph would figure out that she was really trying to kill him, and he did. Ralph confided in Mary, who thought he was absurd. But when she saw Joyce freak out when little Teddy picked up a toy gun, she thought there might be something to Ralph's revelation. After having too much to drink at the country club one night, Joyce told Ralph that if he hadn't threatened to spoil things by telling Don about the baby, Don would never have been shot. Mary investigated on her own and found out that Joyce had "accidentally" run over one of her ex-lovers a few years back. Meanwhile, Joyce had grown tired of being married to a cripple and had started to cheat on Don. As for Ralph and Mary, their mutual concern for Don brought them close together again, and Mary agreed to be his wife. Ralph confronted Joyce about trying to kill him so he wouldn't reveal that the baby's real father was Don, and Don heard the conversation over the intercom. When he confronted her, Joyce swore that she did it all for him, but Don wasn't buying it this time around. Joyce raced to her car and got pinned between the car and the garage door. Ralph saved her life, but Bob diagnosed traumatic shock. Don forgave Ralph for his affair with Joyce, and Ralph urged his friend to have her committed to a sanatorium. Joyce overheard their conversation and escaped, kidnapping Teddy. She merely wanted to say goodbye to Teddy, though, and returned him

home to Mary. Shaken and upset, Joyce drove out of town. Her car plunged off a bridge, but her body was not found.

Mary might have been engaged to Ralph, but she still had feelings for Don. Don's paralysis had led to a deep depression, and Mary was determined to bring him around. Nancy heartily approved of her efforts. One afternoon while Don was showing Mary his physical therapy exercises, he experienced a sensation in his legs. Elated, Mary and Don shared a spontaneous kiss, and Mary bolted. They agreed to try to forget what happened, and Mary went so far as to tell him he better start looking for a new secretary, because after she married Ralph, she didn't intend to work. Mary delayed her wedding, but she remained adamant about marrying Ralph. When he recovered, a disappointed Don told Mary he was thinking of going back to California because he couldn't bear to see her with another man. Nancy suspected Don was in love with Mary, but Mary couldn't bring herself to tell Ralph that she no longer loved him. Even after she accepted his engagement ring, Ralph had reservations about the relationship because he sensed Mary's feelings for Don, and he couldn't let her marry him if she was in love with someone else. So he told her he didn't think it would work out between them, and she gave him back his ring.

Don went to see Jay Stallings about the shopping center he and Ralph were building and saw that the prices on the invoices had tripled. Jay's supplier had warned him that sending out duplicate invoices could land him in trouble. Jay told his supplier to stay cool; no one was going to jail. But after Ralph and Don confronted him, Jay left town to see if he could raise the money he needed to get his construction company back on its feet. When he returned unsuccessful, he confessed what he had done to Carol and said he did it for her and little Amy. Carol understood, but she didn't condone his actions, and she insisted Ralph must know. But Jay wasn't able to be honest with Ralph, and Carol was very disappointed. However, Jay was a knight in shining armor compared to slimy Hank Robinson. Hank sexually assaulted Carol, and Jay was on trial for assault for beating him up. Jay was afraid people would actually believe Hank when he said he didn't rape Carol. Because he didn't want to see his wife's reputation destroyed on the witness stand, Jay offered to plead guilty to the charges. Carol didn't want Jay to go to jail, and she looked for proof to back up her story. Carol discovered that Hank beat up his old girlfriend Linda when he found out she

## Medical Matters

*Kim and Dan hadn't been married long when Dan was diagnosed with an inoperable brain tumor. Kim tried hard to be brave, but she'd waited so long to marry Dan and she loved him so very much! When Dan told her it was time to tell his mother, Ellen, Kim knew the end was near.*

was two-timing him with Jay, but Linda didn't report it, so it wasn't admissible in court. Then Grant produced a tape of Hank offering Grant $5,000 to call off the investigation. The D.A. thought Hank had better get a lawyer. Jay was sentenced to 60 days in prison for the assault and spent the time taking courses in English and law so he could make it in the business world. He wanted Carol and his little girl to have the best that life could offer. While in prison, Jay made a new friend, Matt Kelly. Matt was in jail taking the rap for a car that had been stolen by his older brother, Chip, and Jay admired him for that. When Jay was released from prison, Sandy Thompson insisted on backing his new construction company. Jay hired Matt to come and work for him. Matt suggested Jay hire Chip as well. Jay was not impressed with Chip, but hired him as a favor to his friend. Jay's instincts were right; Chip was bad news. He was borrowing money from a loan shark named Roy Barker, and Matt was very worried about the danger Chip had put himself in. One night when Chip was going to meet with Barker, Matt decided to follow, and Jay came along as well. They witnessed Chip and Barker holding up a liquor store. Chip was shot, and Matt drove him to Memorial. Once there, Chip and Barker took Dan, Kim and John hostage, and Dan was forced to operate on Chip at gunpoint. Barker offered to free the other hostages, but Kim refused to leave her husband's side. In the melee that followed, Dan succeeded in disarming Barker. John was shot in the shoulder, but the wound wasn't serious. The police arrived in the nick of time.

Dan had been experiencing severe headaches, and Dr. Alex Keith told him that the symptoms might indicate a brain tumor. When he got back Dan's test results, Alex's worst fears were confirmed. Annie found a letter Susan had written to David describing her half-brother's illness. When she confronted Dan, he swore her to secrecy. Not even Kim, Ellen or the children knew the seriousness of his condition, and he wanted time to go over his will with Grant. Kim suspected that something was wrong, and she confronted Alex, who told her Dan wanted to spare her the pain of knowing he was sick. Unable to accept the fact that her beloved husband was so desperately ill, Kim went to see the Reverend Booth, who gave her the poem "Look to This Day." It was the same poem that helped her sister, Jennifer, through her crisis. "Look to this day, For yesterday is but a dream, And tomorrow is only a vision, But today, well lived, Makes yesterday a dream of happiness, And every tomorrow a

## Betsy and Kim Grieve for Dan

**BETSY:**

What can I do with memories when I know he's not—My mind's full of questions, Kim—about life and death—about beginning and ending—and I don't have any answers for any of my questions.

**KIM:**

I don't have the answers either, honey.

**BETSY:**

Maybe it's better to try and forget.

**KIM:**

I don't think so. I know some of the memories sting a little now, but you'd be making a mistake if you try to rid yourself of them.

**BETSY:**

But it hurts so much, Kim.

**KIM:**

Yes, it does. But that hurt will disappear, little by little, and in its place you'll have the real thing—the legacy Dan left for all of us.

vision of hope. Look well, therefore, to this day."

Kim tried to be strong, but Ellen noticed she was always crying and thought there was trouble in the marriage. When Dan told Kim it was time to tell his mother of his illness, Kim knew the end was near. They decided to take the children on a vacation so they could be together one last time. While they were away, Dan's condition worsened, and he had to go to the hospital. David, Ellen, Annie and Dee flew to his side. Then Nancy Hughes got the call from Ellen—Dan Stewart was dead. Having only recently found out that Dan was her real father, Betsy had a great deal of trouble accepting his death.

# 1980

In 1980 some fascinating newcomers to Oakdale brought intrigue and adventure to the Hughes and Stewart families. One such character was Brad Hollister, a smooth opportunist who looked rough around the edges but was, in fact, a smooth-talking snake. A land surveyor, among other things, Brad discovered silver on land owned jointly by the Hugheses and the Stewarts. To maximize his chances to make a fortune, Brad charmed Lisa into loaning him money to buy the Hughes portion, then looked to the beautiful Annie as an entrée to the Stewarts' parcel. Nancy and Chris recognized that Brad was a phony because he had conveniently forgotten to tell Lisa about the silver and so had conned her.

While this was going on, Dana MacFarland decided to return to her dancing career, leaving Ian to pursue a new woman—Dee Stewart. But Ian's doctor also began to have designs on the beautiful young Dee, and that doctor was her family's longtime enemy, John Dixon! Dee accompanied Ian to Rome, where he was to conduct a major concert and where they planned to consummate their love. This was John's golden moment to play Svengali to Dee by telling her that Ian was not ready for a late-night schedule because of his fragile heart condition. Ironically, John's attempts to separate the lovers proved medically correct; Ian died of a heart attack while making love to Dee for the first and only time! Dee felt responsible and John promised to protect her. When they returned to Oakdale, Dee was sure everyone could read the guilt on her face, but the only thing Brad Hollister noticed was her beauty. The Stewarts wanted Dee to take an interest in the mine, which meant that Dee and Brad would see each other frequently. John had a good time egging Annie on, saying it looked like there might be competition for Brad Hollister between the Stewart sisters. As far as Brad was concerned, he and Annie were just friends, and Dee couldn't help liking him, even though she fought it. When he tried to kiss her, Dee pulled away, leaving Brad to wonder what he had done. Dee confided in John that she hated it when Brad touched her, and John was not upset. To bury his feelings for Dee, Brad turned to drink and Melinda Gray, with whom he had a brief affair. One day as Brad was taking Dee on a tour of the mine, there was an explosion. Dee was horrified to see Brad buried in the rubble. Had she hurt someone she loved yet again? While recovering at Memorial, both Annie and Dee visited him regularly.

Brad questioned Dee about Ian, and she admitted she couldn't get close to any man. Brad decided to pursue her anyway. Ellen sensed something was wrong with her daughter, especially when Dee ran off to Chicago. John found out where Dee was and followed her there.

When Brad's father had a massive heart attack, he called Brad's younger brother, Eric, but Eric arrived just minutes after his father passed away. Brad was angry because his father had always loved Eric more. Annie overheard and, feeling great compassion, longed to be close to Brad again.

Confused about her feelings for Brad Hollister, Dee fled to Chicago to think. John Dixon followed, and the two ended up having a grand time in the Windy City. When David Stewart found out, he forbade his daughter to see John Dixon again!

Dee and John had had a wonderful time in the Windy City and decided to keep this special time a secret from their friends and family. David was furious when he found out John was there. Dee claimed it was a chance meeting, and besides, John was a changed man. David forbade his daughter to see him, but Dee wasn't about to listen. David went so far as to try to get John fired from the hospital. Dee was infuriated! Unable to have sex with any man since Ian, Dee eventually found herself giving in to John. Brad couldn't bear the thought of her with John, and he tried to convince her she was making a terrible mistake. Dee claimed she would marry John if he asked. Brad confronted John about the hold he had on her, and John simply smiled. Soon after that, he proposed. Annie and Brad resumed their friendly relationship, and Annie told Dee that if Brad asked, she'd marry him tomorrow. Because she still cared about Brad, Dee did her best to hide her feelings. When Dee announced her plans to marry John, Ellen cried, David exploded and Kim, John's former wife, was horrified! David vowed to stop the wedding at all costs.

When Brad decided to give a party by the lake for his employees, Melinda saw her chance to make a move. Unfortunately for her, Brad was thinking about Dee, and he ignored her. Melinda had been drinking and tried her best to get Brad in a romantic mood, but he wanted to be alone. Melinda told Betsy that she and Brad were more than friends and he'd invited her on a speedboat ride on the lake. A drunken Melinda started talking in a loud voice about what a great lover Brad was. Brad warned her she'd be sorry in the morning for making such a spectacle of herself. Eric and Betsy were kissing in the bushes and overheard. Melinda wanted to go to the island across the lake and make love all night. To shut her up, Brad took her out in the boat. When Melinda realized they were headed for home instead of the island, she jumped overboard. Brad tried to rescue her, but she pushed him away, and he struck his head. When he came to, Brad saw Melinda's hair ribbon floating in the water. The police were notified, and they retrieved Melinda's

lifeless body from the lake. Annie did her best to comfort a shocked Brad, while Betsy told the police what she had overheard. The police suspected foul play, and Betsy felt bad about pointing the finger at Brad, but Kim assured her she did the right thing. It was Lisa who comforted Kim as the shock of her niece's death took its toll.

Because she wanted to be married in a church and needed time to convince her family, Dee put off her wedding date. In the meantime, Brad proposed to Annie. David still refused to accept Dee and John, but everyone was happy for Annie and Brad, except Dee. Just as she had done with Beau, Dee pretended to be thrilled, and the sisters agreed to be each other's maid of honor. Annie and Brad were married first, and Ellen and David were as proud as could be. At the reception, David accidentally pushed a drunken John, and plates went flying. Dee was outraged, and she and John left quickly. David felt terrible and begged Dee to forgive him, but she refused. Thanks to John, Dee was becoming further and further estranged from her family. Dee began to have second thoughts about her marriage. The ever-manipulative John told her he could no longer close his eyes to the way she felt about Brad and she would only end up hurting her sister. He also took pains to remind her of Ian. Soon John had Dee thinking he was her only salvation, and they set a firm wedding date. When they announced the date at a Stewart family picnic, David created a major scene and stormed out. After the confrontation, Brad and Dee shared a private moment, and Brad demanded that Dee tell him what made her pull away

## A Loser in Love

Once again, Dee pretended to be happy while she watched her sister marry the man she loved. As she had done with Beau Spencer, Annie got the man Dee wanted when she tied the knot with Brad Hollister, leaving Dee to enter into a disastrous marriage with family pariah John Dixon.

from him. Dee sadly replied that only John would understand. Then she confessed to how she had "killed" Ian. Brad tried to convince her it wasn't her fault. He told her the only reason he had turned to Annie was because Dee had turned to John, but he was still very much in love with Dee. She loved him, too, but could never hurt her sister, and she begged him not to end his marriage to Annie.

Later, John and David met up in John's office, and, unable to control himself, David took a swing at John. As John fell to the floor, David picked up a paperweight. John accused David of trying to kill him and told him that because of what he did, he'd lost his daughter forever! When John told Dee what happened, Dee said she never wanted to see her parents again! Not wanting to lose his daughter, David swallowed his pride and told John that he and Ellen would come to the wedding. John told David that Dee wanted nothing to do with them, and he deliberately neglected to give Dee the message that her parents were willing to come to the wedding.

John didn't stop there. When Annie thought she was pregnant, John checked the lab and found out she wasn't. Knowing that Annie's pregnancy would make any relationship between Dee and Brad impossible, John lied to Dee, telling her Annie was pregnant. It worked like a charm, and they decided to marry that day. When David found out, he tried to stop the wedding but arrived just as Dee and John were saying their vows. Once again David was powerless to protect his daughter.

Tragedy struck suddenly when Jay Stallings was killed in a mine explosion, and a devastated Brad turned to Dee. He told her he understood now what she meant about hurting people and not meaning to. Dee asked Brad about Annie's pregnancy, and Brad confirmed it wasn't true. Dee said she heard it was, and Brad wondered if that was why she rushed to marry John. As Brad became more preoccupied with Dee, Annie sensed that something wasn't right in her marriage.

John wanted his marriage to be romantic, but now his bride wasn't in the mood. When Ellen and David tried to make amends and invited the newlyweds to dinner, John said he would never enter the home of the man who tried to kill him. John then became downright paranoid about his wife! He began to follow her to the mine where she worked, and accused her of being there only because of Brad. When Dee overheard John verbally attack her father, she defended David. John yelled at her

for taking her father's side against him and asked her if she wanted this marriage to work. An angry John warned her to be prepared to face the consequences…

As the Stewart sisters wrangled with their love lives, their buddy Tom Hughes cooled his relationship with Sheila Winston and grew closer to Barbara. But it soon became evident that Barbara had a secret life prior to returning to Oakdale, and it was coming back to haunt her. One day Barbara got a call from a man named Raymond Colfax. He told her "his" condition had worsened and she should come to Philadelphia immediately. Barbara went, and when she returned, she got a call from Raymond's wife, Claudia. The little boy was fine, but Raymond had lost his job and was drinking again. Barbara felt close enough to Tom to tell him she had an illegitimate son. His name was Paul, and he was three years old. She had given him up for adoption to her good friend Claudia. The boy's real father didn't know about him and didn't want to. Tom advised her to sue for custody because it didn't sound like a safe place for the child. He tried to convince Claudia that if she let Barbara take the boy, it might save her marriage. When Raymond saw Tom and Claudia together, he thought they were having an affair and decked Tom. Later, a distraught Barbara told Tom she'd seen bruises on Paul's face. Claudia had been married to someone else when she adopted Paul, and Raymond thought the child was hers. Tom suggested that if she told Raymond the truth, he might let Paul go. The plan worked, and Paul came to live with Barbara temporarily.

Barbara told Tom the sad story behind Paul's conception. When she was an art student in New York, she met a man named James Stenbeck, who was heir to the Swedish throne. She had loved him very much, but she knew he didn't feel the same way about her. Later, Barbara was shocked when Annie told her Brad was bringing James Stenbeck to Oakdale as a partner in his silver mining operation. Of course, the real reason James was coming to Oakdale was to see Barbara. James swore to Barbara he'd never hurt her again, but Barbara remembered the pain of saying goodbye because he was obligated to marry a woman of his family's choosing. James told Barbara his wife had died in an accident and they never had children. But Barbara didn't budge. Since Annie and Brad got married, Barbara had been staying with Lisa, and one day she found James waiting for her there. Lisa had let him see the boy, explaining that he belonged to a friend. In spite of herself, Barbara was touched to see father and son together. When Claudia

Barbara was about to marry Tom Hughes when James Stenbeck showed up and stopped the wedding cold! James proceeded to whisk Barbara away to the Caribbean where they renewed their passion, and James declared his love. Many in Oakdale wondered if it was love for Barbara or the fact that their son, Paul, stood to inherit the Stenbeck fortune that caused James's sudden, intense interest in a woman he hadn't seen for years.

parents. James then wanted Raymond and Claudia to give Paul back to Barbara. For the right price, Raymond would consider it done. Despite Barbara's confusion about James, she became engaged to Tom. Raymond offered the name of the boy's father to Tom for a price, and Tom turned around and told Claudia of her husband's offer. Claudia admitted to Tom that she and Raymond had just received a huge sum of money, which led Tom to suspect that Raymond and James were conspirators. James asked his old aide, Charles Ivenstrom, if he knew Barbara was pregnant when they parted, and he reluctantly admitted he did but explained that James's father didn't want him to know. James was disturbed to learn that Tom and Barbara were planning to adopt Paul, and he begged her for one last meeting. On the day of her wedding, Barbara agreed to meet with James at his hotel. He admitted he didn't come to Oakdale for the silver, he came for her. Was it true that Paul was his son? Barbara reluctantly confirmed that he was, but that she still couldn't forgive James. James

came to take Paul back, Barbara begged for more time, and Claudia agreed. Suspicious, James asked Claudia if she were the boy's mother, and Claudia answered yes. But James was quick to notice that the question upset her. James had his aide check out Paul's parentage and found out that Claudia's first husband died after they adopted Paul, and her present husband, Raymond, didn't adopt him. Even more suspicious was the fact that Barbara paid Paul's medical bills and donated blood when he was ill.

James was awarded the refinery rights he came for, but he decided to stay in Oakdale anyway. When he told his father he would not be returning to Sweden for a while, the elder Stenbeck was not pleased. Desperate to get at the truth about Paul, James bribed Raymond into telling him that he and Barbara were Paul's natural

said he didn't know what she was talking about. Barbara told him how his aide had come to her with the ultimatum that she have an abortion. He said it was what James wanted. James swore he never knew, and Barbara believed him. Then Barbara realized she was late for her own wedding. As Barbara walked down the aisle, tears were streaming down her face, and she stopped the wedding so she could talk to Tom alone. She revealed that James never knew about their child. Suddenly, James showed up, and to everyone's amazement, the wedding was canceled on the spot.

Barbara knew Lisa would hate her for humiliating Tom, so Kim helped her pack up her things and move out. Tom tried hard to make Barbara forget James, and she was amazed that he still cared. But the persuasive

refused; he didn't care what his family thought! Soon afterward, James paid a visit to Grant to make arrangements for naming Paul his legal son and heir. Then he bought a penthouse and hired a large staff for security reasons. He told Barbara it was to protect her and Paul because they were being observed by a mysterious stranger. The stranger swore he would stop the wedding, even if it meant that people would be hurt. When he heard that Barbara and James were planning a masquerade party to celebrate their engagement, the stranger knew he had the perfect opportunity to carry out his plan—or rather the plan of his co-conspirator, Charles Ivenstrom. At the ball, the stranger approached Barbara with the news that a sick guest needed her immediate attention. When he got her into the private elevator, he took out a gun and ordered her to call off the wedding before 6 p.m. tomorrow. If she didn't, James would be killed. In a panic, Barbara ran to James and told him what happened. James set off in search of the

Chris and Nancy Hughes make an elegant entrance at the Stenbeck ball honoring the engagement of Barbara and James.

James persuaded Barbara to go to the Caribbean with him to try to recapture what they had lost. In the Caribbean, Barbara felt guilty about Tom, even though she was beginning to enjoy being with James again. James declared his love. He wanted to marry her.

Back in Oakdale, Lisa tried to persuade Tom to do everything he could to win Barbara back. For her part, Barbara was glad that the truth was out. She told Annie that James made her very happy and that they would marry soon. An unhappy Tom took a leave of absence from the family firm in order to investigate James in Sweden.

When James told his father he was marrying Barbara, his father insisted that James forget all about her and their illegitimate child. James would do no such thing! His old aide, Charles Ivenstrom, arrived in Oakdale and wasted no time in paying Barbara a visit. He accused her of marrying James for his money, and Barbara threw him out. She didn't tell James about the visit, but she wanted to postpone the wedding. James

mystery man and confronted him on the penthouse roof. Just as Barbara arrived with the police, the stranger escaped. James was sure the man was a paid assassin and that Charles was behind the scheme. Charles managed to get to Barbara and take her to the penthouse, where he held her hostage in a dark closet while he lured James to the scene. Charles's gunman tried to force James to sign a document. A struggle broke out, and Barbara screamed. The gun went off, the gunman escaped and Barbara lay bleeding on the floor! Afraid she would die, Barbara asked James to marry her in the hospital; she wanted him to be Paul's legal father. Meanwhile, the gunman filled Charles in on what had happened. Charles was furious. He would fix things. Dressed as an orderly, Charles entered the hospital, crept into Barbara's room as she slept and turned off her oxygen. Fortunately, Bob revived her, and James spotted Charles lurking in the halls. Certain that Charles was behind the attacks, James brought in the police, and Charles confessed. The confession was somewhat disquieting. It seemed that James's grandfather had stipulated in his will that the first child born to one of his grandsons would inherit the Stenbeck fortune. Charles's daughter was married to James's brother, and she was pregnant. He could not allow Paul to inherit his child's fortune! Charles accused James of only wanting to marry Barbara so Paul would get the money, and his accusations hit the newspapers after Barbara and James were married. James swore he would gladly give up his fortune for Barbara and Paul, and she believed him, leaving others in Oakdale to wonder if money were, indeed, James's sole motivation for marrying Barbara.

Lyla Montgomery was concerned that her high-spirited daughter, Cricket, would repeat her mistakes, and she cautioned her that her first sexual experience should be special. The rebellious Cricket told her mother in no uncertain terms that she was 18 and could do what she pleased! And she did.

James's true character was revealed when a new family arrived in Oakdale. John Dixon's old flame from Chicago, gutsy nurse Lyla Montgomery, arrived with her daughters, Margo and Cricket, in tow. Margo was training to be a nurse at Memorial, and James hired her to be Barbara's private nurse. He was immediately attracted to her. They shared a passionate interest in horses, and Margo had taken a part-time job at a stable. The next day, James bought the stable. When James discovered she was riding his special thoroughbred, however, he was furious and fired her on the spot. Margo begged for her job back, but James refused. It was Barbara who intervened and persuaded her husband to give Margo a second chance. Unbeknownst to Barbara, James was informed by his aide, Nels Anderson, that his debt was bigger than his assets. In view of the circumstances, James arranged to have an expensive painting copied. He put the original in his safe and sold the copy for a very high price. Nels was surprised when James paid the bank the money he owed.

As the Montgomerys established themselves in Oakdale, Lyla became friendly with Bob, much to Nancy's delight. Lyla's daughter Cricket baby-sat for Bob's daughter, Frannie, so it seemed they had a lot in common. However, ever-present killjoy John was giving Lyla a hard time at the hospital about taking up with Bob, who thought Lyla was much more pure than the wild, fun-loving woman John had known. Dee overheard John and Lyla fighting one day and wondered about their connection.

Lyla was very concerned that her free-spirited daughter, Cricket, would repeat her mistakes, and she cautioned her that sex the first time should be special. The rebellious Cricket announced that she was 18 and could do what she pleased! Both Cricket and Margo were confused about their parents' divorce. Margo had always sensed that her father, a traveling salesman named Bart Montgomery, had never really loved her. Never at a loss for words, Margo asked her mother if she'd had an affair. Lyla wouldn't answer her but confided to Bob that Bart left her when he learned of her past mistakes. A sympathetic Bob said she shouldn't put all the blame on herself, that everyone makes mistakes. One day at the hospital, Margo heard John yelling at Lyla, and she told her mother she didn't have to take it. Margo asked John why he was always harassing her mom, and John told her to ask her herself. Lyla warned Margo to stay away from John. Alone, she recalled a time when Margo needed blood and her husband's was the wrong type. There was no way he could have been her father!

Betsy and Cricket had developed an on-again, off-again friendship. Betsy missed her father, too, and was feeling depressed. To ease her pain, Betsy began spending more and more time with Eric Hollister. At first Betsy wore heavy makeup and put on sophisticated airs for this "older" man, but she soon learned that it was best to be yourself, and that's what Eric wanted. To Kim's relief, Betsy told Eric that she was not ready to "go all the way" with him, while Cricket made it known that she was more than willing. Betsy's need for a father was soon satisfied, however, when Kim became intrigued by the ruggedly handsome, Greek-born carpenter and restaurateur Nick Andropoulos. They had met after Nick saved Melinda's life when the Wade Book Shop went up in flames a while back and Melinda was caught in the blaze. Nick confided to Kim that his wife and child had died in a fire and that was why he felt compelled to risk his life for Melinda, who had later perished in a tragic drowning at the lake. Bob was not pleased when Kim started seeing Nick, because he was once again developing feelings for his sister-in-law and "pal." Nor was Sheila Winston happy to see Nick, for he was a face from her past that she did not want to see again. Sheila blamed herself for the antagonism between Nick and his hot-headed younger brother, Steve. Nick assured her his grudge was with Steve. He would never forgive his brother for not trying to save Nick's wife and daughter from that terrible fire. He told Sheila that Kim reminded him of his wife, Andrea, and Betsy reminded him of his child. Because Kim had lost someone as well, Nick felt she would understand, and she did.

Kim and Nick were surprised to find Steve at Nick's restaurant, The Plakka, one night. The bitter hatred between the brothers was obvious. Nick had turned Steve out after a violent fight over Sheila—he was trying to make a whore out of her, and Nick wouldn't stand for it. Now Steve was in trouble again and needed a safe place to hide. Sheila urged Nick to get Steve out of town quick. Nick recalled that Steve had once set up a violent man named DuFour, using Sheila as bait. Nick was sure this was the man who was after Steve. Shortly thereafter, a badly wounded Steve was treated at Memorial, and Nick blamed himself because he didn't take him in. The brothers reunited and vowed to fight DuFour together. When Kim went to visit a delirious Steve, he called her "Andrea" and wanted to make love. He swore Nick would never know. Kim was shocked! Once Steve woke up, he begged Kim not to say anything, and as much as she hated hiding the truth from Nick, she agreed. After Steve was released, he went to stay with Nick. At this time, Kim contemplated ending the relationship because she felt Nick's memories of his wife and daughter were getting in the way. Steve told Kim that Nick would spend the rest of his life thinking of his wife as an angel when she was really a fraud. One

night at The Plakka, a drunken Steve accused Nick of blaming him for the deaths of Nick's wife and daughter to hide his own guilt. Kim couldn't understand how Steve could live with his guilt. An angry Steve told her he didn't save Andrea because she was a tramp!

John was getting more and more upset about his son Andy's closeness to Nick and those "gypsies," as he called them. Kim had warned him that she had the legal right to decide how Andy should be raised. Not wanting to be cut out of Andy's life, John decided to investigate Nick and Steve. He discovered that Steve had been arrested several times and used this fact to urge Kim to refuse Nick's marriage proposal. When Kim told John that Steve's record had not changed her mind about Nick, John threatened to take her to court over custody of Andy. John's investigation convinced Steve that he should leave town, but before he could, he was caught in an explosion on his construction job and seriously hurt. Steve needed cardiac surgery, and John was the best, but Nick was reluctant. When Steve was wheeled into surgery, his last word to Nick was "Raven." Nick was baffled. When he woke up from his surgery, Steve told Nick he didn't know what "Raven" meant.

Nick used all his money to buy Kim an engagement ring, but because of John's threats, she still couldn't give him an answer. Hurt, Nick pawned the ring for a one-way ticket to Greece. After Kim checked out her custody agreement and was told John didn't stand a chance of taking Andy away, she told a very happy Betsy that she would marry Nick and informed John of her plans. When Kim called the hospital to see if Nick was with Steve, Margo answered the phone. Kim asked Margo to give Nick a note that read: "Everything is clear to me now. Yes, yes, yes. Love, Kim." As Nick was saying goodbye to Steve, John overheard their conversation and realized Kim had no idea Nick was about to leave the country. John intercepted the note from Margo, lying to her that he would deliver it to Nick. Then he slyly stuffed it into his pocket. By the time Kim arrived at the hospital, Nick was already gone, and Steve told her he was on his way to Greece. Kim couldn't leave things the way they were, and she decided to go to him.

In Greece, Kim traced Nick to his hometown. As she walked along a river looking for him, she noticed a fishing boat and saw Nick on it. She ran into the water and they fell into each other's arms. Betsy liked Nick, and she was happy when she heard they'd found each other. Steve, on the other hand, was not happy, and he told Betsy he knew something she didn't. As Nick and

Kim toured the Greek countryside, madly in love, John went to Steve and told him he knew Steve tried to steal a coveted piece of jewelry known as the Green Fire necklace. John made it plain that he didn't want his son raised by a bunch of thieves. If Kim and Nick married, John would cause big trouble for the Andropoulos family. When Kim and Nick returned from their trip, they were greeted by the shocking news that Nick's wife, Andrea, was alive. She had faked her death. Nick told Andrea that he knew she had deceived him and that he planned to marry Kim. However, Andrea and Nick were still husband and wife, and Kim mistakenly thought Nick had chosen Andrea over her. Nick accused Steve of knowing Andrea was alive, but Steve denied it. Around this time, Steve met Kim's good friend, the newly widowed Carol Stallings. The two became friendly enough for Carol to lend Steve money to go to Greece. Once there, he went straight to Andrea's. Andrea wasn't home, so Steve seized the moment to rummage frantically through her jewelry box.

Andrea wasn't the only woman erroneously presumed dead by Oakdale residents. Joyce Colman, whose body was never found after her car went off a bridge, returned very much alive. She had heard that Donald and Mary were engaged, and she decided to free her husband legally, rather than have him continue to believe she was dead. She told Donald her only reason for living was Teddy, and she swore she'd never tell the boy she was his natural mother. Donald was skeptical. Joyce went to the police station and turned herself in for shooting Don. She admitted she had meant to kill Ralph Mitchell, and she wanted to pay for what she'd done. Donald decided not to press charges. Grant told him it was extraordinary that Joyce stepped forward. This was the Joyce he knew and married in San Francisco. Joyce remembered how her father had walked out on the family, and her mother, blaming her for the desertion, put

After he saved her niece Melinda from a fire at the Wade Book Shop, Kim found herself attracted to ruggedly handsome Greek restaurateur Nick Andropoulos. The attraction soon blossomed into love.

Joyce in a foster home. The only thing she had from her mother was a treasured glass unicorn. Joyce realized that she gave up Teddy because she grew up believing children destroyed marriages, and she feared Grant would leave her if he knew they had a son. Obsessed with Teddy, Joyce egged on Donald to convince Mary that she should let her see Teddy once in a while. Mary agreed to an occasional visit but soon realized Joyce was just as neurotic as ever and reversed her decision, leaving Joyce devastated. Mary even went so far as to bar Joyce from Teddy's birthday party, and she and Donald had a falling out over it. As Mary continued to turn Teddy against her, Joyce turned to Grant as the father of their child, asking him to set things straight. She gave Grant a letter for Teddy, but Mary ripped it up, and the two women had a knock-down, drag-out fight that ended in Mary slapping Joyce. While Donald and Mary's relationship was deteriorating over Joyce, Joyce and Grant were growing closer. Joyce told Grant she wanted to set up a trust fund for Teddy, which made Mary furious. She was sure Joyce was doing this to get Grant on her side. Joyce told Mary that maybe Teddy would be better off if he knew Joyce was his real mother! Upset, Mary told Joyce she planned to leave town with Teddy. As Mary rushed out of Joyce's apartment in a fury, she accidentally

gave Joyce permission to say goodbye to Teddy. Teddy said he knew his "aunt" Joyce didn't hurt his mom and he hoped she'd visit them soon. A tearful Joyce told her son she loved him very much.

Mary was like a second daughter to Nancy and Chris, and it was a sad goodbye. Donald tried to get her to change her mind, to no avail. Soon after she left, Mary was in a terrible car crash and was not expected to live. Teddy came back to Oakdale, and Nancy readied Donald's old room for him. Everyone feared what Joyce's

## On the Road

*When Nick returned to his native Greece to sort out matters concerning his past, Kim followed. In this fantasy sequence filmed at the breathtaking Temple of Poseidon, Kim dreams about being reunited with Nick. The exotic foot-age, shot in Greece, was a first for a daytime serial.*

knocked over and broke Joyce's cherished glass unicorn, escalating Joyce's hysteria. Joyce ran after her, and in the confusion Mary fell down the stairs. When the police arrived, a neighbor told them she saw Joyce push Mary. Joyce was arrested for attempted murder, and if Mary died, the charge would be murder in the first degree! Even Grant had doubts about Joyce's story that it was all an accident. Joyce was sure, though, that when Mary woke up from her coma, she'd tell them the truth. Nancy was taking care of Teddy, and she, too, was certain that Joyce had pushed Mary down the stairs. When Joyce was released on bail, she went to see Teddy, but the boy lashed out at her, saying she'd pushed his mother down the stairs and he hated her! Mary eventually regained consciousness and told the truth, exonerating Joyce. As far as her relationship with Donald was concerned, in Mary's mind it was over, and she planned to return to Laramie. Before she did, she

reaction would be to Teddy's return. Nancy followed Mary's wishes and kept Joyce from seeing Teddy, but Joyce insisted that as Teddy's legal guardian, Grant should be making the decisions. When Teddy asked to play with Joyce, Grant gave the OK, and the boy began to visit with her more often. One night Lisa dropped by and was horrified to find Joyce and Grant alone together! Lisa was certain Joyce was trying to win Grant back, but Grant explained they were just friends and Teddy was the focus of their relationship. Lisa was sympathetic when Grant ached to reveal to Teddy they were father and son, and she was not about to let Joyce come between them! At the same time, Joyce was telling Teddy they'd have to find a way to stop that horrible woman from taking Grant away from them. Later, Joyce stole some stationery from her doctor in San Francisco and contacted someone about a "certain disease." She was definitely up to something.

Grant and Joyce grew closer. While dancing, Joyce complained of fatigue and excused herself to take some medication. Seeing Grant's concern, she was sure he thought she was dying, and he ran to her side. Meanwhile, Lisa was bound and determined to remarry him. But he proposed to Joyce, and she said yes. Joyce couldn't resist spilling the beans and even invited Lisa to the wedding. Shortly, the two were at it once again. Grant warned Lisa to stop harassing Joyce or he wouldn't see Lisa anymore. When Lisa questioned Grant's love for Joyce, he confided about Joyce's "illness," and that he had seen a note from her doctor saying that Joyce had a growth on her brain. Lisa decided to investigate. She looked through Joyce's medicine cabinet and took the medication names to Bob Hughes, who said they were cold remedies. Lisa wasted no time in telling Grant. Furious at Lisa for snooping, Grant told her to leave Joyce alone! Lisa made an appointment for Joyce to see an Oakdale doctor. Trapped, Joyce confessed to Grant that her doctor had made a mistake; she wasn't dying after all. Grant assured Joyce he cared for her, but he wanted to make sure her illness hadn't influenced him, and he thought they should delay the wedding. Then Lisa checked with the doctor in San Francisco and found out that Joyce had never been seriously ill. When confronted by Grant, Joyce confessed. He told her that he never wanted to see her again. Exhausted by his problems, Grant decided to leave Oakdale. Donald Hughes also left to join Mary Ellison in Laramie, and the two were married.

Meanwhile, Kim and Nick were struggling to cement their relationship, but were unhappy that it would take six months for Nick to get his divorce from Andrea. Steve, fed up with Andrea's evasiveness about the Green Fire necklace, demanded that she hand it over, but she said she didn't have it. Andrea warned Kim that Steve couldn't be trusted, leaving Kim to wonder who was telling the truth. Andrea teased Steve about his relationship with Carol Stallings, and he said if she didn't give him the necklace within the week, he'd tell Nick everything. Andrea swore she'd thrown it into the sea, but Steve didn't believe her. When John told Andrea about Kim and Nick's problems, Andrea began to stall the divorce. As Steve was about to reveal their affair, Andrea gave him a map and told him the necklace was

Nick followed Steve to Greece on a quest for the stolen Green Fire necklace and found him at the Temple of Poseidon digging in the dirt. A fight ensued and an enraged Nick came close to smashing Steve's head with a huge rock. Steve fled, and when Kim found Nick, he was sitting at the edge of the temple in shock. The necklace lay at his side.

near the Temple of Poseidon in Greece. Leaving on his quest, Steve said goodbye to Carol, promising to return soon. Kim warned Andrea if she didn't tell her why Steve went to Greece, she would tell Nick about their affair. A frightened Andrea agreed to tell Nick herself and quickly signed the divorce papers. Andrea claimed she didn't know why Steve went to Greece, but Kim had seen Andrea give him a map. Nick said he would find his brother himself. Andrea begged Kim to stop him, telling her about the necklace. If Nick ever found out, he'd kill Steve, so Kim followed Nick. Nick found Steve at the Temple of Poseidon and watched from the shadows as he pulled the Green Fire necklace from its hiding place. Steve, shocked to see him, and with necklace in hand, taunted his brother about how he and Andrea had been lovers. Enraged, Nick started to choke Steve. Then he picked up a rock and held it over Steve's head, but Steve got away and dropped the necklace in the dirt. When

Kim arrived, Nick was in shock. He never had any idea about the affair. Nick asked Kim to go home so he could talk to his brother alone. Finding Steve in a bar, Nick stuffed the necklace into his brother's hand. Steve confessed that he stole the necklace because he loved Andrea and wanted her to go away with him. Everything changed when he thought she'd died in the

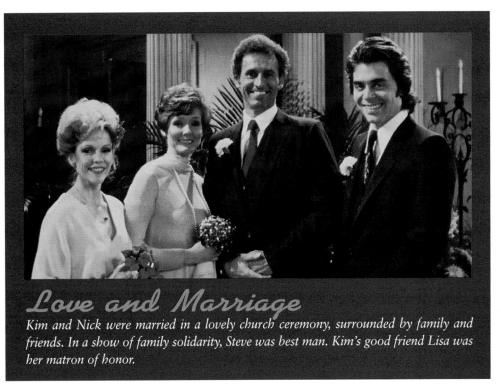

## Love and Marriage

*Kim and Nick were married in a lovely church ceremony, surrounded by family and friends. In a show of family solidarity, Steve was best man. Kim's good friend Lisa was her matron of honor.*

fire. Both Nick and Steve ordered Andrea out of their lives, and Kim and Nick were finally married.

Carol was thrilled to have Steve back, and he came clean to her about everything. She was touched that Steve was determined to make up for his past mistakes and showed his tender side to her little girl, Amy. Carol agreed to accompany Steve to California, where he planned to return the necklace to movie mogul Ari Triandos, the son of the necklace's rightful owner. Triandos's wife observed the handoff. She was none other than Natalie, little Amy's mother. Natalie ordered her lover, Cody Sullivan, to go to Oakdale to check on Carol. By coincidence, Cody was Jeff Ward's half-brother, and he wasn't anxious to go.

Carol and Steve were married in Las Vegas. Andrea threatened to reveal her affair with Steve to his new wife. She would only keep quiet if Nick agreed to watch out for her daughter, Sofia, who was attending college in Oakdale. Nick agreed.

Cody Sullivan arrived in Oakdale, surprising Jeff by paying back an old debt. Jeff was delighted that his half-brother was now a successful moviemaker. He planned to shoot his next epic in Oakdale. Actually, Natalie wanted to be close to the child she had given up. When Cricket met the dashing Cody, she wasted no time in quitting her job for the more glamorous position of production assistant on Cody's film. And both Cricket and Sofia were anxious to win the lead role in the film.

At Steve and Carol's request, Natalie had agreed not to see Amy, but she came to their house on a night she knew they were out and told the baby-sitter she was Carol's cousin. Before she had a chance to see Amy, Annie kicked her out. The next day, an angry Steve ordered her to stay away from Carol and Amy, or else. Natalie wasn't going to let a small-time thief raise her daughter, and she said she could still press charges against Steve about the stolen necklace.

Sofia made her screen debut as the maid in *The Moonlighter*. In exchange for the role, Sofia promised Natalie she would baby-sit for Amy so Natalie could be alone with her. But Steve and Carol came home early. An emotional Natalie told them that Triandos made her agree not to have children and that was why she had to see Amy. Carol was touched by Natalie's words. Steve was not.

Meanwhile, Cricket and Cody started having a secret affair. As the film crew prepared to leave, Cricket told Margo she was pregnant. Margo advised her to tell Cody, but Cricket didn't want him to feel obligated, so Cody departed not knowing that Cricket was expecting their child.

Steve was working at the mine, and business wasn't good. When James Stenbeck asked him about his future, Steve admitted that he'd like to do better for his family. Actually, James was thinking of using the mine in a dope-smuggling scheme and figured the opportunistic Steve could be of service.

John's jealous rages and tyrannical behavior were

causing Dee many sleepless nights. Disillusioned, she asked him to move out. Brad gave her some sleeping pills and told her to go home and get some rest. John went to the apartment and found her in bed, groggy from the pills. Dee thought he was Brad, and by the time she realized who it was, he was already on top of her and she was too weak to push him off. Afterward, John was quite happy, but Dee was crying. Afraid that John would hurt Dee, David showed up. While John was getting a bottle of champagne to celebrate, David found Dee shivering in her slip and sobbing. She said John forced himself on her. David told her that was rape and took her to Memorial, where evidence of forced entry was found. A rape therapist explained to Dee that her husband must be punished. Arriving at Memorial, John couldn't understand why everyone was so antagonistic. He approached David and Ellen, but they told him to go away. Then Brad angrily asked John if he thought he could get away with rape. John was shocked! He called Dee in her room and declared his love. She hung up on him.

Tom Hughes had come home with his new girlfriend, Lyla's younger sister, Maggie Crawford, a lawyer. Maggie was fascinated by the rape case as John was booked. Tom agreed to represent Dee and filled Maggie in on John's background. Meanwhile, Lyla was warned that she may have to testify, since she was on duty when Dee was brought into the hospital. Lyla knew John had a gun, and, afraid that he might threaten her, she took it and hid it in her home. Discovering the gun missing, John confronted Lyla at her home and met Maggie, who, to his surprise, offered to defend him. Horrified by Maggie's offer, Lyla returned the gun when John threatened to broadcast their affair. Later, Maggie told Tom she would be defending John. Amused, Tom said she'd never win. Maggie assured John her relationship with Tom wouldn't affect the case. Actually, Maggie was jealous of Dee. Dee trusted Tom, although Tom was puzzled

when Dee became upset when questioned about Ian McFarland. David spotted John's gun, and John joked that it was a good thing it wasn't loaded.

The trial began with David's impassioned testimony. But Lyla surprised everyone by saying she wasn't sure if Dee had been raped. Baffled, Tom decided to check into Lyla's background and found out that Lyla and John

*Law and Order*

*John thought they were making love, but Dee cried rape and took him to trial. In an interesting twist, Maggie Crawford and Tom Hughes, who were lovers, were on opposing sides: Maggie defended John, while Tom defended Dee.*

attended Northwestern University at the same time. Lyla's ex-husband, Bart Montgomery, then informed him that that Margo wasn't his daughter. Bart agreed to testify. Meanwhile, John swore to Maggie that he first met Lyla at Memorial. Amidst this turmoil, Bob proposed to Lyla, and she accepted. Tom warned his father and thought Bob should attend when Lyla was recalled to the stand. Bart's appearance shocked Lyla. He testified that while they were married, Lyla was seeing another man. When Tom asked if that man was in the room, Bart pointed to John. Maggie tore into John for his dishonesty, and Lyla swore to Bob she'd never loved John. She had kept the affair secret because she thought Bob wouldn't want her. Bob said he didn't know how he felt, and Lyla sadly returned his ring.

Shocked to see their father take the stand, Cricket and Margo were stunned to learn of the affair. Bart said that Lyla lied about Margo being his daughter, and they divorced. Recalled to the stand, Lyla admitted the affair.

Margo screamed, "Tell me who my father is!" Sobbing, Lyla blurted out, "John Dixon!" Margo and John had never liked each other. However, it didn't take long for the two to form a special bond.

When David was on the stand, Maggie asked him if Dee had used the word "rape." She had not. When she asked if David wanted to kill John, David had no answer. John urged Maggie not to hurt Dee, but she questioned Dee about Ian McFarland. Dee lied when Maggie asked her where she was when Ian died, but Maggie caught her in the lie. Dee broke down, confessing that Ian died in her arms. Dee admitted that John lied to protect her, and if she lied then, how could anyone believe her now? David realized John might go free. Dee was afraid John would hurt her, so David found John's gun and hid it. He later took the gun to John's hotel room. A worried Ellen asked her husband where he'd been, and David said he had gone out for a walk. In the morning, David bought a one-way ticket to Chicago without telling his family. Before he left, he told Dee how proud he was that she was standing up to John. Upset that David was now missing, Dee tried to get the trial delayed. She also feared Maggie would bring up her relationship with Brad, and she didn't want to hurt her sister. Meanwhile, John wondered if it were David who had stolen his gun. When Ellen found the gun, she decided to keep it as protection against John.

Maggie asked Dee if there were any other men in her life besides John—perhaps her sister's husband, Brad? Tom warned Dee not to lie because it would ruin her credibility, but Dee insisted that she and Brad were just friends. Under subpoena, Brad confessed that he and Dee loved each other, but they were never lovers. Annie burst into tears and ran from the room. Ellen was furious. But Brad insisted that he wanted to make a life with Annie and the child she was carrying. Unfortunately, Annie left Brad.

In some unknown location, David admitted to a psychiatrist that he left because he feared what he might do to John. When Ellen told him about the exploding triangle, David blamed John, not Brad, and he headed home.

Back on the stand, Dee admitted she lied to protect her sister. She swore that John's jealousy was driving her to a near breakdown, and she feared what he would do to her. Then he forced her to have sex. On the stand, John said he loved Dee and was shocked when she accused him of rape. On the fateful day, they had made beautiful love. John tearfully swore that he didn't rape his wife. Upon cross-examination, John flew into a rage.

Annie lost her baby. David blamed John and the trial. John had hurt yet another member of his family, and this time he would pay. John demanded his gun back. David took the gun and left the house. Ellen was afraid of what David might do. Later that night, John and Annie quarreled at the hospital, and they quarreled. Afterward, Annie slipped out of the hospital unseen. As John walked into the parking lot, a car with an unknown driver raced toward him, hit him and sped away. Ellen was relieved when David finally came home, but he wouldn't tell her where he'd been. And Annie was missing. Dee, tears streaming down her face, came to Brad's hotel room to say goodbye. Frightened that John would hurt her, she had decided to leave town.

Investigating John's attempted murder, Lt. Savage wondered why Annie would run away. When he heard about her fight with John, she was stopped by the police and brought back to Memorial, insisting she had nothing to do with John's hit and run.

When John awoke, he couldn't see. Tests revealed that he might be permanently blind. He told Lt. Savage that either David or Brad ran him down. Ellen said David had been with her all night. The next day, Ellen found a note from David saying he'd left town. Later, Dee and Brad met to discuss their alibis. While admitting they still loved each other, they agreed not to mention her visit to his hotel room. By now, Lt. Savage figured out that David had skipped town.

Dee felt obligated to stay and help John. She asked Tom to end the trial. With Margo and Maggie at his side, John listened as Dee announced she wanted to drop the charges. She realized she might have encouraged him, and he'd already suffered enough. In his arrogance, John thanked her for telling the truth. Annie felt she'd lost her baby for nothing. Depressed, she dropped out of medical school. Lyla was furious when Margo decided she would take John in upon his release from the hospital.

Dashing James Stenbeck had bought Margo a cottage near the stables, and he was not pleased that John would be moving into their love nest. As for John, he didn't like their affair. When the cottage was ransacked, John and Margo suspected David because he was the only one who didn't know that John was still in the hospital. Bitter, John vowed to lure the killer so he could kill him. John moved into Margo's cottage as planned, revealing to no one that he had regained his sight. A round-the-clock guard told him that he'd been told David Stewart was three blocks away, and he wanted to check it out. Just as John settled in with a drink, someone entered the room. It wasn't David. It was James, carrying an umbrella with a large knife hidden inside. Still feigning blindness, John told James he disapproved of Margo's affair with James. He accused James of wanting him dead, and James glibly confessed to the hit and run. John revealed that he could see and pointed a gun at James. He informed him that their conversation was being taped. Either James stopped seeing Margo, or he was a dead man. If he didn't confess to the hit and run, John would turn the tape over to the police. Clever James got his loyal aide Nels Anderson to confess to the "accident."

To Dee's great relief, John agreed to a quick divorce. In the Dominican Republic, she was shocked to find Brad at her hotel. He swore his love for her and said there was no hope for he and Annie. And so Brad and Dee finally made love. But the next morning, Brad said how important money was to him, and how he bought the Hughes and Stewart properties because there was hidden silver. Turned off by his greed, Dee told him they had missed their chance, and he left town.

As things settled in Oakdale, David was in a town called Flat Rock, suffering from amnesia as a result of the shocking events surrounding the trial. Under the name Donald Saunders, he was in love with a widow named Cynthia Haines. Cynthia's teenage daughter, Karen, was thrilled to have a new father figure. But John spotted David and followed him. He learned that Donald/David was planning to marry Cynthia, and he led Dee to the nuptials. Dee ran to her father and hugged him, only he didn't know who she was. Then he keeled over—he'd had a heart attack from the shock. He didn't recognize Ellen either and asked for Cynthia. Still suffering from amnesia, David ironically came to believe

After John's trial, David Stewart left Oakdale and went to the town of Flat Rock. Traumatized by his daughter's rape and his hatred for John, David developed amnesia. Calling himself Donald Saunders, he met and almost married the beautiful Cynthia Haines.

that John was the only one he could trust. David agreed to be injected with sodium amytal, a type of truth serum, and his memory returned, When he finally recalled the night of the rape, David told John that if he ever laid a hand on his daughter again, he'd kill him. When questioned about the hit and run, David was relieved to remember he wasn't driving the car that hit John, and James was relieved that David didn't remember the face of the man behind the wheel. Ellen was ecstatic that her husband was regaining his memory, but Cynthia was heartbroken.

John was not happy to learn that his former buddy-turned-nemesis Rick Ryan, Barbara's brother, was back in Oakdale. Rick assured Bob that he no longer harbored a grudge, so Bob did not object when Rick landed a job assisting Dr. Larry Travis at Memorial's laboratory. Another doctor, Len Howell, owed a sizable gambling debt to an international drug operation. His contact was the mysterious Miranda Marlowe, a sultry brunette and a key figure in the organization. Miranda said the ring would extend his loan if he allowed it to manufacture PCP in Larry Travis's lab at night. Trapped, Len told Rick to conceal the use of the lab. In exchange, Rick wanted to be reinstated as a doctor. Then Rick saw his brother-in-law, James, talking to Len and realized that James was involved in the operation. Len double-crossed Miranda and left for Chicago with a large chunk of money. Soon afterward, Bob discovered that a large sum of money had been embezzled from the hospital. After smelling ether in the lab, Annie realized it was being used to manufacture PCP and informed Lt. Savage. Meanwhile, someone had planted angel dust in Rick's apartment and tipped off the police. Rick was warned that he was being watched, so he planted the angel dust on Larry Travis, who went to jail. When Larry was cleared, Rick left town.

Larry Travis's ex-girlfriend, Connie Wilson, was a gold digger whose brother was a professor working on

James's top-secret project in Egypt. The professor's daughter, Hayley, was attending school in Oakdale. She presented James with a gift from her father. In the box were precious stones from the tomb that the professor was excavating. After examining them, he urgently told Professor Wilson to keep this discovery secret at all costs and that he was coming to Egypt immediately. Barbara begged him to take her with him, but he asked her to stay and keep an eye on Hayley. When Hayley fell ill, Eric Hollister rushed her to Memorial, where John was the only doctor on call. When James returned to Oakdale with the sad news that Professor Wilson had died in a cave-in, John was sympathetic and took Hayley under his wing.

Despite John's warnings, Margo and James continued their affair. Tired of James's neglect, Barbara turned

In 1981, drugs came to Oakdale in the form of PCP, and Memorial's lab was used to manufacture them at night. Eric Hollister was slipped some angel dust without knowing it, and Karen Haines came to his aid.

to Tom for advice. Tom told her that if James lost custody of Paul, he'd lose his fortune. When Margo confided in Jeff Ward that James loved her and would marry her soon, Jeff told her she was a fool.

Recovered from her illness, John offered to help Hayley investigate her father's death. Hayley gave him a tracing of the tomb. Margo told James about the tracing, and James asked her to get it. The tension was

building between these two men as John ordered Margo to end her involvement with James, and James ordered Margo to get John out of the house. James quickly found another object for his affection: Connie Wilson. She was trustee of Hayley's considerable inheritance, and James tried to flatter her into investing in a fashion business he was considering starting. Connie expected some romance, and James didn't discourage her. Since John was staying at Margo's, he offered Hayley his apartment. Hayley was ecstatic, until she learned that Connie would be staying with her. Nels worried about how James would handle these women. Connie might learn about the tomb where her brother died, and it would be dangerous if anyone were to know that Barbara's bracelet and Margo's ring were stolen from the tomb.

James arranged for his associate, Stan Harper, to join his new fashion business. With Connie as an investor and Barbara running the shop, he'd keep two of the women in his life busy. Lisa and Barbara agreed to become partners, and Fashions Ltd. was born. What neither woman suspected was that Stan Harper had been responsible for shipping James's contraband from Egypt to America, and Fashions was to be the front for the smuggling operation. The jewels would be hidden in the clothing. If they were discovered, Barbara would be blamed. Nels reminded James that they were financially dependent on the goods, which were waiting in Egypt. James insisted the jewels remain there until he was sure Hayley wouldn't cause any trouble.

Hayley couldn't understand why her aunt didn't like her boyfriend, Eric Hollister. It was nothing but greed. If Hayley married Eric, Connie would lose control of the estate. When the promised returns did not materialize on Connie's investment in Fashions Ltd., Connie reminded James that the money was Hayley's.

James lied to Margo, saying that Barbara had refused to give him a divorce. Margo stormed into Fashions Ltd. and confronted Barbara. Barbara thought that Margo was crazy and that her infatuation with James had gone too far. James thought Margo was no longer a problem. He and Nels agreed that if Barbara found out about the affair, she'd sue for divorce and James would lose Paul and the inheritance. When Barbara confronted James about Margo, he denied everything. He assured Barbara he loved only her. Nels was worried that if James and Barbara split, James would lose access to Fashions Ltd., and they wouldn't be able to retrieve the jewels or smuggle the drugs. James decided he would use the Hollister mine as a front as well. He had his men drop the drug paraphernalia at the warehouse, where Steve found it. Puzzled, Steve asked James if anyone else had access to the building. When he returned to the warehouse, Steve was taken prisoner at gunpoint. His captor found pictures of Carol and Amy in Steve's wallet and threatened to harm them if Steve didn't deliver their shipments. James gave Steve some money to keep quiet.

John figured out that James had stolen jewelry from the tomb, and he threatened to expose the scheme if James didn't tell Margo that he had never asked Barbara for a divorce. John played the blackmail tape for Margo, but the only thing on it was rock music—Cricket had gotten her hands on the tape. John, however, had a duplicate tape in his safe deposit box. Margo refused to believe her father and asked him to move out.

Meanwhile, Connie complained that Hayley's tuition money was all tied up in Fashions Ltd. Next to Eric, a college education was the most important thing in Hayley's life, and she told her aunt she had no right to invest her money without consulting her first. Connie threatened to tell Barbara about her affair with James if she didn't get the money for Hayley's tuition. James lied and told her he'd ask Barbara for a divorce so they could marry. Impatient, Connie showed up at the penthouse while Barbara was there and questioned James about the money. Shortly thereafter, Connie was found dead in her apartment The police suspected suicide. Hayley married Eric and they left Oakdale, for good.

Stan Harper suspected James, and he sent Cliff Matson to the penthouse to investigate. James admitted that he dealt drugs because he needed the money. Several days later, James and Nels found an attaché case filled with cash. It was the million dollars the organization had promised him. He soon received a box of wilted roses with pictures of him with Connie's dead body slumped on the floor. James assumed Miranda Marlowe sent it as a warning, but she denied it. Summoned to a meeting with Miranda, James planned to tape it so he could offer incriminating evidence in exchange for immunity from prosecution. Miranda then hatched a plot to gain access to Fashions Ltd. and intercept the drugs. She posed as a jewelry designer and acquired Fashions as a client. At this time, an eligible but unlikely man became smitten with this dark beauty—staid and solid Dr. Bob!

## 1982

David Stewart still missed Cynthia Haines, who bought the hospital pharmacy as a way of staying in touch. Confused over his love for two women, David sought advice from his psychiatrist, Matt Butler. In session, David portrayed Ellen as caring and compassionate, but Cynthia made him feel alive. David tried in vain to revive his old passion for Ellen, who was sure David was still in love with Cynthia and couldn't go on living with him. Before he left, David begged her not to get a divorce. He took a leave of absence from the hospital and went to Florida to think. Cynthia was encouraged that there might be hope for them. Meanwhile, Ellen moved into an apartment and tried to adjust to single life. Annie bought the family house without telling her mother. When David returned, he and Ellen agreed to divorce. Annie blamed Dee. David still couldn't tell Cynthia what the future would hold. Meanwhile, Dr. Ben Forrest had become attracted to Ellen, but a strong bond still existed between Ellen and David. Seeing Ellen with Ben upset David and, realizing he was still in love with her, he broke it off with Cynthia. When Ben proposed to Ellen she told him she needed time. Ellen told Annie, and Annie told David, who apologized for everything. He and Ellen were happily reunited.

Cynthia's daughter, Karen, was out to win Jeff Ward. Even though Jeff had begun dating Annie, he gave in to the seductive Karen. When Annie saw them together, she went to Jeff's apartment and found Karen wearing nothing but his shirt. Hurt and angry, Annie ran off. Eventually Jeff told Annie how much he loved her, but Annie wasn't sure of her

As her husband, David, struggled with amnesia and his attraction to Cynthia Haines, Ellen Stewart started seeing Dr. Ben Forrest. But when Ellen made love to Ben, it was David she was thinking of. The two were eventually reunited.

Margo became the assistant to Tom. She went too far when, in an effort to gather information on a case, she disguised herself as a hooker and ended up in jail. Tom bailed her out and then fired her—it was the beginning of a long and beautiful relationship.

feelings, and Jeff turned back to Karen.

It was Jeff whom Cricket called when she went into labor. Arriving too late, "Uncle" Jeff delivered little Billy in Cricket's home. Lyla was getting another addition to her family: Her son Craig was returning to the States from the island of Martinique. Cricket introduced Craig to her friend Ernie Ross, and the men discovered they shared a common interest: chemical engineering. Craig asked Ernie if he could synthesize a formula that made men go crazy around women who were wearing it. When Cricket wore it, Ernie found her hard to resist. When Dee put it on, she was surrounded by swooning men. Dee told Craig she'd put up the money for the essence's production. Ernie would own five percent of the company's interest, and Ellen would be the secretary. James suggested they name the perfume "Deesire." There was trouble in the company almost from the start because Karen got her hands on the formula and blackmailed Craig into hiring her as his assistant. Dee refused to take orders from Karen and threatened to sell her shares.

Ernie liked Cricket, but she refused to see him. Then Miss America came to town, and Ernie asked her for a date. Cricket got jealous when she saw them dancing, and she invited Ernie over for dinner. When Cricket tried to seduce him, he left. Later that day he was seen buying a book on how to make love.

In the spring Annie passed her medical exams and began her residency at Memorial, and Jeff arranged for

her to work with him. Annie finally told Jeff she loved him. When Jeff told Karen, she became hysterical and was admitted to the hospital with no memory of their conversation. Jeff and Annie tried to talk to her, but Karen freaked out and attacked Annie. David was angry at Jeff for leading Karen on, and Annie was upset by her father's devotion to Cynthia's daughter. When Jeff sent Annie a note about a date, Karen intercepted it and changed the time. Then she snuck out and went to Jeff's apartment. Annie arrived and found Karen in a towel. Jeff couldn't understand why Annie was mad at him. Annie finally figured out what Karen was doing and set a trap. Karen found a love note from Jeff to Annie and the message read, "You're caught."

Jeff proposed to Annie, and she said yes, on one condition: After having had two miscarriages, she wanted to find out first whether she could carry a baby to term. Although she pretended to be happy, Karen was furious and made it clear to Jeff that she never gave up something she wanted. Karen found the tests confirming that Annie could bear children, and she altered them. Annie was devastated and Jeff disappointed, but he declared that he wanted to marry her anyway. They were about to get married when Annie started to feel queasy. She was pregnant! Jeff was ecstatic, but Annie's joy was tempered by the fear of losing the baby. David wondered about Annie's test, and when he rechecked, he realized someone had tampered with it. He told Cynthia he suspected it was Karen, and Cynthia advised Karen to tell the truth or leave town. Karen finally admitted responsibility. Then Annie learned that she was pregnant with twins.

As the Stewarts tried to rebuild their lives, the Hugheses unwittingly became entangled with a drug ring. Bob followed Miranda to Paris where, unbeknownst to him, she was to meet with a drug lord who ordered Miranda never to see Bob again and forced her to say she was having an affair with James Stenbeck. Meanwhile, Margo became Tom's assistant. Intrigued with the police investigation into the drug ring, she disguised herself as a hooker and ended up getting arrested. Tom bailed her out of jail and then fired her. Meanwhile, James contacted the FBI. He was met by none other than Stan, who was actually an undercover agent, Holden, not Harper. Stan revealed that he was part of an operation to bring down a drug-smuggling network and offered James immunity if he found out the identity of Miranda's boss. At the same time, Miranda's boss ordered her to seduce James to find out what he

Mr. Big shouted at his "executioner," Bruno, to stop the renegades. But Bruno thought Tom and Margo had earned their freedom, and he let them go.

was up to. The kingpin's name was Mr. Big. He had ordered the death of Miranda's lover Jacques, known as "the Corsican," and Miranda wanted revenge. James went to Paris but refused to tell Barbara where he was going. Margo knew where her ex-lover was going, and she decided to follow him. Disguising her voice, Miranda phoned Tom to warn him that Margo was in danger and that she should get out of Paris and stay away from James. Tom made plans to go to Paris. Miranda and James arranged to meet Mr. Big—who was, ironically, a dwarf—at his greenhouse. James was supposed to wear shoes equipped with sensors so the FBI could track him, but Margo tripped over the shoes when she was in his hotel room and put them out in the hallway to be polished before slipping into his bed. James woke up, startled to find her next to him. He rushed Margo out, but she hid in the hallway, saw Miranda enter and heard the word "greenhouse." Tom soon arrived, much to Margo's surprise.

On the way to his meeting, James realized he wasn't wearing the shoes, but Miranda wouldn't let him go back to get them. Meanwhile, Stan had a tail on Margo, who thought the only thing James was involved in was an affair with Miranda, a story he confirmed just to get her to leave him alone. Shattered, Margo asked Tom to take her home. Then she spotted two thugs following James and Miranda. Remembering what she had heard, she and Tom took off for the greenhouse. The meeting started just as Margo and Tom arrived with the FBI hot on their trail. Mr. Big accused James of being a spy and Miranda of being a traitor. Miranda pulled a gun, but Mr. Big had already removed its firing pin. Seeing the danger they were in, Tom started a fire. In the confusion, Tom and Margo managed to escape, and so did Mr. Big. They spotted a

plane in the field, and, with Margo at the controls, they took off. But Mr. Big was hiding in the back, and before he jumped, he told them the tank was almost empty. Margo managed to land in a deserted area.

When Stan and the FBI arrived at the greenhouse, James tried to plead Miranda's innocence, but Stan arrested her anyway. James felt he should tell Barbara about Miranda's involvement in a drug operation. Barbara, in turn, told Bob and then realized that James must have been involved as well. By the time he returned, Barbara had lost all respect for her husband. After she warned him not to lie, James confessed to his near bankruptcy and admitted that the first shipment of Egyptian jewels came through Fashions Ltd. James swore Miranda blackmailed him with photos of Connie Wilson's dead body and threatened to do the same to Barbara. Hurt and angry, Bob demanded that Miranda furnish him with information that could help him track down Tom.

While searching for civilization, Tom and Margo spotted a castle in a clearing. Upon entering, they found a kitchen stocked with pancake mix and brandy. The phone was dead. A sudden gust of wind slammed the door, and an unseen hand turned the key in the lock.

When Tom and Margo miraculously escaped from Mr. Big's clutches, they ran for their lives!

Exhausted, Tom and Margo went to sleep, awakening to a gourmet meal. Tom wanted to run, but their path was blocked by a 400-pound mute. This silent man, whose name was Bruno, ushered them to the table, and to their horror, Mr. Big joined them. Big blamed them for the downfall of his drug organization.

Mr. Big proceeded to play games with his captives.

Their only escape lay in figuring out clues from classic literature. If they failed, they would die. In the "room of love," Margo stepped on a painted heart and was shot by an arrow. Tom found the clue in a Robert Browning sonnet, and they escaped. The final room was "Alice in Wonderland" with giant chess pieces strewn about. Margo and Tom became trapped on a spinning treadmill. When Margo grabbed onto a Cheshire cat, the floor opened up beneath her, but Tom pulled her out, and they escaped. Bruno thought Tom and Margo had more than earned their safety, and he did nothing. After locking Mr. Big in his office, Bruno led them to freedom.

Safe in Paris, Tom and Margo notified their families. John and Lyla were overwhelmed by the news of Margo's safety. The experience liberated Margo from James, who thanked her for saving his life, but she had finally seen the kind of man he was, and their romance was over. To celebrate, Tom and Margo shared a romantic night in Paris—a night that ended with a kiss. In Paris to greet his son, Bob noticed a new intimacy between Tom and Margo. Margo decided she wanted to become a policewoman, but Tom wasn't pleased. Margo and Tom arrived in Oakdale, and Maggie rushed into Tom's arms. She noticed his reticence, and Tom admitted that he and Margo shared a special closeness. Maggie was miserable; after all, Margo was her niece. She told Lyla, but Lyla stood up for her daughter. Lisa was on Maggie's side. "Her" Tom could never be interested in John Dixon's daughter! To avoid hurting her aunt, Margo tried to avoid Tom, but he hadn't given up on her—not yet.

Margo passed the police academy entrance exams, but everyone worried for her safety. The officer in charge, Capt. Aaron Striker, made it clear that Margo would have to prove herself. She solved one of Striker's cases, and when he tried to take the credit, Margo called his bluff. Striker wanted her dismissed, but Margo caught him in the locker room with a shapely blond officer. Striker realized she'd make one hell of a policewoman and kept her on the force.

Meanwhile, in Paris, Mr. Big infiltrated Miranda's cell and drugged her. He badly wanted something her lover Jacques had stolen from him. But he didn't get what he wanted and booked a flight to Oakdale.

Tom finally convinced Margo of his love for her, and she agreed to see him. One night, Mr. Big arrived at Margo's cottage and searched thoroughly for a hat. Margo had no idea of the hat's importance. She had given Tom the band from the hat, and Tom gave it to Frannie. Later, Mr. Big came back to the cottage, knife in hand, and found the hat. A frightened Margo heard him and called Tom.

Because of the drugging incident in France, Bob got Miranda transferred to a Chicago prison. Then Mr. Big had one of his henchmen deliver a tape to Bob, who played it for Miranda. She warned him that Big was probably close by. Bob warned Tom, who warned Margo, but it was Frannie who was in danger. Mr. Big wanted the hatband back. Margo was duped into going to a nightclub, where there was a magic show. Mr. Big informed the magician that Margo would make a wonderful assistant. She was handcuffed and blindfolded and put in a box. When the box was opened, Margo was gone, as was a cougar. Mr. Big said if she didn't tell him where the hatband was, he would release the cougar. Tom saved Margo in the nick of time, and she told Tom about the hatband, which Frannie had left at Fashions. Miranda told Margo that Mr. Big had said something about his fortune being locked up under his hat. They found a tape sewed into the hatband, which Ernie Ross offered to decode. The only two words they could make out were "Bilan" and "Corsica." Miranda was shocked: Bilan was her daughter by Jacques. She was 17, and Miranda hadn't seen her in some time. Mr. Big also found out about Bilan, and soon he was after her, too. Miranda feared for her daughter. Tom and Margo went to Paris to find Bilan. They found out she was on an island in Africa and was very ill. Big beat them to the island, and the priest in the village church told him where to find her. Tom and Margo were in hot pursuit. One night, Margo went skinny-dipping, Tom awoke and saw her, and they made love for the first time.

Tom and Margo finally located Bilan in a remote village. The village chief thought Margo would make the perfect seventh wife! Margo nursed Bilan until her fever broke, but then Mr. Big kidnapped the girl, with Tom and Margo in pursuit. Mr. Big tried to get Bilan to decode the message. She told him it was part of a poem her father used to read to her. Meanwhile, Tom and Margo swam to Big's boat. They grabbed Bilan and tried to escape, but were caught. Margo begged Mr. Big to spare Bilan. Sure that their time was up, Tom and Margo asked Big, as captain of the boat, to marry them. Bilan then struggled with Mr. Big, and he was thrown overboard. Bilan told Tom and Margo that the message referred to a marked spot on her old convent wall in

## On the Road

*With Jamaica standing in for Africa, Tom and Margo were hot on the trail of Bilan and Mr. Big. When they reached a local village, the chief took one look at Margo and thought she'd make the perfect seventh wife!*

Paris. What they found there were two letters, one for Miranda and one for Bilan. The letters held no surprises and no mention of a treasure. Bilan learned how much her father loved her.

Back in Oakdale, Bob tried to convince Bilan that Miranda was respectable, and mother and daughter had a tearful reunion. Then Tom played a tape of Big confessing that Miranda never killed anyone and was forced to help in the drug operation. The charges against Miranda were dropped, and she was set free. Bob and Miranda were married in a simple ceremony in France. Tom and Margo also became engaged. Lisa had come to love and accept her spunky future daughter-in-law.

Because of how she handled Mr. Big, Margo was assigned to a rape-murder case. The victim said the attacker was wearing a necktie. Because Lisa lived in the same neighborhood, Margo decided to check Lisa's locks. While there, she took a quick nap in Lisa's bed and was sound asleep when a man with a necktie climbed in next to her. As he was stroking her hair, Margo woke up, saw the tie and knocked him uncon-

scious. She was sure she'd caught the rapist, and Lisa was horrified that this occurred in her bed. When he regained consciousness, Margo told him he was under arrest. Lisa was shocked to discover that the intruder was her new husband, an arrogant tycoon named Whit McColl. They had secretly married in Paris. Margo apologized, but Whit's son, Brian, threatened to press charges, and Whit wanted her thrown off the force. Whit went ballistic when he learned that Tom and Margo were to marry. Tom couldn't believe that Lisa had married Whit. Margo was relieved of duty, but thanks to Tom's strong defense, she was allowed to stay on the force. A bitter Whit told Tom that no one got away with crossing him, and Tom advised Whit to keep from Lisa his pending paternity suits.

To add spice to her marriage to James, Barbara hired a medium to entertain at one of her parties. Mme. Koster discovered that Barbara was "sensitive" enough to see into the future. She said that someone at the table should "leap from the arms of death to the arms of life." Barbara jumped up from her chair, and James eyed her

Soon after Barbara had a medium come to her house, she started having visions of handsome men in eighteenth-century clothing: Bianca was Barbara, Jason was James and Geoffrey was the dashing Gunnar St. Clair.

nervously. He advised her to forget the kooky lady, and was sure she was a fake. Shortly, Barbara had visions of handsome men in eighteenth-century clothing. One asked her to dance, another gave her a vase. When James came home with a similar vase, a nervous Barbara locked it in a drawer. After having another vision of herself and a man listening to church bells, she went to the medium for a consultation. Soon the visions had names. Bianca was Barbara, Jason was James, and Bianca's maid Diedre was a double for Dee. Then there was Geoffrey; he couldn't stop staring at Bianca. To assure his control of the Stenbeck fortune, James was quite concerned about Barbara's deteriorating state of mind. When his younger brother, Lars, was killed in an accident, James and Barbara flew to Stockholm for the

funeral. Barbara was shocked to see "Geoffrey" there. His real name was Gunnar St. Clair, and he was an internationally known balloonist, photojournalist and explorer. Gunnar shocked James—they were first cousins! He produced records from the St. Clair orphanage showing that Greta Aldrin, James's ex-nanny, brought him there after his parents died, because James's father (Gunnar's uncle) didn't want him living in the same house. James ordered an investigation and was determined not to let Gunnar claim any rights to the Stenbeck fortune. Barbara couldn't believe the man in her visions was her husband's cousin.

One day, Greta Aldrin's bewitching daughter, Ariel, arrived and informed Barbara that James had invited her to live with them. Settling into the penthouse, Ariel phoned Greta and told her she would do what she came there to do. She began to eavesdrop on James and Barbara's fights about Margo and Miranda. Ariel soon became fascinated by John Dixon. John had written a fictionalized account of the rape trial, titled "The Loner." Ariel left the Stenbecks and moved in next to John. Lisa was writing a gossip column under the pseudonym "Dolly Valentine," and she took great pleasure manufacturing a romance between her nemesis John and Ariel. John accused Ariel of planting the item, but she denied it. When he invited her to dinner, Ariel accepted, and she told John that American women were too aggressive, but European women like herself were "created to make their men happy." John was in total accord.

The Stenbecks were surprised when Gunnar showed up at the penthouse. Electrified by his presence, Barbara mistakenly called him Geoffrey. But she had a troubling vision of Bianca crying in bed. She and Jason had just made love. He was rough and shouted at her, "You belong to me. Wives, peasants and horses, they all have to be taught!" Later in the vision, Geoffrey admitted he wanted to make love to her. James gave Barbara his grandmother's ruby necklace and warned her of a family curse: If she lost it, the Stenbeck empire would fall. Gunnar was intrigued by the necklace and the legend. Although wanting to prove he was a Stenbeck, he claimed he had no interest in the family fortune. One night while the Stenbecks were waiting for Gunnar, someone stole the necklace and replaced it with a music box. James blamed Steve, who was arrested for the theft. While he was in jail, though, a gloved hand returned the necklace to the safe. Steve thought James did it for the insurance money, and he vowed to expose his scheme.

Gunnar paid Ariel a visit at Fashions, where she had become one of the models. James spied them, and his curiosity was piqued. At Fashions, Gunnar saw Barbara holding a blue dress and suggested she buy it. Later she had a vision of Bianca wearing a similar dress for Geoffrey. Whenever she wore the blue dress, Barbara felt loved. Barbara was convinced these visions were premonitions of the end of her marriage, and she was afraid of her attraction to Gunnar. Barbara headed for her cabin in Michigan to get away.

Armond Elliot, a movie producer friend of Ariel's, offered to buy the rights to John's book. Ecstatic, John thought he was going to be rich and maybe even win an Oscar.® His interest in Ariel increased. What he didn't know was that Armond was working for James, who quickly shelved the project. Because John had portrayed James as an adulterer and a crook, James wanted to ensure that the movie would never be made. Dee was relieved, too, since John's "fiction" discussed the inability of a woman to have normal sexual responses. Armond refused to sell the rights back to John. John wanted to know the truth, but Armond wouldn't say. John needed a detective, and Maggie recommended Steve, who had been freelancing as a detective. Steve soon found out that James was the culprit. James, meanwhile, was becoming attracted to Dee. Unable to control themselves, Ariel and John made love in the linen closet at Memorial!

Greta Aldrin visited Ariel and met with James. She fussed over Paul but did not reveal that she was his real grandmother. Before leaving, Greta warned James not to trust Gunnar. James assured her he had everything under control. Greta asked Ariel if she were having an affair with John, and Ariel admitted that it was marriage that intrigued her most. Ariel did everything she could to make John jealous. Afraid of losing her, John went to purchase a diamond ring. The real ones were too expensive, so he bought a fake one. Dee was relieved that John had found someone and wished the couple luck. After Ariel made John promise her a big wedding, a house and travel, she agreed to be his wife. John told Ariel he wanted custody of Andy, but this was not what she had in mind. No one wanted to come to their wedding, so John suggested they marry in Jamaica. John wanted his bride to get pregnant, because he never had the chance to see Margo as a child, and a child would give him respectability. But Ariel's mind was on material things, and when she had her ring appraised, two appraisers verified the diamond was a fake. Ariel vowed to make John pay. First, she went on a shopping spree, then purchased 20 acres of land and made plans to build tennis courts and a pool. Despite his anger, John was still attracted to Ariel, and after making love, she showed him the blueprints and told him the house would cost around a million dollars. And she'd already made the down payment. John gave Ariel an ultimatum: no children, no house. Ariel agreed to have children, and John threw out her birth control pills. Soon after, James saw Ariel renewing her prescription.

When Barbara got into her car at the cabin, a masked man put a gun to her head. Barbara's captors were Charles Ivenstrom, the man who had once ordered her death, and his daughter, Ingrid, widow of James's younger brother, Lars. Ingrid blamed Barbara and James for her husband's death. Lars and James would have had to share the Stenbeck fortune, and Ingrid said Lars futilely begged James to keep him out of bankruptcy. Desperate, Lars got drunk and died in an accident. In revenge, Ingrid vowed to kill Barbara, and Charles was helping her get back the money that was rightfully hers. The kidnappers mistook Gunnar for James, and demanded $2 million in cash for Barbara. They insisted Gunnar make the drop, but captured him as he approached. Alone in a dark cellar, Gunnar and Barbara declared their love. They escaped and hid in a nearby barn. As they slept, a little girl wandered in and told her parents, who contacted the police. James arrived to find Gunnar and Barbara sleeping in each other's arms. Alone with Barbara, James accused her of having an affair with Gunnar, which she denied. Gunnar found a painting of a woman who bore a striking resemblance to Barbara/Bianca and bought it, telling Barbara the picture meant they were destined to be together. Then he proposed.

When John found out about James's affair with Brenda, he tried blackmail to get his film rights back. Barbara overheard John yelling at Dee that Barbara was a fool to stay married to the man who ran him down and who was having an affair with Brenda. Shocked, she told James she and Paul were moving out. Nels warned James about losing control of the Stenbeck fortune. He begged Barbara to reconsider and warned that she and Gunnar would never get custody of Paul. Barbara ignored him and went to Switzerland with Gunnar, leaving Paul with Kim and Nick. While she was away, James broke into Matt Butler's office and stole Barbara's files, which contained information about Mme. Koster and the visions. He bribed Mme. Koster into becoming his co-conspirator. Barbara had moved into the Stewart house, and on James's instructions, Mme. Koster sent a woman named Sylvia to apply for the job of housekeeper, and Barbara hired her.

James planned to drive Barbara crazy so he could get custody of Paul. Sylvia began tormenting her. She made noises and terrified Barbara with an image of the Everett painting on the wall. When she turned on the lights, the image vanished. Then, James dressed up as Jason. When Barbara spotted him, she fainted. Gunnar promised to keep her safe. One night, James/Jason lured Barbara into a raging storm. He then left her and told Paul that she was missing. The next morning he "found" her and made her feel guilty for leaving Paul alone in the house. Everyone was worried about Barbara's state of mind, but Gunnar suspected James and installed round-the-clock surveillance. Meanwhile, Sylvia was drugging Barbara's coffee, and Barbara started acting strangely. Even Paul backed away when she reached out for him. Finally, while Barbara was drugged, James ripped her dress, cut her arm lightly and placed a letter opener in her hand. She awoke screaming and terrified Paul. James committed Barbara to a sanatorium, and Gunnar arrived too late to stop him. The doctor, Henry Moller, was a cohort of James. Gunnar accused James of having Barbara committed in order to take Paul away, and he refused to leave until he got her out. James told Barbara that Gunnar had left. Barbara was alone and frightened, and the drugs made her lash out at everyone—even Kim. Gunnar found her and gave her a locket. He told her that if she weren't sure he existed, she should look at the locket, and she would know. They tried to escape but were captured. Barbara was sedated, and James found the locket and got rid of it. The nurse tried to convince Barbara that she had imagined the locket, but Barbara knew better, and Gunnar continued to defend her sanity. One night he was able to whisk her away and told her they would "spend their future together." Ariel and John agreed to testify on Barbara's behalf at the custody trial. However, Ariel and James were becoming closer, so Ariel changed her mind. When she told Greta about her feelings for James, Greta headed for Oakdale.

As Ariel and James flirted, Greta called and ordered James to send Ariel home. She asked Ariel if she was in love with James, and Ariel said not yet. Greta told Ariel to stay away from James. When she wouldn't listen, Greta blurted out that James was Ariel's brother and confessed she took the real Stenbeck child to the orphanage and placed her own son in the Stenbeck house. Greta insisted James shouldn't know, but Ariel couldn't resist. To James's horror, he realized that Gunnar was the true Stenbeck heir.

John found out because he had a tape of James screaming that he wanted the birth certificates destroyed. James went to Stockholm to retrieve them. John followed and found the birth certificates in Greta's house. When James arrived, John escaped out the window with the documents. He put copies in Greta's car, where Greta and James found and burned them. On one of the tapes, John had heard Ariel and James talk about getting rid of him. With glee, John began to plot James's ruin. John was out driving when his brakes failed, and he lost control of the car and crashed. When he came to, John told Margo that either Ariel or James was trying to kill him. John cut Ariel out of his will and insurance policies. Then he gave her sealed envelopes containing copies of James's birth certificate and addressed them to Gunnar, Barbara and the *New York Times*—to be delivered in the event of his death. John pasted cut-out letters to form the question, "When is a Stenbeck not a Stenbeck?" James suspected John, but Ariel was sure John had no idea that James was not a Stenbeck. John's next note read "Sweet Dreams," and with it John sent a copy of James's birth certificate. James accused Gunnar and warned that he would make things tough for Barbara.

In a rage after John refused to sign the deed to the new house, Ariel destroyed her engagement ring, but told John not to worry—she'd get another one, and this time it would be real. Maggie soon arrived with divorce papers. Ariel heard John listening to the tapes and realized that it was John who was behind the blackmail and the notes. Ariel stole the tapes and played them for James, who went wild. James assured her that he'd handle the situation. After Ariel left, James vowed that he would kill John Dixon. He read up on undetectable poisons. Then he left a message for John saying Dee's life was in danger. John ran out, and seconds later James poisoned a jug of water on John's desk. John returned to his office and drank some water. Soon he was lying on the floor, gasping for air. Simultaneously, James was searching for the birth certificates. When he didn't find them, he called Dee. James was in the middle of declaring his unconditional love for her when the doorbell rang. It was John, and he had a gun. John was supposed to be dead. James intended to marry Dee. Hoping to upset John, James urged her to tell him of the coming event. John got on the phone, but Dee wouldn't listen to John's ranting and hung up, saying, "I hate him so much, I could kill John Dixon right now!" John forced James to admit to the murder attempts and said he had proof that James wasn't a Stenbeck. Instead of killing him, John demanded a million a year for his silence. "You should have killed me, John. It was the last chance you'll ever have," James said. The first installment of James's blackmail money, $100,000, was missing, and Ariel didn't deny stealing it. John handed her the divorce papers and told her she could consider the money her settlement. Then he ordered James to deliver the remainder to his new house or be exposed. James had a plan that included a gun and a way to dispose of a body without detection.

Ellen knew David was angry at John for harassing Dee and feared he was headed for John's. She followed him and found John's body on the floor. Afraid that David did it, Ellen called the police. When they arrived, there was blood, but no body. James was stunned to learn that John was dead. He took pains to conceal the reason for his visit. A shoe found near the lake was John's, but a dragging of the lake failed to turn up the body. A memorial service was held for John.

Dee confided in Brian McColl, and it was apparent that she was emotional over his death: "I had to find some way to get him out of my life, to make him leave me alone.... I had no choice but to try and end it." She was talking about her marriage, but at her parents' wedding, Dee was arrested for the murder of John Dixon. Tom offered to defend her; Margo was enraged that he would defend the woman accused of murdering her father.

Meanwhile, Annie and Jeff became the proud parents not of twins, but of quadruplets: two boys and two girls. Annie received a call from President Reagan congratulating her on the birth. Thrilled, they named their youngest daughter Nancy, after Nancy Hughes and Nancy Reagan. The pressure of work and fatherhood soon proved to be too much for Jeff, and he turned to Dexedrine to keep him going. One day Jeff froze in surgery, and John was forced to finish the operation. Once home, he took a downer. Annie questioned him about some amphetamines she found, and Jeff admitted

## Issues

In 1983, Jeff Ward suffered from an increasingly common problem in the medical profession: prescription drug addiction. A new father of quadruplets, Jeff faced mounting pressures in his personal life, and his surgery schedule was grueling. Having easy access to drugs, Jeff gave in to the temptation and started taking amphetamines. When Jeff hit bottom, his family persuaded him to seek help at a drug treatment center. He returned home briefly for his children's first birthday, and eventually he was able to turn his life around.

to having taken them twice. Then one of the quads developed symptoms of Reye's syndrome, and David confirmed the diagnosis. When the baby got sicker, only Jeff was available to do the surgery. He could get through it only by taking a pill. Jeff gradually sank into a morass of drug abuse, complete with street pushers and a near-fatal car accident, finally hitting rock bottom in a seedy motel, where he went through withdrawal. He eventually checked himself into a drug treatment center, returning for the quads' first birthday. He was able to salvage both his family and his career.

Tom informed a happy Barbara that he had papers validating her sanity. Paul had been staying with Ariel because James said the boy was afraid of Barbara. When Maggie issued James a copy of the decree ordering visitation rights for Barbara, James tore it up. He threatened Gunnar and demanded they meet at the Stenbeck refinery. Barbara grabbed a gun and arrived just as James was about to throw Gunnar from a catwalk. Barbara tripped, and the gun went off, the bullet hitting James in the stomach. He told Barbara he'd make her pay for what she'd done. He told Paul Barbara had shot him, that she was a very sick woman and could hurt him, too. When Barbara saw Paul, she reached out for him, and the boy ran away in terror!

Ever since Steve had smuggled drugs for James, Steve and Carol's marriage had been coming apart. Carol told Kim that two men had been watching her building, and Kim blurted out that she thought Steve fled because he was part of James's drug operation. Unable to forgive Steve and fearing for her family's safety, Carol had Steve arrested and divorced him. She then married a minister named Norman Frazier.

Nick ordered Kim not to visit Steve in prison, but she went anyway. He did not like to be disobeyed. Kim informed her husband that she didn't take orders from anyone. When Steve was released, he hired Maggie to handle his divorce. Once Steve got a job on a construction site next to Maggie's office, they saw each other often. Maggie was intrigued by Steve. Soon the lawyer and the hardhat found themselves making mad, passionate love. But Betsy would win Steve's heart. She sympathized with Steve when Nick refused to stake him in a trucking company venture. Betsy offered him her trust fund money in order to jump-start his business, which Steve couldn't accept. They became involved, much to Maggie's horror, who accused Steve of dumping her for a child.

Betsy knew Kim and Nick would never approve of her and Steve; Stan spotted them at a bar, however, and when Betsy got home she knew she was in trouble. Steve and Nick exchanged bitter words, and Kim accused him of taking advantage of Betsy's innocence and sweet nature. When Steve told Kim to trust Betsy's judgment, a stunned Kim realized he was in love with her step-daughter. Steve claimed only frienddhip, but he warned Kim that if she persisted in controlling Betsy, she would only rebel. Anxious to prevent an explosion, Kim decided not to tell Nick. Steve told Betsy about his conversation with Kim, and Betsy was so outraged she impulsively gave Steve her trust fund money. When Betsy told Nick she was dating Steve, he stormed over to the construction site where Steve was working and lunged at him, accusing him of wanting Betsy for her money. Terrified that the brothers would hurt each other, Betsy promised never to see Steve again. By now, Nick's attitude concerned Kim, and she confided in her new boss, Stan Holden, who now owned a detective agency.

Betsy didn't keep her promise, and soon she and Steve took a trip up to the lake. Nick followed. When he demanded that Betsy return to Oakdale, she refused and said she loved Steve. Nick was irate. Steve entered, and Nick turned on his brother. His last words before he collapsed were, "I should have killed you!" He made Betsy promise she'd never see Steve again, and then Nick died. Steve reluctantly agreed not to see Betsy, and Kim told Betsy she must keep her promise to Nick. She resumed her studies at Oakdale University. Craig Montgomery's interest in Betsy was obvious. Steve tried to persuade Kim to free Betsy from her guilt, but Kim told him he was unsuitable for Betsy. Steve was adamant and was sure Betsy loved him, too, but she told him they must go their separate ways.

Steve was working part-time for Whit McColl, hauling material to his factory. Craig also worked for Whit, and he was told that tough union negotiations were approraching. Craig thought Steve would make the perfect scapegoat. He vandalized Steve's truck, and the union was suspected. This was only the beginning of the problems between these two men. Craig was developing feelings for Betsy; he next planted a bomb in Steve's truck that would destroy his plans to join the union and, he hoped, destroy Steve as well! The plan backfired when Craig found out Betsy had gone to meet Steve and was waiting for him in his truck. Craig saved her but got caught in the explosion. He was hospitalized with injuries that would haunt him in the years to come.

Betsy and Craig's wedding kicked off 1983. But this was not a happy day for the bride, because her thoughts were with Steve. As the wedding procession began, Steve arrived at the church and hid behind a pillar. By the time Craig and Betsy were pronounced husband and wife, Steve was standing outside the church in the rain, tears streaming down his face.

When they returned from their honeymoon, Craig and Betsy put on a happy facade for their friends and relatives, but the truth was that Craig was unable to make love. The problem was residual nerve damage from the truck explosion. An out-of-town doctor informed Craig that the impotence might be temporary, but the sterility was not. Craig didn't tell Betsy he was sterile; instead, he said his impotence was caused by the knowledge that she was in love with Steve. Betsy was appalled by the accusation and by Craig's jealous fits over Steve. She took Kim up on her offer to get away and stay with a friend in Ronda, Spain. When Steve found out where she was going, he scraped together the money to join her.

Meanwhile, Whit's wild daughter, Diana, flew in from Paris. One look at this gorgeous blonde and Craig realized his potency was returning. In Spain, Steve found Betsy, and she tried to hide her feelings about him. But Steve knew different, and a picnic lunch in the olive groves led to passionate lovemaking. Steve thought it was the first time, but Betsy denied it. They returned to Oakdale with the intention of staying together and going public with their love, only to have a rejuvenated Craig stage a romantic "honeymoon night" in celebration of his wife's return! Betsy felt trapped. How could she tell Craig she wanted to leave him now?

Diana McColl insinuated herself further into this romantic quadrangle by coming on to Steve. But when he snubbed her, she let it slip out to Craig that Steve had borrowed money for a plane ticket to Spain. Craig realized Betsy and Steve had been together and was crushed. One day while Betsy was out, Craig took a call from her doctor and was stunned to learn she was pregnant! Although Craig had regained his potency, he knew he was still sterile, which meant Betsy was carrying Steve's child! David knew about Craig's sterility from the hospital records and was shocked as well. After keeping quiet for a long time, he finally told Ellen. Ellen wanted to tell her granddaughter, but David said it would be a violation of doctor-patient confidentiality and could cause serious problems at the hospital.

Torn between her love for Steve and the belief that she was carrying Craig's child, Betsy stood Steve up on a day they had planned to go away together. Although Betsy reluctantly chose to remain with Craig, Steve could not accept the idea that she didn't love him anymore. And Craig went to great lengths to rub in the fact that Steve and Diana seemed to be an item now.

The newly married McColls were having their share of problems, too. When Lisa found out that her ex-husband Grant was very sick, she hurried to his side. Whit could barely conceal his jealousy, because he knew Lisa had told Grant that she'd never stopped loving him.

*On the Road*

To escape her troubled marriage to Craig, Betsy went to Ronda, Spain, and Steve followed. A picnic lunch in the olive groves led to a night of passion under the stars. For Betsy, it was the first time.

Later, Whit was aghast when ex-chorus girl Charmane L'Amour arrived at his office unannounced and introduced herself as his long-lost wife! As proof, she showed Whit their marriage certificate and explained that they were married five years ago during a wild weekend in Vegas. The lawyer who supposedly divorced them never filed, so the decree Whit received was a phony. Whit said he was now married to another woman, and Charmane replied that he had better get a divorce from her fast! When Whit tried to pay her off, Charmane refused and told him he had 24 hours to break the news to Lisa. Whit called his lawyer only to find out that Charmane's

When Lisa threw a gala costume ball for Whit's 55th birthday, Diana thought she'd snagged her man when Steve agreed to be her date. But Steve's heart was and always would be with Betsy. That night, Betsy's jealous husband, Craig, framed Steve in a coin robbery, forcing him into hiding.

story was true—they were legally married!

Shortly after Grant recovered, Lisa returned to Whit and threw a gala costume party for his 55th birthday. Charmane came dressed as Martha Washington and told Lisa she was Whit's long-lost sister. Then she proceeded to inform Whit that she was ready to move into his mansion! The party provided the perfect setting for Craig to exact revenge on Steve. Craig contacted con man Ike Slattery, who, posing as Steve, stole some rare coins from Whit's collection while the party was in full swing and planted one in Steve's apartment. When Whit discovered his coins were missing, Craig convinced him Steve was the culprit, and when the police searched Steve's apartment, they found one of the coins. Confronted by the cops, Steve bolted, and the police opened fire. Steve was hit in the leg but managed to escape.

Later, Betsy, who had been out shopping, got into her car and found Steve in the back seat! She took him to the boathouse and lovingly tended to his wounds. Meanwhile, a grateful Whit promoted Craig to vice president at the factory. Betsy enlisted Steve's friend Tucker Foster to help them find out who framed Steve. She thought it was Whit, but Tucker was sure it was Craig! David caught Betsy sneaking into the supply room at Memorial to get medicine for Steve. She begged her grandfather to come and examine him. David discovered that Steve was suffering from blood poisoning and gangrene and would die unless he got treatment. With Betsy's help, David operated on Steve right there in the boathouse.

Aware of his granddaughter's feelings, David wondered if she were sure she'd married the right man. Betsy said she was committed to Craig, so David kept quiet about Craig's sterility. Steve worried about Betsy's safety, especially in light of her pregnancy, so he departed, leaving a note for her at the boathouse. Upset by the note, Betsy started experiencing severe cramps and was rushed to Memorial. As Betsy recovered, Craig and Diana made plans to open a nightclub on the Stenbeck yacht, which Whit had bought as a present for Diana. The club was to be called the Anemone. Betsy wasn't pleased. They were already building a house in expensive Ruxton Hills, so where was all this money coming from?

Tucker and Steve located one of Whit's missing coins at a pawnshop, but by the time they got together the money to buy it, it was gone! Still on the lam, Steve got a job with a traveling circus. One day, Kim took Andy to the circus, and when Andy recognized the voice of the clown, he blurted out, "Uncle Steve, is that you?" Tucker decided to move Steve to another location. The only problem was, the police were tailing Tucker!

One of Whit's rare coins had been bought by a Bobbi Maxwell and her boyfriend, Lonnie. They traced Tucker from the pawnshop and called him for a meeting. Betsy and Steve joined the "coin hunt" and arrived for the meeting to try to buy back the coin. Lonnie told Bobbi that a Mr. Maurice Vermeil had one of the coins and was anxious to get another. Steve and Betsy, along with Tucker, set off after Vermeil.

The threesome found out that Vermeil did have the stolen coin and was planning to auction it off on a cruise to Bermuda. Betsy paid for Steve's passage, and he joined the cruise pretending to be wealthy playboy Daniel Bishop. When Betsy discovered Vermeil was a mobster, she knew she had to warn Steve. She told Craig that her doctor had recommended she take a cruise, and he believed her. Actually, Craig was relieved, because now he could spend more time with Diana. But when Betsy told Craig she was going to call her broker and sell some stocks to get money for the cruise, Craig panicked. He had made some bad investments and had lost all her money in the stock market! The Montgomerys were broke, only Betsy didn't know it yet.

Suddenly Craig remembered the cash receipts from the Anemone. With them, he was able to give his broker the money he'd put up to cover him. He also found out that Ike Slattery had sold a coin to Vermeil, who was headed for Bermuda. What a happy coincidence that Betsy was on the same boat! Craig made plans to join the ship in Nassau, with the intention of selling his own coin to Vermeil. Luckily, Steve and Betsy found out about Craig's arrival beforehand, and Betsy pretended to have a happy reunion with her husband.

Being careful to conceal his identity, Craig met with Vermeil, who offered him a measly $10,000 for the coin. Craig tried to negotiate, but the crafty coin dealer held firm. When Steve got wind of Craig's attempted deal, he informed the captain there was a stolen coin on board and contacted the police in Bermuda. To avoid being caught, Vermeil was forced to throw the coins overboard. Seeing Betsy and Steve together, Craig made plans to return to Oakdale without Betsy. When they reached Bermuda, Steve and Betsy checked into a hotel as Mr. and Mrs. Bishop, and they reconfirmed their love.

By this time, Vermeil knew that "Mr. Bishop" was an impostor and was busily plotting Steve's ruin. Unaware that Vermeil was on to him, Steve decided to infiltrate his organization in hopes of finding out who set him up. He was in luck when Ike Slattery, the man Craig hired for the job, showed up. As Steve and Betsy bid each other a sad goodbye in Bermuda, Craig was proposing to Diana in Oakdale. Diana, however, didn't love Craig—she loved Steve. When she arrived home, Betsy told Craig she was leaving him.

Upon returning from a romantic evening with Steve at the boathouse, Betsy went into labor. It was a breech birth, and Steve had to get her to the hospital quickly! Still a wanted man, he waited in the shadows of the emergency room. Diana discovered him there and tried to get him to leave, but Steve couldn't tear himself away from Betsy, who gave birth to a healthy but tiny daughter. In remembrance of her father Dan, she named the child Danielle. Craig told his wife how much he loved her, and now that they had a child, he hoped things would be all right between them. That night, Vermeil ordered his security people to find Steve and kill him! Diana helped Steve escape by hiding him in her room, and he rushed back to Memorial just as Betsy took a brief turn for the worse. Craig spotted him, though, and had his rival arrested. But Craig's sister Margo outsmarted him and got Ike Slattery to give her enough information to free Steve. After all was said and done, Betsy told Craig she still planned to leave him for Steve.

Meanwhile, Whit figured out the only two people who knew the combination to his safe were Lisa and Craig. He confronted Craig, who was unable to lie his way out of it, and Whit fired him. Then there was the question of who had embezzled funds from the nightclub. When Diana didn't buy his excuses, Craig pleaded poverty. Diana said she wouldn't call the police if he handed over his half of the club to her. Craig told Betsy he had been fired because Whit said he spent too much time with the baby, and Betsy bought the story. Betsy was moved when she heard Craig talking to his sleeping daughter about his losses, and weakly told Steve she couldn't leave Craig right now. When Steve exploded, Betsy stormed out, saying they were through! Diana was supportive of Steve and tried to help him start up his construction company again, although what she really wanted was to get him into her bed.

On Kim's advice, a sad Betsy wrote a note to Steve telling him how much she loved him. Craig found the note, tore it up and forged a new one saying Betsy loved Craig and regretted having to betray him. When Steve read it, he went to Betsy's house and through the window watched her feed the baby. Drawn to her by this tender moment, he was about to tap on the window when Craig entered. Seeing this family picture, Steve was convinced the letter was true. He returned to Diana and, grateful for her support, made love to her. The next morning, when Betsy came by to see Steve, Diana answered the door wearing only Steve's shirt. Devastated, Betsy decided she couldn't stay with Craig, so she moved in with Kim.

Ever the schemer, Craig found an offbeat way to better himself: He signed up for stunt school because he wanted to learn how to fall down stairs! When Betsy arrived to get the rest of her things, Craig picked a fight with her and "fell" down the stairs. Craig then cried "paralysis," getting Betsy to move back in with him. Certain that Craig was faking, Steve brought in his ex-cop cousin, Frank Andropoulos, to investigate the slippery Mr. Montgomery. Frank went undercover as a hospital worker at Memorial, where he met Lyla. At first, his interest in her was strictly as a source of information, but he soon came to like her very much. Unfortunately, Lyla took their friendship to mean more and fell in love with him. Frank and Lyla became lovers, if only briefly.

As heinous as Craig was, he proved to be a rank amateur compared to James Stenbeck. One night, recovering from his gunshot wound and groggy from the medication, James thought he saw John Dixon standing at the foot of his bed! The figure told James there was no way Dee was going to be convicted of murdering him, because he was going to make sure she got off. Scared to death, James closed his eyes. When he opened them, the apparition was gone. James was sure he had been hallucinating. He told Barbara he would take her

In Spain for Paul's birthday, James lured Barbara to a bullring, where he'd planned a little surprise. As Barbara walked to the center of the ring to pick up a bouquet of flowers James had placed there, a sudden noise made her turn. To her horror, she saw a bull charging toward her.

to trial for attempted murder unless she signed an agreement giving him full custody of Paul. An angry Barbara tore up the agreement and threw it in his face.

As Dee's trial got under way, Tom angered Dee by trying to prove that James wanted John dead. Meanwhile, Karen Haines accidentally discovered John's tape in Maggie's safe. After listening to James tell Ariel he wasn't the true Stenbeck heir, Karen realized she had the evidence Tom needed to indict James for the murder. The prosecutor, Brian McColl, was harshly cross-examining Dee on the stand when a man appeared at the back of the courtroom and shouted at him to stop. When he removed his wig and his beard, everyone in the courtroom gasped—it was John Dixon, back from the dead! After the trial, John took great pleasure in telling Ariel to pack her bags and leave, while James proposed to Dee, and she said yes. But the greedy Karen blackmailed James into marrying her instead, threatening to reveal his true heritage if he didn't.

Upset and confused, Dee decided it was time to leave Oakdale and start a new life. Because of her work at Fashions Ltd. and the perfume company, she was

offered a job with *Flair* magazine in New York. Many people were sad to see her leave, especially John.

James promised Karen a married life of hell and, with Ariel as their witness, they said, "I do." When they got home, James told Karen she'd be sleeping in the maid's quarters.

Karen tried to make friends with Paul, but James said it wouldn't be necessary, since Paul was going to Europe soon. Karen divulged this to Barbara. Barbara and Gunnar went to Maggie and told her that if she couldn't do anything legally, they were going to take Paul. Maggie warned them there could be serious consequences if they did. When James got wind that Barbara and Gunnar had seen the District Attorney about Paul's custody, he knew he had to stop them. He came up with the perfect "accident." James invited Barbara to a private bullfighting demonstration he was presenting in Spain in honor of Paul's birthday. With James, Karen, Barbara and Gunnar in attendance, the birthday bullfight was a great success. The next day, James told Paul to call his mommy and ask her to meet James at the bullring for a surprise. Gunnar suspected foul play but was detained by one of James's men. Barbara arrived and walked toward the center of the ring to pick up a bouquet of flowers that James had strategically placed there for her. A sudden noise made her turn around and, to her horror, she saw a bull coming straight at her. As Barbara frantically tried to dodge the animal, she saw James smirking on the sidelines. Gunnar arrived just in time to see his panic-stricken lover. He called out for her to remain still, and he diverted the bull's attention while Barbara ran to safety.

James took off and Gunnar followed him to an old castle, where James grabbed a sword from the weapons room and engaged his rival in a "duel to the death." They were both expert fencers, but Gunnar got the best of him and, with a sword at his throat, James was forced to sign the custody papers. James bade Paul a tearful and surprisingly heartfelt goodbye. Barbara and Gunnar happily claimed Paul as their own and told him they were going to be a real family now. What started as a vision had now turned into a dream come true as Barbara married Gunnar. In honor of their marriage, Barbara made good use of the Stenbeck fortune by giving an endowment to the St. Clair Orphanage, where Gunnar had spent his childhood years.

James told Karen he had lost Paul and revealed that without him, there was no Stenbeck fortune. Karen called him a coward for giving up. She had married him for the fortune and now felt entitled to look elsewhere. A down-and-out James was forced to sell his penthouse. As soon as he put it on the market, it was snapped up by none other than his adversary, John! John threatened James with public disclosure of his true identity as Jimmy Aldrin. John even took great pleasure in calling him "Jimmy."

On a happier note, in true Tom and Margo fashion, this passionate couple tied the knot in a very unusual ceremony. Since neither was known for their conventionality, why should their wedding day be any different? Friends and family were called to the park on an "emergency." It was come as you are. The minister arrived in an ice cream truck, the mother of the bride was in a housecoat and curlers, and the bride and groom made their grand entrance on a motorcycle!

Love was in the air for another member of the Montgomery family in 1983. In the spring, a tipsy Ernie Ross finally got up the courage to make love to Cricket, although he did call his friend Craig for pointers first. When he saw Cricket in a sexy nightgown, he ran into her arms like a man out of control. The morning after, Ernie was bowled over by the discovery that sex could be so much fun, and Cricket was ecstatic as well. Soon, though, Ernie got a job offer in Los Angeles and they parted ways. Then Cricket found herself pregnant! For his sister's sake, Craig called Ernie in California,who was quick to return to Oakdale and propose. In the middle of their wedding, Cricket went into labor. Determined to tie the knot, the couple completed their vows in the ambulance, with Lyla and the minister in attendance. As they were pronounced husband and wife, their baby girl was born. The new Ross family moved to California to set up house.

Two more characters now entered the chaotic Stenbeck saga. A handsome but bitter man named Burke Donovan approached James and suggested they form an alliance against Gunnar. Burke's wife Nicole had had an affair with Gunnar but later died and left Burke with a son, Dustin, called Dusty. When Ariel investigated Burke, she began to suspect Gunnar was actually Dusty's biological father. It was then that Ariel

realized Dusty could be the true Stenbeck heir. Ariel talked James into hiring Burke as his horse trainer. During Paul's riding lessons, Burke ran into Gunnar. The horseman's hatred for Gunnar was blatantly obvious. Ariel, meanwhile, found herself attracted to Burke, especially since his son might possibly be the heir to the Stenbeck fortune. But she didn't dare reveal this possibility to James.

Karen's curiosity was aroused when she saw how much time Ariel was spending with the new horse trainer. Ariel claimed she and Burke had once been lovers, but now they were just friends. Karen didn't buy this and asked Burke, who replied he'd known Ariel for only three weeks! The persistent Karen got the name of Burke's late wife's parents and told James she was going on a trip. When she met with them and brought up Gunnar's name, it was obvious that because of their affair, they blamed Gunnar for their daughter's death. On the plane home, Karen realized that Ariel was after Burke because she'd figured out that his son could be the true Stenbeck heir.

After his failed attempt to kill Gunnar by rigging a beam in the stables, Burke decided to pursue Barbara as a way of evening the score with Gunnar for stealing Nicole away from him. James was intrigued, to say the least, by Burke's vendetta against Gunnar. For the life of him, James couldn't understand what Karen and Ariel saw in a lowly stablehand. Burke's teenage son Dusty was also a troublemaker, and he talked Paul into shoplifting a bracelet from Fashions Ltd. The juvenile

*On the Road*

In Spain, Gunnar proved to be Barbara's knight in shining armor. He saved her from the bull and fought James in a duel. Holding a sword to James's throat, Gunnar forced him to sign the custody papers for Paul. Gunnar and Barbara were now able to claim Paul as their own and assured the boy that they were going to be a real family now.

pranks came to a head when a firecracker exploded in Paul's face, narrowly missing his eyes. Gunnar wasted no time in threatening to fire Burke if he didn't keep Dusty away from Paul. This encounter sent Burke on such a rampage that he mysteriously blacked out. When he went to the hospital for tests, Ariel forced Dusty to stay with her, but Dusty hated every minute and ran to the sympathetic Karen. John told Burke the tests indicated he had a possibly fatal disease. Burke didn't want Dusty to find out, and privately he began speculating about who would make a good stepmother for his son.

When James asked Burke about his wife, Burke sadly recalled the argument that led to her death. She had just told Burke she was leaving him for Gunnar. They struggled, and Nicole fell off the balcony to her death. James thought this incident was just the ammunition they needed to destroy their mutual rival. The plan was to make Gunnar believe he drove Nicole to suicide, thereby wreaking havoc in his marriage to Barbara. James hired a Nicole look-alike to haunt Gunnar, who saw her face in the window one night and woke up screaming. Barbara wanted to know what was going on, and he told her about Nicole and their affair.

The relationship between Ariel and Burke eventually got hot and heavy, and before long the two agreed to marry. Burke collapsed during the ceremony and was taken to the hospital. But Ariel got him to agree to finish the wedding ceremony in the hospital. When Dusty admitted he didn't want Ariel as a stepmother, Karen, wanting to stop the wedding, urged him to tell his father how he felt. The ceremony was well under way when Dusty arrived and voiced his objections. Torn between his love for his son and his love for Ariel, Burke was forced to delay the wedding.

Meanwhile, Gunnar was plagued by further visits from "Nicole" until he finally captured the impostor in his camera lens! Gunnar and Barbara tracked "Nicole" down at the Hayloft and persuaded her to help them seek revenge on James. She tipped them off about her next meeting with him, and James was caught red-handed.

Fearing that he was going to lose his visiting rights, James lured Paul away from camp and took him on a trip. When Barbara found out, she was frantic! In a hotel room in Cheyenne with James, Paul saw a news bulletin about his disappearance and realized his father had lied to him. Barbara and Gunnar arrived in Cheyenne and traced James to the hotel, but all they found was Paul's teddy bear lying in the middle of an empty room. When they returned home, however, Paul was there to greet them! The ever-manipulative James claimed his son had asked him to take him out of camp, and once they saw the news and knew how worried everyone was, they had come home. Barbara had had it—James would never see his son again! When Barbara and Gunnar tried to explain this to Paul, the boy blamed Gunnar for keeping him away from his father.

Never one to miss an opportunity, James tried to turn Paul against Barbara as well. Once Karen learned that James had kidnapped Paul from camp, she sided with Barbara and Gunnar and left James for good. With nowhere to go, she took John up on his offer of an extra bedroom. They talked about Burke, and about John's desire to find a cure for Wilhelm's disease so he could save Burke before it was too late. Before the night was over, Karen and John found themselves in each other's arms.

From the hospital, where he was secretly scheduled for surgery, Burke called Ariel and told her how much he loved her. Remembering Karen's wish for a son and knowing how much Dusty disliked Ariel, Burke wanted to make arrangements for Dusty in case anything happened to him. Maggie drew up a custody agreement that named Karen as guardian, and Burke was relieved when it was signed. After the surgery, John reported that the heart muscle was badly damaged and it was unclear whether the operation was a success.

In the meantime, the Justice of the Peace contacted Ariel and explained that after reviewing the videotape of her first ceremony, Burke had indeed said, "I do," and therefore they were legally married. Ariel couldn't wait to tell Burke. John finally persuaded Burke to tell Ariel and Dusty the truth about his illness. Burke told Dusty he had something important to tell him, but that he wanted Ariel to be there, too. Thinking that his father was going to marry her again, Dusty ran away and hid out at Paul's. When Burke heard Dusty had run away, he and Ariel decided to keep their marriage a secret. When Dusty returned, Ariel pleaded with him to stay for his father's sake.

Since everyone finally seemed to be getting along so well, Burke told Maggie the custody agreement was no longer necessary. But before anything could be done about it, Burke collapsed and was rushed to Memorial, where he died. Gunnar and Barbara were stunned to find out Ariel was Burke's widow. Ariel blamed Gunnar for his death; she told him Burke hated Gunnar for causing Nicole's death. After this sank in, Gunnar realized Dusty could be his and Nicole's son. From the intensity of Ariel's reaction, it was clear to John and Karen that she truly loved Burke.

Karen was all set to divorce James, but the custody agreement for Dusty stated that she had to be married. John volunteered for the job and presented her with a ring as a token of his sincerity. When Karen told Dusty his father had made her his guardian, he thought living with her would be much better than living with Ariel. Meanwhile, Ariel informed a stunned James that Dusty, not Paul, was the true Stenbeck heir. Since Karen had custody, Ariel told him he had better get her back at once! But Karen was already on her way to getting a quickie divorce. James traced Karen and John to the island of Hispanique and set out with Ariel to stop the divorce. By the time James and Ariel arrived, Karen and John were legally married. Ariel tried in vain to persuaded Dusty to live with her. In search of an answer to Dusty's parentage, Gunnar hopped a plane for Hispanique as well. Desperate, James locked Dusty in a hut with Gunnar and set the hut on fire, but they were saved by Karen and John. Because there were no commercial flights leaving the island that night, Gunnar and John arranged for a private jet to take them home. On the plane, John confirmed Gunnar's suspicions that Dusty was his son. Little did they know, however, that James was at the controls. The plane lurched, and the cabin reached freezing temperatures, and one by one, the passengers passed out, leaving James free to kill Gunnar. But Gunnar came to, and in the struggle that ensued, Gunnar accidentally pushed James out of the open door that was meant for him. James seemingly fell to his death.

Traumatized, Paul refused to talk about his father's death, and Dr. Zachary Stone was called in to help him through this difficult time. Because of Paul's feelings toward Gunnar, Barbara and Gunnar decided to part, if only temporarily, until Paul could accept him as his stepdad. On the way home from the zoo, Barbara and Paul got a flat tire on a deserted road. A truck approached with two men inside, and the driver mentioned that someone had recently escaped from the Brighton Hospital for the criminally insane. The truck stopped, and a man by the name of Richard Fairchild got out and offered to fix Barbara and Paul's flat tire. Paul liked him a lot and suggested that he ride back to Oakdale with them. Richard portrayed himself as the scion of a

Not one to give up on a vendetta, James trapped John, Karen and Dusty on a plane, but his real target was Gunnar. Just as it looked as if James were going to succeed, Gunnar accidentally pushed James out of the open door and watched him fall through the sky to his death.

wealthy family, but when they reached town, he checked into a flophouse, convincing the clerk that he was a rich man who had been robbed.

Richard visited Fashions Ltd., ostensibly to solicit advice from Barbara about opening a string of boutiques. Richard had become obsessed with Barbara's beauty and was determined to destroy anyone who came between them. Under an assumed name, he met John on a flight from Detroit. John was still banned from Memorial and, low on research funds, was looking for a teaching post. He almost had one but was disqualified because of a condemning recommendation from Bob.

Richard engaged John in an eerie conversation about enemies. John thought this stranger was joking when he suggested that he'd kill John's enemy, Bob, if John would kill his enemy, Gunnar. Later, when Bob got an emergency call and left the hospital, Richard lay in wait, gun drawn. As Bob opened his car door, Richard opened fire. Margo and Tom found him lying on the ground, semiconscious. All the doctors were occupied with car-crash victims, and an inexperienced resident asked for John. Tom didn't want John near his father, but when Bob's condition worsened, John asked Tom if he were going to let his personal feelings get in the way of saving his father's life. After much agonizing, Tom let John perform the surgery. John saved Bob's life, and Bob thanked him, but he still could not approve readmitting him to the hospital staff. He did agree, however, to abstain when the board voted on the proposal. Unfortunately, all evidence in the shooting pointed to John, and he was booked for attempted murder.

Meanwhile, Richard, Bob's true assailant, befriended Dusty by pretending to be a friend of John's. When Dusty mentioned that John had saved Bob's life, Richard was stunned and gave Dusty a message for the good doctor: "Now it's your turn." The next day, when Richard paid John a visit, John realized it was Richard who had shot Bob, but Richard fled before John could stop him. Knowing that he might try to kill Bob again, John called the police, but they didn't believe John's story, and neither did Tom.

Around this time, Whit McColl got a call from his black-sheep son Kirk. Kirk had been thrown out of the military school his father had forced him to attend in the hopes of straightening him out, and now he was in jail. This wasn't the first time Whit had to bail his son out, and he refused. Diana and Kirk had grown very close, and when she heard about it, she posted Kirk's bail. As far as Kirk was concerned, though, he'd rather spend the summer in jail than with Whit. Lisa thought Frannie would be a good influence on Kirk, and she arranged a dinner party so that the young people could meet, but it turned out they already had—Kirk had earlier rear-ended Frannie's car, and they didn't like each other one bit. Later, to their chagrin, they learned they were in the same English class. The teacher convinced the studious Frannie to tutor Kirk. Once she got to know him a little better, Frannie saw through Kirk's tough act and realized he was a boy who just wanted some of his father's love and attention. Kirk and Frannie soon found they had a lot in common, and they started dating.

On the other hand, Bob and Miranda realized they had nothing whatsoever in common. Miranda found Bob and his family to be hopelessly provincial but was still determined to make the marriage work—that is, until her suave old flame, Antoine Bisset, arrived in Oakdale. Antoine played on Miranda's ambivalence about Bob and talked her into running away with him to Paris. It would not take Bob long to get over this hasty marriage.

# 1 9 8 4

A major storm ushered in the new year. After it had passed, Betsy's boathouse was on shaky ground. Not about to give up on doing Steve in and knowing that he was already scheduled to work on the boathouse, Craig loosened a support beam so that it would fall on Steve's head. However, Steve and Betsy had decided to work together to salvage their special place, and the beam landed on Betsy instead. Luckily, Steve was able to save her from the wreckage. With the boathouse now destroyed, Craig knew he was sitting on valuable lakefront property. He located a Colonel Jameson, who eyed the property as a potential site for a chemical plant. Jameson shrewdly promised Craig a top-level job if he were able to talk Betsy into selling it. But Betsy had other ideas. She surprised Craig by telling him she planned to build a home for abandoned children on the lot and call it the Refuge. Steve's construction company put in a bid. Diana heard about Steve's plans, got hold of the other bids and changed them, making Steve's the lowest. Steve and Tucker's company got the job.

One night, when Betsy couldn't go through with a romantic evening, Craig left in disgust. Upset that Steve was hindering her marriage, Betsy tried to destroy everything that reminded her of him. She found the book of Greek poetry Steve had given her when they first met and decided to give it back to him. When Betsy arrived at Steve's apartment, she tried to say she was through with him, but the chemistry between them was too strong, and they fell into a passionate embrace. Betsy and Steve agreed not to make love until after she had left Craig; unfortunately, Diana saw them kissing and was quick to inform Craig. Diana was also suspicious that Craig was faking his paralysis. She threw a cup of tea in his lap, and when Craig jumped up, she knew he could really walk and threatened to tell Steve. But the intrepid Andropoulos cousins were already on the case. Steve and Frank got Craig's address book and found the number of the stunt school. The instructor confirmed that Craig had come to the school to learn how to fall down a flight of stairs.

One night Steve took Betsy to the partially constructed Refuge and expressed his pride in the project. Diana, angry that Steve told her there would never be anything romantic between them, told Craig where they were. After Steve and Betsy left, an angry Craig destroyed the site. Heartbroken about the vandalism, Steve paid Craig a visit and implied that he had damaging evidence against him. Then he put an envelope on the mantel and left. Betsy arrived home and almost caught Craig getting out of his wheelchair to get the envelope. He accused her of getting love letters from Steve and threw the envelope in the fire.

As gently as possible, Betsy told Craig their marriage was over. Then she went upstairs to pack and discovered that Danielle was gone! Craig said he couldn't let Betsy take her away, so he hid her. Craig threatened to leave town with Danielle if Betsy called the police, and if she went to Steve, Craig told her, she'd never see her daughter again. Up to this point, Lyla had sympathized with Craig in his attempts to stay married to Betsy—or rather, the attempts she knew about. But once Craig used his own child, Lyla realized how twisted her son was. Out of guilt, she traced Danielle to the home of Mrs. Hoffman, a stuffy nursemaid whom Betsy had fired previously, and Danielle was returned to her mother. Diana finally confessed to Steve that she knew Craig was faking his paralysis. Steve found Betsy at Kim's, and when she told him she'd left Craig for good, they had a joyful reunion.

Craig may have been twisted, but Richard Fairchild was downright psychotic. He would have stabbed Gunnar if John hadn't intervened. John planned to surprise Richard by injecting him with truth serum and then rushing him to the police station to tell his story. But the plan backfired when Richard injected John instead, getting him to admit he was only pretending to be Richard's friend and never intended to live up to his part of the bargain and kill Gunnar.

To get the goods on Richard, John planned to go to New Orleans with Gunnar, Karen and Dusty to track down Richard's father. Meanwhile, Richard became increasingly disturbed by flashbacks of a boy named Davey being warned not to play with matches and playing with them anyway. In New Orleans, Mr. Fairchild Sr. told Karen and John his son was dead. Karen and John checked out the cemetery and found Richard's crypt. Mr. Fairchild's butler, Winston, who had followed them there, closed the doors of the crypt behind them and

*Troubled Triangles*

*Steve's cousin, Frank, found himself smack-dab in the middle of a romantic triangle. Lyla was just getting serious about him when he fell head over heels for her sister, Maggie.*

turned the key. Meanwhile, Dusty spotted Richard in the hotel lobby and called Gunnar. At the cemetery, some Mardi Gras revelers freed a grateful John and Karen from the tomb.

Back in Oakdale, Richard sank further into madness. He saw an apparition of Barbara telling him to kill Gunnar without delay. He tried to slash Gunnar with a razor as he slept, but when Margo, the investigating officer, called for reinforcements, Richard fled the scene. John then came up with an idea of how to catch the madman. Barbara would tell Richard she was leaving Gunnar for him, and Margo, dressed as Barbara, would be used as bait to trap him. Richard took the bait. But once Richard figured out he was being framed, his anger built to a fever pitch. He quickly changed the meeting place to the Refuge, and when Margo arrived, he knocked her out with chloroform.

Winston arrived in Oakdale and identified himself as Davey's, a.k.a. Richard's, father. He explained that Davey had taken his brother Richard's identity after Richard died in a fire started by Davey. On their way to the Refuge, Tom and the lieutenant heard the report that "Richard" had been in prison for arson.

Steve and Betsy were with Kim when she got the call that the Refuge was on fire. Craig arrived at the site without his wheelchair and rushed in to save an unconscious Margo, surrounded by flames. Richard plunged into the basement and perished in a ball of fire. Margo was promoted to detective, but Craig had done so many terrible things to the people he loved that he felt he deserved to be punished and decided not to fight the charges against him. Lyla was so angry with her son for what he had done to Danielle that she refused to go to the trial. Craig was sentenced to five years in prison.

Determined to reform, he even finally admitted to Betsy that Steve was Danielle's father.

Bart came to town to visit his son in his time of need, but Craig didn't buy his father's sudden concern. Through her police contacts, Margo learned that Bart's show store was under surveillance for selling hot merchandise. Margo persuaded Bart to come clean. Bart told Craig he regretted all the rotten things he had done, especially not being a good father.

Just as Steve and Betsy thought their problems were over, Diana McColl found herself pregnant with Steve's baby. Although she made a point of saying she didn't want to ruin Steve and Betsy's future, Diana secretly hoped Steve would marry her and was encouraged when he was adamant about taking responsibility for the baby. Steve told Betsy the news, and a shocked Betsy told Diana this would not change her love for Steve. Diana said she understood, but she gave Betsy fair warning—she was in love with Steve, too.

Lyla was becoming serious about Frank, but he in turn found himself attracted to Maggie. Maggie was representing Frank in the NYPD corruption case and knew nothing about his relationship with Lyla. Frank was wowed by Maggie's successful representation of him, which brought them to New York together. After Frank was acquitted, he and Maggie celebrated with champagne and ended up making mad, passionate love. Afraid that he would drive a wedge between them, Frank neglected to tell Maggie that the "other woman" whom he promised to end it with was her sister. When Maggie found out it was Lyla, she felt she had to bow out for her sister's sake. But Frank knew he and Maggie belonged together, so he gently broke the news to an irate Lyla that he was in love with her sister. Maggie felt guilty and lied to Frank by telling him she'd accepted a marriage proposal from another man. She went so far as to get Brian to pose as her fiancé. Soon afterward, Maggie became attached to an abandoned baby she found in the bushes near Memorial.

Believing things were definitely over with Maggie, Frank formed a close friendship with Diana and offered to marry her to give Diana's baby a name. Even though they would dissolve the marriage as soon as the baby was born, Diana told him she was going to marry his cousin Frank. It almost worked as a ploy to catch Steve. Steve told Betsy he couldn't let them marry when he was really the baby's father, so Betsy selflessly suggested Steve marry Diana. Steve couldn't find it in his heart to do that, a decision that disappointed Diana. Just as

Frank was about to marry Diana, Maggie told him she and Lyla had worked things out, and now Maggie and Frank could be together. But it was too late. Frank told a heartbroken Maggie that the baby Diana was expecting was his.

Despite her career-driven exterior, Maggie desperately wanted a child. She tried to get custody of Jill, the baby she found in the bushes near Memorial, but she was informed that custody had been awarded to a married couple. Then the couple changed their minds, and Maggie was awarded temporary custody. There was one stipulation, though: The adoption board had been made aware of Maggie's relationship with Frank, now a married man, and they warned her to keep her distance. Diana offered an annulment to Frank, who was sure she was doing so only because Steve was still free. Finally, Steve forced Frank to admit that Diana's real motive was to get Steve to marry her.

Trapped, Diana feigned a episode of pre-eclampsia. When a drunken Whit arrived at the hospital, the social worker overheard him accuse Frank of having the morals of an alley cat because he was running around with Maggie Crawford while his wife was pregnant! Maggie knew Whit's comment would jeopardize her attempt to get custody of Jill. Meanwhile, Diana was hit by a stab of pain. The pre-eclampsia turned out to be real. Against Diana's wishes, Whit warned Steve to stay away from his daughter, but he refused. Diana became so distraught by her father's tirade that she miscarried, and Steve blamed Whit for the loss of his child.

Right around this time, Frank's mother Irene revealed that the late Costas Andropoulos wasn't Steve's natural father. This sent Steve and Betsy on a quest to Greece, where they traveled the countryside talking to relatives who remembered Steve's mother Marina, and questioning them as to whom she might have loved. The name that kept popping up was Michael Christopher, but no one seemed to know what had happened to him. In the village of his birth, Steve and Betsy found a locket belonging to Marina. Inside was a picture of Marina, and on the back was the inscription M.C. Steve knew now that Michael Christopher had given this keepsake to his mother. As a token of his own love, Steve gave the locket to Betsy. They also found a love poem, a symbol of Michael and Marina's love, which became a symbol of Steve and Betsy's love as well. After this romantic interlude in Greece, Steve and Betsy returned to Oakdale and were married in a traditional Greek Orthodox ceremony.

Love was also in the air for Steve's friend and construction partner, Tucker. One day Heather Dalton, a beautiful law student and singer, turned up at his door. She was working for a congressman and had a survey for him to sign. It was love at first sight for Tucker, and he started to pursue her despite the fact that Heather didn't show the slightest bit of interest in him. When Tucker found out Heather sang in the church choir, he joined the choir, too. Heather was amused and charmed by his terrible voice and decided to give him a chance. Tucker offered to get her a job at Diana McColl's nightclub. Unfortunately, Heather's father Lionel was a deeply religious man who wouldn't stand for his daughter singing in a place where people smoked and drank. Heather resisted the offer, but Tucker was able to talk her into at least auditioning. When Diana heard Heather sing, she promptly offered her a job. Because her father was out of work, Heather accepted.

On her opening night, Lionel walked into the club, ordered her off the stage and forbade her to see Tucker again! Heather tried to obey her father, but she had already begun to fall in love. Together she and Tucker were able to convince Lionel that there was no shame in what Heather wanted to do, which was to share her voice, her gift from God, with the world. After that, Heather began to sing regularly at the club.

But she had a rival for Tucker's affections in Beverly Taylor, an ambitious young woman intent on climbing the corporate ladder. Beverly arranged for record executive Otis Sutton to come to hear Heather, knowing Otis would love her voice and sweep her off to a new life of recordings and tours, far away from Oakdale and Tucker. Beverly was right—Otis thought Heather was sensational. He immediately offered her a deal, and Tucker encouraged her to sign.

While Betsy and Steve were settling into married life, two mysterious people got word that Steve Andropoulos had been asking questions about Michael Christopher in Greece. They were beautiful concert pianist Juliette Hanovan and her adoptive father, Raymond Speer. Together they came to Oakdale, where Juliette planned to give a concert. At the same time, Betsy discovered there was a picture behind the one of Marina in her locket—a photo of Michael Christopher wearing a uniform with an insignia. Betsy and Steve had the photograph enlarged and saw that the insignia was a bird.

Raymond Speer met Kim, and they started to see quite a lot of each other. One night, Steve mentioned the picture of Michael Christopher and the bird on the insignia, and Raymond vowed silently to get hold of it before Steve could figure out what the insignia meant! As Kim and Raymond grew closer, Juliette caught the eye of Brian McColl. At her Oakdale recital, he waited backstage and silently handed her a rose before her fiancé, Kent Bradford, whisked her away. Raymond asked Juliette when she planned to marry Kent, and she looked fondly at Brian's rose. Raymond was against Juliette's staying in Oakdale, but she felt she must find out why Steve was so set on finding Michael Christopher. After all, Michael was her father.

Beautiful and mysterious Juliette Hanovan wasn't in Oakdale long before she caught the eye of Brian McColl. Juliette turned out to be Steve's half-sister, and they became embroiled in a mystery involving Russian spies.

Brian McColl abandoned the budding political career his father Whit wanted so much for him and started publishing a competing newspaper. Unlike Whit's sensational *City Times*, Brian's *Argus* was a serious investigative paper. Brian asked to interview Juliette about her concert as an excuse to be alone with her. The two soon became romantically involved, and Juliette confided to Raymond that she'd like to break off her engagement to Kent. Raymond advised her not to throw everything away and told her to stay clear of the Michael Christopher situation; it would be disastrous if Steve connected Michael to him. Steve and Betsy, in their continuing search for Christopher, decided to run his picture in the paper.

Meanwhile, someone brought Raymond a sealed file on Christopher, and he ran it through the shredder. Raymond then told Betsy he had news of Michael Christopher and instructed her to go to the airport so that he could search the Andropoulos cabin while she was gone. On her way to the airport, Betsy picked up a young girl, a hitchhiker, and they got into a terrible accident. Marina's locket was found near the body, so it was assumed that Betsy had perished in the accident. Betsy's family, especially Steve, mourned the death of this beloved daughter, wife and mother. But little did they know that Betsy wasn't dead…

Steve was a broken man, but he decided to continue the search for his father. He came across papers in Nick's belongings that made reference to Davis State Penitentiary. Convinced that Nick had gone there to visit Michael, Steve had Frank canvass the prison for some answers. Frank reported that there were no records of Michael at the prison, but he had spoken to a guard who had worked there for six years. Though Raymond claimed the FBI file said he had died ten years ago, the guard remembered Steve's father very well.

Then Brian told Juliette that Steve was looking for his father, Michael Christopher. When Juliette relayed this information to Raymond, he told Juliette not to tell Steve because he would be devastated to find out his father was a convicted spy. Raymond proceeded to bring in Craig, who was now in a halfway house where Raymond had arranged for him to stay on a work-release program. Raymond had in his pocket a psychiatrist named Dr. Johnson, whom he ordered to conduct mind-control experiments on Craig. The plan was for Craig to kidnap Danielle and distract Steve from his search for Michael Christopher. But Maggie grew suspicious of Johnson's claims that he needed to keep Craig incommunicado for extensive psychiatric testing, and she obtained a court order for Craig's release.

Welcomed home by his family, Craig couldn't stop looking at a picture of Danielle, which he later stole. Then he went to Steve's cabin and watched her through the window. Raymond wanted Craig deprogrammed, but Dr. Johnson continued his experiments behind Raymond's back. He planned to activate Craig by adding a special musical piece to Juliette's upcoming recital. Juliette played the piece, and Craig disappeared. By this time, Steve was certain that Juliette and Raymond were somehow involved with Michael Christopher and were trying to sabotage him. When Steve confronted Juliette, she finally admitted that Michael was their father and he had been caught selling government secrets to the Russians.

As Steve wrestled with this revelation, he was unaware that Betsy was alive in a Vermont hospital—suffering from memory loss and being treated by a Dr. Russ Elliot. It soon became obvious that Russ was desperately and obsessively in love with Betsy. To keep her in his clutches, Russ lied and told her that she was wanted by the police. When he asked her to marry him, a lost and lonely Betsy, with little recollection of her past, said yes. Before the ceremony, she had a memory flash of Oakdale and asked Russ to take her there. In Oakdale Russ heard Heather sing "Nobody Loves Me Like You Do" on a television show. When she told the history of the couple whose song it was, Russ had a good idea who the couple was.

Diana saw Russ lunching with a woman at Le Club and thought there was something familiar about her. Tracing Russ's license plate to Vermont, Diana presented him with a proposition: She wouldn't tell Betsy who she was if Russ kept her away from Oakdale and Steve. But Diana was foiled again. Steve discovered that an autopsy had never been performed on Betsy and was convinced she was alive! On the day she was to marry Russ, Betsy read the inscription on her old wedding ring—FOR ALL TIME—and she ran back to Oakdale. Craig saw her first and recognized Betsy by looking into her eyes. Craig filled Betsy in on her missing past and reunited her happily with Danielle.

Always in search of greener pastures, Ariel left town to pursue a European count. But with her gone, John was about to meet a far more formidable woman: Lucinda Walsh, a successful business tycoon with several marriages under her belt. Lucinda remembered John as a young doctor in Chicago. Back then, he'd saved her mother's life, and Lucinda had developed quite a crush on him. John and Lucinda were deep in conversation when Lucinda suddenly fainted. John discovered an aneurysm and had to operate quickly to save her life.

Lucinda blatantly pursued John, and John loved the attention. But she had another motive for staying in Oakdale: the destruction of Whit McColl. A business rival of Whit's, Lucinda began a campaign to buy up enough stock in McColl Enterprises to give her a voting edge. Lucinda was eventually able to seize everything Whit had built. Her motivation was at once simple and tragic. She blamed Whit for driving Martin Guest, her late husband and Whit's business associate, to suicide.

Thanks to Lucinda, John had little time for his marriage to Karen. It didn't help Karen's cause when Lucinda bought further acquiescence by sponsoring John's latest research project. Soon Karen had reason to suspect that John was thinking about a divorce, and the marriage began to disintegrate. They briefly considered a reconciliation for Dusty's sake, but Karen was angry at how he had treated her, and she told John she "wouldn't live with him for all the tea in China." Karen bade Dusty a sad farewell and left Oakdale, leaving John to care for the boy.

Another Oakdale marriage was in trouble, and surprisingly it was Barbara and Gunnar's. Gunnar had led Barbara to believe he was having an affair with another woman, and Barbara was on the verge of divorce as he prepared to go to New York. But before he left, Gunnar told John to give his love to Dusty and to "make sure the boy is well cared for." This piqued John's curiosity, and he discovered Gunnar was suffering from a fatal blood disease. Fortunately, John persuaded him to return to Barbara and tell the truth about his condition. Shortly thereafter, Barbara and Gunnar were overjoyed by the news that Gunnar's disease was in remission. But instead of spending the time with Barbara, Gunnar wanted to realize his life-long dream of flying to Australia in a hot-air balloon. Barbara supported his decision even though she knew she'd probably never see him again, and Gunnar left Oakdale for the land Down Under.

Lucinda's daughter Lily came to town in June, and the first person she met was Dusty Donovan. At first, Dusty saw Lily as a stuck-up rich kid, but he was soon impressed by her expertise with horses, and the two became fast friends. When Dusty took Lily to a local rock 'n' roll club, John and Lucinda were so livid that they forbade the young people to see each other. Dusty was so furious he broke into John's lab and trashed it. When John and Lucinda found him, he was sitting in the debris, sobbing. While he was cleaning up afterward, he knocked over a test tube containing toxic chemicals. His

*Spring break in Daytona would be a turning point in the young lives of Marcy, Kirk, Frannie and Jay.*

vision blurred, and he became disoriented, collapsing in the snow. Found later by Steve, Dusty was very sick, and as the search for the source of his illness continued, his condition worsened. John was finally able to save him with the help of his old adversary, David Stewart.

Another young person arrived in Oakdale that year, but she wasn't nearly as elegant as Lily. Her name was Marcy Thompson, a troubled high school senior. Painfully shy and withdrawn, Marcy was living with her uncaring mother, Peggy Thompson. Frannie befriended her and brought her home to meet Bob. When Bob was sympathetic to her, Marcy misinterpreted his kindness and convinced herself that Bob was in love with her. One day, she dropped in on him at the hospital, and turned an innocent conversation into a sexual invitation, offering herself to him. As she was taking off her blouse, John came down the hall and caught a glimpse of what was going on. With the confused Marcy's help, he got Bob charged with sexual harassment, but at the hearing she admitted Bob had never shown her anything but kindness.

Frannie still wanted to be Marcy's friend, even encouraging Kirk to be nice to her, but once again, she took a man's concern too seriously and found herself falling in love with Kirk. When Peggy Thompson left town, forcing Marcy to come under the jurisdiction of a social worker, Miss Davis, Frannie came up with the idea of having Charmane pose as Marcy's mother.

With his new mansion completed, Whit brought his loyal housekeeper, Dorothy Connors, up from his Florida estate to run his new home. After the death of Whit's alcoholic wife, Dorothy had become much more than a housekeeper. She was a friend, a confidante and a mother figure to his children, especially Kirk, who was the same age as her son, Jay. When Jay arrived in Oakdale, he and Kirk instantly revived the close friendship they'd shared as boys. Whit firmly believed Jay was a bad influence on Kirk, but in reality Jay usually took the rap for Kirk. The boys' friendship was threatened, however, when Jay found himself falling secretly in love with Frannie.

It was spring break in Daytona, a turning point in these young people's lives. Frannie, an excellent gymnast, took advantage of a great opportunity to participate in gymnastics meets around the state, and she arranged for Marcy to travel with the team as an assistant. One night, a date of Frannie's tried to get physical with her. They had gone to the observation deck of a lighthouse, and after Frannie told him she wasn't interested, he angrily locked her on the deck. When Frannie didn't come back that night, Marcy panicked and called Kirk, who headed for Florida with Jay. Frannie was released by a security guard the next morning and started back along the beach. The first person she saw was Jay, who'd been searching for her, and she melted into his arms. Frannie wasn't in the mood for fun the rest of the week, so Kirk spent most of his time with Marcy. Finding themselves alone, Frannie and Jay admitted their feelings for each other and shared their first kiss. But once they were back in Oakdale, they decided to stay apart because of Kirk.

Frannie suggested that Marcy stay in the McColls' mansion for a while until she could find a decent place to live. Lisa had never forgiven the girl for falsely accusing Bob of sexual harassment, though, so she called Miss Davis to come and get the girl. But Marcy ran away. Kirk decided to go to Jay for help, and he burst in on Frannie and Jay just as they were about to kiss. Shocked and hurt, Kirk ran off into the woods, where he was caught in a freak accident that left him blind.

Jeff operated on Kirk and restored his sight, and the first person he saw was Marcy, who told Frannie she liked Kirk, but she was sure nothing would come of it because he was rich and she was poor. So she vowed to find a way to become rich. When the *Argus* ran a Cinderella sweepstakes at Heather's suggestion, Marcy entered and won. Ecstatic, she hoped the win would make an impression on Kirk. At the lavish Cinderella Ball at the Country Club, Jermaine Jackson and Whitney Houston performed Steve and Betsy's special love song, "Nobody Loves Me Like You Do." Shortly after Kirk's recovery, Jeff was offered a post at a hospital out of town and left Oakdale with Annie and the quads to begin life anew.

Lisa McColl wasn't happy about having a housekeeper and her son forced on her. But Whit wanted Dorothy there, and when they were together, it was obvious they were more than just friends. Whit had uncharacteristically admitted defeat when Lucinda succeeded in buying up the McColl stock, and Dorothy was there to pamper her boss. When Diana and Kirk wanted to live at home to help their father through this rough time, Dorothy dissuaded them and then told Whit his children had deserted him. She made it clear that she, Dorothy, had always been there for him.

It was August 2 and Whit McColl wasn't having a very good day. He had had a bitter fight with Steve over Diana's losing the baby, and each blamed the other for the tragedy. Steve went to a bar, where he ran into Craig, and they argued about Danielle. Whit also got drunk that night at the Country Club, and Jay expressed his anger at Whit for abusing his mother's loyalty. Then Jay left to keep a date with Frannie—it would be the first time they made love. When Whit got home, he summoned Craig and pressured him to work for Raymond Speer in order to determine his connection with Steve. Craig refused. Just then, Steve drove up. Craig overheard Steve and Whit arguing fiercely again about Diana. Steve arrived at the cabin, battered and bruised, with no idea where he'd been or how he had torn his shirt. Lucinda Walsh paid Whit a visit that night, too. Her takeover of the McColl empire was almost complete, and she had come to gloat, unknowingly losing an earring in the process. Later that night, Lisa returned from a buying trip to Chicago and found her husband dead on the library floor.

When the McColls gathered for the reading of the will, Maggie announced that Dorothy would receive $500,000, but instead of being happy, Dorothy seemed hurt. There were certain stipulations for the others. Brian wouldn't get his money until he took over Whit's business; Diana, raised like a princess but acting like a tramp, wouldn't get hers until she married and gave birth to a legitimate offspring; and Kirk, the playboy, would have to lead a stable life before collecting his.

Whit's untimely death brought up many painful memories for Lily. It was Lily who had found her father's body after he committed suicide, and she told her mother she felt it was somehow her fault. Lucinda was able to convince her daughter that she'd had nothing to do with it. She was certain Whit McColl was the cause of her family's trauma, and she vowed to make the McColl children suffer as Lily had.

At this time, Raymond was preoccupied with a trip to Amsterdam. The excursion was ostensibly for Juliette's recital, but it was in fact a mysterious mission connected to Michael Christopher. When Juliette overheard Raymond telling someone that Christopher was alive and coming to Amsterdam, she quickly called Steve. Although he was about to be booked for Whit's murder, Steve couldn't lose this chance to reunite with his father, and he flew to Amsterdam—only to have Raymond's men intercept him at the airport and drag him away. In a panic, Juliette enlisted the help of Kim, who was Raymond's guest at a concert. Kim called Bob, who flew to Amsterdam. When he arrived, Raymond's men escorted him to a wine cellar where Steve was being held prisoner. Bob and Steve smashed the guard over the head with a wine bottle. Then Bob went to look for Kim while Steve went after Raymond.

When Bob found Kim, they were stopped by Raymond, who ushered them into a limo and promised to explain everything soon. Then the driver turned around. It was Steve. They headed for the airport. On the docks, a KGB officer pried open a crate marked for delivery to Raymond—and pointed his gun at the man inside. The man was Michael Christopher. Father and son soon found each other at the airport, while on the docks Raymond disappeared with the Russian agents. He had traded himself for his friend's freedom and was

now in the hands of the Russians.

When Steve returned to Oakdale, he discovered that his beloved Betsy had since returned home, and the separated lovers were reunited. They had but a few blissful days together before Steve turned himself in to stand trial for the murder of Whit McColl.

During the trial, Steve testified that he saw Jay's car return to the McColl mansion on the night of the murder. Jay admitted that he was there and angrily related how Whit had constantly insulted his mother. A distraught Kirk yelled out, accusing Jay of murdering his father. Suddenly, Dorothy stood up and confessed to the murder of Whit McColl! She admitted she had had an affair with Whit 19 years ago, and the affair had produced a son—Kirk! When Whit's late wife Joanna lost her baby, Whit let her think Kirk was her own. On the fateful night of August 2, Dorothy struck Whit with a paperweight after he fired her for telling Jay she was in love with Whit. As Dorothy collapsed after telling her story, Kirk ran frantically from the courtroom. Jay promised to stand by his mother.

Lisa persuaded Kirk to see his mother, and despite the awkwardness, he couldn't help but be touched by Dorothy's outpouring of love. As for Lucinda, she had a field day with the City Times headline, which read, "Bastard Son Of Whit McColl Exposed At Trial."

After the trial, feeling confused and alienated from his family, Kirk turned to Marcy. In the meantime, Frannie wanted to give up her freshman year at Yale to be with Jay, but Jay wouldn't allow it. By the time Christmas break rolled around, their affair had cooled, and Frannie told him it was over. Soon after, Jay took a job with Andropoulos Construction.

Maggie had represented Steve in Whit's murder case, and her hands were full. She was preoccupied with Frank and Diana's impending annulment, as well as with her new little girl, Jill. Then Craig persuaded her to represent his scruffy former cellmate, Cal Randolph, who had been temporarily released from jail on a robbery charge. Cal claimed he had been set up, and Maggie believed him. Maggie picked him up from prison and brought him to her apartment, only for Cal to recognize Jill as his little girl. Cal's former wife had run off with another man and abandoned the baby. Then Cal's conviction was reinstated, and he was ordered to return to jail. Cal wanted to go to St. Louis and find the man who could give him an alibi—a card shark named Missouri Spats. Cal had been playing poker with Spats when the robbery occurred. Maggie refused, so Cal pulled a gun and forced her to go, taking Jill. Cal owed Spats lots of money, and when Maggie made good on his debt by beating Spats at one hand of poker, Spats agreed to testify.

Driving back to Oakdale, Cal and Maggie grew closer, and Maggie said she wouldn't press kidnapping charges. Although Maggie told Frank the gun Cal used on her wasn't loaded, Frank vowed Cal would get what was coming to him. He did some detective work and found out about Jill, as did Diana. Greedily eyeing her inheritance from Whit, which stipulated that she have a family, Diana made a play for Cal, who told Maggie the only way she could keep Jill was if she married him. Maggie said she couldn't do that because she was in love with Frank. To force him to sign over custody, Frank lured Cal out to a nearby island. When he refused to sign, Frank tried to abandon him. This treatment only angered Cal more, and he went to the welfare board, demanding that custody of Jill be given back to him.

Unaware of all of this, Maggie was planning a party to announce her wedding to Frank on Christmas Eve. Frank suspected Cal was up to something, and he headed to Cal's armed with custody papers. After Frank left, Cal went to Miss Davis, Jill's social worker, who told him Cal's custody papers took precedence over Frank and Maggie's, and he could claim Jill anytime he wanted. Frank and Maggie's party was in full swing when Cal arrived and announced he was there to get Jill. He accused a confused Maggie of being in on his "abduction" and left with his daughter. When Frank admitted taking Cal to the island, Maggie blamed him for the loss of her child and asked him to leave. But it didn't take her long to forgive him.

Cal resumed his plans to marry Diana and give her the "instant family" she needed. But as they stood before a Justice of the Peace, he suddenly bolted. At a nearby church, Maggie and Frank were married. Cal then walked down the aisle and handed baby Jill to Maggie. He had decided that Jill would be better off with her after all.

Diana was infuriated by Cal's desertion, but she quickly recovered when Lisa offered to invest money in Le Club. Her happiness was short-lived, though, when Brian was forced to liquidate the company that owned the yacht. Although her family offered to help, for the first time in her life Diana was determined to stand on her own two feet.

# 1985

Brian resolved to buy back the yacht when it was offered at auction. Lucinda also wanted it and sent Craig to do the job. The bidding was fierce, but at $1,700,000, Diana got the boat. She offered the renovation job to Steve and cut Cal into the deal as her manager. She soon regretted hiring Cal when two federal agents caught him trying to buy liquor without paying taxes. To avoid jail, Cal worked undercover on a gambling sting and made Diana's new nightclub a government front. She was livid.

Crime was rising in Oakdale, and Margo and Frank were partnered by their crusty boss, Lt. Dan "Mac" McClosky. When Maggie tried having Frank designated as one of Jill's legal guardians, Cal refused this request. Then Maggie received a top-secret assignment from the D.A. having to do with a gambling sting at Diana's club. Maggie had to make sure the surveillance tapes were admissible. But her contact was Cal, and they would have to meet nightly while Frank was at work.

On opening night, Mitch, posing as the headwaiter, told Diana that Jake Haskell, a representative from the gambling syndicate, would soon arrive. Haskell moved his gambling equipment into the club, and Diana wore a recording device. Haskell took the bait. The gaming tables were a hit, and Haskell persuaded Diana and Cal to continue the gambling. Just then, a young Briton, Lord Stewart Markham Cushing, broke the bank. Cushing announced that all his winnings should go to Memorial Hospital.

But the night's excitement was just beginning. While staking out Diana's, Margo and Frank saw a searchlight across the water, which Frank went to investigate. He warned Margo that the bootleggers were monitoring the police radio. Det. Moran joined Frank while his partner, Churchill, called McClosky. The bootleggers heard Churchill, and they caught Margo in their spotlight. Moran was killed, and Frank was seriously injured. Margo ended up deaf.

Maggie blamed Margo, but Frank defended her. Nevertheless, Margo felt guilty. Tom pushed her to come out of her depression, and John warned him to go easy on his daughter. Margo eventually regained her hearing. At the inquest, many of her fellow officers still held her responsible for Moran's death. Stung, Margo requested a leave of absence.

Meanwhile, the gambling sting climaxed when Cal taped Haskell telling him to set Cushing up for a loss at blackjack. Concerned for his sister, Kirk confronted Diana, who told him everything. Despite her warnings, Kirk decided to write an exposé for the *Argus* and joined Haskell at the blackjack table as part of his research. But Kirk developed an addiction that would lead to monumental debt. At one point, his desperation forced him to steal $15,000 from Brian's safe at the *Argus*.

As part of the sting and to fool Haskell, Maggie and Cal pretended to be an item. One day, with Frank out of earshot, Cal told Maggie that Haskell knew she worked for the D.A., but he insisted they must continue to pretend to be lovers. Frank overheard Cal tell Maggie that she had to lie, and he pressed his wife and accused her of having an affair, which Maggie vehemently denied. When Frank went to the yacht, Haskell tried to sweet-talk Frank into working for him. Frank agreed. It was the perfect way to keep an eye on Maggie and Cal and help fight crime undercover.

Diana was guilt-ridden when Kirk's debt reached $40,000 and Haskell's goons roughed him up. She'd finally had enough, and she disappeared into the safety of the Witness Protection Program. Cal wanted to stop her, but the operation was over, and the Police Department was ready to make arrests. But Haskell had his equipment moved out, so the attempted bust went bust, and McClosky resolved to try again.

Amid this chaos, Kim and Bob were falling in love. Bob realized there would never be a better woman for him than Kim. They were already best friends. Kim was considerably more hesitant, and she decided to spend some time at her cabin. When a severe winter storm was predicted, a worried Bob followed. Kim had had an accident, and Bob found her semiconscious and hurt. As Bob tended her wound, they talked about their feelings. With much difficulty, Kim confessed that she had planned their rendezvous in Florida and that she had never stopped loving him. Bob loved her and wanted to spend the rest of his life with her. They made plans to marry at Eastertime. The occasion became a family reunion. Nancy and Chris came in from Arizona, Penny arrived from Europe, and Donald flew in from Laramie. Something else made this wedding quite unusual: It was on the night of the police action at Diana's. True to form, Lisa took center stage on the day her ex-husband married her best friend. Haskell caught her snooping in his cabin and took her hostage. He then escaped and took her aboard his plane while the police arrested Bob and Kim at Diana's. Luckily, Tom and Margo saved Lisa in the nick of time. In the end, Haskell was booked, Margo

At Easter, longtime friends and onetime lovers Bob and Kim were finally married. For their nuptials, they decided on a sunrise ceremony at the Oakdale Botanical Gardens and a sunset reception on Diana's yacht. The ceremony went off without a hitch, but the reception came to an abrupt end when a gambling sting went down and the unsuspecting bride and groom began their married life in jail!

returned to the force, and Maggie and Frank made up.

Maggie was stunned to learn that Lyla and John were getting close again. The one obstacle was an attractive but very young lady named Shannon O'Hara. She saw John sitting alone at a table in Diana's and promptly joined him, making a point that she had no money. John paid for her dinner and left, but she found his address and showed up at his door. He let her stay the night, and she promised to leave the next day. Instead, Dusty helped persuade John to let her stay. Lyla was baffled by John's new "maid" and wondered why Shannon was staying at John's despite his complaints that he couldn't wait for her to leave. Lyla wanted John out of her life permanently. John got so drunk that Shannon had to put him to bed. Then she crawled in next to him. The next day, Shannon placed a call to her "brother," identified herself as Erin Casey and said that everything was going fine. In a later phone call, she claimed that a man was following her.

Shortly after Shannon's arrival, Kim found a body in her backyard. The police computer was able to turn up a match. Someone fitting the dead woman's description was reported missing at O'Hare Airport six weeks earlier. Margo told Tom that, according to Forensics, an E. Casey might be the murderer. Meanwhile, over at Fashions Ltd., Lisa was interviewing Shannon and learned that she had arrived in Oakdale six weeks before. Shannon was alarmed to see E. Casey plastered on the front pages of the newspapers. Since her name was found among the deceased's belongings, Shannon feared for her life. Nervously, she took a handful of diamonds from a pouch. The police identified the body as Evelyn Stone, and evidence showed she worked for a mobster. Evelyn had died from a deadly poison that the lab identified as indigenous to the small country of Montega. Further investigation revealed that E. Casey arrived in the United States several weeks before the murder. When Shannon saw a headline linking Evelyn to a jewel-fencing case, she tried desperately to contact a man named Guy Howard. Meanwhile, Frank discovered that the stolen gems were priceless diamonds known as "Tears of the Crocodile" and that Guy Howard, a well-known fence, was believed to be involved. Shannon called Tom for help. Tom told her she should go to the police immediately. Frank deduced that Erin Casey was supposed to give the diamonds to Evelyn Stone, so Erin was either the murderer or the next victim. After successfully contacting Guy, Shannon was warned to hand over the jewels or else. Terrified, she went to Tom, and when he asked if she were Erin Casey, she didn't answer.

One day, two "policemen" grilled Kim about the dead body and the whereabouts of the diamonds. They turned out to be thugs and demanded the jewels. Margo soon arrived, and she and Kim jumped the thugs. As Margo arrested them, they admitted to working for Guy Howard. Guy confessed to Evelyn's murder, but Shannon admitted nothing. She instead offered the diamonds to an unidentified man overseas and was told that someone would contact her.

After Whit's death, his son Brian began dating Barbara. But Barbara was ambivalent because she continued to hope that Gunnar was still alive. With Brian's help, Barbara began a search for her missing husband. Brian's Australian contact, Matt Wilson, discovered a life jacket and a roll of film where the hot-air balloon

was last seen. The photos showed that Gunnar was very much alive. Barbara made arrangements to go to Australia. Brian followed and unknowingly booked the hotel room next to hers. Barbara was grateful for his presence once she learned Gunnar had been killed when his balloon crashed in the outback. One night, they found themselves in an embrace and made love.

Barbara and Brian had to deal with Paul's disapproval of Brian. No one could replace his father, rotten though he was. In an effort to get to know Paul better, Brian took him to a baseball game. But when Brian went to get hot dogs, Paul ran away. Brian found the boy calmly waiting for him at Barbara's. They had a fight, and Paul punched Brian several times. As Barbara entered, Brian instinctively raised his hand as if to hit Paul back. Paul made it seem as though it was Brian's fault. Barbara was furious. But Paul eventually told the truth, and Brian and Barbara made plans to marry. Unfortunately, Barbara put off committing herself to Brian. Incensed that Barbara was letting her son call the shots, Brian told her that they should move on with their lives.

Brian began frequenting a singles bar in town, and he soon connected with Shannon, who fled, afraid that he would blow her cover. Intrigued, Brian put her picture in the *Argus* with the headline "Do You Know This Woman?" Shannon came to his office, and Brian offered to pull the picture if she would join him for a drink. She agreed, and over drinks, Shannon spoke of her fabulous life, but Brian sensed her loneliness. John kicked Shannon out, and, when Brian got wind of that action, he offered to set her up in an apartment. No strings, Shannon warned, right before they kissed. Brian had a hard time staying away from Shannon, and she had a hard time putting him off. Meanwhile, in Nice a man received a sketch of Shannon taken from the picture Brian had published in the *Argus*. Smiling, he said, "For such a little bird, Shannon managed to get pretty far away." Lisa pushed Barbara not to give up on Brian and persuaded her to drop by his apartment. Barbara was shocked when Shannon opened the door wearing Brian's robe. She left before he could explain. Shannon urged him to go after her, but Brian had put his past behind him and told Shannon that he loved her. Barbara hid her feelings from a suspicious Lisa, and she vowed she was no longer going to be victimized by men.

Shannon was planning a Halloween party at the creepy Corbman estate, where Verna Corbman had hanged herself. Shannon thought it would be the ideal place. When she went to check out the house, a bag lady identified herself as Harriet Corbman, Verna's granddaughter. It turned out this woman had a sizable nest egg, and she and Shannon became fast friends. They decided to turn the Corbman house into a homeless shelter. On Thanksgiving, Shannon held a dinner for the homeless. One of the "guests," Smitty, seemed to be following Shannon around, and Harriet asked Brian to keep an eye on him. Another "guest," Fingers, lifted Smitty's wallet and found out Smitty was a phony. Smitty turned out to be a private detective hired by Barbara to investigate Shannon. Smitty found a letter to Shannon from a man named André in Nice. When Brian pressed her, Shannon admitted she was hiding from her ex-lover, André Montrand, the leader of an international underworld society. She also said her real name was Erin Cavanaugh, but she later told Harriet she didn't tell Brian everything: Smitty was Barbara's private detective. Shannon had earlier approached Smitty about finding a man by the name of Earl Mitchell, who she knew was looking for her. She and Barbara ran into each other and had it out. Shannon soon received a mysterious phone call from a man who said their paths would cross again. She tried to maintain a facade for Brian, but privately worried that Det. Daniels, a.k.a. Smitty, would check into her past. She asked Barbara to call him off. "Never," replied Barbara. When Shannon accused Barbara of jealousy, Barbara slapped her. The new, independent Barbara threw a Christmas party to celebrate changing her name from Stenbeck to Ryan. Brian was there, and under the mistletoe Ms. Ryan turned a friendly kiss into a passionate one.

After Diana left, Kirk stopped gambling and became an ace reporter for the *Argus*. When Kirk and Marcy went to the Stratford Arms to pick up some things Diana had left behind, they found an old woman named Daisy Simmons shivering in her bed. They took her to Memorial and were shocked to learn Daisy was being victimized by the owners of the seedy hotel. Kirk decided to do a piece on the hotel and its occupants. He discovered that the owner was none other than his family's nemesis, Lucinda Walsh, and he played it to the hilt in his article.

In the wake of the raid, all of Oakdale was intrigued by Lord Cushing. A world-renowned tennis player, he was the son of a British stage actress and an aristocrat. He had supposedly arrived in Oakdale to build a sports complex, but Lisa discovered the truth when she dropped by his room to invite him to a dinner party. She noticed a letter with a return address from the Wade Book Shop and went on to read part of it. It was signed, "Love, Paul." She excitedly rushed off to see David, and he confirmed that Paul Stewart had lived for a while above the Wade Book Shop. Lisa told Stewart she had read the letter, and he said he suspected that Paul Stewart was his father. Lisa introduced the young man to Betsy. When Betsy showed him the family photo album, he was stunned to see one of the pictures torn in half. He produced the other half, which he always carried with him. It was a picture of his mother. Betsy identified the man in the photo as her uncle Paul, and Stewart had all the proof he needed. David and Ellen welcomed him into the family as their grandson. Stewart was charmed by the sweet, plain-spoken Marcy Thompson.

Kirk was too busy to notice Marcy's preoccupation with Stewart. A hard-working cub reporter, he also planned with Jay to open a new restaurant, the Grand Prix, on the site of the old casino. When a gang set fire to the restaurant site, Stewart saved the boys from the flames, and Marcy hailed him as a hero. But she couldn't help noticing his distress until she found his journal and discovered that he blamed himself for his mother's death in a fire. Stewart saw her reading the journal and was troubled because he didn't know what she had read. She, in turn, was troubled because of what she had read and worried that she may have lost him as a friend. Stewart had been warned by his valet, Alfie, not to write down his secrets. He locked the journal in a drawer.

Stewart's trust fund was tied up pending a Scotland Yard investigation into his mother's death, which meant it might have been a murder. Stewart was a likely suspect. He retained Tom to represent him, although he had some misgivings after learning that Stewart had fought with his mother on the night of her death. Heeding Tom's advice, Stewart decided to go to London and see the case through. Determined to help, Marcy followed him to London. She was shocked to discover that Lady Cushing wasn't the loving mother Stewart made her out to be. Then Tom learned that Lady Cushing had been killed not by the fire, but with a poker. When a stableman placed Stewart's car at the scene of the crime, Stewart was arrested for murder. The situation looked grim until Tom was able to prove that the real culprit was Alfie, who had been Lady Cushing's lover. Soon after this ordeal, Stewart asked Marcy to marry him, and she accepted. They agreed they would go to England to live. And so, among the ruins of an old castle on an island off the shores of Oakdale, Marcy and Stewart were wed in a fairy-tale ceremony befitting a prince and his fair lady. Kirk left Oakdale to pursue his journalistic career in New York.

When Bob and Kim returned from their honeymoon, Chris and Nancy decided to move back to Oakdale. Chris wasn't well, and Bob wanted him nearby so he could keep an eye on his condition. Andy later confided to his mother that he was having trouble adjusting to living with his stepgrandparents. Not wanting to be a burden, Chris insisted that he and Nancy move out, but Bob and Kim persuaded them to stay. Bob solved the problem by converting the garage into an apartment for Nancy and Chris.

To add to the mix, a troubled Frannie was home from Yale—she had been expelled for poor grades. Her former boyfriend, Kevin Gibson, followed her to Oakdale begging for another chance. But Frannie refused because he had impregnated another girlfriend, Marie Kovac. She also blamed Kevin for causing her so much stress that her grades fell. Bob and Kim were supportive of Frannie, as was Jay, who hoped that he and Frannie could still have a relationship. Then Kevin revealed that Marie had lost the baby and they were no longer together. Frannie said they had to take it slow, but she introduced him to her family, who were all charmed except for Bob. Kevin moved to Oakdale, landing a spot with Lucinda's training program for junior executives. He told Frannie that Marie's baby wasn't his. But when Frannie later told Kevin she had written a letter to Marie, he inexplicably blew up. Caught off guard by his strong reaction, Frannie began to suspect that Kevin might not have told her the entire truth.

Meanwhile, Kim started receiving flowers and phone calls from a secret admirer. She was intrigued, and Lisa happily observed that Bob seemed jealous. Lisa still carried a torch for Bob and could barely conceal her delight when Kim's secret admirer became a sore point between them. Kim soon received long-stemmed apricot roses, her favorite. The florist said an attractive woman signed for them. Kim thought the woman might have a clue to her admirer's identity. Then she received a locket, which contained an old publicity shot of her from her days as a singer. Kim thought her secret admirer must be

a former fan. But when Margo checked out the fingerprints, they belonged to Bob, Kim and Lisa. Lisa wondered if John might be behind it, since he had a history of causing trouble. Then Kim's former piano player, Ken Wayne, came to Oakdale to play at a new restaurant called Caroline's. Suspecting Ken, Kim agreed to meet him for lunch. Ken said he'd been "longing to see her"— the very same words that appeared on one of the letters. Then a gift arrived for "Kimberly Sullivan," a paperweight with a spray of pink feathers. Lisa noticed they were from a stole Kim had worn when she was a singer. Margo investigated Ken and discovered he had been harassing other women with flowers and presents. Kim and Bob decided to get away to the cabin. While they were away, Lisa accepted another gift for Kim, and Ellen mused that the gifts always seemed to arrive when Lisa was around. Ellen told Nancy, reminding her that Lisa was capable of doing anything to get what she wanted, and she wanted Bob. Nancy remained loyal and insisted Lisa was not behind the plot.

Bob and Kim shared a blissful weekend while Tom took the latest package to the police. This one had a note that read: "Kimberly, you have carried the key to my heart and always will." Later, Kim received a letter from Ken warning her that some of his personal mementos had been stolen. Bob and Kim realized Ken was not the culprit. They agreed to have the phone in the cabin tapped. They arrived to find a package waiting for them. It was a photo of Bob and Kim on their honeymoon. Meanwhile, Lisa admitted to Barbara that she was still in love with Bob.

Frannie's relationship with Kevin deteriorated when Marie suddenly arrived in Oakdale. She told Frannie that Kevin had lied: Her miscarriage was really an abortion that Kevin paid for. Marie showed Frannie a letter from Kevin that accompanied the check to cover the abortion. She swore that was the last time she'd heard from him, and Frannie believed her. Kevin was upset and vowed to get Marie's diary, which would prove everything, even if he had to strangle her to get it. When Kevin confronted Marie, she told him he belonged to her, not Frannie. After Kevin left, Marie started a new diary. In it she scribbled about how she and Kevin had passionate, violent sex that night. Then she gave herself bruises to make her story more believable. When Frannie saw the bruises, Marie told her Kevin had raped her, and she warned Frannie to be careful. Frannie didn't know what to think. Kevin was quick to deny everything and stormed out to find Marie, while Jay comforted Frannie. Frannie finally told Kevin it was over. Marie, intent on getting him for herself, decided to stay in Oakdale. Kevin thought she had returned to New Haven, and he went to get her diary. At her apartment he was arrested for breaking and entering. Tom managed to bail him out, and Frannie and Kevin reached a shaky understanding. Meanwhile, Marie took a job at Caroline's. Unaware that Marie worked there, Frannie decided to check out the new hot spot before it opened, and she and the handsome owner, Douglas Cummings, ended up checking out each other. It was obvious to both Marie and Doug's right-hand person Marsha Talbot that their boss was very interested in Frannie. Marie warned Doug that Frannie was nothing but trouble and fed Frannie more lies about Kevin. Determined to win Frannie back, Kevin got a job at Caroline's and soon realized Doug was going to be his competition.

As Doug prepared for Caroline's opening night, Marsha told Frannie and Lisa about his tragic past. Pointing to a portrait of a beautiful woman, she identified her as Doug's beloved, Caroline, who was killed in a freak riding accident. Frannie was delighted when Doug

Lucinda wanted Craig Montgomery in the boardroom and the bedroom. Although he and Lucinda did share one night of passion, Craig fell in love with Lucinda's daughter Sierra, and much to the "boss lady's" chagrin, he became her son-in-law instead.

asked her to attend opening night. Tony Bennett was scheduled to make a guest appearance. The party was a smashing success, and as Doug celebrated with Frannie, Jay and Kevin jealously looked on. When Doug was called away to attend to restaurant business, Marsha took a moment to turn to Caroline's portrait, murmuring under her breath that she was watching after Doug, just as she promised she would. Kevin got Marie's address. Marie was in the middle of seducing Ken Wayne when she was interrupted by a violent knocking on the door. Recognizing Kevin's voice, Marie refused to answer and quickly called the police, who arrested Kevin on the spot. A "shaken" Marie wanted to press charges. Frannie, Lisa, Tom and Margo converged on

the police station. Marie begged Lisa to warn Frannie that Kevin was dangerous. As for Kevin, his problems were just beginning—it seemed that Marie was pregnant again. Marie told Frannie that Kevin had tried to rape her again. A furious Kevin told Jay he was going to bribe Marie to tell the truth. Jay reminded him that Tom had warned him to stay away from her. Jay offered to talk to Marie for him, making it clear, though, that he was doing it for Frannie. Marsha overheard Marie talking to her doctor about her impending pregnancy. Unaware that Marsha was on to her schemes, Marie played yet another one by seducing Cal. Following her tryst with Cal, Marie was intrigued when Jay dropped by with a check for $1,000 and a confession for her to sign saying that everything she said about Kevin was a blatant lie. Loving her power over Kevin, Marie said she'd think about it, and she kept the check. Marie joined the list of Marsha's enemies when Marsha overheard Marie tell Doug she'd noticed how possessive Marsha was of him.

On the night of Shannon's Halloween party, Kevin demanded that Marie either sign the letter or return his check. Marie refused. Within earshot of all the guests, Kevin shouted that she had better do it or he'd kill her. Later in the evening Kevin called Frannie, and she told Doug that his voice sounded strange. When Doug went

When Lucinda forced her daughter Lily to attend a gala costume ball with preppie Harrison Blake, a jealous Dusty got his friends Jay and Kirk to dress up as the Three Musketeers and crash the party. It was not a good idea. When Harrison and Dusty met at the punch bowl, fists flew, and Lucinda threw the lovesick Dusty out.

to deliver Marie's paycheck, there was no answer, and the landlady thought she'd skipped town. But over at the Corbman place, Kevin found a body—it was Marie.

Frannie turned to Doug for comfort, and much to Marsha's chagrin, they began spending more and more time together. Hopelessly in love with Doug herself, Marsha tried to reunite Frannie and Kevin, but Frannie sadly told Kevin it was too late. Hearing this, Marsha took Frannie aside and told her Doug would never love anyone but Caroline.

Marie Kovac's murder left behind a string of suspects, most notably Kevin, Cal and Ken. Cal suffered briefly from blackouts but later remembered seeing Jay at Marie's door.

Convinced that Jay stole Marie's diary, Kevin maintained his innocence to Frannie. Later he received a call from "Cal" to meet him at the yacht basin; he had Marie's diary. Kevin went, only to find Cal floating face down in the water. Seconds later, the police arrived, and Kevin was arrested on suspicion of murder.

Asked to cooperate with the police, Kevin told them that a wealthy man named Tad Channing was the father of the baby Marie lost. Margo was assigned to the investigation and interviewed Iva Snyder, another woman from Tad's past. Iva explained that she knew Marie had threatened to tell Tad's wife about their affair. With great difficulty, Iva told the police that she and Channing were having an affair as well. Thus when Tad arrived in Oakdale, he had an airtight alibi. But another layer was piled onto this mystery when Frannie and Doug found Marsha dead, a black ribbon tied around her neck. At the same time, Betsy was also frightened to discover Steve was receiving a series of death threats.

In his new position as up-and-coming junior executive at Walsh Enterprises, Steve's nemesis, Craig Montgomery, was given an unusual assignment. His boss, Lucinda, was distraught to hear that Jacobo Esteban, a dear friend, had been kidnapped by guerrillas in Montega. Lucinda was inordinately concerned that Jacobo's daughter, Sierra, was also in danger and asked Craig to fly to Montega to find the missing girl. In the war-ravaged country, Craig found a boy burying Jacobo in a secret ceremony. The boy called himself Carlos. As bullets flew overhead, "Carlos" took off his hat and revealed that he was a she—Sierra Esteban. When they reached the safety of Craig's hotel, they talked about their families, and he discovered Sierra was a nurse, as Craig's mother had been. It was obvious that there was a spark between the two. The next day, Craig and Sierra were offered exit papers from a government contact who was none other than Steve's father, Michael Christopher. They spent the night hiding in a peasant shack and the following day went to see Jacobo Esteban's loyal servant, Artemio. He gave Sierra an emerald earring that had belonged to her mother. They decided it would be safer to take separate routes to the city. While Craig, who was holding Sierra's emerald, waited for Sierra, two Montegan militiamen forced him to go to the airport. When Sierra arrived, Michael told her Craig was in danger and had to leave immediately. Then he gave Sierra her passport and told her to contact Steve and Betsy in the United States but not to contact Craig, for everyone's safety. Craig still had the emerald, and he swore he would see Sierra again.

Sierra arrived in Oakdale and was welcomed warmly by Betsy and Steve. The two young women quickly bonded, but it was clear that they knew two completely different sides to Craig. Betsy described Craig as the man who kept Steve from her because he was jealous and sick, and Sierra described the Craig who helped her in Montega as wonderful, kind and gentle. Meanwhile, a shadowy figure lurked outside Betsy and Steve's cabin dressed as a policeman. One night, the shadow telephoned Steve and ordered him to meet him that evening. Instead, Steve headed for the police station but was assaulted by a man who chloroformed him and dragged him into the bushes. After hours of waiting for word of Steve, Betsy learned that he'd been found and rushed to the hospital. Posing as "Nan Stephans," Sierra joined Betsy at the hospital and narrowly missed running into Craig, who had returned from Montega. Just as Craig looked to be the culprit, Betsy was shocked to discover Russ Elliot injecting a mysterious substance into Steve's IV. Completely deranged, Russ showed up later at Betsy and Steve's cabin, where he chloroformed Betsy and laid her out in the dress she was to have worn at their wedding. When Betsy woke up, Russ was about to strangle her, but Craig broke down the door, and Russ fled into the night. To make up for all the pain he had caused Betsy and Steve, Craig offered to help trap

Russ at the hospital. Craig's plan succeeded. With Betsy and Steve reunited, a dejected Craig turned to Lucinda for comfort, and they shared a night of passion. Sadly, though, Steve's buddy Tucker left town when Heather's father, Lionel, proved a detriment to their romance.

His night with Lucinda notwithstanding, Craig couldn't get Sierra off his mind. Sierra shortly received word from Montega that she was finally safe. As a thank-you for his help in saving Steve from Russ, Betsy arranged a joyful reunion between Craig and Sierra. Sierra wanted to meet Lucinda and thank her, and when Lucinda was uncharacteristically soft with the girl, Craig began to suspect that Sierra meant more to Lucinda than she let on. That night, Lucinda privately took an exquisite jewel from its secret hiding place. It matched the emerald Artemio had given Sierra in Montega—the only thing she had left of her mother. Meanwhile, Sierra accepted Lucinda's invitation to stay at the mansion. As she watched Sierra sleep, Lucinda remembered the time when her baby was taken away.

Hoping to learn more about her past, Sierra went back to Montega with Craig. They went first to her father's house, where they found a faded picture of Sierra's mother. As they were studying it intently, Michael Christopher arrived and told them Sierra's mother wasn't buried in Montega as they had thought. When Craig and Sierra returned to Oakdale, they questioned Lucinda, who told them that Sierra's mother, Mary Ellen Walters, had died in Peoria, Illinois. Thinking that Lucinda was hiding something, Craig accompanied Sierra to Peoria. But Lucinda had gotten there first, and Craig and Sierra reached a dead end.

Convinced that she would never have a mother to call her own, Sierra couldn't wait to be a mother herself. Knowing he was sterile, Craig was tortured by the thought that this fact could come between them. He begged David Stewart to treat him, but David said it was unlikely that the condition could be reversed. When it became clear that Sierra didn't know about Craig's sterility, Steve warned Craig that he couldn't make plans for the future without telling her the truth, and although Craig agreed, he couldn't bring himself to do so. Sensing that something was going on and determined to break up the couple, Lucinda managed to gain possession of Craig's medical file. She informed Sierra about Craig's sterility. Unaware that she already knew, Craig finally told her the truth himself and released her from any commitment, but Sierra told him she loved him, and they could always adopt. Lucinda was distraught to learn Sierra and Craig were now closer than ever, and Sierra made plans to move out of the mansion. Lucinda and Craig had it out, and Craig discovered she had revealed his sterility to Sierra first. Desperate, Lucinda blurted out that she loved him and didn't want to lose him. Craig gently told her he wanted to start over—with Sierra. Craig cautioned Sierra not to trust Lucinda, but Sierra refused to think ill of a woman who had already lost one child. Then Craig was shocked to learn that Mary Ellen Walters had not died. When he confronted Lucinda, his suspicions were confirmed. Mary Ellen Walters was, in fact, Lucinda.

Enter John Dixon. He was thrilled when he overhead Craig telling Lyla about Lucinda. When Lyla told Craig that John knew, Craig feared that John would use the information in a way that could hurt Sierra. Meanwhile, Lucinda broke down and told her lawyer/confidant, Ambrose Bingham, that she was Sierra's mother. When she learned that Craig and Sierra were engaged, Lucinda was shattered. Afraid that she would lose Sierra's trust if she knew she was her mother, she plotted to ensure Craig's silence.

Meanwhile, John couldn't wait to get his sweet revenge. Because of his work on the cure for Wilhelm's disease, John wanted a spot on the board. So did Lucinda. They vied bitterly, and even though John found the cure, Lucinda had the big bucks and she won. This was his chance to get back at her. Unaware that John knew her secret, Lucinda arranged Sierra's promotion to John's lab assistant. As for Craig, he'd been pushed to the limit, and Lucinda was shocked when he announced he'd had enough of her interference and was resigning from his position at Walsh Enterprises. Craig warned her that John knew about her secret as well. While Craig and Sierra planned a romantic weekend at Foxwood Lodge, Lucinda told Ambrose that she had to find a way to prevent their marriage. Lily overheard and lashed out at her mother for trying to run Sierra's life. To protect Lily, Lucinda was now more determined than ever to prevent John or Craig from telling Sierra the truth. Just as Craig and Sierra were about to make love up at Foxwood, the phone rang. It was Lyla. Tonio Reyes, Sierra's ex-fiancé, had been found alive in a Miami hospital.

Around this time, an incident occurred in Oakdale that affected many lives. Lucinda continued to meddle in the affairs of her loved ones, and Dusty was angry that Lucinda had forced Lily to be escorted by preppie Harrison Blake Jr. to one of Lisa's gala costume balls.

Dusty and his buddies Jay and Kirk decided to crash the ball as the Three Musketeers. Lily's "suitable" date turned out to be a fast mover. When Dusty and Harrison met at the punch bowl, Harrison bragged that Lily was an easy score. Dusty started a fight, and when a confused Lily denied that Harrison was upsetting her, an outraged Lucinda threw Dusty out. Dusty jumped on his bike and, while speeding down an empty road, was hit by a car. The driver was Craig. After covering him with a blanket, Craig drove to a phone and called 911, but the connection was bad, and he was unable to report the accident. Things went from bad to worse when Craig's car wouldn't start and he had to get back to Dusty. He ran the four miles only to find that Steve and Frank had already arrived on the scene and were furious about the hit-and-run. Racked with guilt, Craig's fear got the better of him, and he didn't step forward. Dusty was rushed to Memorial, where he soon regained consciousness, but he was unable to identify the driver who had hit him. Desperate to keep his involvement a secret, Craig visited an ex-con named Tyrone and paid him to fix the dent in his car. Craig's jumpy behavior convinced Lucinda that something was up. To test him, she asked him to write an article about the hit-and-run for the *City Times*. Meanwhile, Tyrone demanded $10,000 to keep quiet. Craig wanted to tell Sierra what had happened but couldn't follow through.

As the police investigated the hit-and-run, Craig had a talk with Dusty and decided to tell everyone the truth. Trying to protect him, Dusty urged Craig not to ruin his life for nothing. But Lucinda broke into Craig's apartment and found Dusty's scarf. When John and Lyla found her there, Lucinda gleefully told them of her discovery. Just as Craig and Sierra were finally about to make love for the first time, John burst in, demanding an explanation for Dusty's accident, and Craig admitted the truth. Sierra ran out in horror, and Craig turned himself in to the Oakdale authorities. Lucinda made Craig an offer: If he signed a new contract with her company, she would take care of everything. Craig refused until Lucinda offered to throw in the telephone number of the place where Sierra was staying. Craig signed, only to learn that Dusty had persuaded John to drop all the charges against him.

Then Lily entered the fray. The young girl was staggered to overhear Lucinda warn Craig that if he ever told Sierra she was her mother, Lucinda would tell Sierra she and Craig were lovers. Craig caught up with Sierra, but

At the end of 1985, the Snyder family began to make its presence felt in Oakdale. Mama Emma was a widow who lived in Luther's Corners and ran the family farm with the help of her sexy son, Holden. Iva, the eldest daughter (right), returned home after many years away and was soon followed by Meg (left), a boy-crazy teenager who liked to stir things up.

she rejected him. This left Sierra vulnerable to the attentions of John, who was becoming quite taken with her. John constantly taunted Lucinda with his attraction to Sierra and blackmailed her into underwriting his research. When Sierra went to Miami to visit Tonio, John decided to follow at Lucinda's expense. As Lucinda and John continued to do everything they could to keep Craig and Sierra apart, Lily threatened to tell Sierra everything she knew. And John told Lucinda that if she didn't resign from her hospital seat, he'd tell Sierra who her mother was. But Lucinda remained adamant; her secret must be kept. Craig warned Lucinda that John's attachment to her daughter was more than just a way to make Lucinda miserable. Sierra soon told Lucinda that John had persuaded her to reopen the search for her mother. Craig became an unlikely ally by agreeing to help Lucinda stop John from destroying Sierra. He was giving Lucinda a supportive hug when Lily walked in and assumed they were having an affair again.

Harrison Blake was up to no good as well. He planted a marijuana cigarette in Lily's birthday present, for which Lucinda blamed Dusty. Fed up with her unreasonable mother, Lily decided to run away. She got as far as the stables before placing a call to Dusty to tell him where she was. Lily was asleep in the stables when she was attacked by a drunken Hank McPherson, the stablemaster's son. Luckily, Dusty found her in time, and Lily thanked him by warning him that Lucinda would do whatever she could to prevent Sierra and Craig from being together. Lily confided in Dusty that Sierra was her sister. Despite Dusty's advice, Lily refused to confront her mother. Instead, she waged a silent competition with Sierra, vowing to be the better rider. Lily's campaign was not as easy as she thought, given her explosive relationship with Lucinda's new young stablemaster. His name was Holden Snyder, and he was the brash younger brother of Tad Channing's former mistress Iva. Although her first real kiss was with Dusty, Lily couldn't help being attracted to the smoldering young man. Lily and Holden clashed over a prize horse, Big Max. Holden said she wasn't ready to handle him yet, but Lily ordered him to saddle the horse up anyway. Several hours later, Lily returned with the injured animal. After Dusty went to England for back surgery, Lily found herself spending more and more time at the stables with Holden. He gave her a cat, which she named Ma'am, because that was what Holden had called her when they first met. Lily was upset when Lucinda took a trip to Dallas with Sierra, which meant she might not be able to take Lily to London for Thanksgiving to see Dusty, as she'd promised. A neglected Lily told Holden that even if Lucinda returned on time, she was going to spend Thanksgiving at the Snyder farm instead.

Holden's new job at the Walsh estate was a source of great pride to his mother, Emma, a widowed farm woman who lived in the nearby town of Luther's Corners. Unlike his sister, Iva, Holden had been a great comfort to her. Even though Holden urged his mother to give Iva another chance, Emma was afraid of being hurt again. One evening when Emma was reading one of Iva's letters, Iva appeared at the door. She'd been gone for a long time. Later, Tad Channing showed up and offered to underwrite the farm and divorce his wife in an effort to win Iva back, but Iva refused to have anything to do with him.

At this time, Lucinda was being taunted by a caller who threatened to expose her secret. The caller always asked to speak to Martin Guest's widow…

# 1986-1990

The world had been turning in Oakdale for 30 years. At the start of this particular year, a couple who almost made it to the altar once discovered each other again—Barbara Ryan and Tom Hughes. There was a hitch this time around, though: Tom was married to Margo. The irony was that Margo had once had an affair with Barbara's ex-husband, James Stenbeck.

Impressed with an outfit Barbara designed, Lisa encouraged her to turn her hobby into a career. Tom heartily approved, and together they came up with the name, Simply Barbara, for her new dress company. Career-minded and ambitious, Barbara made Tom her business manager and insisted he accompany her to the promotion of Simply Barbara in New York. With mixed feelings, Tom agreed. Barbara was a smashing success, and Tom found it hard to keep a lid on his emotions. Getting caught up in the moment, Tom gave Barbara a good luck "kiss," then backed off and told her it would be impossible for him to handle her business affairs any longer. Barbara persisted. How could he think of walking out on her now? Relenting, Tom followed Barbara to a party and got plastered. After pouring him into bed, Barbara decided to get in, too. The morning after found Tom speechless. Barbara assured him it was great, just like the good old days. Consumed with guilt, Tom couldn't go near his wife. A rejected Margo suspected something was wrong and asked Tom point blank: "Did you sleep with her?" Although Tom had no idea what happened that night, he was caught off guard and answered yes. Hurt and angry, Margo accepted a six-week assignment in Washington, D.C. When Tom told Barbara he felt lost without his wife, Barbara suggested he throw himself into his work—that's what she did. Funny, but Tom still couldn't remember "that night." Barbara could, and, according to her, it was perfect. An irate Lisa suspected that her friend and partner had something to do with Tom and Margo's breakup, and if she did, Lisa would never forgive her. While Tom remained upset about the state of his marriage, Barbara was right there to comfort him. Then Jerry Halpern came to town. Jerry was the PR man for Simply Barbara in New York and was with them that fateful night. Jerry saw Tom pass out cold and knew he was in no shape to handle romance or anything else.

Margo decided she wanted a divorce. But Tom didn't, and when she finished her assignment in D.C., he enlisted friends and family to help win Margo back. Barbara was just as determined not to let that happen. Making a TV appearance to discuss the instant success of her Simply Barbara line, Barbara rhapsodized about her business manager, Tom Hughes, while Margo listened intently at home. Things reached the point of no return when Tom was served with divorce papers from his alienated wife.

Tom and Margo had been out of circulation a little too long to enjoy the single life. But every time Margo was on the verge of taking her husband back, Barbara turned up like the proverbial bad penny. When Margo found out she was pregnant, it didn't change how she felt. Margo and Tom were two stubborn, proud people, and although they were loath to admit it, they loved each other and always would. One summer night, Tom arranged a romantic dinner in the park where they had been married, and Margo said she might consider a reconciliation. No sooner had they settled in when Tom tried to persuade Margo to quit working until she had the baby. Margo had other ideas: There was a big drug case going down, and she wanted to be in on it. Soon afterward, a car bomb meant for Margo injured Det. Hal Munson and his partner, Nick Castello, and someone with a raspy voice threatened Margo on the phone. Despite the threats, Margo was determined to solve the case, especially when she got a lead from teenage hooker Judy Baldwin. Judy led Margo to the base of the drug ring's operations and split. "Raspy" stepped out from the shadows and warned her that if she wanted to keep her unborn child, she better drop the investigation. Tom was furious at Margo for taking a risk. So was McClosky, because both Judy and "Raspy" had turned up dead. Margo was sure they'd been iced by the drug lord known as the Falcon.

Not content just to cause havoc between Tom and Margo, Barbara was busy making trouble for Brian and Shannon. If Barbara couldn't have Brian, nobody could. There was something about Shannon's past she wasn't telling, and Barbara was going to find out what it was. Shannon was worried that Barbara's detective might have found out about Earl Mitchell, which meant it wouldn't be long before Brian did too. She tried in vain to contact Earl in Nice. Then she decided to go there to hand over the priceless jewels. At the same time, Earl was catching a flight to Chicago, and they ran into each other at the airport. To Shannon's dismay, he moved in with her, threatening that if she tried to throw him out, he'd tell the police about her part in the diamond caper. Barbara got word that her rival had a new "roommate" and innocently suggested that Brian call Shannon and tell her how much he missed her.

Just when Shannon thought it was safe to resume her relationship with Brian, she got more bad news from Earl. The diamonds she returned were paste. Earl was now broke and would be forced to rely on Shannon for assistance. When Brian got suspicious, Shannon confessed that Earl was her uncle. Although Brian wanted to believe her, he couldn't. When Shannon went with Earl to confront him, a seductive Barbara answered the door. Convinced they'd made love, a devastated Shannon decided to leave town. Harriet and Earl persuaded her to have one more talk with Brian, and Shannon knew she had to tell him the truth: Earl had been using her to smuggle jewels. That was a little too farfetched for Brian, and he accused her of making it up. Hurt and angry, Shannon swore that Barbara would not win.

Harriet Corbman found some Walsh stock that had belonged to her grandfather and gifted Shannon with it. Desperate for money, Shannon cashed it in, and Lucinda bought her out. Earl was ecstatic; he had his eye on Lucinda, and he needed money to impress his little "pigeon," as he called her.

While Earl had his eye on both Lisa and Lucinda, Shannon had eyes only for Brian. With Earl's encouragement, she took out an ad in the paper, just like the one Brian ran to track her down. Touched by her overture, Brian suggested a romantic dinner at Diana's. In the meantime, Barbara was thrilled to learn that Shannon was really Erin Casey, the woman the police were looking for in connection with the stolen diamonds. Hoping to humiliate her, Barbara contacted the police. As Det. Roy Franklin was arresting her, Lucinda's *City Times* photographers were clicking away. Earl convinced Det. Franklin that his niece was blameless, and she was released. Soon after, Brian asked Shannon to be his wife. Shannon was evasive and confessed to Earl that there was a little problem Brian was not aware of. Not knowing how Barbara felt, Earl asked her to design Shannon's wedding gown. Steaming, Barbara called Det. Daniels, telling him she wanted anything and everything he could dig up on Earl Mitchell. Meanwhile, Shannon, ignoring

Harriet's advice that the truth would set her free, avoided setting a wedding date. Running out of excuses, she consulted a private detective, warning him that what she had to say was highly confidential, and when he made inquiries, he should be asking about "Scotch Terrier." Shannon was very relieved to find out that Scotch Terrier was dead. But no sooner had she set the wedding date than her detective informed her he'd made a mistake. Scotch Terrier didn't die in an avalanche—he was very much alive! As her wedding approached, Shannon grew more nervous. When Barbara's detective learned that Scotch Terrier was in Switzerland, Barbara was determined to bring him to Oakdale before the wedding. As Brian and Shannon said, "I do," Duncan McKechnie, a.k.a. Scotch Terrier, made his entrance. How could Shannon possibly marry Brian when she was already married to Duncan?

A dashing Scotsman, Duncan married jet-setting Erin Casey on August 21, 1978, in Antibes. She was a mere 18 and very drunk. The marriage was never consummated. As for Duncan, the kind of woman he sought—older and very rich—found the fact that he was already married very attractive. An angry Brian insisted on an annulment. Duncan had his eye on Brian's private island, and he tricked Brian into selling it to him in exchange for an annulment. But Duncan sent an impostor to sign the papers, rendering the annulment worthless. Duncan made arrangements to bring his grandfather's castle to Oakdale and rebuild it on Brian's island. With the castle came Duncan's sister, Beatrice, a disturbed young woman who'd spent considerable time in a sanatorium. Her guardian, nurse Rosalind Hatchley, accompanied her.

Shannon decided to get a quickie divorce in the Dominican Republic. When she arrived, she found a message from Brian saying he was waiting for her in her room. Shannon raced to the room and jumped into bed, but instead of finding Brian, she found Duncan. Her divorce was foiled once more.

As for her charming Uncle Earl, he was courting Lisa and working for Lucinda. He was also quick to make friends with Duncan. While visiting the castle, Earl noticed the name Thomas Beeton on one of the tombstones. Beeton was Beatrice's betrothed. Walking toward the moat, Earl was sure he heard a faint moaning in the air. When Brian came to the island to blast Duncan for visiting Shannon in the Dominican Republic, Beatrice rushed into his arms. She thought he was her dead fiancé, Thomas, and begged him to marry her and take her away. Duncan explained that Beatrice's fiancé was killed on her wedding day, and Brian bore a striking resemblance to her dead lover. When Barbara dropped by the castle, Beatrice confused her with a devious woman named Suzanne Duprés, who had stolen Thomas away.

By this time, Barbara had fallen for Duncan, and everyone was worried. Margo was sure the dashing Scotsman was up to something, because all the women in his life, including Suzanne, to whom he was once engaged, had died under mysterious circumstances and left their fortunes to him. Since Suzanne's body was never found, Duncan had yet to collect on her. While pretending to be Thomas for Beatrice's sake, Brian tried to dig up information on Duncan, who he suspected was involved in the Oakdale drug ring.

One night, when they were making love, Barbara heard a scream coming from the castle's secret passageway. Duncan investigated and found his lawyer, Hensley Taggart, who lived at the castle, cut and bleeding. Hensley was obsessively jealous of Duncan and Barbara, and he had planted dynamite fuses in the castle walls. But a mysterious stranger wandering the halls stopped his scheme. Soon after, Rosalind Hatchley turned up dead. It seemed Rosalind was a former duchess who'd run off with Duncan. Margo now thought Duncan was the Falcon. Meanwhile, Brian was receiving threats about articles he wrote in the *Argus* about the drug ring. He persuaded Shannon to fly to Las Vegas and establish residence so she would be out of harm's way.

Margo was planning to start her maternity leave when she received a frantic phone call from Barbara. She was at the castle and was very frightened. Bent on revenge because of Barbara and Duncan, Hensley took advantage of Duncan's being away by locking Beatrice in her room and luring Barbara to the island. He was trying to poison Barbara when Margo and Brian arrived and heard her screams. Brian went to check on Beatrice, who was in total shock and no longer saw him as Thomas, while Margo took off after Hensley. As she chased him into the secret passageway, Margo tripped and was knocked out. She was revived by a mysterious man in a monk's robe and hood. When he took off his hood, he revealed himself to be James Stenbeck! Like a cat with nine lives, he had survived his fall from the airplane. All of Oakdale was in shock. Hensley lost his life that day, and although James saved Margo, she lost her baby.

Much to John Dixon's dismay, Lucinda made a cause célèbre of James and had the *City Times* churn out favorable articles about him. Unbeknownst to the people of Oakdale, James had become involved with Ellen and David's granddaughter, Emily Stewart, during his absence. Lucinda, who wanted him for herself, persuaded him to work for Walsh Enterprises. Because of John's vendetta against his lifelong enemy, James was forced to submit to an inquest. Much to Dixon's dismay, Stenbeck was exonerated, even though he'd once tried to murder Dusty Donovan and several other people. As for Emily, she'd had quite a past for one so young. When the police found her name in Hensley's black book, they wondered if she'd known a Lester Keyes (the name James used when he worked with Hensley and supposedly had amnesia). "No," Emily lied sweetly.

Barbara was shaken by Margo's miscarriage. After all, Margo was trying to help her. Dr. Samuels told Tom and Margo they would have to wait two years to try again. They tried to put up a brave front, but mostly they didn't talk about it, and Margo turned to her partner, Hal, for comfort. Although there was a definite attraction between them, Hal didn't want to come between Margo and Tom, and when she poured her heart out about the loss of the baby, he gently told her that she should be telling this to Tom.

Other Oakdale relationships were in trouble as well. Ever since Beatrice snapped out of her illness and no longer thought of Brian as Thomas, Shannon noticed a growing attraction between them. However, love was in bloom for Shannon's uncle Earl and Lisa, especially after she accompanied him to New York on a press campaign for Lisa's nemesis, Lucinda. Although Lisa was disturbed by Earl's constant disappearing acts, she was nonetheless completely charmed, and they decided to marry in a double ceremony with Shannon and Brian.

While Tom was attending a special commission on organized crime in Washington, D.C., he was shocked to learn that Earl was an Interpol agent assigned to the Falcon. Earl told Tom he believed the Falcon was operating out of McKechnie Castle and had enough dynamite there to destroy the island and everyone on it.

On the day of the wedding, in front of a stunned congregation, Shannon announced that she couldn't marry Brian, and no one was more surprised than her husband-to-be. But when Shannon asked him if he could deny his feelings for Beatrice, he admitted he couldn't. However, the second wedding went without a hitch when Lisa took her sixth trip down the aisle, with Earl.

He's back.... Last seen plummeting out of an airplane, James Stenbeck returned to Oakdale and was found wandering the halls of Duncan McKechnie's castle, dressed as a monk. Barbara and all of Oakdale were in shock.

Marriage was in the air in 1986. A blissful Sierra was making plans for a Valentine's Day wedding with Craig, while John was silently seething. Taking his frustrations out on Lucinda, John warned her that if she didn't resign her board seat, he would tell Sierra that Lucinda was her mother. Desperate, Lucinda turned to Craig, who was on his way to Wisconsin to have surgery to correct his sterility. Craig gave Lucinda his own ultimatum: If she didn't tell Sierra, he would. He couldn't continue to deceive Sierra and marry her in good faith. But John couldn't deny his feelings for Sierra any longer and blackmailed Lucinda into calling off the wedding. Trapped, Lucinda pulled some strings and arranged for Sierra's childhood sweetheart, Tonio Reyes, to come to Oakdale and work for Walsh Enterprises. Despite the last-minute appearance of her former fiancé, Sierra refused to change her plans.

In Wisconsin, Craig learned that Betsy inadvertently had tipped Sierra off that John was in love with her. Suspecting the worst, he hurried back to Oakdale to tell Sierra about Lucinda before it was too late. John got there first. "The honest man" in her life, John told her, had been keeping things from her—things like the fact that Lucinda Walsh was her mother! As Sierra reeled from the shock, John said Craig had known all along. Sierra bitterly confronted Lucinda, who tried to explain. When Jacobo Esteban found out Lucinda was in love with Martin Guest, he threatened to kill Martin unless Lucinda left Montega and her baby behind. Sierra listened in stoic silence. Craig wanted to tell his side of the story, even if Sierra didn't want to hear it. But weak from surgery, he collapsed before he could explain that he and Lucinda were lovers and that was why he couldn't tell the truth. Sierra found out anyway. When she and Lily faced each other as sisters for the first time, Sierra told her she knew everything and was trying to find it in her heart to forgive Craig. Lily wondered how she could, since he'd slept with their mother. Crushed by this revelation, Sierra left town. Lily confessed to Craig what she had said, and when Craig went to find Sierra, she was gone. Lucinda hired a private detective, and she and Craig searched frantically for her. John was so depressed that he gave up on his research. Lucinda was far from sympathetic; after all, he'd ruined her life. John begged to differ—he wasn't the one who'd abandoned Sierra as a child. They traced Sierra to San Francisco and found her in Tonio Reyes's hotel room, dressed in a flimsy nightgown. The slick Tonio introduced her as his wife. Craig listened in shock as Sierra admitted it was true and told Craig she never wanted to see him again. Later, when she and Tonio were making love, it was Craig she was thinking of. Lucinda warned Tonio if he didn't bring her daughter back to Oakdale, he'd be out of a job. Sierra tried to persuade him to find work elsewhere, but Tonio was adamant about staying with Lucinda. When Craig heard that Sierra and Tonio were setting up house in Oakdale, he decided to leave Walsh. Ever the astute businesswoman, Lucinda tried to dissuade him. But the lure of Craig's job at Walsh had always been security and Sierra, and now he wanted out. Meanwhile, Sierra was learning that being Tonio's wife wasn't exactly the way to get out of a bad situation. Tonio was such a male chauvinist that he wouldn't let her go out after 9 p.m. without an escort and working as a nurse was out. Her job was to raise a family.

Lily was moved when Sierra told her she didn't blame her for anything. Tonio overheard Sierra admit to Lily that she was still in love with Craig, but he was much too ambitious to let a little thing like Sierra's love for Craig get in his way. Lucinda was grooming him to take over her company, and in exchange he'd agreed to smooth things over between mother and daughter—not an easy task. Meanwhile, Tonio was becoming increasingly impatient with his wife's cold demeanor, and when beautiful Barbara Ryan caught his eye, he liked what he saw. However, Tonio continued to be jealous of Craig and threatened to kill him if ever came near Sierra again.

Craig couldn't deny it anymore—he loved Sierra. The star-crossed lovers finally had their night together, and they made passionate love. But when Sierra remembered Tonio's threat, she lied and told Craig it was over. Hurt and lonely, Craig found comfort in the arms of Iva Snyder. Soon after, Sierra found out she was pregnant. Miserable in her marriage, Sierra went to London alone. While she was away, Craig proposed to Iva, but Iva knew he was on the rebound and said no. As Sierra longed for Craig, Tonio's roving eye found Meg Snyder.

Meg was Emma Snyder's youngest daughter, and she had been living with her aunt Elizabeth and uncle Henry. When she returned home, her mother and siblings had their hands full with this headstrong, boy-crazy teenager. When Lily saw Holden at the pond with her, she thought Meg was his girlfriend, and she was jealous. Lily was rude to Meg. Feeling snubbed, Meg declared war. Meg had her eye on Dusty, so watch out, Lily! Dusty found fun-loving Meg a pleasant change from moody Lily. Although Lily continued to be afraid of her physical attraction to the sullen, handsome Holden, they did finally share a kiss.

With all the commotion over her sister, Lily was desperate for love and attention, and Meg seized the opportunity by offering to play confidante. What Lily didn't know was that Meg was only using her to get information about Dusty. When Dusty came to the farm expecting to see Lily, Meg was there to greet him and stole a kiss.

After Lucinda was in an automobile accident, Lily came to stay on the Snyder farm. Living under the same roof as Holden, it wasn't easy controlling her feelings or her hormones. Holden was puzzled as to why Iva seemed so protective of their houseguest. And Meg was disturbed about the fact that Dusty and Lily were getting close again. When Meg learned John was intent on Dusty's getting into Harvard, she made her move. Thanks to her, John suspected that Lily was distracting Dusty from his studies. Dusty was feeling so pressured

by John, he wondered if he could go on much longer. After an argument with John, Dusty skipped the graduation banquet and headed to a New Mexico ranch where he used to ride rodeo. Determined, Meg followed and seduced him, although he regretted it later, especially when Meg blabbed about their one-night stand to Lily.

Meg managed to impress Lucinda enough for the tycoon to offer her money to go to nursing school. She even persuaded Lucinda to let her live at the Walsh estate, a move that fulfilled Meg's fantasy of living the rich life but angered Lily. Then Meg set out to trap Dusty into marriage. Switching pregnancy tests with Sierra, she suggested to Dusty that they marry and then divorce after the baby was born. Because he felt he had to do the honorable thing, Dusty told Lily about the pregnancy and his plans to marry Meg. He was very much relieved when Dr. Samuels told him the lab had made a mistake and Meg was never pregnant. By threatening to tell her mother about the fake pregnancy, Lily was able to force Meg out of the house. Instead of going home, Meg turned up on head nurse Lyla's doorstep.

Lucinda was intent on separating Lily from Holden and was happy to see the farm boy beginning to pay attention to Emily Stewart. The effects of the good life weren't lost on Holden as he'd struggled long and hard to help his mother on the farm. Emily advised Holden that he should promise Lucinda he'd stay away from her precious daughter in exchange for a junior executive job at Walsh Enterprises. The Snyder clan thought working for Lucinda was a bad idea, but that didn't stop Holden. When Lily saw the former stableboy in suit and tie, she wasn't sure she liked Holden the businessman. Despite Lucinda's efforts, Lily and Holden were getting closer. She tried to manipulate them by making sure they were on different continents when Thanksgiving rolled around, but once again her plans were foiled when Lily and Holden spent their second Thanksgiving together on the Snyder farm.

Over at the Andropoulos home, Betsy and Steve discussed the possibility of having another child. Betsy was concerned about finances, since the dream house Steve was so intent on building was going to cost $300,000. Steve assured her they could afford it, but Betsy was having a hard time going along with his grandiose plans—the cabin suited her fine. Steve thought Betsy should want what he wanted, and Betsy was upset that he hadn't changed his chauvinistic ways. But his new assistant at Andropoulos Construction, Iva Snyder, liked him just the way he was. When Iva's married ex-lover, Tad

Channing, tried to pressure her into a reconciliation, Steve was there to comfort her. When a blizzard forced them to spend the night in the construction trailer, although nothing happened, Iva felt confused.

Gradually, Betsy and Steve's marriage began to disintegrate. When Craig started up his management consulting firm, Montgomery Associates, Betsy put off having another child in order to work as Craig's girl Friday. When her work kept her from accompanying Steve to Chicago on a business trip, Steve invited Iva. Reluctant because Tad Channing was there, Iva eventually changed her mind and decided to go. Iva and Meg were often at odds over Meg's boy-crazy schemes, and Meg got back at her by telling Tad that Iva was going to the Windy City. Tad appeared right on schedule and tried to seduce her. He was infuriated when Iva resisted and vowed revenge through Steve by undercutting him in a construction bid. With Andropoulos Construction in a terrible bind, Steve was relieved when Tonio offered to use his position at Walsh to throw work his way. But soon Tonio was forced to admit there'd been a change in plans, and the jobs would be going to Channing instead. Iva put two and two together and realized Tad and Lucinda were in cahoots. Tad was plotting to sabotage Steve's subcontracting work, thus destroying his firm and leaving Iva jobless. When Betsy confronted Tad, he was very amused. He liked a woman with a temper and decided to get back at Steve through Betsy. Soon afterward, Betsy got a phone call from a woman who said she was her half-sister, Emily. She said she was in Los Angeles and was in trouble. Betsy made plans to go, and so did Tad. When he joined the bikini-clad Betsy at the pool, his private detective clicked away. Although nothing happened, the photos made it look like something had.

Tad planned to juggle the books to sabotage Steve and offered Holden a job as bookkeeper. He intended to make Holden the fall guy for the "fixed" books. Then he made sure Steve saw the "incriminating" pictures of him and Betsy, and Steve was convinced they were having an affair. Tad blackmailed Lucinda to the tune of $3 million after overhearing her talk to Ambrose about something extremely confidential concerning Lily. He went on to attack Sierra but was stopped by Tonio. Not to be outdone, Tad took great pleasure in telling Sierra that Tonio was having an affair with Barbara Ryan. As if that weren't enough, he tried to rape Meg.

Everyone was looking for Tad, including Barbara.

He was blackmailing her, too, demanding she fire signature model Denise Darcy, who had posed as Emily and made the frantic calls to Betsy. Denise knew about Barbara's affair with Tonio, and Barbara had signed her on to keep her quiet. Meg's older brother, Seth, was in town, and he, Holden, Tonio and Craig were all gunning for Tad. When Margo and Hal investigated Tad's whereabouts, they found his hand protruding from the hardened cement of the Walsh Towers foundation!

The murder left behind a slew of suspects. As he investigated the crime, a lonely Hal became smitten with Denise Darcy. When someone started terrorizing her, Hal was sure it had something to do with Channing's murder, especially when a poster of Simply Barbara's beautiful signature model was slashed. A briefcase bearing the initials "T.C." had washed ashore, and Duncan brought it to the police station. Inside was a paper with cryptic numbers written on it. Margo discovered they were code numbers for porno movies. Hal got the connection and searched Denise's room for the shoe with the missing heel that matched the one stuck in the cement near Channing's body. He found it. It seemed that Denise was being framed by Channing because of the porno flicks, and she was the one who did him in.

Lucinda was still getting troubling phone calls for Martin Guest's widow, and she finally agreed to a meeting. On the way, she was involved in a car crash and was rushed to Memorial. Her adversary, John, saved her life. Lucinda told Ambrose she had to find out what this woman knew about Martin Guest's death. John lurked outside Lucinda's room long enough to catch part of the conversation. He knew she was hiding something, and he'd find a way to use it. Craig was very interested to learn from Lily that her father was being blackmailed when he died, and he decided to do some investigating on his own.

Lucinda was finally able to keep her appointment with the caller and was stunned when it turned out to be Iva Snyder. In a shocking revelation, Iva explained that Lily was her daughter. She had given her up for adoption 17 years ago. A Chicago lawyer, Clifford Breyer, handled the adoption. Breyer turned out to be a crook and was eventually murdered. Iva had obtained a journal from the lawyer's widow, and next to her baby's name was the notation "M. Guest." That was how she found Lucinda. Stunned, Lucinda set out to destroy Iva. Checkbook in hand, she went to the farm. Iva didn't want a check. While Lily was on the farm, Iva recalled that she was starving for attention while Lucinda ran her empire and manipulated other people's lives. All she wanted was for Lucinda to be a good mother or she'd tell Lily the truth. Undaunted, Lucinda planned to use the farm to keep Iva in check. The Snyders were badly in debt, and Lucinda used her financial power to exert pressure on them to pay up. Lucinda did try to be a good mother, but it seemed she was not cut out for the job, and Lily was sick of Lucinda's running hot and cold. One minute she was loving, the next minute she was obsessed with her latest smear campaign. Lily overheard Lucinda say there was something irregular about her father's suicide. But whenever she asked, Lucinda changed the subject. Alone, Lucinda recalled that fateful day when she was holding her baby in her arms, and Martin came home with the news that the adoption was illegal. He said he was sick to death of the blackmailing lawyer and planned to take care of him once and for all. Soon after, the lawyer was found dead, and Martin took his own life.

Iva considered leaving town, but Craig talked her out of it. She and Lucinda squared off about the farm: If Lucinda tried to foreclose, Lily would know the truth. Lucinda backed off. As for Lily, she was happy to spend most of her time at the Snyder farm, with Holden as the main attraction. When Iva caught them almost kissing she was shocked—Holden could be kissing his niece.

Iva finally told Seth why she ran away from Uncle Henry's farm and hadn't contacted the family all those years. When she was 13, Iva was raped by her cousin Josh, and Lily was the product of that rape. Both Holden and Meg overheard the conversation. Thinking that he was Lily's uncle, Holden knew he couldn't see her anymore, and Lily was hurt by a rejection she couldn't understand.

When Iva was finally able to tell Emma the truth about the rape and how she felt about Lily's being a child of incest, Emma revealed some family secrets. Iva was adopted at a time when she and Harvey didn't think they could have children, and Josh wasn't Uncle Henry's real son. Iva was stunned and relieved at the same time.

Another mystery hit Oakdale concurrently with Tad Channing's murder. Marsha Talbot, last seen with a black ribbon tied around her neck, had faked her own death to throw suspicion on Ken Wayne and was very much alive. Margo learned that Marsha was a black belt in karate and could have easily overpowered murder victims Marie Kovac and Cal Randolph. Meanwhile, Doug

was rattled when he received a call from a woman whose voice was identical to his "dead" wife's. Frannie told Marsha about the call, and Marsha later chided a mysterious friend to be more careful. Then she placed an anonymous call to the police advising them to check out a connection between Lucinda and Marie. Marie had found some personal papers of Lucinda's that had to do with Lily's being adopted, and she was holding them over Lucinda. When the police questioned her, Lucinda lied and claimed the papers had to do with business. Shortly thereafter, the police arrested Ken Wayne, accusing him of being Kim's secret admirer and Marie's murderer. Doug was pleased. Thanks to him, the authorities had all the evidence they needed against Wayne: Marie's diary and the same typewriter used to write the letters to Mrs. Hughes.

Someone was following Kim. She was sure it was her secret admirer, and when he was the victim of a hit-and-run, Kim couldn't help but be relieved. But soon the gifts and roses began to appear again, and the nightmare started anew. Kim was so unnerved that Bob suggested she get psychiatric help. John noticed her emotional state and thought Andy should come to live with him. Kim informed him that she was quite capable of taking care of their son. Then she found out that she and Bob were expecting. Dr. Samuels warned Kim that any emotional stress could cause her to lose the child. Having suffered a miscarriage while carrying Bob's child all those years ago, Kim wondered how Bob would take it if she told him and then ended up miscarrying again. She decided to confide in Lisa.

Meanwhile, someone was typing Kim's name on an envelope. Next to the typewriter was an autographed picture of her that read: "Best wishes to my lost little lamb." Kim shortly received a package with a locket she thought she'd lost. She tried to piece together all the clues and finally traced them to an unlikely source—the lyrics to the Gershwin standby "Someone to Watch Over Me." Meanwhile, her secret admirer sat in his secret room listening to a recording of her singing the same song. That secret admirer was Doug Cummings!

Kim never would have guessed that her stepdaughter's new boyfriend was the one who'd been sending her strange messages and apricot roses. Marsha chided Doug for taking too many risks. How would Frannie feel if she knew the truth? Doug vowed that by the time she did he'd be a part of Bob and Kim's family. Frannie was speechless when Doug proposed, and she accepted. Doug told Marsha the good news: He'd taken care of

Marie, Cal and Dr. Henry Strauss (the victim of the hit-and-run), and nothing was going to stop him now. Doug dreamed that his union with Frannie would bring him closer to Kim, but Marsha burst his bubble when she told him Kevin had become suspicious. Doug swore that was another problem he'd take care of. An ecstatic Frannie made the rounds—showing off her ring, a ring that had belonged to Doug's dead wife, Caroline. Hearing that the woman he loved so much had become engaged, Kevin was distraught. He was convinced that Marsha and Doug were up to something. Just as Marsha feared, Doug was getting careless. When Heather spotted a key and picked it up, Doug tried to strangle her. Left for dead, Heather was rushed to the hospital, where she lapsed into a coma. Desperate to prevent her from awakening and telling the truth, Doug tried to turn off her life-support system.

Marsha received a visit from a woman named Elaine who'd been worried about her lover, Henry Strauss. Marsha lied and assured her that Henry was bound to turn up soon. As it turned out, Dr. Strauss was Doug's psychiatrist, and he knew about Doug's obsession with Kim. Certain it was Caroline's death that triggered Doug's psychosis, Strauss had followed Kim in an attempt to protect her.

Haunted by encounters with Kim when he was a busboy and she a popular songstress, Doug vowed not to let anything interfere with his plans. One way or another, he'd make Frannie his wife and Kim a part of his family. Soon after, Frannie came across the secret room and a half-crazed Doug tried to tell her his story. Shocked, Frannie backed away. Doug told her she didn't have to be afraid, but as he moved closer, Frannie fainted. Kim arrived, and when Doug started to tell her how he felt about her, Kim realized he was the secret admirer. Then Marsha entered, pulled a revolver out of her purse and stopped Frannie and Kim from leaving. Clearly demented, Doug vowed he'd have the family he always wanted and forced the three women to board his jet.

When Heather came to and named Doug as her attacker, Bob was stunned to learn that his wife and daughter had been kidnapped by this madman. To add to Bob's torment, Lisa told him Kim was pregnant. Doug landed his jet safely in Colorado and led his captives to the renovated millhouse where he was born. He had named it Dream's End. Much to Kim and Frannie's relief and surprise, Marsha offered to help, but her plan to have Frannie use the helicopter radio backfired when

The revelation that clean-cut restaurateur Douglas Cummings was Kim's psychotic stalker and that he had committed several murders rocked Oakdale. Cummings kidnapped Kim and Frannie and whisked them away to his Colorado "dream house." Bob and Kevin came to the rescue, but unfortunately Kevin took the bullet meant for Frannie. Douglas died, the victim of a spurned and jealous lover, Marsha Talbot.

Doug found his fiancée sneaking away. Smiling, Doug led the terrified Frannie back to his lair. Their escape foiled, Kim and Frannie were distraught to hear that Doug had installed a security system, and if anyone tried to get through, they'd be blown to bits. Suddenly Kim winced in pain, and Frannie realized she was pregnant. Meanwhile, Bob and Kevin had put everything together and were on their way to Colorado. It was a race against time as Bob and Kevin neared the millhouse. His dream shattered, Doug intended to blow the place up. In an effort to stall him, Frannie swore she still loved him. Doug wanted a terrified Frannie to prove it. As Bob and Kevin neared the house, they heard a blood-curdling scream. Kim rushed into Doug's room and found him dead—stabbed by a letter opener. Frannie was on the floor sobbing that Doug had tried to rape her. When Marsha saw the dead body of the man she loved, she went berserk and pulled her gun just as Kevin and Bob rushed in. Kevin jumped in front of Frannie and took the bullet. He died in her arms.

Back in Oakdale, Kim told everyone that she was the one who killed Doug and vowed that no one would ever know the truth. The ordeal left Frannie drained. Thanks to her, Kevin was dead, and she was haunted by nightmares. Unaware that Kim was covering for her, Frannie couldn't remember anything after Doug tried to rape her. The police learned that Doug was impotent, so how could he rape Frannie? Marsha insisted that

## Love and Marriage

*On the 30th anniversary of "As The World Turns," Chris and Nancy Hughes celebrated a milestone of their own: their 50th wedding anniversary! Friends and family from far and wide joined in their celebration.*

Frannie and Kim killed Doug in cold blood. She'd inherited a considerable sum of money from Caroline's family and was willing to spend every cent of it to convict Kim and Frannie. Meanwhile, Doug made Frannie his heir. She was a wealthy woman, but she didn't feel she deserved the money.

Frannie and Kim were unnerved when they learned that Marsha intended to take full blame for the kidnapping, making Doug the innocent victim. Unsure of what to think, Bob pressed Kim to tell him again what happened. Kim repeated her story—she killed Doug to protect Frannie. Determined to remember what had happened the night of the murder, Frannie went to Doug's secret room and remembered him calling Kim's name. McClosky ordered Det. Roy Franklin to get another statement from the women. Franklin learned that at no time did Doug use a gun. If that were true, the D.A. could make a case that Frannie killed Doug out of malice, not self-defense. What's more, the prosecuting D.A., Avril Hobson, noticed discrepancies in Kim's and Frannie's stories. They all went back to Dream's End to see if the visit would jog Frannie's memory. Based on what they saw there, Kim couldn't possibly have stabbed Doug the way she claimed, so Hobson handed the matter over to a grand jury. When Tom told Kim that the stories conflicted, Kim didn't care—she was going to protect Frannie. On grand jury day, hell-bent on destroying her beloved Doug's fiancée, Marsha entered the courtroom wild-eyed and without a lawyer. Marsha had nothing to lose. Her appearance jolted Frannie's memory, and she remembered that Doug had been trying to rape her when Marsha entered and was distraught to find them together. When Doug told Marsha he didn't

love her, Marsha killed him with the letter opener in a rage. She was sentenced to life in prison. Kim and Frannie had a heart-to-heart talk about how much Kim loved her sister's daughter and had wanted to protect her. It was then that Frannie asked Kim if she could call her Mom.

After the trial, realizing he'd never get Frannie back, Jay Connors left Oakdale for good. But two new men came to town that year, and both had their eye on Frannie. When Emma collapsed from exhaustion, Seth, her oldest son and father figure to the family, moved to Oakdale to help his mother and keep the Snyder farm from going under. The other new arrival was Dr. Casey Peretti, a protégé of John Dixon's. Casey, a resident at Memorial, was boarding at Lyla's. Casey and Seth vied for Frannie's attention. Seth was ahead. Lyla encouraged Casey not to give up, but things got complicated when his old flame, Taylor Baldwin, came to town and went to work in the Memorial lab.

The danger wasn't over for Frannie, because being behind bars didn't stop Marsha from plotting revenge on her for stealing Doug away. Marsha managed to escape, kidnap Frannie and take her to a deserted cabin. Frannie's competing suitors, Seth and Casey, found her in the nick of time.

After the ordeal of the trial, Bob and Kim took Frannie and Andy to the cabin for a holiday. They invited Casey along. No sooner had they arrived than Nancy had a bad fall, and Bob had to go back to Oakdale. While he was away, Kim went into labor and Casey delivered his first baby. Kim and Bob named their son Christopher after the beloved patriarch of the Hughes family.

Hoping to put time and distance between her and the events of the past year, Frannie decided to go back to school and chose Oxford. Before she left, she and Seth acknowledged their love. When she arrived at Heathrow Airport, Frannie spotted a woman who could be her double, and she was determined to find out about her. While Seth was visiting her, they tracked down a clue that led them to a woman named Mona Simms. When they arrived at her cottage, they found Mona's body. Rummaging through her things, they saw the name "Sabrina" on a birthday card. She had been born on the same day as Frannie—they could be twins! Mona had one living relative, Peter Marsden. Frannie was upset, though, because he didn't know anyone named Sabrina.

At year's end, Bob, Kim, Frannie and little Chris gathered in London for the holidays. Little did they know they were being followed by the woman Sabrina.

Year's end also found Steve Andropoulos struggling with his failing business and troubled marriage. He was distraught when Iva had an accident that almost left her paralyzed, and he realized he'd let her medical insurance lapse for lack of funds. He'd taken a loan from Lucinda, which he couldn't pay back, and he was too proud to accept money from Betsy's ex-husband Craig. Demoralized, Steve left to start over in Greece. Betsy and Dani stayed behind.

By holiday season, Lyla Montgomery was in love with an unlikely person—her boarder, Casey Peretti. He was young enough to be her son, but Casey didn't care. He was in love, and everyone noticed that Lyla was walking on air.

It was a year of beginnings in Oakdale's business community. Lisa bought Caroline's from Frannie, who'd inherited it from Doug. Then she went into partnership with Craig and renamed it the Mona Lisa. It quickly became a success.

John and Emma grew closer after he treated her for her heart condition. Emma would prove to be a very good influence on Dr. Dixon.

Heather thought she'd found love, too, with Det. Roy Franklin. Her father, Lionel, thought he was a much more suitable match for her than Tucker Foster. But things did not turn out so well. Roy had a sister, Nella, whose boyfriend Frank was involved in drugs. There was a shootout, and Frank was killed by Roy. Heather was sympathetic, but Nella's father, Leonard, went ballistic and threw Roy out. Leonard hated the police for having killed another young man who'd been involved with drugs—his son, Larry Jr. Facing another postponement of her wedding to Roy, Heather left for Los Angeles to pursue her singing career.

The centerpiece of this 30th anniversary year was the golden wedding jubilee of Nancy and Chris Hughes. Penny and Don Hughes were there, as were Annie and Dee Stewart and bad seed Rick Ryan. Susan Stewart, Emily's mother, attended, and David Stewart called in from Africa, where he was doing AIDS research. Sadly, only months later, Chris Hughes, the beloved patriarch of the Hughes family, died quietly in his sleep. Nancy, who had shared his life as wife, partner and friend from the early days when she helped him through law school, to the sunset years of their lives, led the memorial service for family and friends.

## 1987

The New Year began with the engagement of Frannie and Seth and the mystery surrounding Frannie Hughes's look-alike, Sabrina. Bob, Kim and Seth were in England scouring the missing pages of Mona Simms's journal for clues. When they talked to the groundskeeper on the Fullerton estate where Mona once worked, he was startled by how much Frannie looked like the Fullertons' daughter, Sabrina. Then Bob paid a visit to Peter Marsden, Mona's only living relative, and he sensed something suspicious and frightening about the man.

As for John, his past acts were coming back to haunt him. After overhearing that John was responsible for the New Mexico fiasco with Dusty and Meg, Emma felt she could no longer see him. Then Margo started to grill him about his connection to Howard Lansing, who used to be Memorial's chief administrator. Lansing was blackmailing John, and John complained bitterly to Rick Ryan about it. Something was going on. It turned out that Howard Lansing had been posing as Peter Marsden, and soon afterward, the real Peter Marsden was found dead.

Sensing she was in danger, Sabrina booked a seat on the Orient Express. The detective investigating Marsden's murder learned from Sabrina's art teacher that she'd left London for Venice because she thought she was being followed. On her trail, Lansing found Sabrina's circular for the Orient Express and chartered a flight to intersect with the train. When Frannie, Seth, Bob and Kim learned of Sabrina's plans, they headed for the Orient Express as well. On board, Bob was shocked to come face-to-face with Howard Lansing. Kim tried to find out why Bob was so upset after seeing Lansing, but Bob was close-mouthed. He called Lyla and asked her to check hospital records as to whether an ob/gyn patient named Fullerton was admitted to Memorial in December of 1965, and if so, what doctor signed the birth certificate for the daughter who was born to her. Then John received a cryptic message from Lansing: "Mission almost completed." Not knowing what it meant, John confronted Rick, who filled him in. Apparently Sabrina didn't die in a train wreck with her parents as they had thought, and now Lansing was going "to make the lie the truth." John told Rick they might have to pay the price they should have paid 21 years ago.

Lansing and the Hugheses searched for Sabrina in

mazelike Venice. Lansing spotted her on a boat heading for the island of Torcello. Seeing her as well, Frannie, Seth, Kim and Bob followed in separate boats. On the way, Bob finally told Kim what he thought he knew about Sabrina's true identity.

Rick and John beat Lyla to the hospital records room, and Rick stole Sabrina's file, but Lyla managed to locate proof of Mrs. Fullerton's admission on December 10, 1965.

On the island of Torcello, Frannie came face-to-face with her mirror image in an old Venetian church. But before they could connect, Lansing opened fire. Kim ran to get the police, while Bob and Seth went after Lansing. Once Lansing was finally in custody, a passionate Bob demanded to know if Sabrina was Kim's daughter. Lansing wasn't talking. Nevertheless, Bob and Kim felt it was time to tell Frannie and Sabrina that 21 years ago, they'd had an affair and conceived Sabrina out of love.

The police inspector found the missing pages from Mona Simms's journal in Lansing's hotel room. She wrote of a quarrel between Sabrina's father and Lansing about the illegal baby switch. Edgar Fullerton paid Mona £50,000 to keep quiet.

When the Hugheses returned from Europe, John confessed to the police that he'd heard about the baby swap from Howard Lansing two years after he told Kim she'd given birth to a stillborn boy. John insisted that at the time, he understood Sabrina had died with her parents in a train wreck. John was desperate to have his story corroborated, but Rick Ryan fled to the Caribbean, and Howard Lansing hanged himself in jail.

John's confession wasn't the end of it—the hospital board had to decide if the withholding of information constituted a criminal act. Much to everyone's amazement, especially John's, Lucinda defended him before the board, and the hospital cleared him of any wrongdoing. The newfound kinship between John and Lucinda was undermined when the *City Times'* tabloid reporter smeared the Howard Lansing/Sabrina story all over the front page, leaving John feeling very much betrayed.

The news of Sabrina's origin was difficult for Frannie to swallow. She was no longer Bob's sole prized daughter, and it was hard for her to adjust to the fact that her father had an affair with Kim all those years ago. Barbara was also upset because Sabrina was a living reminder of Bob's infidelity to Barbara's mother, Jennifer. With their customary grace and fair-mindedness, Bob and Kim welcomed Sabrina into the family. They were not so understanding with John, for, after all,

he'd kept their daughter a secret for 19 years! They told him he was not welcome in their home and never would be, and Andy was caught in the middle. Making matters worse for John, Margo, who was usually John's champion, sided with Kim and Bob. It didn't take Sabrina long to realize she was a controversial presence in Oakdale, as she was well aware of Barbara's coldness and Frannie's feelings of displacement. Frannie was so upset that she stopped calling Kim "Mom." Seth was the only one who made Sabrina feel comfortable, and she greatly appreciated his kindness. They began to spend a great deal of time together talking about their mutual artistic pursuits—his writing and her art. Despite her friendship with Seth, Sabrina sensed she would never fit into the Oakdale landscape, and she decided to return to England.

Because of the newspaper articles about the Sabrina affair, Lucinda had already lost ground with John. When she sent a reporter to talk to Andy, that was the last straw. John stormed into the mansion. Lucinda had just had a massage, and John locked the door so she couldn't escape. Then he told her what he thought of her. The soap dishes and the accusations flew until the two ended up in the hot tub, where anger turned to "steamy" passion. In the blink of an eye, John and Lucinda hopped aboard the Walsh jet and were married in Las Vegas. It was not clear whether it was a marriage made in heaven or in hell, but it was an interesting match to be sure. Emma arrived at John's apartment to tell him she'd had a change of heart and forgave him. She was too late.

Margo and Bob went down to the Caribbean to extract the truth from Rick Ryan. When they found him, Rick, who'd had a strong dislike for Bob for many years, pulled a gun and insisted that John was the guilty party in the baby switch. Although there was no love lost between him and John, Bob didn't believe Rick was giving the true story. Then Rick let it slip that Lansing had approached John two years after the swap. Margo felt a bit better about her father, but not enough to accept what he'd done.

Back in England, Sabrina had a quick fling with her ex-lover, Colin Crawley. When Sabrina told him she was returning to Oakdale, he wondered if the reason had to do with some new man in her life. Upon her arrival, Sabrina quickly picked up on tension between Frannie and Seth. Sabrina had been gradually altering her appearance to please Seth, and she looked even more like Frannie than before. Seth was thrilled to have her back, while Frannie was more reticent. Sabrina's roots in Oakdale deepened when she was commissioned to paint a mural in the hospital cafeteria. She was not pleased when Colin showed up, claiming he was there only because his artwork was being shown in a Chicago gallery. Sabrina told him to get lost, and although she was thrown off course by his occasional kisses, she insisted that there would be no romantic connection and headed to the cabin to work on her mural. Colin went after her. Despite his best efforts, it was obvious Sabrina had her sights set on Seth. Colin chastised her insensitivity toward her new-found half-sister and predicted that Frannie might regret having saved her life in Venice.

One evening Seth snuck up on a woman he thought was Frannie and drew her into a passionate kiss. Sabrina was well aware of the mistake and let the kiss linger. When Seth realized who she really was, he was embarrassed and decided not to tell Frannie about it. Frannie had requested that they not make love until their wedding night. She had finally found a kind man to spend the rest of her life with, and she didn't want to repeat her past mistakes. Seth was frustrated, but he understood and promised not to push. After all, Frannie had changed his life, too. She'd made him realize he had the right to follow his dream of being a writer. However, Frannie was less than thrilled when he called his current novel *Sabrina*.

Iva had trouble telling Sabrina and Frannie apart, and when she passed the Snyders' moonlit pond one night, she thought she saw Frannie enjoying a swim. Iva told Seth, and he went to join her. Sabrina was wearing only a towel, and Seth, thinking she was Frannie, got very turned on. Sabrina did not resist. Thinking Frannie must have changed her mind about sex before marriage, Seth didn't ask questions when Sabrina let him make love to her. By the time he realized who she was, it was too late. Seth was devastated. Sabrina confessed she'd wanted this to happen, but she offered to leave town if that would set things right. Before she packed her bags,

## On the Road

*"As The World Turns" traveled to Venice to follow Bob and Kim as they tried to solve the mystery surrounding Frannie's looka-like, who turned out to be their daughter.*

Sabrina thought she should tell her half-sister what had happened. Frannie was crushed, especially since she and Seth had never made love. She called off the engagement and returned his ring.

Sierra was trying to balance two lovers as well, her husband and Craig. While Craig was having a second operation to reverse his sterility, Lucinda warned Tonio that if he had another affair, his career would be over. Nevertheless, Tonio continued his romance with Meg Snyder. When Craig told Sierra that Tonio was having an affair with Barbara Ryan as well, Sierra made up her mind to get a divorce. She told Tonio her plans and threatened to name Barbara as co-respondent if he contested. Tonio was afraid that without a wife and a job, he could be deported. Tonio eavesdropped on Lucinda telling Ambrose to find Mrs. Clifford Breyer, the widow of the murdered adoption lawyer, because she couldn't let Iva or anyone else discover why Martin Guest had committed suicide. Tonio found the woman first, and when she recalled that her husband had mentioned Martin Guest a few days before he was tragically murdered, Tonio felt a renewed sense of job security. But he still had Seth on his back, telling him to stay away from Meg. Even after Meg moved back to the farm, she continued her affair with Tonio.

When Craig told Lucinda about Tonio's current fling with Meg, Lucinda tried to fire him, but Tonio threatened to tell Lisa everything he knew about Martin Guest's death. Lucinda hired a detective to follow Tonio. She was determined to find something to use against him if he came close to telling Lily what he knew.

In her eighth month of pregnancy, Sierra got tangled up in phone wires and had a bad fall. Tonio found her unconscious and rushed her to Memorial. When Craig arrived and learned that Tonio hadn't informed Lucinda of Sierra's injury, he called her immediately. A furious Lucinda threatened to keep Tonio from seeing his child. But when Sierra went into labor, Tonio was there helping her with her breathing and pushing, while Craig was in the lobby, wringing his hands. Sierra gave birth to a son, and Tonio was elated. The thrill was short-lived, however, when Dr. Samuels examined the newborn and discovered the child couldn't possibly be Tonio's. Everyone was baffled except Casey, who had a theory that if the first surgery to reverse his sterility was a success, Craig could be the father. Craig was only too happy to accept Casey's theory and rejoiced in the birth of his son. He and Sierra were married in her hospital room with little Bryant in attendance. Tonio and Iva watched silently from the open doorway, knowing they'd have to let go of their former loves. When Lucinda ordered Tonio to train Holden in the Management Consultant Division, he feared she was grooming Holden to take over his own job, and he was more determined than ever to tighten his hold on Lucinda. After talking to Meg, Tonio thought he'd put two and two together and claimed to know the identity of Lily's father. Lucinda demanded he tell her what he knew. Tonio said he would if she assured him job security, company stock and Walsh Enterprises when she eventually stepped down. Lucinda threw him out of her office and told Craig about the blackmail. Craig swore that if Tonio ever did anything to hurt Lily, Iva, Sierra or anyone else Craig loved, he'd destroy him. Aware that his enemies were breeding, Tonio put a letter in a safe-deposit box and gave the key to Meg, along with instructions to open it if anything happened to him.

With Sierra's support, Craig decided to follow Betsy to Greece to find Steve. Betsy was touched by his willingness to help. Following a lead, Craig and Betsy hired a small airplane. The plane went down in midflight. Betsy survived, but Craig was missing. David flew to Greece to attend to his injured granddaughter, and while he was there, Betsy learned that Steve had been arrested for drug trafficking. Alarmed, Betsy assured her grandfather that Steve couldn't possibly have known what he had been transporting.

With Craig out of the picture, Tonio was sure things were on an upswing. But when the truth about Lily's parentage was revealed, he lost his leverage with Lucinda, and she wasted no time in kicking him out of her company. Divorced and unemployed, Tonio stood an excellent chance of being deported. Not one to give up, he persuaded Meg to marry him. But clever Meg, knowing he was using her to stay in the country and having her eye on the good things in life, made Tonio sign a prenuptial agreement. Iva felt that out of respect for

Craig's memory, they should boycott Tonio and Meg's wedding reception, and Meg was deeply hurt when her family refused to attend.

There were other problems on the farm as well. Josh and Uncle Henry had a terrible fight in which Henry attacked Josh with a bullwhip and then suffered a heart attack. Emma and Iva were shocked when Henry died, and Josh disappeared. Meanwhile, Lucinda hired a new stablehand, Rod Landry, who hailed from somewhere "out West." One day he helped Betsy with a flat and was disappointed when he noticed her wedding ring. Rod and Betsy became good friends. Lily was also quite taken with Rod, with whom she quickly felt a connection.

At this time, Lily was asking many questions about her father's suicide, and a shaken Lucinda swore she'd told her daughter everything. When John told his wife that Lily should learn the truth from her rather than from someone else, Lucinda misunderstood and thought John knew Iva was Lily's mother. Iva was able to catch Lucinda before she let the truth slip out in front of John.

Still vengeful over Lucinda's part in Whit's death, Lisa was determined to use the *Argus* to reveal the reason Martin Guest killed himself. She hired Jessica Griffin to look into the suicide, and Jessica discovered that Mrs. Breyer had passed away and her secrets were in a journal, which was locked safely away in Iva Snyder's safe-deposit box. Jessica was able to locate the woman who ran the home for unwed mothers where Iva stayed when she was pregnant with Lily. Lisa did too, and after offering a sizable bribe to look at the record books, she found Iva Snyder's name in the ledger. When Lucinda heard Lisa had this information, she thought it was time to tell Lily the truth. But before she could get the words out, Craig told her that he'd persuaded Lisa to keep quiet. Even though Lisa believed Martin Guest had killed Clifford Breyer because he was blackmailing him about the illegal adoption, she would never hurt Lily.

When John moved into the Walsh estate, he and Lucinda told Lily they'd like Dusty to move in with them. This upset a jealous Holden, but Lily was impressed with how gracious her mother was about accepting Dusty and Andy into the family. On a roll, Lucinda encouraged John to invite his teenage niece, Pamela Wagner, to spend the summer, and she accepted.

One day Emma received a phone call from Josh. He wanted to talk to the Snyder family about the time he molested Iva. Emma tried to dissuade him from coming back to the farm, but Iva soon discovered Josh was already back in Oakdale, using the name Rod Landry! When Iva saw her cousin's face, the memory of her childhood nightmare overwhelmed her, and she told him to get out of Oakdale. Josh refused to leave until he knew what had happened to the child he'd fathered. When Iva told her brothers who Rod Landry really was, Seth went to the stables and beat him to a pulp. Josh tried to make the Snyders understand that Uncle Henry had abused him as a child, and perhaps that had affected his behavior toward Iva. Emma checked his story with Aunt Elizabeth, who replied that Josh was lying. Despite being bruised and battered by the Snyder boys, Josh refused to leave town. He didn't believe Iva had told the truth when she claimed the child they'd conceived was stillborn. Josh received support from Betsy and Frannie. Through her relationship with Doug Cummings, Frannie had seen firsthand how childhood abuse could lead to psychosis later in life; it was what had inspired her to pursue a career in psychology. The Snyder boys went crazy when they saw Josh with anyone they loved. When Holden saw Josh with his arms around Lily after he'd helped her down a ladder, he was convinced Josh had to go. But Josh had established ties in Oakdale and wasn't going anywhere. One of those ties was with Betsy. She had been confiding in him about her problems with Steve, who was still in Greece. When Betsy decided to go to Greece, Rod declared his love for her. Betsy gently told him he'd mistaken kindness for love. Ashamed, he told Betsy he planned to leave town. Iva was very relieved. Lily lobbied for him to stay and was happy when he changed his mind. Rod started seeing Dr. Michaels and was finally able to admit to raping Iva. Dr. Michaels saw this as a big step, but Iva was not impressed.

When Craig told Sierra that Lily was illegally adopted, Sierra urged her mother to tell Lily right away. Lucinda promised she would, right after Lily's graduation. Lucinda and Iva agreed on a plan in which Lily would learn she was adopted but would never find out that it was Iva who gave birth to her and gave her away.

Meg overheard Tonio and Lucinda exchanging threats about Lily's adoption. Although Lucinda had enough on Tonio to silence him, she perceived Meg as a loose cannon, so Lucinda did her best to appear extra nice to Tonio in order to appease her. Despite appearances, Lucinda was conspiring to set Tonio up for a fall by giving him an insider-trading stock tip, and Tonio fell for it.

In Greece, Betsy learned that Steve could face a life sentence for his crime. She tried to visit him in jail, but Steve refused to see her. She was devastated when she learned that Steve gave up his U.S. citizenship three months ago. It was discovered that Steve participated in the transport of leather boxes, which resembled the one Shannon found in connection with the Falcon case. Steve had apparently gotten himself involved in the Falcon's drug ring. Extremely hurt and feeling vulnerable, Betsy realized she needed Josh in her life.

With Betsy away, Josh began spending more time with Lily and felt very protective of her. When Lily invited Josh to go swimming, the entire Snyder clan exploded in fury and fear. They were convinced that Josh would hurt Lily, if not rape her. Iva panicked and headed to Lucinda's stable to tell Josh to leave Lily alone. When Iva arrived, she thought she saw Josh making a move against Lily. Iva grabbed a pitchfork and screamed at Josh to stay away because Lily was his child. Lily and Josh were stunned. Josh pleaded with Iva to tell Lily the whole truth, and Iva confessed that she was Lily's mother, and Josh was her father. Overwhelmed by a sense of betrayal, Lily told Iva she hated her and never wanted to see her again, and she ran away from Oakdale.

Iva told John and Lucinda that she was raped by Rod/Josh when she was 13. Lucinda hired a detective to find Lily and then confronted Rod or Josh or whoever he was and fired him. Josh claimed he wanted to be a father to Lily, and Lucinda swore he'd never get near her daughter, and if she had anything to say about it, his next home would be jail!

Dusty thought Lily would listen to him because he never hid anything from her, unlike Holden, who had known for a long time that Iva was her mother. Holden told Dusty to go back to Harvard and leave Lily alone, but they both went off to find her. Lily was trying hard to fend for herself. A trucker found her asleep by the road and drove her to a diner, where she got a job and a room out back. She called Sierra, but when Lucinda tried to talk to her, Lily told her she was no longer her mother. A man overheard the conversation and realized Lily could be worth big bucks. Lily gave him her watch to buy his silence and took to the road again. A little while later, Holden heard two men talking about Lily's watch and demanded to know where she was. Lily was near the Badlands, taking shelter in a cave. A Native American named Keith found her and invited her to stay on his reservation. That's where Dusty found her, and Lily was thrilled to see him. But she refused to call home. Dusty called John and told him Lily was all right. Lily and Dusty hit the road together and made their way to Wyoming and a place called Grace's Brookside Cafe. It was there that Holden caught up with them. When Lily learned that Dusty had called John, she felt it was another betrayal. Defeated, Dusty left Lily and went home, where John's niece Pam tried to distract him from his woes.

Lily asked Holden if he had known the truth about Iva all along. Holden started to tell her but stopped himself when she said how angry she was at all the Snyders who'd kept the secret from her. Lily now thought Holden was the only person she could trust.

Lucinda feared Lily and Holden would do something crazy, like get married. Dusty became even more concerned when he found out that Holden had known the truth about Iva. Dusty called Lily, but Holden picked up the phone. The two started to have it out, and when Lily got on the line and Dusty heard her fragile, loving voice, he couldn't bring himself to tell her that Holden had been lying to her. Lily turned 18 in Wyoming, and Holden gave her a peridot ring. Holden's sole focus was on Lily, but when he heard that his mother had collapsed from exhaustion on the farm, he was very concerned. With Holden gone, Emma was having a much harder time maintaining the farm, and she feared foreclosure was near. When she suffered a heart attack after two close calls, Holden and Lily hurried back to Oakdale. As the Snyders waited for word about their mother, Lily maintained her distance. Lucinda believed Holden was encouraging Lily's lack of forgiveness toward her and warned him that if he ever wanted his old job back at Walsh, he'd better help heal things between Lily and her. In addition, she threatened to tell Lily that Holden had known the truth all along.

When Lily learned that Emma thought she might lose the farm, she decided to use part of her trust fund to pay off the debt. Despite her general anger, Lily always maintained her affection for Emma, calling her Grandma. Emma pleaded with Lily to listen to Iva's side of the story.

Aunt Elizabeth arrived to check on the ailing Emma, and Josh begged his mother to tell the Snyders what he'd endured as a child. Elizabeth finally let herself feel her son's agony and told the Snyders that Josh had been abused. Emma apologized, while Iva, Seth and the rest of the Snyders tried to accept this information.

At Emma's urging, Lily began to communicate with Iva, but she refused to do the same with Lucinda. Before Lily could reconcile with anyone, she was kidnapped by James, who was blackmailing Lucinda for the money he felt she owed him. After Josh saved her, Lily was forced to deal with her feelings for her father and her need for family. Little by little, Lily started trusting people again. Thinking she'd finally found some solid ground, she decided she wanted to marry Holden. Holden was thrilled. Even with the secrets he was holding back, Holden felt their love could survive anything. Lucinda had other ideas, though, and when Lily announced her plans, Lucinda told her Holden had known about her parentage all along, which meant he'd been lying to her.

With Lily's trust in Holden destroyed, she ran to Dusty, and they made love. For Lily, it was the first time; for Dusty, it was a dream come true to have her back. Lily moved in with Dusty. Holden was devastated and vowed to get revenge on Lucinda.

Lyla Montgomery and young Casey Peretti were having their struggles with romance as well. After John's tirade over their age difference, Lyla became concerned about how people would view her romance with Casey, and when Casey offered to move out, she agreed. Lyla couldn't tolerate the separation, so she decided to defy public opinion and asked him to return. Their bliss was challenged by Casey's old flame, Taylor Baldwin, who had joined the Memorial staff. Taylor's arrival stirred Lyla's insecurities, and Casey feared that if Taylor learned about his romance with Lyla, she'd try to come between them. Once again, Lyla had to keep her romance under wraps. Taylor managed to find out about it anyway and was undeterred in her quest—Taylor always got what she wanted. Casey confronted her about the way she'd been ingratiating herself into his life. The showdown led to a kiss, and Taylor took great pleasure in telling Lyla about Casey's passionate slip. Lyla told Casey it was either she or Taylor. Knowing that he'd be crazy to lose her, Casey took Lyla into the hospital linen closet and proposed. Because of their age difference, and because she was not interested in having more children, Lyla was hesitant. Casey responded by telling her over and over how much he wanted to marry her, but Lyla was still uncertain. Casey was relentless, and Lyla was just about to give in when she learned that he'd proposed to Taylor when they were involved. Although she was very torn, Lyla told him no. Casey moved first out of the bedroom, then out of the house.

Lisa had persuaded Lyla to sing at the Mona Lisa. On her opening night, Casey brought her a single rose, and Lyla was touched. Heather's former manager, Otis, was at the opening, and he offered Lyla a gig in New York and a possible recording contract. Although Margo and Casey thought Lyla was running away from a marriage she truly wanted, Lyla accepted Otis's offer. Hurt and alone, Casey made Taylor dinner one night, had too much to drink and dozed off. When Casey woke up and realized how much he had drunk and who he was with, he freaked out. Realizing what he'd almost lost, Casey flew to New York to be at Lyla's opening. Lyla was thrilled to see him and sang her newest song, "From Now On," to him. After Lyla's singing engagement, she and Casey toured New York, and she realized she couldn't live without him. To Casey's great delight, Lyla accepted his umpteenth marriage proposal.

Love was in the air for another Oakdale couple, although it took some doing. Shannon had left Brian because she believed he loved Beatrice, and she urged Beatrice to tell Brian how she felt. Brian was flattered, but he'd been an emotional wreck since Shannon walked out on their wedding, and he wasn't ready for anything new. Depressed, Beatrice left for Edinburgh, and Shannon persuaded Brian to follow. When Beatrice had her tea leaves read and learned that Brian would find happiness with an Irish lass, she presumed the lass was Shannon. But Brian found her and insisted her interpretation was wrong. Beatrice was flabbergasted when Brian proposed, but she said yes. To Brian's surprise, Duncan disapproved. When Brian tried to persuade him to give his blessing, Duncan confessed he was overprotective because Beatrice wasn't his sister—she was his daughter. Beatrice was the product of his teenage romance with Mary Callaghan. Duncan's parents adopted the baby when she was born. So the tea leaves were right—Beatrice was the Irish lass Brian was destined to marry. But when Duncan demanded that Brian keep this secret from Beatrice, Brian called off the wedding. Beatrice demanded an explanation. Duncan finally confessed and told Beatrice that Brian had refused to marry her until Duncan admitted he was really her father. Stunned, Beatrice digested the news and told Duncan she loved him more than ever. Brian and Beatrice decided to move to Scotland, and on their way they paid a visit to Beatrice's mother, Mary Callaghan.

Lucinda suggested to Kim that she host a talk show on her TV station. What she was trying to do was put John in a position to gain custody of Andy, because Kim would be working. Unaware of Lucinda's motives, Kim agreed. Kim named her new talk show "Patterns." Lucinda wanted a glamorous topic for the show's premiere, but Kim elected to do her first show on teenage depression and suicide. "A Teenage Hotline" would be flashed on the screen. The topic hit closer to home than Kim anticipated when Andy's girlfriend, Kathy Evans, called in after overdosing on pills and booze.

Andy had been having a very rough time when he met Kathy. Sabrina's arrival had stirred a lot of confusion in him about the kind of people his parents really were. When Kim and John fought over what John knew about Sabrina's birth, Andy felt torn between his parents. Kim and Bob were out of the house a lot, focusing on their work, and with John moving into Lucinda's mansion, Andy's inability to communicate with his family increased. On top of this, Andy's best friend, Paul, had gotten him involved in Paul's plan to reunite with his criminal father, James. Lying wasn't easy for Andy, and with the flurry of changes he'd had to endure recently, he was desperately struggling to gain some sort of control over his life. He began spending a lot of time with Kathy, whose overly strict and negligent parents had caused her to turn to drink. One night Kathy offered Andy champagne, and he accepted.

When Kim and John learned Andy had covered for Paul when Paul lied to the police, they grounded him. Andy couldn't take Kathy to the prom, and he was very upset. He snuck out of the house to visit her, and they shared a drink. Andy was staying with John at the time, and when he got home he expected some sort of punishment, but none came. John was trying to keep his son on his good side for the time when he would ask for full custody. Soon after, Kathy learned that her parents were sending her to boarding school, and she freaked out. Andy tried to calm her down to no avail, and Kathy drank heavily. On the night of the "Patterns" premiere, Kathy overdosed but managed to call the hotline. Kathy was taken to the ER, where Casey was instrumental in saving her life. When Andy told John he couldn't talk to Kim about Kathy's problems because she was so busy with her new career, John started seriously contemplating a custody fight.

John's arch-enemy, James Stenbeck, was on the loose in Oakdale. Working for Lucinda, the nefarious James had many schemes up his sleeve. Beatrice found a letter indicating that Suzanne Dupres was involved with James during the time he was calling himself

Lester Keyes. She told Duncan, who flew to Edinburgh to investigate further. While he was gone, Beatrice found James going through Duncan's things, and James admitted he knew Suzanne. James was planning the takeover of Walsh Enterprises. Ambrose tried to warn Lucinda about James, but her hormones overrode her business sense.

Shannon and her pal Harriet followed Duncan to Edinburgh. When they caught up with him at the McKechnie home, Shannon overheard Duncan tell his loyal housekeeper he was out to prove James killed Suzanne. James called his henchmen in Scotland to stop Duncan from returning to Oakdale with any evidence linking James to Suzanne's death. Soon, Duncan's house went up in flames, and Duncan returned to Oakdale empty-handed, his proof turned to ashes.

Barbara was touched by Hal's sensitive handling of Paul during the investigation into Stenbeck's disappearance. Hal tried to convince Paul that Barbara was a wonderful mother and wanted only to protect him. A grateful Barbara accepted Hal's invitation to take them to a hockey game, and the elegant designer even agreed to share a beer from Hal's six-pack.

One day, Duncan received a phone call from McNeil. Now that Stenbeck had fled with McNeil's money, he, too, was out to get James. Duncan went to Cape Cod to meet with McNeil. Shortly thereafter, McNeil's body washed ashore. Shannon was positive Duncan was innocent, but Earl was not so sure. Duncan insisted he never even saw McNeil, and ballistics tests showed McNeil could not have died by Duncan's gun. However, suspicions of Duncan's being the Falcon persisted, especially after the shack on the island where James allegedly worked for Hensley Taggart burned to the ground. Earl and Hal warned Shannon to stay away, but Shannon continued her pursuit, even though Duncan told her to leave him alone. Duncan felt he had to protect her from the danger that seemed to follow him everywhere, and Shannon began to think that perhaps he did have too many secrets.

Before Brian left for Scotland to marry Beatrice, he named Earl editor of the *Argus*, and Earl, together with Lisa, vowed to uncover the identity of the Falcon. But it was Shannon who discovered new evidence when she accidentally knocked over a lamp and found letters to Emily from James and a secret cache of jewels. Among the treasures was an emerald necklace. Earl suspected Duncan had seen this necklace before, and indeed, he

had once given it to his fiancée, Suzanne Dupres, who later died. The police were intrigued by Duncan's knowledge of the gems. They didn't know, as Shannon did, that Duncan had a pirate's trunk full of jewels. Earl made note that the love letters James wrote to Emily were from all the places where Duncan had major distributors for his import/export business. Feeling the heat, Duncan had his man Pierson relocate their operations. When Duncan's falcon, Angus, escaped from his pen, Duncan panicked. Fearing the curse would once again fall on the McKechnie Castle, he ordered his ships back to safe harbor. But no catastrophe occurred; instead, he received a package of rubies worth a fortune.

The Oakdale police thought a post-office box was the clue to James Stenbeck's whereabouts, but all they found in the box were a list of Paul's friends and a map of McKechnie's castle. Margo and Hal were sure Paul knew where his father was. Paul gave the post-office box key to Andy to hide, and when the police questioned him, Andy covered for his friend. John overheard Paul warning James's Oakdale contact that the police planned to put a wiretap on Barbara's phone. John told Margo about the conversation. Paul's increasingly suspicious role in the case heightened the tension between Margo and Barbara. Frustrated by Margo's late-night phone calls to Hal just as she and Hal were getting closer, Barbara confronted her. Margo said that if Barbara ever hurt Hal, she'd have to answer to her. Barbara retaliated by insinuating that the reason Tom had stayed so long in D.C. was because he was having an affair.

Duncan's falcon, Angus, returned to the castle with a broken neck, and Duncan sadly buried him. Meanwhile, Shannon came across a map of the island hidden in Duncan's pillow. The map detailed strange markings in the cemetery. Shannon dug up Angus's casket but found nothing. After she left, someone else dug up the same area and discovered Duncan's latest shipment of jewels. Duncan was convinced Earl was the culprit. Then Lisa heard Earl tell someone on the phone his plans to accompany Duncan had changed because Duncan was gone, and Shannon was nowhere to be found. Trying to throw her off the track, Earl presented Lisa with a double strand of perfect pearls as a present to mark their six months together.

Barbara was upset when she learned Margo had assigned a plainclothes policeman to follow Paul. Considering that her son was hiding important information, Margo found Barbara's attitude appalling and suggested Barbara hadn't done a very good job convincing

Paul of just how evil his father was. An insulted Barbara told Margo that since she was not a mother herself she had no right to give parental advice. Margo, who had suffered two miscarriages, one of them after trying to save Barbara at the castle, was incensed by the cruel remark. She told Barbara that if she ever made another crack like that again, she'd tear her apart. The confrontation between Margo and Barbara pushed Margo further into the emotional deep end. Still angry at Tom, and with her feelings for Hal escalating, Margo plotted to undermine Barbara. When she learned that Italian businessman Franco Visconti had invited Barbara to his hotel suite for a meeting, Margo tried to prove that Barbara was having an affair. An embarrassed Margo later confessed to Hal what she had done, but she still accused Barbara of being a liar and of using men. Sensing her pain, Hal took her in his arms, and the physical contact stirred confusion in them both. Hal reminded Margo that she was a married woman and the sexual tension was happening only because she was vulnerable. Barbara guessed that Margo had squealed about her visit to Franco's suite, and she assured Hal she would never jeopardize their relationship for a fling. When Margo learned that Tom was expected home any day, she told Hal she planned to tell him Hal was the man she wanted. Touched by Margo's feelings toward him, especially since he felt the same way about her, Hal replied that it would be foolish to do anything that could destroy her marriage. When Tom did not show up in Oakdale as planned, for Margo it was the straw that broke the camel's back.

Looking for a way to communicate with his father, Paul got Andy to let James contact him at the Hughes home. Andy was upset with Paul for involving him and couldn't understand why Paul would leave his family and friends for James. But under questioning, Andy lied again to protect his friend, saying he had no knowledge of Paul's contact with his father. Desperate to get Paul to stop protecting James, Barbara told him about her past with his father and how James had tried to kill her and commit her to a mental institution. Paul feigned distress

to fool his mother, but told Andy he didn't believe a word she said. He was convinced Barbara was trying to trick him into abandoning his father. The next time Paul spoke to James's contact, he told him he couldn't last in Oakdale much longer.

As Margo became more convinced that her marriage was over, Hal became more confused, and Barbara

## *Husbands and Lovers*

*Once upon a time, Barbara was engaged to Tom, and after he married Margo, Barbara led him to believe they'd slept together, even though they hadn't. But Margo had slept with Barbara's husband-to-be, Hal, while they were in Greece searching for her brother. It wasn't the first time Margo had had a husband of Barbara's; when Barbara was married to James, Margo was his mistress on the side.*

took note of how distracted he always was around Margo. Margo was stunned when Tom sent her a diamond watch for their anniversary, yet she still met with Ambrose to discuss divorce proceedings. Hal urged Margo to go to D.C. and talk things through with Tom. Margo agreed, but she told Barbara that if it was over with Tom, she'd be going after Hal with all she had.

Shannon put herself in a precarious position when she hid out in Duncan's speedboat. Now in the Florida Keys, stowaway Shannon was surprised to learn Duncan knew she was there all along. When a furious Shannon tried to slap him, Duncan stopped her with a kiss. Not wanting Shannon to get too close to his operations, Duncan shipped her home. The police found Duncan's visit to the Florida Keys quite suspicious, since James had first resurfaced in that part of the world under the name of Lester Keyes. Things looked worse for Duncan when Officer Nick Castello discovered a body in the castle. The corpse belonged to the caretaker, George. Duncan hired Simon and Geraldine Cutler to be his new caretaker and housekeeper, unaware that they were working for James. Back at the castle Shannon discovered a ruckel in a box emblazoned with the figure of a falcon. Before she could decide whether to turn it over to the police, she received a call from a strange man, instructing her to leave the box in an airport locker or Duncan would die. Shannon delivered the box to the police anyway, and they questioned Duncan. While Shannon was at the station, a Doris Pierpont arrived, rendering Duncan speechless. Doris was one of the wealthy women with whom Duncan had had an affair, but he thought she was dead. Doris explained James knew she was hiding something and wanted her eliminated, so she faked her death. She told Duncan she remembered seeing Hensley and Stenbeck in Edinburgh with a small collection of leather boxes just like the one Shannon discovered at the castle. With this flurry of evidence, Earl was becoming even more obsessed with the Falcon case. His focus greatly concerned Lisa, while Lisa's pearls greatly concerned Doris and Shannon. Duncan confided in Doris that the pearls once belonged to Suzanne Dupres.

M̲argo's time in D.C. did little to convince her that her marriage could survive. Then she learned that Craig's plane had gone down in Greece. When Margo decided to look for him, Hal went with her, leaving Barbara abandoned and alone. In Greece, Margo and Hal grew closer. One afternoon on the beach, Margo told Hal that when Craig reformed, it was as if she had gotten her brother back. How could he leave her now? Hal comforted Margo. The solace turned into a kiss, and they gave in to their passion and made love. When they returned to Oakdale after failing to find Craig, Margo and Hal were shocked to learn that Tom had returned to rebuild his marriage. But Tom wasn't wearing blinders, and Barbara had taken pains to let him know just how close Hal and Margo had become. Soon after, Margo moved out of the cottage.

Emily returned to Oakdale and told the police James had forced her to take part in kidnapping a coin dealer named Jarvis, who had one of the ruckels. Emily wasn't the only one who'd returned—James was lurking in the shadows, emerging only to see Paul. On Paul's birthday, he received a sports car from his mother, but her efforts to win him over were thwarted when James gave his son a key to a locker at the Yacht Club. When Paul opened the locker he found cash—a lot of it. Paul idolized his father, and as the day when he would join him for good grew nearer, he became more evasive with Andy. Meanwhile, Emily was receiving threats instead of gifts from her former lover. James swore he'd frame her for the murder of Nigel Cromwell if she told anyone he was back in town. Cromwell was the captain of a ship in the Florida Keys, and he had been stabbed with Emily's nail file.

J̲ames surprised Lucinda in the ladies' room of her television station and told her that if she called the police or told anyone she'd seen him, she'd never see Craig alive again. If Lucinda gave him the $255,000 she owed him for the salary, commissions and stock dividends he didn't get when she ousted him from Walsh, his men would release Craig.

Emily visited Paul before he left for summer camp and tried to warn him to stay away from James. Again, Paul pretended to believe his father was evil, and he wanted nothing to do with him. When Barbara said goodbye to her son, she noticed an extra key on his ring. Gloating, Paul told her it was for his locker at the Yacht Club. He neglected to tell her about the money. Barbara was relieved when Paul called to say he'd arrived safely at camp, but in reality he never went—Paul was at the Stewart cabin with James.

Duncan asked Barbara for her help in tracking down Stenbeck, but Barbara told him she'd prefer to handle the situation on her own. When Meg overheard Barbara tell Duncan that if she found James she'd shoot him on sight, she reported what she'd heard to Margo and Tom. Then Doris Pierpont informed Duncan that she'd figured out who James's Oakdale contact was but that she didn't want to go to the police. They arranged to meet and discuss the matter, but Doris never showed up. When Duncan returned to the castle, he was horrified to find Doris's lifeless body on his bed.

James ordered Lucinda to make the first of four payments to a bus station locker, and Lucinda followed through without telling a soul. John was aware that his wife was keeping something from him and tried to trap her in a lie. Soon after, James appeared at Barbara's apartment and gleefully explained to his ex-wife that Paul had been a willing accomplice and was now with him. James allowed Paul to call Andy. With Tom standing nearby, Andy was unnerved. He told Paul that he was making a big mistake. When Tom pressed Andy for information, Andy claimed he knew nothing. Having Paul didn't stop James from continuing his sexual exploits as he maneuvered his way into the beds of influential Corinne Lawrence and her debutante daughter, Monica. Continuing his blackmail of Emily, he lured her to the cabin and persuaded her to pretend they were still lovers so that Paul wouldn't doubt him. Regardless of everything she knew, like Margo, Barbara and numerous other women before her, Emily let James seduce her yet again. Despite this charade, Paul caught on that his father was manipulating both Corinne and Monica and became wary of his father. James allowed Paul to call his mother, but Barbara didn't learn much. She was, however, able to ascertain that Paul was in the Oakdale area.

With Craig's disappearance, a vulnerable Sierra was left responsible for the financially strapped Montgomery & Associates. She opted not to sell the company to Lucinda, thinking it would be better off in the hands of a third party. She was very receptive to a Marvin Jurrow, who offered to buy the company and then sell it back should Craig reappear. Sierra signed the contracts and arranged a meeting with the executive in charge of managing the company for Jurrow. Imagine her surprise when she discovered he was Tonio. After gloating a bit, Tonio went to his first company meeting—under the docks. It was there that Tonio was shocked to find that his new business partner was none other than James Stenbeck! James thanked Tonio for making his plan work like a charm.

James continued to call Lucinda, and Lucinda continued to pretend it wasn't he. One day she slipped and called him by his first name, and John and Ambrose grew suspicious. James told Lucinda he wanted to move into Steve and Betsy's dream house, which Lucinda had acquired when she called in Steve's loan. First Lucinda wanted proof that Craig was safe, and James promised to arrange a time when Craig could call Sierra. Sierra soon received a phone call from someone who might have been Craig, but there was static on the line. Stenbeck continued to make the fake phone calls; Sierra even received a flower arrangement exactly like the one she had received from Craig the day he disappeared.

Meanwhile, Shannon didn't trust Duncan's supposed ally, Charles Pierson, and her instincts were right—Charles was working for James and had been stealing inventory sheets and other items that could be used to frame Duncan. Charles congratulated James on

the Scottish accent he had used when he told the Greek police Duncan was the Falcon. Shannon realized the date in question, March 22, was Beatrice and Brian's wedding day. Duncan was relieved to have an alibi. Emily was warned by James that the police might be asking her about March 22, so she swore she and James were in Toronto on that date, although Betsy remembered Emily telling her they were in Greece.

Because of their mutual involvement in the Falcon case, Tom and Margo were forced to work together. Margo accused Tom of using the case as an excuse to see her, and Tom saw that she was truly in love with Hal. A hurt Tom confessed he almost had an affair in D.C., but he never went through with it.

Shannon O'Hara was a thorn in James Stenbeck's side. She quickly became wary of Duncan's new housekeeping couple and got Earl to investigate. Stenbeck told Charles it was time to use Shannon to teach Duncan a lesson. Charles told Duncan that Shannon's room had been ransacked. A panicked Duncan returned to the castle and saw what he thought was Shannon's body floating in the moat. Duncan was about to dive in when he heard her voice behind him. Although he was enraged by the trick, Duncan was relived that she was alive. The realization led him to give in to the passion he'd long carried for her, and they made love—but someone was watching.

Duncan told Shannon he was a descendant of pirates, and the cherished maps were found hidden in the castle walls. He was receiving shipments of jewels that his ancestors had buried long ago. Duncan had developed a secret method of transporting the jewels that was working smoothly until Stenbeck took advantage of his network and started using it for his drug smuggling. Duncan was unable to prove ownership of the jewels. Appalled to hear the steps he'd taken to avoid taxes, Shannon left.

Tom and Earl were becoming increasingly suspicious that someone on the police force was in contact with James. While Roy knew the castle inside out, Tom had his eye on Hal. However, the mole was rookie cop Nick Castello. When Nick delivered Lucinda's latest cache of blackmail money to James, Stenbeck told him he wanted him to plant a ruckel and the matching leather box on Duncan. Then the police got a tip and headed to the castle with a search warrant. It was Nick, of course, who found the leather box and the ruckel in Duncan's bedchamber, and Duncan was arrested. But

## Dueling Divas

*Emily had an affair with Barbara's now ex-husband, James, then seduced her son. Lucinda stole Barbara's business and blackmailed her with the knowledge of her husband's illegitimate child. Although Barbara was the only one he married, all three had liaisons with James, and all three were suspects when Stenbeck perished, yet again, in a fire in Ruxton Hills.*

but when he got to the cabin, it was deserted. Alone in the cabin, Nick heard Hal's voice over a bullhorn ordering whoever was inside to come out and surrender. Cornered, Nick tried to bluff his way out, claiming that he'd beaten his fellow officers there after he heard the call over the police radio. Nick's ability to skirt the truth lasted only momentarily until Tom caught him in a lie. When Tom confronted Paul and told him he knew Nick was James's contact, Paul's shocked expression told him he was right.

James was waiting for Meg under the sheets. He told her that Tonio was working for him and if she said a word about this visit, he would tell Tonio she had seduced him. When Tonio came home and found that someone had been wearing his robe, he accused Meg of adultery. Later, Meg overheard her husband arrange a meeting with Stenbeck at the docks.

Meanwhile, a frustrated Duncan broke out of jail. He tried to persuade Barbara to join forces, but she was too afraid for Paul. When he went to Shannon, she urged him to turn himself in. At the same time, a naive Nick, not fully aware of how much suspicion he was under, asked for a leave of absence to attend to "a family emergency." This triggered

Nick's prized discovery sparked suspicion in Tom, and he decided to check out his file.

With Duncan in jail, Shannon confronted Emily and Barbara. Shannon warned Barbara that she could go to jail if she were helping James in any way. She then went to Margo and Hal and told them she knew Stenbeck was in town and suggested they do something about it. Barbara and Emily confessed to each other what they knew about James. They learned the police were on the way to the Stewart cabin, and, fearing for Paul, they decided to warn James. Nick also went to warn James,

Margo to do some snooping at Nick's apartment. Tom went after her. Margo could tell by his new stereo, clothes and other items that Nick had had a recent rush of money. Then Nick arrived and got Margo's gun. Proud of his allegiance to Stenbeck, Nick admitted to working for him ever since he had entered the police academy. Then he announced he planned to get rid of Margo the same way he got rid of Doris and George. Nick believed if he dispensed with Margo, he'd be free, but Paul called and warned him Tom now knew he was James's contact. Nick escaped just before Tom arrived.

Margo was grateful to Tom for saving her life; however, it was Hal whom she embraced when he arrived on the scene.

Duncan was still at Shannon's when she learned from Lisa that the police were on their way to get him. Duncan fled and ran into Nick at the docks. Duncan overpowered him, taking back Margo's gun, but Nick escaped again. When Hal and Margo arrived, they found a blazer button. At home, Meg noticed Tonio's blazer was missing a button.

It was Lyla's nightclub opening in New York, and Margo and Tom had come there, albeit separately. On the way home, they found themselves sitting together on the plane. With a little help from the awful airline food, which was not unlike Margo's cooking, Tom made his estranged wife laugh for the first time in months. Tom reminded Margo they'd been through a lot together, and their history was much longer than the three months she'd spent with Hal. When Lyla and Casey asked them to be matron of honor and best man at their wedding, the couple realized just how inseparable their paths were.

Emily was having nightmares about James. In the latest one, James was threatening to kidnap Dani if Emily didn't help kidnap Paul. In the dream, Emily shot James to protect Paul. She soon learned that she had another reason to be concerned: She was pregnant with James Stenbeck's child. Emily was not the only one contemplating murdering James. Barbara admitted to Kim and Bob that she would gladly kill James to keep him away from Paul. However, Barbara need not have worried so much about her son; he was finally doing everything he could to avoid his father. This greatly frustrated James, who was hiding out with Nick at Monica Lawrence's mansion and playing all his cards to get his son back. Paul overheard Emily and Barbara talking about James's intention to steal him away, and he saw Barbara load her gun. Afraid of what she would do, Paul waited for her to leave and removed the bullets. The police continued to track down James and, as Shannon suspected, they discovered Duncan's servants were working for Stenbeck and had a history of poisoning their bosses. Duncan and Shannon were soon confronted with a poisonous snake the servants had left behind. Duncan killed it just in time.

James felt the wagons circling around him. Tonio refused to help him get Paul. Lucinda wouldn't assist him in luring Paul to her ridge, where James could kidnap him. Obsessed with his need for his son, James knew he needed to do something drastic, so he got Nick to kidnap Lily. With Lily in his grasp, James called Lucinda and told her to cooperate or she'd never see Lily again. Trapped and knowing she couldn't confide in John or the police, Lucinda turned to Ambrose. However, Margo was putting the pieces together, and when she confronted her new mother-in-law, Lucinda tried hard to hide her obvious distress.

Josh overheard Hal and Margo confer about why James might have kidnapped Lily, and Josh left to find his daughter. Meanwhile, a handcuffed Lily freed herself and clobbered Nick over the head. She almost escaped, but unfortunately James appeared and stopped her. When James left, Nick started to come on to his young hostage. A clever Lily seduced him into taking off her handcuffs. At that moment, Josh appeared and jumped Nick from behind. Josh and Lily escaped, but not before Josh was shot by Nick. Lily ran home and told the police everything, and happily Josh survived.

James suffered another setback when Corinne Lawrence found him in her daughter Monica's bed. Corinne told James if he set one foot on her estate again, she'd shoot him. As for Tonio, he didn't budge when the police asked him to explain his missing blazer button, and he insisted he had no part in the Falcon case. Angry at Stenbeck for trying to involve him, Tonio went to Lucinda and threatened that if she revealed Stenbeck's hiding place, he'd kill him for her. Stenbeck was secluded in Steve's empty Ruxton Hills estate. He called Emily at Fashions Ltd., where she was working, and arranged for her to meet him there. Emily took the gun that Barbara kept in her office and left. Innocently playing into James's hands, John suggested to Andy and Paul that they go riding to let off some steam. When Lucinda heard this, she panicked. She told John that if Paul rode his horse up to the ridge, James would kidnap him. Lucinda confessed the blackmail scheme to John, who immediately chased after the boys. Just as Stenbeck arrived and was reaching for Paul, John came to the rescue. John succeeded in knocking the gun out of his old enemy's hand, but James knocked him out and was just about to crush his skull with a rock when, to save Andy's dad, Paul called out, "I'll go with you anywhere!" By the time the police arrived, James and Paul were long gone.

John was furious with his wife for keeping him in the dark, and he refused to sleep in their bed. Lucinda decided it was time to call Tonio and take him up on his offer to kill James. Holden overheard the conversation and decided to do some investigating himself. At this point, the police were looking for Emily, and Barbara hid the fact that her gun was missing and that Emily had left a note saying where she had gone. Meanwhile at Ruxton Hills, the lights went out, and James told Nick to get the generator going. Finally alone with him, Emily tried to persuade James to let Paul go by telling him she was pregnant with his child. Even if he didn't have Paul, he'd have an heir. James was elated by the news but thought Paul should decide for himself.

Lucinda had given Tonio directions to the Ruxton Hills house, and Meg, suspicious of her husband, followed with a gun. After reading Emily's note, Barbara decided to head there too. Since she was being watched by the police for her own protection, Barbara was forced to sneak out her bedroom window. At the same time, James called Monica to come to the house and signal him by blowing her horn three times. Corinne overheard and trailed Monica. Emily tricked James into allowing her a moment alone with Paul. Then she gave him her car keys and told him to go out to the car. When James returned and found his son gone, Emily pulled the gun on him—but it was empty. Outside a horn blew three times, while downstairs Nick was struggling with the generator. Smoking to alleviate his tension, Nick was unaware that gasoline was leaking onto the floor. Nick tossed his cigarette butt on the ground just as he heard gunshots and a blood-curdling scream that sounded like James. Upstairs, Barbara watched in horror as Lucinda, gun in hand, stood over Stenbeck's body. Then James grabbed Lucinda's ankle. She broke free and ran screaming from the house. Nick was unable to get out of the basement in time. Seconds later, the generator exploded, and Steve's dream house went up in flames. When the police arrived, Hal was worried that Barbara was still inside the house, but there was too much smoke to go in to save anyone. Then a disoriented Barbara emerged, limply holding a gun in her hand. Once the fire died down, the police sorted through the rubble and found what appeared to be James Stenbeck's corpse. However, they found only one body, and Paul and Emily knew that Nick had been inside, too.

There were cover-ups galore. Still bickering over each other's involvement with James, Meg and Tonio tried to get their stories straight before the police called them in for questioning. Meg, however, admitted to Iva that she was afraid Tonio might have killed James. Barbara told Paul to talk to her before he said anything to the cops, and she instructed him not to tell Hal how the gun got to Ruxton Hills. Corinne told Monica they had to destroy all evidence that connected them to James.

Margo, Hal and the rest of the force had their hands full trying to unearth the truth. John admitted to Margo that he had gone to the house to kill James but had changed his mind. He said that as he drove up to the house, another car whizzed by him, and he couldn't see the driver. It was Margo's hunch that Tonio killed James before Lucinda found the body. Andy sensed Paul wasn't telling him everything about the night of the shooting, and Tom overheard Andy pressure his friend for more information. As for Barbara, she would have loved to give more details to the police, but the trauma of the whole event left her straining to remember anything at all, including how the gun, which she did not bring to the house, ended up in her hand. But forensics discovered the corpse was shot twice in the back with the gun Barbara was holding, and ballistics determined that the gun was the one Barbara kept in her night-table drawer, not the one Emily took from the office. In addition, dental charts seemed to prove it was James who died in the house that night. Desperate to remember something so that she could defend herself, Barbara sought help from Memorial's Lynn Michaels, and they worked together to break though Barbara's mental block, but time was running out. Even though Stenbeck was hated by many, Tom was feeling pressured to make an arrest in the murder. Barbara was not the only prime suspect. When Holden told Tonio he had seen him at Ruxton Hills that night, Tonio suspected Barbara might have seen him, too. He was relieved to learn about Barbara's memory block. Things looked especially bad for Tonio when Charles Pierson's address book was found. It listed many of Stenbeck's contacts in Greece and elsewhere, such as the detective who was in charge of the mock search for Craig—Tonio Reyes. Margo, thinking Tonio might have been withholding information, not just about James, but about Craig as well, gave him the third degree. Even though Tonio insisted he was not in contact with James, Margo vowed to nail him.

Monica Lawrence was unable to hide her connection to James after Shannon spotted her wearing a brooch that had belonged to Duncan's ancestor Margaret. Monica publicly stated that James gave her the brooch as a sign of his affection. She also confessed that she wrested her mother's gun away from her in front of the Ruxton Hills house but that neither of them ever went inside.

The plot thickened…

The year did not start off well for Barbara Ryan, who was on trial for the murder of James Stenbeck. With the help of psychiatrist Lynn Michaels, Barbara tried to piece together what happened the night James was killed. The police knew she would do anything to protect her son, and Barbara's attorney, Jessica Griffin, thought Paul knew more than he was letting on. She wanted to put him on the stand during the court hearing. When she did, Paul said he took an empty gun to the house, and when he came back to get it, he saw John Dixon. Tom doubted the credibility of Paul's testimony, and Paul later admitted to his mother that he'd perjured himself. Meanwhile, Emily told Holden she hadn't been waiting for Paul in the car on the night of the murder; she had instead walked around the house and had run into Monica and Corinne. Then she saw Duncan with a bloody arm, and they made a pact not to tell anyone what and whom they had seen.

Barbara had an unlikely ally in Lucinda, who believed her former son-in-law Tonio Reyes was the man the police really wanted. Lucinda begged Holden to tell the police whether he saw Tonio at the murder scene. Holden admitted to the police that he saw Tonio at the house the night of the murder. Margo told John that if Barbara were cleared, Lucinda would become the prime suspect. Barbara had another ally in Lisa, who went so far as to spend the night in Lucinda's closet to try to find out how she was involved. But time had run out. Jury selection was complete, and testimony began in the case of *the State of Illinois v. Barbara Ryan*.

Meanwhile, down in Martinique, Corinne Lawrence met up with James's flunky, Nick Castello. Later, Corinne was found dead of a drug overdose. Before she died, she gave two names to her daughter: Nick and Tonio. Then Monica remembered she had failed to tell the police she saw Tonio at Ruxton Hills on the night of the shooting. Tonio admitted being in the house but denied killing James, and forensics showed that his gun had never been fired. Tonio claimed he saw Barbara leave the house after he heard the gunshots. Barbara berated her ex-lover for lying on the witness stand. With the evidence stacked against her, the jury handed down the verdict: guilty of murder in the second degree. Barbara received a ten-year sentence.

Seeing the tremendous pressure Tom was under while prosecuting the Stenbeck case, Margo told Hal that they should release each other from their commitment until they decided what they wanted. Margo canceled her plans to divorce Tom, and eventually she was able to assure him that her relationship with Hal was purely professional.

Barbara's family rallied around her. Hal was at her side, and even longtime rival Margo assured her she'd always believed in her innocence. Paul sadly admitted to Andy that he'd lied on the stand to protect his mother, but the lie had backfired. Facing the reality of prison, Barbara decided to take Lucinda up on her offer to buy Simply Barbara and put the proceeds in a trust fund for Paul. Then she signed a custody agreement naming Bob and Kim as guardians for her son.

Meg was getting calls from Nick Castello. Nick told Meg he saw Tonio shoot James, and he wanted money to keep his silence. Even though the case was closed, the calls made Meg and Tonio nervous. Meg wanted to let the police know where Nick was, but Tonio stopped her. He was quite satisfied to let Barbara sit out her prison term.

Margo believed that Paul had killed James, but Barbara flatly refused to even entertain the notion. Before she went to prison, Hal professed his love, but Barbara told him not to wait. Behind bars, Barbara ran into an old employee of hers, Denise Darcy, who was doing time for the murder of Tad Channing. Denise offered to show Barbara the ropes and warned her that because she was wealthy and beautiful, the other prisoners might not take a liking to her. Denise started to ask Barbara for protection money. Unbeknownst to Barbara, the request was a scam, and if Barbara stopped paying, she was as good as dead.

One day Hal received a package from Martinique. It contained Corinne's robe. In the pocket he found a note implicating both Emily and Tonio in James's murder. Hal hoped this new information would help Jessica reopen the case. He was sure the numbers in Corinne's note, 2-2-9-8-8, stood for February 29, 1988. On that date Emily was in Edinburgh to meet with Stenbeck's Scottish lawyer to discuss her inheritance, which was half of the Stenbeck estate. Was it a coincidence that soon all the suspects in the Stenbeck murder were in Edinburgh, except for Emily, who had returned to Oakdale? Lucinda, John, Meg, Tonio and Duncan, whose hometown was Edinburgh, converged on the city. Hal was there also, and he kept a watchful eye on all of them. Back in Oakdale, while searching through her daughter's things, Susan found a note from Nick threatening to tell the cops he saw Emily shoot James.

Hal visited the house Stenbeck lived in while pretending to be Lester Keyes, and he found a hollowed-out copy of *Treasure Island* with a note inside. Just as he was about to read it, someone fired a gun at him. Lucinda returned to her hotel from a mysterious late-night errand only to find her husband missing. Meg was wondering where Tonio was. She found a note in his briefcase identical to the one Susan found at Emily's, threatening to tell the cops that Castello had seen Tonio shoot James. When Tonio returned, he assured his wife that Nick wouldn't be telling Hal anything. Little did Tonio know that Hal had escaped injury. Hal later learned that the bullet that was fired at him came from Nick Castello's gun.

Following up on a lead about Nick, Hal found himself on the doorstep of Mrs. Fiona McBurny, who said that her husband had disappeared. Mrs. McBurny gave Hal the number of the warehouse where her husband stored his files. Hal was followed by someone hired by Duncan, who was worried that the files in the warehouse might link him to Nick Castello. In the warehouse Hal learned that Castello had murdered McBurny. When he got home, Hal told Barbara that he almost had the proof to clear her. Hal's theory was that James only pretended to be shot when Lucinda found him. He thought James murdered Nick and planned to use his body as a substitute for his own. It was James, not Nick, who was writing the notes and making the calls. Hal ordered an exhumation of the body. He was convinced that McBurny, a dentist, was hired by James to duplicate his own dental work in Castello's mouth. Sure enough, when Monica Lawrence returned from Scotland, she told Hal she'd seen Stenbeck alive. Barbara was a free woman.

Barbara soon learned that freedom had its price. Lucinda refused to sell Simply Barbara back to her for at least a year, and Barbara refused Lucinda's offer to work for her. Barbara decided it was time to settle a few scores, especially with Tonio and Emily, who she was sure had put her away. Barbara accepted Hal's marriage proposal, but Paul was indifferent. Barbara and Hal were married in an elegant ceremony at the Lakewood Towers.

Barbara planned revenge on Lucinda. She decided to start a new company, Barbara Ryan Originals—BRO for short—and began a search for investors. Lucinda was appalled to learn that Lily withdrew $100,000 from her trust fund to invest in her mother's arch-enemy's new company. Holden also happily invested in BRO.

Shortly thereafter, Emily, Paul and Barbara started to get phone calls from James. Hal promised to protect his wife and stepson, and Tonio vowed to protect Emily, who was now his mistress. Barbara had settled back into her work with handsome new designer Hank Eliot, and they burned the midnight oil working on the new clothing line. She unveiled her fall collection at the castle. In honor of the event, Stenbeck sent her a bouquet of black flowers, and Barbara tried hard to allay her fears. One of the models had taken sick, and Hank hired a striking woman he'd met a few days before named Isabella.

Tom and Margo were enjoying renewed bliss in their marriage when a knock at the door changed everything. Lien, a 17-year-old Amerasian girl, arrived on the Hughes doorstep claiming to be Tom's daughter from an affair he'd had with a Vietnamese nurse during his tour of duty in Vietnam. Tom immediately accepted Lien as his daughter, but Margo was uneasy. When she discussed her trepidations with Hal, Tom was upset that she felt more comfortable talking with Hal than with him. Lien picked up on Margo's feelings and considered leaving Oakdale. This shook Margo up, and she decided to try to adjust to the situation. Lien quickly assimilated into life in Oakdale. Soon after, Margo discovered she was pregnant. She was very surprised, since she and Tom had been practicing birth control since their reconciliation. This could only mean one thing—Hal was the father! Margo made the decision that Hal must never know about the baby. An immigration officer told Tom that in order for Lien to be declared an American citizen, they would have to appear before the board in Washington, D.C. When Tom and Lien returned, Margo was gone. Lien blamed herself for the disappearance, but her new friend Paul Stenbeck tried to convince her otherwise.

Andy had a crush on Lien, and when he realized just how much she liked Paul, he turned to the bottle for solace. On the night of John and Lucinda's first anniversary, a drunken Andy pulled into the garage, and after the door closed, he fell asleep with the motor running. Luckily, Pam found him. Andy survived, and the Hughes and Dixon families agreed to intensive family therapy. Recovering alcoholic Susan Stewart helped Andy deal with his alcoholism.

Andy's sister, Margo, was now in Akros, Greece, assisting Inspector Haniotis in the search for Craig. She wrote to Tom that he should accept the end of their marriage and move on, as her feelings for Hal hadn't gone away. Casey warned Lyla to stay out of the matter, but Lyla only wanted to know where her daughter was and if she were all right. Lyla showed up in Greece. Haniotis told her that Margo was safe, and he had reason to believe Craig was being held by a Greek crook. The man agreed to give Craig up in exchange for another hostage. Margo volunteered, but Casey had followed his wife to Greece and insisted on being the decoy.

While waiting for Craig's return, Sierra decided to rebuild Jacobo Esteban's home in Montega. Tonio advised her to wait until current tensions in their homeland eased up. But Sierra was determined, so she took her infant son and headed for Montega.

In a Greek jail, Craig was near death from a hunger strike, but with Casey's help he escaped and contacted his mother and sister. In pursuit of Margo, John had taken Lucinda's jet to Greece. Little did he know that Hal and Barbara were honeymooning in Akros. John reached Margo and found out the truth about her pregnancy at the same time Barbara and Hal were visiting Hal's old friend, Inspector Haniotis. It was a close call.

It was obvious to Craig that he'd missed out on a lot during his time away. His most traumatic dis-

## Issues

*Tom and Margo were back together when a knock on the door changed everything. Lien, a young Amerasian girl, arrived on the Hughes doorstep claiming to be Tom's daughter from an affair he'd had with a Vietnamese nurse during his tour of duty. Along with the normal share of teenage problems and angst, Lien had to deal with the prejudice of a history teacher who'd fought in the Vietnam War and saw her as the enemy. Like her American father, Lien chose law as her profession after she graduated from college.*

covery, though, was that Sierra had gone to Montega with Bryant while the country was in the throes of a revolution. Craig immediately flew to Montega. He found his son, but Sierra had been captured by the rebels and executed in the square with other patriots. A devastated Craig left Montega with Bryant. Lucinda refused to accept her daughter's death.

Tonio told Lucinda his friends in Montega had financed his new business venture. Lucinda, who was sure her daughter hadn't died in the mass execution, offered to pay them a lot of money if they could provide information on Sierra. Craig refused to give money to Tonio at first but eventually relented. Neither of them knew that Tonio planned to use the money to advance his business.

With Margo gone, Tom tried to file for divorce on the grounds of desertion, but Casey wouldn't give him the address to send the legal papers. Meanwhile, Tom and Shannon were becoming good friends, although it was clear that she still pined for Duncan.

Craig wanted to be with Margo in Greece when she gave birth. He left his phone number with Barbara and told her to call in case Tom was getting close. Barbara copied the number down, and Hank mistakenly put it in a note for Lisa. When Lisa realized what it was, she gave it to Tom, who promptly flew to Greece. Tom called Margo and told her he was only a few blocks away, but she hung up on him. Margo went to the island of Livia to look for the woman who had taken care of Craig after his plane crashed. Tom followed and finally saw how very pregnant his wife was. Margo cried out, "It's not your baby; it's Hal's!" Then she delivered a baby boy. In search of a name for her son, Margo asked the woman who had been so kind to Craig to tell her the name of the son she had lost at sea. His name was Adamus, and Margo decided to name her newborn Adam. Tom realized he couldn't leave her and decided that in the name of love, he would live a lie and let the world think Adam was his child. Tom fabricated a story that Margo had run off to Greece because she thought her pregnancy would jeopardize their reconciliation. When Hal called Greece and spoke to her, Margo told him she'd had Tom's baby and would be coming back to Oakdale soon. Back home, Margo fumbled her way through the explanation to anyone who would listen. The news did not sit well with Barbara, and she quickly counted the months that Margo had been away. Meanwhile, Lucinda commented that baby Adam was quite robust for a premature baby, and she took note of the attention Hal paid the child. John warned his wife to keep her mouth shut about his grandson. Kim wondered why Margo would leave town when she was pregnant. When Margo was asked by Barbara for more facts, such as the date of conception, she told Tom she was afraid Barbara was catching on.

Adam wasn't the only child involved in a deception. Emily was alone and pregnant with Stenbeck's child. Holden was alone, too, now that Dusty and Lily were together, and he'd always been attracted to Emily. The two were married quietly in the campus chapel.

Holden overheard busybody Meg say that Emily was pregnant. Realizing he didn't want to have children with Emily, a sad Holden knew that their marriage was a mistake. He told Lily it was she he loved and they should be the ones having a baby! Soon after, Emily had an attack of conscience and told her mother that her unborn child was sired by James Stenbeck. Susan agreed to keep quiet and counseled her daughter to do her best to convince Holden that he was the baby's father. True to form, Susan advised her to "use sex, Emily." The apple hadn't fallen far from the tree. But Holden discovered Emily had been making phone calls to Scotland and began to suspect that the baby was James's.

One day Paul got into a street fight with some bullies who were giving him a hard time about being Stenbeck's son. In the melee, Emily was knocked down, and by the time she reached Memorial, she'd lost the baby. While she was in the ER, Bob heard her murmur, "James…our baby." Margo conjectured to Hal that since Paul was so upset over Emily's miscarriage, the baby must have been James's.

Before he got news of Emily's condition, Holden told Seth his marriage was over, but once he got to the hospital, he changed his mind. He begged Emily's forgiveness for doubting the paternity of the child. Of course, Emily, who had decided to tell Holden the truth, said nothing. After the miscarriage, Emily made a career change and left Fashions to work for Tonio at Montgomery & Associates. But working for Tonio had its pitfalls. At a meeting in Franco Visconti's hotel room, Franco came on to Emily, and Tonio came to the rescue. The clever Tonio told her she owed him one, and Holden was livid that Tonio thought the best way to close a deal was to use Emily as bait.

In a public restroom, Andy told Paul he was disgusted to hear Emily and Holden discuss having another baby when he knew the one she lost was really James's. Paul reminded Andy of his promise never to tell anyone about that. After they left, Holden emerged from a stall—he had heard everything. He confronted Emily angrily. Emily turned to Tonio, and it wasn't long before they ended up in bed. When Holden confirmed that Tonio and Emily were sleeping together, he moved out. He also backed out of his deal with Tonio and decided to set up his own business, with BRO as his first client. When they separated, Holden turned over his shares in M&A to Emily. Holden was able to persuade Craig to join him, and the two set out to destroy Tonio.

Basking in the afterglow of their indiscretion, Tonio assured Emily that Meg was unaware of their relationship. But Meg had been on to them for some time. Meg decided the best way to end her husband's affair was to lie and tell him she was pregnant. The story worked, and Emily abruptly ended the affair. Meg was surprised when Dr. Samuels told her that she was, indeed, with child. When Meg overheard Tonio tell Emily they could continue their relationship, a hurt Meg turned to her cousin Rod for comfort.

Emily's half-sister, Betsy, was having her romantic problems as well. With her husband in a Greek jail for drug trafficking, Betsy had also found solace with Rod Landry. Kim warned her against getting involved with a man who seemed every bit as hot-headed as Steve. One day, Rod picked Dani up at preschool without telling Betsy. Remembering his past with Iva, Betsy didn't want Rod alone with Dani, and he was hurt that she would think her daughter was in danger with him. They made up, and Rod confessed he hadn't been with a woman since he raped Iva. It wasn't long before Betsy and Rod made love. When David returned to Oakdale from Zaire, where he had been conducting AIDS research, he was shocked to learn his granddaughter was dating a known rapist.

Sabrina was unnerved when her ex-lover Colin Crowley showed up in Oakdale to paint Shannon's portrait. When Arnold Bennett, a publisher who had rejected Seth's novel, attended her gallery opening in Chicago, Sabrina gave him a painting he'd admired and offered to subsidize the expense of having Seth's book published by his company. Seth was ecstatic. He asked for Sabrina's hand in marriage, and Bob and Kim approved. Sabrina planned on telling Seth she'd paid for his novel to be published, but she didn't want to do it just yet. Emma and Iva knew the truth and urged her to come clean. Seth was doing some accounting for Sabrina, though, and he found out the truth. He wasn't interested in her explanations and ended their engagement. Sabrina quietly left Oakdale, promising never to return. Shortly thereafter, Seth received news that Sabrina and Colin were married in Venice.

Kim thought Betsy could help Seth overcome his anger toward Rod. Seth did, indeed, find a friendly ear in Betsy, and Rod admitted he was jealous of the attention he paid her. Betsy's welcoming Craig back from Greece with open arms made Rod jealous, too. Betsy decided she'd had her fill of jealous men, so she said no when Rod proposed. Rod then turned to his cousin Meg, who was disillusioned about her marriage, and eventually the two kissing cousins made love.

When Meg found out she was pregnant, she decided to stick with Tonio; after all, he could give her and the child the good things in life she'd married him for in the first place. As for Tonio, the news that he was going to be a father drove him to tell Emily they could be business partners and nothing more. When Rod heard Holden tell Meg he didn't mean to upset her in her "delicate condition," he concluded the baby must be his, but Meg insisted it was Tonio's. Satisfied that Tonio would be faithful, Meg told Rod that although their relationship might be over, she would always care for him.

Rod wanted to try again with Betsy, but Seth was already falling in love with her. Betsy had figured out that Rod had been seeing Meg, and she berated him about his sexual relationships with Snyder women. A despondent Rod tried to return to Meg. She told him if Tonio found out the truth, they were both as good as dead. But when Tonio left for a business trip, Meg foolishly invited Rod to the penthouse. Emily stopped by to drop off some papers for Tonio and took note, waiting for the right moment to flaunt Meg's dirty linen in her husband's face.

Emily vowed revenge on Tonio because of the way he'd used her. She confided to Susan that she was going to help Craig get his business back from Tonio. When she told her mother that she would like to keep Betsy and Holden in the dark about her affair with Tonio, Barbara overheard and tucked the information away for future reference.

Weary of her problems in Oakdale, Betsy moved to the Wisconsin office of the construction firm that had taken over Steve's company. At the same time, Seth went to New York to see about getting a literary agent with the help of Hank Eliot's friend Charles, who was in the publishing business. When he returned to Luther's Corners, Seth admitted he'd always felt trapped by the farm. Emma encouraged him to follow his heart and start a new life, so Seth got on the next bus to Wisconsin, hoping for a relationship with Betsy.

Tonio was furious when he found Meg at Rod's. Rod swore that if Tonio ever hurt Meg, he would kill him. When Meg told Tonio that his jealousy was probably a product of his guilty conscience because of his affair with Emily, Tonio began to rough her up. Emily caught him and threatened to expose their affair if he didn't stop hurting Meg. Later, Emily was cornered by Meg, who told her she'd known about the affair all along. Meg did not appreciate Emily's concern and resented her request that Meg keep quiet about the affair to Craig until Emily could tell him herself.

Tonio turned to the beautiful model Isabella for solace and sex. One night, Duncan found him at her door in a bloody heap. Tonio told Hal he thought Craig had beaten him up. But Craig was in bed with Emily at the time. Rod confessed to Meg that he was the one who beat up Tonio, and he made a deal: If Tonio stopped mistreating Meg, he would stay away from her. Rod later left town for Kansas.

## Issues

*Handsome Hank Eliot came to Oakdale as Barbara Ryan's designer when she started her new BRO line. Hank and Iva seemed headed for romance until Hank told her he was gay. Iva reacted well, but many in Oakdale did not. When Hank told Andy, he freaked out. Paul, too, was upset that Hank had kept the secret from him for so long. Eventually, the citizens of Oakdale embraced Hank as a member of the community. But Hank had a lover, Charles, who was dying of AIDS, and he left town to care for him in his final days.*

Meanwhile, Emily's plan to ruin Tonio's business was succeeding. Tonio got a call from James Stenbeck offering financial backing. Tonio also got news from his doctor that the tests that were run after the beating showed that he was sterile, so he couldn't possibly be the father of Meg's baby. When Meg heard Tonio was found outside Isabella's hotel suite, she decided to leave him once and for all, and she left a message for Rod to call her as soon as he got to Kansas. Then Tonio showed up, shouting that he wasn't going to pay the bills for another man's child and demanding to know if Rod was the father. A struggle broke out, and Meg fell down the steps, went into early labor and lost the child. Rod flew back to be with her, but Meg decided not to tell him the baby was his. Tonio informed Meg that unless she wanted to tell the police that it was Rod who nearly killed him, they would

remain husband and wife. Meg gave in and didn't admit to Rod that Tonio was holding something over her. Nevertheless, she told Tonio that they would be occupying separate bedrooms, and she would be keeping her door locked. With Tonio's threat looming over their heads, the young lovers did not want to admit their feelings, but eventually they gave in. Meanwhile, Tonio had recouped his business losses and rented spacious new offices. One day Meg overheard him thanking James Stenbeck for his support and saying that he would be happy to return the favor. But later when James called Tonio for some assistance, Tonio told him to bug off and proceeded to hire a bodyguard. Tonio continually threatened Meg with sending Rod to jail, and Meg finally lashed out, telling him that at least Rod was man enough to make her pregnant. Wrongly assuming that she cared about Tonio, James placed a call to Meg telling her that he was responsible for Tonio's financial success and that if Tonio crossed him, they would both be sorry. Meg knew it was time to leave.

Meg returned to the farm and proudly graduated from nursing school at the top of her class. She was particularly grateful to her mentor, Lyla Peretti. Meg then planned to marry Rod as soon as she could get a divorce from Tonio, much to the chagrin of Seth, Holden and Emma.

Millionaire oil man Cal Stricklyn arrived in town looking to make a deal with Tonio, Craig or Lucinda. He enjoyed a home-cooked meal at Emma's and took a shine to her right away. Cal Stricklyn was the name taken by the former Rod Landry—Cal was Rod's long-lost father. Rod was not thrilled about meeting him, but eventually they made amends. The happy couple began to make their wedding plans. Meg told Rod the baby she lost was his, and they mourned their loss together.

Lucinda decided she needed a new golden boy to

help run her empire, and that was when Kirk Anderson came to town. Kirk knew one other person in Oakdale, Iva Snyder, with whom he'd shared an interesting encounter on his incoming flight. Kirk promptly told Lucinda that part of his job would not be filling her lonely nights, as had been the case when he worked for Adelaide Fitzgibbons. Lucinda had also recruited Dusty Donovan, and Lily wasn't pleased. Kirk had several schemes in mind, one of which was sending Dusty off to the London office. Lucinda liked the idea and hoped Lily would join him and stop working for her nemesis Lisa at the Cellar. John was concerned that Lucinda was manipulating his ward, but Dusty assured him that London was too good an opportunity to pass up.

John told Lucinda that if she and her new lackey Kirk tried to get just one acre of the beloved Snyder farm to build new homes, he'd be long gone. He was also appalled at her behavior toward Barbara. As Lucinda spent more and more time on business, John was getting lonely, and he sought the company of his good friend Susan Stewart. When Dr. Taylor Baldwin left Oakdale, John replaced her at the hospital with Susan and told her he would help her with her research, a project that was funded by his wife. Lucinda wasn't happy. Soon, Susan invited John to stay the night, but John said he didn't want to use her. When the two women got into an argument over their claim on John, Susan lied that she had a sexual past with John. Lucinda was more worried about Kirk, though. Corinne Lawrence had recommended him to her before she died, and everyone knew Corinne was James's cohort. Maybe Kirk and James were in cahoots. Kirk had a talk with Addie Fitzgibbons, who told him Lucinda suspected they were both involved with James. Soon after, Lucinda got a call from James, and she and John went straight to the police. Lucinda wanted to take over the Snyder farm and develop the land. But Kirk had his eye on Iva and didn't want to get involved in the scheme. Lucinda said if he didn't like it, he could quit. Kirk prepared the papers.

With all this pressure on her, Lucinda still had time to worry about Barbara. Barbara had refused to buy back Simply Barbara, and Lucinda had to find a way for the company to turn a profit. Lucinda was sure Barbara had figured out, as had she, that Hal was Adam's father. She blackmailed Barbara into designing for Simply Barbara by threatening to tell Hal that Adam was his son. Barbara told Lucinda

that her tall tales concerning her stepgrandson were ludicrous, but she valued her marriage and eventually gave in. Not to be outdone, she told Hank Eliot to get going on BRO and give it all he had. Lucinda encouraged Pam to baby-sit for Tom and Margo and find out what she could. Pam told Craig that Aunt Lucinda had suspicions concerning Adam's paternity, and when Craig told Margo what Lucinda was up to, the two figured out Lucinda had blackmailed Barbara into designing for her.

Kirk, who was busily making the rounds in Oakdale, got his hands on a new gown from the BRO line. Barbara had a fit when she saw her design on a Simply Barbara model and vowed war. Kirk had taken a shine to Iva, but the feelings weren't mutual, and he couldn't understand why she would turn down a hot single man like himself to pine away for recent widower Craig. The Snyders, however, were thrilled that both Hank and Kirk were paying attention to the oldest Snyder daughter. One night at the Mona Lisa, Kirk followed Iva into the ladies' room and pulled her into a passionate kiss. Iva couldn't say she didn't enjoy it, but she warned him not to play games with her heart.

Hank was somewhat embarrassed one night when he came upon Kirk and Iva kissing. But Iva and Hank had grown closer—so close that they almost kissed, until Hank pulled back. Hank told Iva that he was gay and was involved in a relationship with a man named Charles in New York, which explained his frequent weekend trips to the Big Apple. Iva was very understanding, and the two became good friends.

Hank was interested in taking over the garage apartment after Nancy moved out. Andy was a little disappointed because he'd wanted it for himself. If he was going to be living next door, Hank thought it was time to tell Bob and Kim about his sexuality. They were fine with it, but they wanted him to tell Andy himself. When he did, Andy freaked out, saying that he almost always went out of his way to avoid gay guys at school.

Ambrose had been tracking down Iva's real parents, and she was elated when he found her father, Jared Carpenter, a wealthy businessman who made his home in Southampton. Kirk did whatever he could to dissuade Iva from meeting with Jared and his family, but Iva was determined. Kirk cautioned her not to mention his name. When Lucinda heard about Jared, she wanted to do business with him, but when

Jared learned Kirk was working for her, he hung up. Kirk explained he once had a deal with Jared that went sour. Lucinda decided to do some digging on her own. When Kirk slipped and called her Lenore, Lucinda told her detectives to find out who "Lenore" was. Soon after, Kirk got a mysterious phone call from Lenore, and he couldn't fathom why she would be calling him after all those years.

When Iva came face-to-face with her birth father, she found out that her mother, Caroline, had died a few years before, but she had a sister, Elizabeth. Elizabeth told Iva that Jared was dying and made it clear this was not a very convenient time for Iva to appear for her share of the inheritance. However, Iva and Jared got along famously, and she also got on with her cousin Lenore. Iva invited Jared to visit Luther's Corners, where he was welcomed with open arms by the Snyder clan. The reunion was a rousing success until Jared collapsed. Elizabeth and Iva took him back to Southampton. Iva cautioned her family to keep Kirk's name out of the conversation, even though she still didn't know why Jared hated him. A curious Lucinda advised her daughter's other mother to find out exactly what the root of the problem was.

In other Snyder news, son Caleb returned to Oakdale from Chicago and announced he would stay at least through the summer. There had always been a rivalry between Holden and Caleb. Holden claimed Caleb did nothing unless there was something in it for him. Ellie Snyder, also living and working in Chicago, was unaware that Caleb had quit his job. Caleb had told Ellie that he had to leave in a hurry and didn't want anyone in Chicago to know where he was.

Caleb lacked the home spirit of the other Snyder siblings. That piqued the interest of Kirk and Lucinda, who eyed him as someone who could push Emma to sell the farm to developers. Kirk told Caleb, whose eyes were full of dollar signs, that if he ever wanted to sell his share of the farm, he should let Kirk know. Meanwhile, Caleb was getting calls from a young woman named Angel, and he asked her to keep her father and brothers off his back. When Caleb found out that his brother-in-law Tonio had a meeting with his former boss, Henry Lange, he asked Tonio not to mention his name, as he and Lange had had a parting of ways. Then Iva and Emma got a call from Chicago—Ellie was in trouble. They were imme-

diately en route. Caleb also left, telling Holden he was going to see Ellie as well. But Caleb went to see Angel, even though her father and brothers had threatened to kill him if he did. Apparently, when Angel got pregnant with Caleb's child, a butchered abortion made it impossible for her to ever have children again. Caleb made Angel promise to stay away from him and Ellie. He found out that Angel's family had hired a hit man to beat Ellie up. Not long afterward, Angel arrived at the Snyder farm. She was actually the daughter of Henry Lange, who was meeting with Lucinda, Tonio and Craig to decide which management consultant firm in Oakdale would handle his multinational corporation. When Caleb came home and discovered Angel, he hid her in the hayloft until the coast was clear. Then Caleb put Angel on a bus back to Chicago and went to speak with Lange privately. Little did he know that Kirk had an ear to the door. Henry tore into Caleb about Angel's back-alley abortion. When Henry returned to Chicago, he locked Angel in her room.

Kirk reported back to Lucinda that Caleb was their ace in the hole when it came to dealing with the Snyders and the Langes. He offered Caleb a loan if he agreed to sign his share of the farm away as collateral. Kirk reasoned that when Caleb defaulted, as he surely would, Walsh would own a sixth of the Snyder farm. Henry told Holden about Caleb's sordid past with Angel. Enraged, Holden blasted his brother for what he did to Angel and for getting close to Lily because she was an heiress. Holden managed to clinch a deal with Lange, bringing the account into the M&A fold. Henry seemed to like the young man and offered him the use of his private jet whenever he wished. Holden told Angel he didn't think Caleb ever loved her. Henry Lange was pleased as punch that a fine, upstanding young man like Holden was willing to make amends for what his callous brother did.

Lucinda threw a fabulous party for Lily's birthday, but Lily was disturbed by Holden's absence. Angel was falling hard for Holden as well. When Holden was in Chicago on Lange business, Lily borrowed Lucinda's jet and flew to see him. Just as she arrived, she saw Holden and Angel kissing—a kiss instigated by Angel. Lily ran off before she could hear Holden tell Angel it was Lily he loved and always would. By the time Holden returned to Oakdale, Lily was with Caleb. The brothers had a fierce fight. When Henry sent Holden to check out his plant in North

Carolina, Holden was surprised to find Angel on the flight, and a distraught Lily was told that Holden was with Angel. The star-crossed lovers were once again apart and would be for some time, as Henry was considering opening a showroom overseas and Holden was the man for the job.

Lily was touched when Caleb confessed his past with Angel to her. Soon after, she received a letter from Holden saying he'd decided to go to Europe to sort out his life.

As Holden was leaving Oakdale, Ellie was returning, and she set her sights on Kirk, Craig or any man with money. When Emily saw Ellie and Craig kiss, she was furious, and when she heard about Ellie's past, which included an early marriage and a miscarriage, Emily decided she wanted to know more, and she hired a private investigator to dig deeper.

Shannon O'Hara loved Halloween. While she was

## Troubled Triangles

*It was a dark day when Duncan introduced Shannon, the second Mrs. McKechnie, to the first Mrs. McKechnie. Psychotic, unstable, daring and dangerous, Lilith McKechnie had plunged a knife into Duncan's back on their wedding night while they were in the throes of passion. She was institutionalized for 12 years, but now she was back and ripe for revenge. After Duncan and Shannon married, a jealous Lilith abducted her rival and sent back her shrunken head as proof that she was dead.*

planning her spooky shindig, she found a portrait of Duncan's great-great-grandmother Margaret in the attic and decided to hang it up in honor of the occasion. Then she received a special delivery from Scotland—it was Margaret's casket. Shannon wanted to bury Margaret next to her husband, Angus, in the family plot and didn't understand why Duncan was so vehemently opposed. It seemed Margaret had had a child by another man. Because of her infidelity, Angus let Margaret die in childbirth, and he cursed the future generations of McKechnie women: If they gave birth to a girl, they would die in childbirth, too. Then Shannon started to hear the cries of what she believed to be Margaret's ghost. She thought the only

way to break the spell was to hold a séance and summon Margaret's spirit. Duncan told Shannon that if she returned Margaret's portrait to the attic, he'd commission a portrait of Shannon to put in its place. He went to Europe to commission Colin Crowley. While he was there, Duncan hoped to persuade his pregnant daughter Beatrice to have an amniocentesis to determine the sex of her unborn child in case she stood to inherit the McKechnie curse. When Duncan was away, strange things began to happen around the island: Mirrors shattered, a boat disappeared, and Angus's headstone was broken in two.

When Colin arrived from Europe, he was taken by Shannon's beauty, a passion that aroused Duncan's jealousy, although it was Sabrina whom Colin really wanted. The ghost of Margaret did not approve, and Colin soon found his sketchbook soaked and his sketches ruined. One night, Shannon had a dream in which she was Margaret, Duncan was Angus and Colin was Jeremy, Margaret's lover. In the dream, Jeremy told Margaret how much he would miss her when the portrait was finished.

For her séance, Shannon enlisted the services of medium Lydia Konstantin. During the séance, Lydia went into a trance and wrote down the phrase "enough tears to fill Loch Lomond." Colin reported he felt an icy hand on his neck. Duncan was fretful because his daughter was in labor, and he was worried that she would be a victim of the curse. Duncan thought he felt Margaret's presence in the room, and he spoke to her: "I don't want to believe that you were an adulteress." "I wasn't," she replied. Then Brian called from Scotland—Beatrice had given birth to a healthy baby girl, and mother and daughter were doing fine.

Shannon decided to take the bull by the horns and propose to Duncan. When he turned her down, Shannon was livid. She didn't waste any time establishing herself as one of Oakdale's hottest swingers. When she returned to the castle to get her portrait, Shannon found the name "Lilith" written on it. Shannon thought that Lilith was Duncan's new mistress. Meanwhile, Duncan was worried about Lilith, who was his first wife, especially after he learned that a Dr. Sylvestre, her psychiatrist, was missing. When he found out Dr. Sylvestre had been murdered, Duncan realized he had to protect Shannon.

Duncan let Barbara use his castle for the premiere of her BRO line. During the fashion show, Duncan was horrified to see Isabella modeling Barbara's designs—"Isabella" was really Lilith McKechnie.

Lilith was quick to make friends with Tonio and invite him to her suite at the Lakeview. When Duncan found them there together, he threw Tonio out. Duncan introduced Lilith to Shannon, insisting that Shannon was merely his decorator. Lilith couldn't resist hiring Shannon to redecorate her hotel suite. An agitated Duncan sought comfort with good friend Jessica Griffin, and the comforting led to a kiss. Lilith suspected that Shannon and Duncan were once lovers, and it made her blood boil. It turned out that Lilith's brother, Roderick, got the information that Duncan was in Oakdale from none other than James

Stenbeck. Duncan sent Jessica to investigate, but Lilith warned her brother that if he helped Jessica, she would tell the authorities what had really happened to Dr. Sylvestre, and she'd order Jessica's death. When Lilith saw Shannon's portrait, she was enraged. Duncan reminded her of their wedding night when, in the throes of passion, Lilith had plunged a knife into his back. Lilith insisted she was cured, but Duncan wasn't taking any chances.

In a short time, all of Oakdale heard the news that the beautiful Isabella was actually Lilith McKechnie, Duncan's wife of 13 years. For Shannon's protection, Duncan told her that Lilith had been institutionalized for 12 years. He insisted that Lilith was a violent psychopath with revenge on her mind and that Shannon was a likely target. Lilith told her brother, Roderick, that Lisa's husband was an Interpol agent who was trying to bring Stenbeck to justice. Roderick promised to get the message to James, who got in touch with his Oakdale contact—Duncan's supposedly loyal servant, Theresa—and told her to let it slip to Duncan that Lilith had been proclaimed cured.

James hadn't even arrived in Oakdale when the bodies began piling up. Theresa was killed, and so was Tobias, Duncan's manservant, because they were getting too close to the truth. The detective who was protecting Barbara was found dead, and so was Duncan's guard, by Lilith's hand. Duncan was horrified to find Theresa's prints on the gun that killed Tobias. If Theresa were working with James, then she probably lied about Lilith being cured. James asked Lilith to get in touch with Paul for him. When she did, in a moment of compassion she advised the confused teenager to stay far away from his father. Lilith was closing in fast on her prey and managed to stab Shannon with a letter opener. Luckily, Duncan heard Shannon's screams and found Lilith standing over her wounded body brandishing the bloody weapon. Unfortunately, Duncan and the police lost the deranged Lilith's trail in the thick island fog.

After Lilith's disappearance, Shannon bid her uncle Earl goodbye as he took off on an alleged investigative reporting jaunt for the *Argus*. Later, Lisa was surprised when her ex-husband Grant Colman paid her a visit and inquired about Earl's whereabouts. Earl was missing, and he'd left a message for Lisa: "James found out about me." Then a reporter named

Glenn Harrington showed up in Oakdale looking for Lisa. He said he'd met Earl while doing a story on James and was under the impression that Earl had gone to South Africa. Tom and Margo discovered that Glenn was an undercover agent, not a reporter. Soon after, Earl's trench coat was found in a hotel room in South Africa. His passport was still in the pocket, the coat was stained with blood that wasn't human, and his luggage had been given to someone who had a letter authorizing its release. Glenn was sure someone was trying to make it look as if Earl were dead. Because Grant had been asking questions about Earl's intentions and had been negotiating to take over the management of Lisa's business interests, all eyes were on him.

Glenn agreed to stay in town and work undercover as a reporter for the *Argus*. Privately he told Shannon that he worked for the FBI. Glenn speculated that Stenbeck was holding Earl prisoner, and Shannon was curious as to who told James that Earl was with Interpol. When Lisa confided to Shannon that she'd heard Earl's voice in the apartment, Shannon was sure her mind was playing tricks on her.

Jessica told her lover, Thornton Converse, that she didn't think he could cope with being married to a black woman, and she moved in with Roy. However, their arrangement got off to a bad start when Jess discovered Roy was a slob who was used to having his mother pick up after him.

One night, while driving near Veterans Park, Bob spotted a young woman struggling to fight off an attacker. Bob chased him away and urged the woman to report the incident. Her name was Laura Simmons.

Pam Wagner, John's niece, was working in Memorial's emergency room when a young man was brought in with a cut leg and a twisted ankle. He said his name was Beau Farrell and, like the man who had attacked Laura Simmons, he was wearing a red scarf. Beau claimed he was passing through Oakdale when he was mugged. Pam felt sorry for him and offered him lodging in her aunt Lucinda's stables. Later, Beau heard Bob talking to Laura on the phone about going to the police. He called her at home and told her she shouldn't have done that. When the police put together a line-up for Laura, she wasn't able to identify her attacker, and neither was Bob.

John and Lucinda disapproved of Pam's friendship with Beau, but kind-hearted Lisa gave him a job

at the Mona Lisa waiting tables and playing the guitar. Beau swore he wasn't leaving town until he finished what he came for. Meanwhile, Laura was growing closer to the Hughes family, and Kim offered her a job baby-sitting little Chris. Laura confided in Kim about her own children, Darren and Jen, and how her ex-husband took them away from her. When Laura ran an errand for Kim, Beau emerged from the bushes and followed. He rented a room near Kim and Bob's so he could keep an eye on her. In his wallet, Beau carried a picture of himself standing next to Laura in a wedding dress. When Bob gave Laura a small gift, John and Susan noticed her elation. They spotted Bob making purchases on his Fashions account for Laura, causing Susan to remark, "The baby-sitter, my foot."

Kim offered Laura a job at TV station WOAK. When Frannie found her studying a tape of Kim on "Patterns," Laura told her Kim was her role model. Laura began dating Herb Petrie, a studio executive. As Bob and Kim were celebrating three years of wedded bliss, Laura heard them referred to as the "perfect couple," and she grew more and more depressed. Meanwhile, Beau told Laura that Victor was looking for them. Beau and Pam finally made love, and he surprised her by proposing.

While Kim was on a business trip, Laura put on Kim's nightgown and slipped into bed next to Bob, whispering that she loved him and asking him to tell her that he loved her, too. Bob was taken aback, to say the least. He told her he was sorry if she'd misinterpreted his feelings. Laura accused him of lying— why, he'd been telling her that he loved her since they first met in the park. Bob suggested she get professional help and tried to send her home, but Laura lingered in the bedroom. When Andy saw Laura coming out of the bedroom, he completely misunderstood the situation. Bob had no choice but to fire her, but the next day Laura showed up for work as if nothing had happened, and Bob was forced to fire her again. Meanwhile, Beau went to Laura's. Calling himself Billy, he insisted she would always be the most important woman in his life.

When Kim returned from her trip, Laura told her she and Bob were having an affair. Beau stopped by later and told Bob that he was the man Bob saw with Laura in the park; he was actually Laura's brother, Billy. Beau went on to relate his sister's history of serious mental problems. She had never recovered from their father's death, for which she may have been responsible. When her ex-husband, Victor, realized how unstable Laura was, he took the children away.

Nancy found Kim's nightgown slashed to ribbons, and the Hughes family began to wonder if Laura was capable of doing them harm. Later, Laura met Herb Petrie for a tryst at the Yardley Motel. In her twisted mind, Laura saw Herb as coming between her and Bob, and she took a letter opener that she'd stolen from Kim and Bob and killed the man. After leaving the corpse in the bathtub and calmly putting a "Do Not Disturb" sign on the door, Laura called Mrs. Petrie and said Herb was in serious danger from Bob Hughes. Then she called her landlady and told her she would be returning to Ohio with Mr. Petrie.

After getting the message from Laura's landlady, Beau called his mother, who said she hadn't heard from Laura and had no idea who Mr. Petrie was. A frightened Pam locked herself in the Hughes house with Christopher, while Beau went to the Yardley and discovered Herb's bloodied body in the tub. Beau called Pam and told her to leave the Hughes place at once. Pam fled through the back door just before Laura arrived. After smashing Kim's picture, Laura settled in to wait for Bob. Bob arrived and found her dressed in Kim's nightgown and brandishing a knife. She told him if he didn't declare his love for her, she would commit suicide and make it look as though Bob had killed her. Beau, who'd been watching this scene from outside the house, burst in and grabbed the knife. Before she was taken away, Laura pleaded with Bob to tell her that he loved her, and the always kind Dr. Bob said, "For all of the good in you, I do love you." Heartbroken over his inability to help his sister, Beau broke down. It was later revealed that Laura had been sexually abused by her father from the age of 12.

All was not bleak in Oakdale in 1988. The year did have its share of love stories. One of the most touching and romantic was the union of Dan McClosky and Nancy Hughes, the beloved matriarch of the Hughes family. They had dated quietly for several months and were married in a simple backyard ceremony at Bob and Kim's with all of the out-of-town Hughes and Stewart family members in attendance. With nearly a century of wedded bliss between them, these two seemed headed for their twilight years filled with contentment and joy.

## 1989

As 1989 got under way, Margo thought all the controversy surrounding baby Adam's birth had died down. But Hal began asking questions about Adam's conception. At the same time, Emily got to look at Margo's file and learned that Adam was Hal's son. Margo told Tom she'd have to leave the country or risk losing her son. She went back to Greece, leaving Tom to face the family. Unable to lie to his father, Tom admitted that Adam was Hal's child. Bob was deeply troubled by his son's deception, and Kim was saddened that her worst fears were realized.

When Emily and Craig offered Paul a job with Montgomery & Associates, Barbara was opposed— no way was her son going to be working anywhere near Emily Stewart. Emily warned her not to interfere unless she wanted Emily to tell Hal the truth about Adam. When Margo called Oakdale, she learned that all her relatives knew the truth, except for Hal. Barbara realized she had to get to Hal before Margo did, but Margo found him first. At the courthouse, where they'd shared many an honest conversation, Margo told him he was Adam's father. Hal felt he'd been played for a fool. When Barbara arrived, she found a broken-down Margo in her husband's arms. Hal's pain was intense, and Barbara's attempts to comfort him did little to help. Tom and Margo tried to figure out a compromise, but joint custody was not attractive to Barbara because it meant Hal would have to be even more involved with Margo. Barbara tried hard to help Hal forget about the whole mess, but her attempt to seduce him didn't work. Although she had been taking birth control pills, she was now ready to have a child, especially if a baby would strengthen her bond with Hal. And when Margo tried to get Tom to make love, he accused her of trying to conceive a baby of their own to soothe his ego.

Hal decided he had to get out of Oakdale. He requested a leave of absence and went home to Kentucky for a rest, though it was anything but. Hal had never gotten along with his father, and when they had it out, Harold Sr. admitted he'd always wondered if Hal were an illegitimate child. The confrontation caused Hal to reconsider the situation with Adam, and when he returned to Oakdale, he went to see Tom and Margo. His feelings hadn't changed about how they'd betrayed him and cheated him out of the first ten months of his son's life. Nevertheless, he thought it was fine for Adam to live with Tom and Margo, as long as Hal was still included in his life. But the next time Hal visited, he had some new conditions: Paul was Hal's stepson now, and he wanted to tell him the truth. Tom objected because he didn't want Lien to know. Hal told him he was sick and tired of Tom and Margo making all the decisions, and it was his turn to make a few. Hal told Paul, and Andy was upset that Margo hadn't told him earlier. When Tom finally told Lien, she was shocked and dismayed; her parents were not as honorable as they had seemed. Lyla didn't want anyone else to know about her grandson, but Lucinda pointed out how easily secrets could backfire, and she should know—just look at her situation with Lily! News of Adam started to spread. Tom and Margo informed John that Lucinda was using Adam's paternity to blackmail Barbara into designing for Simply Barbara. Lucinda vehemently denied the accusation and asked Kirk to back her up. Realizing he could lose his job over this one, Kirk admitted it was his idea.

Barbara felt she was fast losing her grip on her husband as he became more focused on his relationship with his newfound son. Hal didn't realize that she had known the truth before he did, and this information could destroy them if she didn't find a way to bond him to her permanently. As Adam's christening drew near, everyone involved was at each other's throats. Barbara confronted Margo and told her it was all her fault, and Margo accused Barbara of being the one who started the ball rolling when she got Tom drunk and led him to believe they'd had an affair. Despite the turmoil, Adam was christened Adam Christopher Harold (for Hal) Hughes. Hal would be the boy's godfather. Barbara continued to try to distract Hal by talking about having a child together, but Hal remained focused on Adam. He asked Barbara if she would be willing to adopt the child should anything happen to Tom and Margo. It was not a question Barbara could easily answer.

When Hal's father became ill, Hal wanted him to see his first grandchild. Barbara couldn't go to Kentucky because she needed to be there for Paul, so Margo went instead. Margo and Hal realized how

easy it would be to become lovers again. When Margo told Hal's dad the story of Adam's conception, Harold asked his son how he could let another man care for his child, and how long could he pretend not to be in love with Adam's mother?

Margo was estranged from Tom when she and Hal went to Greece in search of Craig and shared a night of passion on the beach. Margo later reconciled with Tom, and Hal married Barbara. Soon after, Margo found herself pregnant with Hal's child. She named the boy Adam, and Tom agreed to raise him as his own. Although he adores his "Uncle Hal," Adam thinks of Tom as "Dad"—a situation that often grates on Hal.

Ever since the Hugheses moved out of Margo's cottage and into their new home, a shadow had been hovering around them, and one day she materialized while Pam was baby-sitting Adam. The woman said she was looking for the Bensons, the family who used to live in the house. The police figured out that Pam's visitor was Anna Benson, ex-wife of Arnold Benson, who was doing time for mail fraud. Anna had some of the $20 million Arnold was convicted of stealing. Soon afterward, a mysterious man got into the Hughes home and ransacked the attic.

Margo and Tom pieced together some details about the Bensons. When Anna lived in Oakdale, she worked at a savings bank. After the bank was robbed, she became an assistant postmaster to her husband, Arnold. Arnold was jailed, and he and Anna divorced. That was 13 years ago. Margo and Hal decided to pay Arnold a visit in prison. In the meantime, a man called George McLellan, the head of security at a Florida hospital, was looking for Anna and was skulking around outside Tom and Margo's house.

Arnold clammed up when Hal and Margo pressed him about his postal-theft conviction. After they left, Anna appeared and told her ex that an Erik Rykov was back and looking for "the money." Later, Pam found George McLellan, alias Mel Asher, dead in Riverfront Park. Margo learned that George worked with Anna in the bank when it was robbed 22 years ago. Anna came to the police frightened because Rykov was stalking her. When Rykov confronted Anna, he swore he didn't kill George and did his best to convince her that Arnold had taken out a contract on George's life. Rykov believed that some of the money from the bank robbery was hidden in Tom and Margo's house. When Tom and Margo discovered a leak in Adam's nursery, Rykov posed as a repairman, and he tore up the room looking for the cash. Tom found out that the contractor never sent a repairman and called Margo and told her to take the baby and get out as fast as she could. Aware that something was up, Tom and Margo invited Anna to the house. Anna seemed especially preoccupied with the nursery. Ironically, it was Pam who eventually made the discovery—she found a U.S. Mail bag in the ripped-up ceiling and was pulling it out just as Rykov entered. Pam managed to call the police before Rykov pulled a gun and took her hostage. The police arrived with Beau, but it was Glenn Harrington who made the capture. The mailbag didn't contain any money; instead, it held letters from 1969, one of which was addressed to John, and five rare stamps worth $2 million!

The letter to John was from a Rosemary Kramer. John was a bit baffled by the 19-year-old letter, which seemed to suggest that Rosemary was pregnant when she left Oakdale. Lucinda was dying to know what was in it and what Rosemary Kramer had meant to John. John decided to track Rosemary down in Seattle and asked Margo to help him. Lucinda interpreted the letter to mean that Rosemary was carrying John's child when she left Oakdale. Margo discovered that Rosemary was dead, but she did leave a son whose name was Ian Kramer. John's focus on the implications of this discovery unnerved Lucinda—she wanted her husband all to herself. Even though she'd

opened her arms to Andy, Pam and others of John's kin, the thought of John chasing after this boy made her uncomfortable. Lucinda insisted there was no way he could possibly be John's son. Susan encouraged John to seek him out in the hopes that her enthusiasm and help might win him over romantically. Susan suggested John hire a detective, but Lucinda beat her to the punch. Lucinda had a dream in which John found out she'd hired a private detective to search for his son, and he left her. When her detective found the boy's grandmother, Lucinda told him to pose as a social worker and extract some information. Unfortunately, John overheard. He couldn't believe his wife could go behind his back and continue to keep secrets after all they'd been through. As far as John was concerned, it was over between them. Lucinda tried to stop him from flying to Seattle. She even went so far as to order Rex Whitmore, the hospital administrator, not to give John the time off he'd asked for. John quit his job, and Susan joined him, with Lucinda in hot pursuit. In Seattle, Lucinda was not pleased to find her husband working with Susan Stewart, and John was not pleased to find Lucinda, period. But it was Lucinda who found the boy's address. When John phoned, Ian, who called himself Duke, hung up on him. The ever-resourceful Lucinda paid Duke's grandmother, Edith, a visit to try to find out the identity of her grandson's father. After Lucinda left, John and Susan arrived and told Edith about Rosemary's letter. Edith promised to look for more letters and then contact the couple. Duke, who had been hiding in his grandmother's closet, confronted John and Susan about what he perceived to be a scam, and when Lucinda arrived, he was sure the three of them were in cahoots. John realized Lucinda could undermine his entire effort to get to know Duke, so he ordered her to leave Seattle. Fed up with his wife's manipulations, John had too much to drink, kissed Susan and then fell asleep, leaving her high and dry. Back in Oakdale, Susan got Duke's medical records and discovered he and John were the same blood type. Undaunted, Lucinda asked Hal to find out if Duke had a criminal record. At the same time, Julie Wendall, Duke's girlfriend, was trying to convince him to take a job with a drug dealer named Vince, since his boxing career wasn't exactly raking in the dough.

Before she died, Duke's grandmother made a call and told the person on the other end that if anything happened to her, Rosemary's papers should be destroyed. Just when John was about to tell Duke he might be his father, Edith died, and Rosemary's papers vanished. John wanted Duke to come to Oakdale. Eventually Duke agreed.

Lucinda confided in her old boyfriend, Niles Mason, that her marriage was on the rocks. Niles flirted with Lucinda, and she enjoyed their banter, but John was her passion, and Niles was unable to distract her. When John returned with Duke, Lucinda was thrilled, or so she said. John was straight with her—either she welcomed them both in her home or it was over. Lucinda rolled out the red carpet for Ian or Duke, or whatever his name was. Despite her outward ebullience, Lucinda was dreading having the lower-class, sweaty, dirty Duke under her roof. Kim was concerned as to how the move would affect Andy. After all, Duke might be his son from an affair John had when he was married to Kim. Kim warned John to be sensitive to Andy or he'd answer to her. Meanwhile, Lucinda was having a hard time keeping up a happy facade with "Neanderthal" Duke in her midst. She could hardly control herself when he broke a treasured Ming dog vase and tried to put it back together with Crazy Glue. Duke was enjoying his new life. To him, the mansion was a wild place. He loved to flirt with Walsh heiress Lily, especially when he saw how much his intentions bothered Caleb. Lily, however, was not impressed, especially when he kissed her without warning. John persuaded Duke to take a job as an orderly at Memorial, and to everyone's surprise, he proved to be a diligent worker.

One night, Duke got Paul and Lien to join him at the Silver Dollar Roadhouse, where they could get a beer without a hassle. The kids had a grand time until Duke, who was driving, ran a stop sign and was arrested. When Tom and Margo got word that Lien was at the police station, all hell broke loose!

Lien went on a class trip to Washington, D.C. While visiting the Vietnam War Memorial, her unstable history teacher, Mr. Patelli, started hearing gunshots in his head. The veteran imagined he was back in Vietnam and began to attack Lien as if she were the enemy. Andy rescued her from the crazed teacher.

While playing the loving stepmother, Lucinda kept looking for ways to rid herself of Duke. A plan fell in her lap and her name was Julie Wendall. When Lucinda learned that Duke broke up with Julie when he found out she wanted him only for the money he was getting living with John, she knew she'd found a weak spot. Behind John's back, Lucinda flew to Seattle, paid a visit to Pam's father, Larry, and tracked down Julie. She told her all she had to do was get Duke out of town, and Lucinda would amply reward her. Since Julie had just lost custody of her two kids and was up to her ears in debt, she was vulnerable to Lucinda's bribes. Lucinda funded a makeover for Julie and gave her a pep talk. In the meantime, Duke made no progress in endearing himself to Tom. During Andy's housewarming party, one of the guests decided to spike the punch. Lien drank more than she should, and Duke drove her home. Later, Tom found an empty vodka bottle in the back of Duke's van and accused him of "taking advantage" of Lien by intentionally getting her drunk. When Duke told John about the incident, John was more concerned about Andy and the alcohol. But Andy had already given in to temptation.

The new and improved Julie Wendall came to town, and Duke was wary of her sudden interest in him. John was none too thrilled to see Duke's ex-girlfriend insinuate herself into his life, but Lucinda was elated. Julie soon realized that she had a lot of power and it would be in her best interest to use it. It didn't take long for Julie to seduce Duke. Lucinda warned John that he'd only push them closer together if he expressed his disapproval. Lucinda was sure Julie was the answer to her prayers, but little did she know the type of creature she'd lured to Oakdale. Julie moved into Beau's old basement apartment and got a job at the Yacht Club, where she caught Andy's eye. Later she told Lucinda she wanted $300 a month or else she'd spill the beans about who brought her to Oakdale and why. Lucinda did not appreciate being blackmailed, but she was amused by Julie's spunk and agreed to pay up. John offered Julie a check to get out of town, which Lucinda instructed her to rip up. Duke and Andy were giving Julie tons of attention, which was making Lien somewhat jealous, as she didn't think she could match Julie's sex appeal. Julie was reveling in her newfound power— she even got Duke to sleep with her between John and Lucinda's satin sheets. When Duke made up the bed, he accidentally left his wet bathing suit in it. Later, as John and Lucinda settled in, they happened upon the

Julie Wendell came to Oakdale under the auspices of Lucinda to help her get John's son, Duke Kramer, out of town. Kim was horrified that under Julie's influence Andy started to wear an earring—but that was the least of it! Andy fell hard for this sexy redhead, and she became his first love. Julie cared for Andy, but she cared for the good things in life more, and she left him for greener pastures. Andy turned to drink. It would be a long road back for this heartbroken and sensitive young man.

damp clump. John was curious why Lucinda was not more outraged when Duke confessed.

To complicate matters, Larry Wagner arrived in town to celebrate his daughter Pam's birthday. John was intrigued that Larry knew Rosemary Kramer. Larry suggested to Julie that they work together in extorting more money from Lucinda. But first, Julie had to take care of some business for Ms. Walsh. Sobbing hysterically, Julie called Duke and told him to come over right away or she'd kill herself. When Duke arrived, Julie announced she was pregnant. Duke made her have a sonogram, which revealed she'd been pregnant for more than two months, and

she'd been in Oakdale for less than that.

When Lucinda learned about Julie's pregnancy, she decided to dispatch her back to Seattle post haste. Her plan was foiled when Duke walked in while she was giving Julie her final payment. An angry Duke told Lucinda he was moving out. He confided in Susan, who went straight to John. John saw this as a new low, even for Lucinda, and he moved out as well. Susan was more than happy to provide a new home for John, not to mention a new bed. On his first night away from Lucinda, John and Susan became "involved."

An insecure Lien was longing for the kind of attention Julie so easily received. One night she and Andy were becoming passionate, but after an intense kiss, Lien admitted she was afraid that if she went one step further, she'd lose control. Andy assured her that he respected her too much to go "all the way." As for Julie, her scheming days were over, her life was a mess and, to top it all off, she was pregnant. Julie was very needy, and Andy enjoyed the role of protector. The two got closer and eventually made love. When Duke came knocking on the door looking for a place to stay, he found Julie in Andy's bed. Lien was hurt by the change in Andy's behavior toward her, but when she saw him kissing Julie, she realized why. Meanwhile, Julie went to Chicago to take care of "female problems" and later returned to be with Andy.

Lucinda realized she'd really done it this time. John was gone, and he wouldn't accept her phone calls. When Pam learned Lucinda bribed her father to help get Duke out of town, she moved in with Lyla. To add insult to injury, Susan gloated that she and John had slept together. Lucinda pleaded with Craig, Kirk and Ambrose to help her get John back, but they told her that her ploys wouldn't work this time around—Lucinda would have to change her ways. John offered her a quick and easy divorce, but Lucinda would have none of it. When Niles tried to seduce her, Lucinda realized adultery wouldn't help her case. However, she did give in to a kiss, which unfortunately John was privy to.

Andy continued to protect Julie, hiding her in Oakdale. But when Olivia Wycroft asked her to be one of her models, Julie decided it was time to resurface. John, Duke and Lucinda were floored to see "Little Miss Seattle," as John liked to call her, on the runway! While Andy was seeing Julie, Duke was becoming interested in Lien. Duke wasn't pleased to hear about his half-brother's attachment to Julie. In Andy's presence, Duke forced Julie to reveal the circumstances of her arrival in Oakdale. A lot of what she said went against what Andy had been brought up to believe was right, but Julie was his first sexual experience, and he adored her. Julie truly cared for Andy but thought she should leave town. A lovesick Andy persuaded her not to go. Julie told Kim that Andy had changed her life and assured his horrified mother that she'd never do anything to hurt him. Kim asked Susan for advice, and Susan told her that Julie was trouble. Bob was sure Andy's infatuation was a passing phase, but Andy was changing. For starters, he began to wear a gold earring that Julie bought for him. Worse, he was missing his Alcoholics Anonymous meetings, saying that Julie made him feel so good that he didn't need them. When John got wind of what was happening, he hit the roof! He knew all about "Little Miss Seattle" and her past. Andy couldn't take the criticism coming from all directions, and so he moved into Julie's basement apartment.

Seeing some of herself in the fiery young woman, Lisa gave Julie a job as hostess at the Mona Lisa just as John was ready to run her out of town. Tonio offered to help Julie with her modeling career. The flirtatious Tonio lured her to his apartment, telling her that Andy would never have to know. Tonio continued to appeal to Julie's love of money and glamour and filled her head with dreams of being a fashion model. With his help, Julie began modeling for Veronica Leathers. When Julie and Tonio went to New York together for a shoot, Tonio made his move. Julie rejected his advances but accepted his champagne. When she returned, Andy confronted her, but she insisted no harm was done. Besides, Tonio was already having an affair with Veronica Tucci.

Julie wanted to be a successful model so bad she could taste it. When Tonio gave her an ultimatum— sleep with him or forget her career—Julie gave in. The more Julie stayed out, the more Andy drank. He finally confessed to Frannie, who told Susan what was going on. Aware of his drinking, Julie offered to stay out of Andy's life, but Andy panicked and told her that without her he had no life.

Kim knew it was time to tell John about Andy's relapse. The two started to spend a lot of time together trying to figure out what they could do for their son. Bob began to feel left out and started to spend more time with Susan Stewart.

Lucinda was still hoping to find Sierra alive, and as Tonio continued to milk as much money from her as he could with his "searching for Sierra" scam, John warned him not to capitalize on Lucinda's grief.

Meanwhile, Craig continued to have his hands full with the women of Oakdale. Emily, desperate for him to give her another chance, hired a private investigator to dig up dirt on Craig's current companion, Ellie Snyder. Emily soon got her ammunition and eagerly reported to Craig the details of Ellie's sordid affair with a married man. Her plan backfired, though, because Craig had already learned about it from Ellie, who was well aware of Emily's plan.

Despite Meg's warnings, Lily gave money to Tonio, while a suspicious Lucinda called the State Department to check on Tonio's so-called contact in Montega, Juanita Perrera. What Lucinda didn't know was that Tonio had been paying Juanita to lie to the authorities about the search for Sierra.

Perceiving Sierra as Craig's weak spot, Emily offered Tonio more money to help with the search, and Tonio took full advantage of it. When Margo investigated, she discovered that Tonio's Montegan contact didn't even live there. Lucinda confronted him about the lack of information concerning her daughter. If he'd been robbing her all this time, he was a dead man. Tonio told Lucinda what he knew to be a lie: that Sierra was alive and well and fighting for the Montegan resistance, but there was still a contract out on her life. Craig heard this and considered going to Montega, but Lyla and Margo dissuaded him.

When Holden called to say he'd be making a trip back home this summer, Lily wondered if she'd made love to Caleb too soon. She was very protective of Caleb when Lucinda offered him a job at Simply Barbara. Caleb went to work for Simply Barbara's designer, Olivia Wycroft. When Olivia flirted with him, Caleb explained he was in love with Lily and reported the incident to Lucinda. Lucinda wasn't pleased; she wanted to keep Olivia happy so she would be competitive against Barbara's new line of designs. Caleb was fired. The news came that Holden had married Angel Lange in Europe, and unable to deal with her grief, Lily turned away from everyone. Caleb realized he was no more than Holden's surrogate, and he found comfort with Pam. Lucinda was thrilled that Lily was finally over the Snyder boys.

Lucinda was out to get another man—intense, young Brock Lombard. But this was business. She wanted to sign him and his company to Walsh. Ellie had other ideas, and she tried to persuade Kirk not to pursue Lombard. Brock was Ellie's ex-boyfriend, and she didn't want him around. When Emily got wind of the situation, she advised Tonio to go after Lombard, and Tonio succeeded in signing him. Brock arrived in Oakdale eager to do business with Tonio and taunt Ellie about their past affair. He was immediately taken with Emily. As for Ellie, she deeply regretted "that September night" when she did things for Brock that continued to haunt her. Brock was turned on by what he saw as Ellie's enticing mix of prudishness and sensuality.

Craig got word that refugees from Montega, possibly including Sierra, had escaped an island prison by boat. He immediately made arrangements to go to Cuba. Lucinda chose not to tell Ellie until Craig was gone. Now Ellie had oodles of time to think about Brock, and she couldn't get him out of her system, even though he was married, and she was frightened for her life because of what she'd done for him in the past. Brock continued to bait her while also flirting with Emily.

Tonio was surprised when Bianca Marques, a Montegan refugee, appeared on his doorstep with Sierra's wedding band. Tonio welcomed Bianca into his home, but he didn't give the ring to Craig. Tonio told Bianca they were doing the right thing, but Bianca felt guilty.

Needing something to distract her after learning about Holden's marriage, Lily asked Bianca to help her find Sierra. She asked about the people in Florida who had helped Bianca come to Oakdale. When Lily got to Florida, Bianca's contacts, the Delgados, tried to discourage her from searching for her sister alone. But Lily was persistent and was soon introduced to a man named Sawyer, who agreed to serve as her guide. Lily took the name "Snyder," donned fatigues and braved the Montegan jungle. Her first day was cut short when Sawyer was shot, and she was taken pris-

Julie wanted to be a successful model so bad she could taste it! So when sexy, sleazy Tonio Reyes gave her an ultimatum—either sleep with him or forget her career—Julie gave in. She was disgusted with herself, but she wanted the money and the work.

oner. Lily tried to pass herself off as a cocaine buyer, but her captors weren't fooled. The captain wanted to punish her for her lies and had his lackey cut her cheek deeply. The Montegans wanted to know the real reason Lily entered their country—they were quite aware that she could be worth a large ransom. Then a guard entered with Duncan! Duncan was posing as a drug dealer while searching for his psychotic wife, Lilith. That night Duncan helped Lily escape, and they made their way back to U.S. soil. Duncan told Lily he wouldn't be joining her in Oakdale, but when her wound became infected, he realized Lily needed medical attention, fast. When Lily returned from Montega, Lucinda was horrified to see the very visible scar on her cheek. She wanted the best plastic surgeon possible to remove it, but John said it was too soon to operate.

The scar made Lily more insecure than ever. When Lucinda threw a party for Niles and his son and daughter, Lily elected not to attend. While sulking at the poolhouse, she encountered a young man who wasn't much in the mood for a party either. The stranger turned out to be Niles's son, Derek. Lily found Derek charming, but his sister, Trish, told her that her brother had a reputation for loving and leaving, and Niles confirmed that this was true. Soon, Derek and Lily were on their way to London on Lucinda's jet. When they returned from England, they made a dramatic reappearance at the AIDS ball and informed their parents they were married! Lucinda and Niles were shocked. Derek's wedding present to his wife was a stone cottage by the river. Lucinda was not enamored of the primitive abode, and Lily's bliss was further undermined when she heard Niles and Derek arguing. Niles accused Derek of marrying Lily for her money, while Derek accused the pot of calling the kettle black, considering Niles's recent interest in Lucinda. Lily's hopes dimmed when Derek went to New York on business with his assistant, Karen. Lily hopped on a plane to see for herself if Karen was gorgeous, and Derek was amused by her jealousy.

When Holden reappeared in Oakdale, he wasn't greeted with open arms, but that didn't stop him from seeking Lily out. He surprised her at the hayloft and tried to rekindle their romance, until Derek arrived and put a stop to his attempt. Emma told her son it was time to get over Lily once and for all—he was married, and so was she.

Niles was planning to steal Lily's worldly holdings. When Lily rewrote her will, she left her entire $25-million estate to Derek. Niles enlisted the help of the corrupt Jeff Dolan. Derek was aware of the plan, but now he wanted out. Niles was upset that his son was backing out of the deal they had made to take Lily for all she was worth, kill her and split the money. Niles had Jeff douse the cottage with gasoline. Then he shot Jeff and made it look like Derek did it. When Derek showed up to warn Lily, the cottage exploded in flames, trapping them both inside. The rescuers found Lily's wedding ring outside the cottage, which was a signal that she might have gotten out alive. Lucinda was devastated. John was there to console her; both her daughters were now missing, and he knew she was at a loss.

Hal found a letter in Derek's glove compartment describing the plan to kill Lily. Hal put out an APB on Niles, who eventually turned himself in. Then Lily called the farm. She said she didn't want anyone to come looking for her. Her bandaged hand hung up the phone, and she gave the receiver to a nun. Lucinda told Ambrose to hire detectives immediately.

In another match not made in heaven, the sexual tension between Brock and Emily was rising fast. Brock told Ellie that he'd drop Emily in a second, if she would take him back. Ellie said there was no way she would go back to Brock. When the cocky Lombard kissed her, she slapped him hard. However, it was Brock who turned violent when his wife Marjorie appeared in Oakdale. Marjorie wanted a divorce, and Brock was delaying things. She saw Brock in an embrace with Emily and ordered a background check on her husband's latest companion. When Brock overheard this, he knocked her down and threatened greater punishment if his wife continued to snoop in his affairs. Marjorie got the dirt on Emily and wasted no time in informing Brock of Emily's history with James Stenbeck. Brock confronted Emily and called her a slut. Emily said she'd stack her reputation against his any day. Later Emily told

Paul what had happened and how James still haunted her to this day. Because he was James's son, Paul was probably the only person who could empathize with the scars Emily lived with. He comforted her and held her in his arms. Their attraction built, and they kissed. Paul stayed, and they made love.

Emily felt affection for Paul and told him she was glad she was his first. However, she knew Barbara would have a fit if she found out. A smitten Paul sent Emily flowers and letters to commemorate the occasion. He no longer saw himself as the teenager he really was; he was a changed man, and he owed his new maturity to Emily. Emily appreciated his admiration, but she wanted to get on with her life. Paul was not letting go so easily, though.

Meanwhile, Tonio was like a drug supplier, giving members of the Oakdale community addictive doses of information about Sierra for a price. For a long time, his goods had been in great demand, but now his customers were dwindling. When Craig returned from Miami, he announced he was through giving him money. Tonio tried to lure Craig back with a new lie: Stenbeck was holding Sierra prisoner! The ploy didn't work.

Lucinda was not the only one who was unhappy that Ellie and Craig's relationship had intensified. In the wake of his breakup with Emily, Brock realized he wanted Ellie back more than ever, but because of his father Philip, he was unable to divorce Marjorie. Philip controlled Brock's life completely, and he let his son know in no uncertain terms that he was not to leave his wife for the lowly Snyder. Brock was determined to break all ties with the Lombard network and fortune so that he could be with Ellie. But at that very moment Ellie was passionately making love to Craig at the Snyder pond. Hurt and bitter, Brock asked Ellie if "it" was as good with Craig as it was with him. Ellie was quick to tell him "it" was better, because Brock knew nothing about tenderness.

Philip thought Brock had gotten too soft, and his emotions were clouding his judgment concerning Ellie. After all, Ellie, merely by being alive, put the whole Lombard operation in jeopardy because she knew what had happened "that September night." Philip put a gun on Brock's table and told him to keep his libido under control. Brock assured his father that Ellie wasn't a threat anymore, but Philip wasn't so sure.

Brock was needier than he'd ever been in his life.

He wanted to reform, but he was not sure how. One night, Emily's doorbell rang, and she found Brock on his knees begging for a chance to explain his behavior. Emily told him her history with James left her in no position to be superior. The sexual attraction was clearly there, and Brock and Emily made love. Then the doorbell rang again. It was Ellie, trying to warn Emily about Brock, but she was too late.

Emily and Brock did not hide their rekindled affair. At the AIDS ball, they performed a red hot tango that amazed everyone. Paul was jealous of Emily's relationship with Brock. He'd been writing her love letters, and Hal noticed his crush was growing. When Paul asked Emily what she thought of his letters, she tried to tell him gently that their romance was just a one-night stand.

Tonio revealed Sierra's wedding ring, and Craig was flabbergasted. Up to this point, he'd been able to focus solely on his relationship with Ellie. Craig wanted to know where the ring came from, and Tonio demanded more money for the information.

Lucinda headed for Montega now that she felt she'd ruined her marriage for good. She wanted to know the truth about James. Was he alive, and did he have Sierra? In Miami, Lucinda met Sawyer, Lily's guide in Montega. Sawyer refused to risk his life again, until he saw Lucinda's briefcase filled with money. They landed in Cartagena and waited in a hotel room while the war raged on in the streets. Sawyer was attracted to Lucinda's gusto as well as her body, and they enjoyed the energy of adventure together. After a passionate kiss, they leaped into bed. Their post-sex glow was put on hold, however, when two soldiers arrived and held them at gunpoint. Lucinda tried to bribe the soldiers, but they insisted their fate lay in the hands of Colonel Araca. The arrogant Araca told Lucinda that Sierra was dead, but Lucinda refused to believe him. The junta contacted Craig and demanded $5 million in ransom for Lucinda in 48 hours or else. Craig went to Montega with the money. Just as he was arriving, Lucinda and Sawyer managed to escape. A shot rang out, and Sawyer was hit. A second shot was fired, and Lucinda fell to the ground. When a soldier turned over her body to see if she was alive, the feisty Lucinda fired her gun and blew him away. Sawyer urged Lucinda to find Cordova, the man who was commanding the opposition. When Craig met up

with Cordova and showed him the money, Cordova placed him under house arrest.

John returned from a weekend with Susan to the news that Lucinda had been taken prisoner. Bianca was also upset and told Tonio if anything happened to Craig she'd tell Margo the truth about Sierra's ring.

When Lucinda met up with Craig, she collapsed in his arms. Lucinda and Craig learned little about Sierra. They talked to Sierra's old nurse, Flora, who told them that Sierra was executed a year ago. Flora claimed she received Sierra's wedding ring from a guard and sent it to the United States, a story proving that Tonio had been lying all along. Lucinda and Craig found Sierra's name on the wall of martyrs by a mass grave. Forced to accept the fact that she was really dead, they headed back to Oakdale. Soon after, a bereft Lucinda adopted Tonio's ward, Bianca, and she came to live with her at the mansion. John and Lucinda grew closer, and a passionate kiss made Lucinda wonder if starting over again were possible. John had second thoughts, too, and he told Susan he was planning to give his marriage a second chance. Susan called John and feigned being upset by an anonymous phone call. John rushed to her side. He returned to the mansion to find Sawyer in his robe, emerging from the sauna. Unable to control her desire for one-upmanship, Lucinda introduced Sawyer as her lover, and considering his affair with Susan, John knew he'd be a hypocrite if he said anything. Nevertheless, Lucinda and John continued to have contact, and Lucinda admitted to being wrong about Duke, but she still wanted proof that he was really John's son. One day Lucinda and Susan had an all-out brawl over John. Lucinda pushed her adversary, sending her crashing into a ladder. Unaware of the seriousness of the fall, Lucinda left a crumpled, unconscious Susan on the floor. Susan starting taking pills for her excruciating back pain and threatened to tell John the truth about how it had happened. As Susan continued to take painkillers, Bob grew more concerned. Lucinda wanted to prevent John from learning she was responsible for Susan's injuries. She tried to bribe Susan, but Susan continued to hold the threat over her head. While John continued to try to work things out with his wife, Susan found herself alone and in pain on Christmas Eve.

While John, Lucinda and Susan were having their romantic troubles, the Perettis were gloriously happy and expecting a child. Lyla was enjoying her pregnancy in Boston, being cared for by Casey's folks. Their happiness was marred, however, when Casey began to experience spells of numbness in his arm and other unusual symptoms. He soon felt too weak to work and asked John to remove him from the surgical roster. Then he collapsed in the hospital cafeteria. Tests showed Casey had Guillain-Barré syndrome, a disorder of the nervous system. It wasn't long before the paralysis spread to his neck. Casey realized his life could be threatened if the paralysis attacked his respiratory system, but he was encouraged when he began to experience some sensation in his hand. When Lyla's water broke, Casey checked himself into her Boston hospital. Lyla gave birth to a daughter, and they named her Kathryn Ann, Katie for short.

When Iva returned from tending to her father, she went straight into the arms of Kirk Anderson. But Lucinda was out to undermine their happiness. First, she made sure to mention Kirk's name to Jared's niece, Lenore, the woman Kirk had wronged. Although Lenore wasn't sure if she could attend Meg and Rod's wedding because of Kirk, Lucinda sailed into the Snyder kitchen and informed everyone of her imminent arrival. Lucinda knew damn well that Lenore was the key to Kirk's scandalous past with Jared, and she wanted it to all to come out. After much thought, Lenore decided to attend the wedding. She also elected to bring her two children. It was a disaster! This was one predicament that Kirk couldn't worm his way out of, as it became clear that he and Lenore were once married and that Kirk had deserted her and their two children, Stephen and Linda Ann, for Adelaide Fitzgibbons. Even worse, that Kirk got a lot of money from his relationship with Adelaide, and none of it went to Lenore and the kids. Jared and Lenore opted not to attend the wedding reception. When Lenore told Iva her side of the story, Iva told Kirk to get out of her life for good. Craig was

there to comfort Iva, while Lucinda tried to comfort Kirk, who didn't trust her. Even Cal comforted Kirk, since he'd also abandoned his wife and child. And Emma urged Iva to forgive him. Meanwhile, Lenore fled to Quebec, and Kirk followed. He arrived just in time to save her and the children from a burning

When Brock walked out on her, Paul and Emily shared a night of tender love. She was Paul's first, and he was smitten, but Emily soon returned to Brock (left). At the AIDS ball they performed a red-hot tango that amazed everyone!

cabin. When she heard that Kirk had rescued Lenore, Iva was impressed, but Lenore left the hospital without saying thank you or goodbye. Eventually, she returned to Oakdale and had a change of heart. She gave Kirk visitation rights so he could get to know his kids. Kirk was on cloud nine and hoped Iva would give him a second chance. Iva wasn't ruling it out, but she wanted to take things very slowly. When he asked Iva to marry him, she said yes. The Snyders were overjoyed. But Kirk got ahead of himself when he announced he wanted full custody of his children. When Iva heard about his demand, she wondered if Kirk were really a changed man after all. Kirk and Iva were having other problems as well. Every time they started to make love, Iva had devastating flashbacks of being raped by Rod. Finally, Iva left him a note saying she wasn't sure if they had a future together, and she decided to seek therapy.

Lucinda decided to recharge Kirk's competitive motor by hiring businessman Blake Stevens, her first African-American executive. Blake planned to stay only six months, and he quickly succeeded in winning clients away from Kirk and his former employer Adelaide. However, Blake was not so lucky with Jessica, who turned him down every time he asked her out.

Roy and Jessica's relationship was undermined when they fell on different sides of a domestic violence case. Amy Phillips had accused her husband Lloyd of beating her. Roy thought he had enough evidence to arrest him. Believing she had enough evidence to prove Lloyd's innocence, Jessica decided to represent him. Roy couldn't understand why she would even think of taking such a case, and their arguments led them to a parting of ways. Amy broke down and admitted that Lloyd didn't beat her, and the man who did could be anywhere by now. Although hurt and disappointed, Roy was drawn to Amy and wanted to be a part of her life. When she disappeared from Oakdale, he followed her to Arizona, to Jessica's dismay.

Another Franklin had her eye on someone. Nella had long been attracted to Beau, who had eyes only for Pam. Beau's singing career had really taken off, but it was jeopardized when he lost his voice and couldn't get it back. He was able to talk, but when he tried to sing, nothing came out. Pam was sure the failure was psychosomatic. Beau's manager replaced him on a big concert tour, and his replacement arrogantly planned to include the love song Beau had written for Pam. Beau lost his temper, grabbed the microphone and sang the song himself. His voice had returned. Beau broke up with Pam after he found out she unwittingly gave his list of songs to the replacement singer. Pam turned to Caleb, and Nella comforted Beau. When Beau decided to move to Los Angeles, Nella followed. And when Pam graduated from nursing school, she, too, left Oakdale for good.

James Stenbeck was keeping an eye on Tonio Reyes. Tonio had agreed to go to the Dominican Republic to divorce Meg. Meg and Rod went to the Dominican Republic together and stayed in the hotel across from Tonio's. Unbeknownst to them, Stenbeck had planted an assassin in their room with orders to shoot Tonio. Rod almost walked in on him, but the man avoided being seen and was able to get a shot at Tonio and then hide his rifle in Rod's suitcase, making Rod the prime suspect. Meg's intuition told her that Stenbeck was responsible, and she warned Tonio that either he inform the police of his connection to Stenbeck or she would. Afraid of the repercussions if he were to confess, Tonio concocted a story of attempted murder by a Montegan who knew he was involved in the search for Sierra. Soon after, Meg and Rod were married in the Snyder barn. Rod officially changed his name to Josh, and they made plans to move back to Waco.

Romance was in bloom at the Snyder farm as Cal and Jared competed for Emma's affections in an unusual way—by vying to replace her faltering kitchen appliances! Emma chose Cal. The Snyders were all astir when Mama wasn't there to make breakfast. When Cal and Emma appeared, an embarrassed Cal assured the family he intended to marry their mother. Emma was quite surprised and not at all pleased with his presumptuous announcement.

Lisa Mitchell was having a hard time sleeping. Her fears about Earl's whereabouts and his absence caused her to turn to sleeping pills. One night, while walking in a fog, Lisa was aware she was being followed, and she ran for her life, crashing into Grant. A vulnerable Lisa was happy to take comfort in his arms. When she was searching through Earl's suitcases, Lisa found a letter addressed to a Jennifer Hobart. Oddly enough, Grant knew her from San Francisco. Lisa panicked—maybe Earl was having an affair. She called the woman, who had the nerve to ask Lisa if she were Earl Mitchell's widow. Lisa decided to go to San Francisco and confront this woman face-to-face. Grant, who was now Lisa's financial manager and primary confidant, tried to dissuade her from going, but his efforts were in vain.

At this time, Hank confided to Barbara that his lover, Charles, had been diagnosed with AIDS. Bob arranged for him to have a test for HIV, and John got involved when a lab technician refused to perform it. Then John learned the test concerned AIDS, and the patient was Hank. Andy had rethought his initial reaction to Hank, and John wasn't thrilled that his son was so accepting of this man and his homosexuality. He warned Andy he might be judged by the company he kept. Hank was relieved to learn he was negative, but he soon walked into an unexpected showdown with Paul. Paul lashed out, calling Hank a "queer." Paul felt betrayed not only by Hank's homosexuality, but also by his secrets. Barbara condemned her son for his obnoxious behavior, and an angry Paul moved out of his mother's apartment into a fraternity house on campus. James seized the opportunity to enlist an Oakdale contact to help get his son back into his grasp.

Kim agreed to join Lisa in San Francisco. They missed their scheduled flight, which was fortunate, since the plane crashed! When they got to Jennifer Hobart, she showed them a picture of the young Earl and said they'd recently rekindled their relationship. They'd planned to meet over the holidays, but when he didn't show up, Jennifer called some friends in Egypt, who told her he was presumed dead. Lisa found her story hard to swallow. When Kim and Lisa returned to Oakdale, Grant headed out to San Francisco. After he got there, Jennifer Hobart died of an overdose. Grant tried to persuade Lisa to cut Earl out of her will, and she did so, leaving a large sum to Grant. Lisa then received a call from someone claiming to have information about Earl. He wanted her to meet him at Lookout Tower. On the way, Lisa's brakes failed, and she lost control of the car. A highway patrolman dragged an unconscious Lisa out of her car, and when she came to, she learned the brakes had been tampered with. Lisa felt she was losing control over her life. She even thought she heard Earl in the apartment. Grant was convinced it was her imagination and what she needed was rest. He even went so far as to suggest a mental clinic on an island where a friend of his could take care of her. Kim and Bob knew Lisa always had a flair for the dramatic, but insane she was not. Lisa had her own doubts when she saw a man who looked like Earl come into the Mona Lisa. Soon after, she received a bouquet with a card signed "Earl." Lisa decided to get a checkup, and she signed her power of attorney over to Grant. As suspicions about Grant were increasing, Roy Franklin grew wary of the heroic Glenn Harrington. Then Shannon found Earl's bloody trench coat in Lisa's penthouse, the same coat Lisa swore she had seen.

Shannon brought the coat to the police. Glenn told her he wanted to end his undercover work and have a real life—a normal life—with her, and they shared a night of passion.

One night when Shannon was due to meet Glenn at Lisa's penthouse, an Earl look-alike named Benjamin unlocked the terrace door and let himself in. At the same time, Roy decided to search Glenn's room. He found a photograph of Shannon and Lisa inscribed to Earl and a tape of Earl's voice calling out to Lisa. Roy called Hal and Margo and told them to get over to Lisa's right away. Meanwhile at the penthouse, Glenn was pouring Lisa a brandy laced with drugs. Then he told her that Grant was James's contact in Oakdale, and she believed him. Woozy from the brandy, Lisa went out on the terrace to get some air, and in her drugged confusion, she saw Earl's look-alike. Glenn was just about to push her off the terrace when Shannon arrived and pounded on the door. When Glenn heard Shannon's voice, he hesitated, and the police were able to get in. In the confusion that followed, Glenn got away. It was revealed that Glenn was after Earl's money, which would go to Shannon if Lisa died. He planned to marry her, then kill her, but he fell in love and decided that they could live happily ever after and share the money. It was Glenn who'd smothered Earl in his hotel room in Egypt and used Grant as a smokescreen.

Not wanting to have any secrets between them, Meg confessed everything she knew about Tonio to Josh: that he didn't have a contact in Montega searching for Sierra, and that James was responsible for Tonio's financial well-being. Josh insisted they go to the police with the information. Meg agreed to tell Tom and Margo everything she knew. The police brought Tonio in for questioning, but he refused to talk until his lawyer, Fred Greer, arrived. Meg offered to help the police by hiding a tape recorder on her when she confronted him. But a suspicious Tonio noticed she was especially nervous and seemed to be hiding something in her pocket.

When Barbara, Hal, Hank and Paul went to New York for Barbara's fashion show, Paul used the opportunity to arrange a meeting with his father. Lien discovered a note about the meeting and showed it to Hank. When Paul snuck away to rendezvous with James, Hank followed. The crafty James was circling over the city in a helicopter, accompanied by Glenn.

## Love and Marriage

*She'd married Tonio for his money, and she was miserable, so Meg turned to Rod Landry, Lily's father and reformed rapist of sister Iva, for comfort, and they fell in love. The Snyders weren't pleased, especially Holden, Seth and Caleb, but Meg and Rod were eventually married on the Snyder farm. Rod officially changed his name back to Josh, and he and his "Meggie" made plans to move to Waco.*

Paul arrived at the heliport, and Hank ran after him. When Glenn realized what was happening, he ran to Hank, only to be shot and killed by James. Pursued by the NYPD, Stenbeck's chopper crashed in the East River. Horrified by his father's actions, Paul hurried to comfort a bleeding Hank and realized he owed his life to a man he'd spurned merely because he was gay. And so Hank became the heroic figure in Paul's eyes, replacing James. Barbara dedicated her new collection to her talented designer and friend. Hank recovered from his bullet wound, and when he felt well enough to travel, he decided to visit Charles. When Charles's condition grew worse, Hank announced his

plans to move to New York. Kim snagged him for an interview on "Patterns," and he was given a heartfelt send-off.

Shannon got a call from Duncan's demented "wife," Lilith, who vowed to return to the castle and get her revenge. Around the same time, Mark Harrington, Glenn's brother, arrived in Oakdale. Mark was a Philadelphia policeman whose wife had recently left him. He brought with him a letter Glenn had written to Shannon the day before he died, and Shannon learned she was to inherit the contents of Glenn's Swiss bank account. Shannon offered Mark a room at the Castle, which she planned to convert into a home for runaways. Mark opted to stay at Lyla's but agreed to help set up the center. Shannon's budding romance with Mark continued as smoothly as their work in transforming McKechnie Castle. Shannon began to feel dizzy. She wondered if this could be morning sickness, and if the child could be Glenn's from the one night they had made love. When Shannon went to the hospital to see Dr. Samuels, she was shocked to run into Duncan, who had just returned from saving Lily in Montega.

Shannon's coziness with Mark made Duncan more than a wee bit jealous. Hoping to prove there was still a lot of love between them, he kissed her passionately. But Shannon was adamant that it was too late for them, and she told him she was pregnant. Shannon was confused—she liked the idea of Mark raising his brother's child, but the passion she had for Mark didn't match what she had with Duncan. When Shannon told Duncan the baby she was carrying was Glenn's, not Mark's, Duncan saw the fetus as cursed and told his beloved lassie she should get an abortion. Shannon was appalled by his lack of sensitivity.

Shannon named her shelter the Earl Mitchell Center. One of the runaways, Buddy, captured

Duncan's attention. Mark thought Duncan was using his attachment to Buddy as a way to get closer to Shannon. When Mark told Duncan he hoped to marry Shannon, the fiery Scotsman swore he'd see his soul burn in hell first. Meanwhile, Buddy was heard saying that Duncan was a real pushover and would probably give him a job at one of his warehouses soon.

Tonio started to receive phone calls from James, who was last seen before his helicopter crashed into the East River. James warned Tonio that he was coming to get him. Stenbeck was closer than Tonio imagined. When Barbara moved into a townhouse that her husband and son weren't crazy about, she hired a new gardener, Shavez—but it was James in disguise. The clever James was able to find work with both Barbara and Lucinda, as well as around McKechnie Castle, where Buddy was his contact. It was Buddy who found James on a beach in Staten Island after his helicopter crashed and helped him hide out from the police. But Lucinda was nobody's fool. When he finally got her alone, she knew that he was James.

When Shannon was taken to the hospital with false labor pains, both Mark and Duncan spent time at her bedside. Duncan felt guilty for telling her to have an abortion and prayed she'd be all right. But Shannon remained distant. One night Duncan got drunk and approached his friend and lawyer Jessica Griffin, who gently let him down. Jessica convinced him that the best thing he could do was to give Shannon some space. Then Shannon's condition worsened and she miscarried. Aching to put his arms around his lassie, Duncan told her instead he was going to Scotland. Although she had mixed feelings, Shannon bid him goodbye. Realizing how she felt about Duncan, Mark said goodbye as well. Sad but determined, Shannon resolved to get on with her life. Missing her with all his heart, Duncan turned his plane around and came back to Oakdale.

James was manipulating the residents of Oakdale like puppets. He told Lucinda she had better do as he said, or he'd kill Sierra. He gave her a letter that she was sure was a forgery until Tonio showed up with Sierra's wedding ring, and Lucinda began to believe Stenbeck's story. James learned that Adam was Hal's child. He also heard Paul say he hoped his father was dead. This hurt James to the quick, but it didn't stop him from wanting his son back.

When Emily received a dozen pink roses that both Brock and Paul insisted were not from them, she knew James was stalking her again. Paul took Hal's service revolver and gave it to her for protection. When Paul finally got a call from his father, he contacted Emily, and they decided to go to the police together.

Soon after, James appeared on Tonio's balcony threatening death if Tonio didn't help him kidnap Paul. He ordered Tonio to make sure Paul was at Emily's apartment the following night. Luckily for Tonio, Emily had invited Paul to dinner that evening. She put his love letters in an envelope and planned to return them to him that night. Emily placed the envelope on the dining room table. Suddenly, James appeared on the terrace. He was sure his plan would work but got derailed when he found the envelope and discovered his son's love letters to his ex-mistress. A terrified Emily found an enraged Stenbeck in her living room. Paul arrived carrying flowers and heard Emily's screams. He rushed inside and found Hal's gun. When Paul saw his father strangling Emily, he fired. James crumpled to the floor. Emily checked his pulse and found none. Together they agreed to burn the love letters before they called the police.

As the cops arrived and outlined James's corpse with chalk, Emily wondered if Paul could face the consequences of what he'd done. In his statement Paul said he shot his father to save Emily. Hal and Barbara were in Kentucky visiting Hal's family when they learned what happened. Margo brought the evidence from Emily's apartment to the station and did a double-take when she found the flowers from Paul and the card that went with it. When Emily learned Lucinda had harbored James in her stables, she was furious.

From the grave Stenbeck continued to affect the lives of Oakdalians. Duncan refused to believe he was dead until he saw the corpse. Tonio continued to deny any connection to him, but phone records from Lucinda's stables told a different story. When James's journals were recovered, Hal found one entry particularly interesting—it concerned a conversation Barbara had with Lucinda about Adam's paternity while James was eavesdropping. Hal saw this as yet another lie from Barbara.

The police were curious as to why Jessica was called before they were, and Margo was convinced that Paul and Emily were holding back vital information. When Hal asked Emily what she had burned in her sink, she claimed it was love letters from James, and forensics reported that the charred bits were too small to identify. The police said James's death was not a clear-cut case of self-defense. Barbara was upset that Paul was taking all the heat when it was Lucinda who'd harbored the criminal. Barbara stumbled on her son telling Emily that he was afraid "it will all come out tomorrow," and Emily reassured him that "it can't, because we're the only ones who know." Barbara didn't know that what they were hiding was not a conspiracy to kill James, but the sexual history they had shared. Paul was indicted for second-degree murder. An enraged Barbara accused Emily of killing James and making Paul take the rap. Paul considered telling Jessica the truth about the burned love letters, but Emily was vehemently opposed. Brock warned Emily that Paul's feeling of guilt about their liaison was bound to trip up his defense.

Because of Brock Lombard's association with Emily, his face was everywhere, which greatly disturbed his father, Philip. Philip tried to blackmail Emily, and Brock threatened to turn state's evidence on his father if she were harmed. Emily finally explained the whole story to Brock—that James was trying to kill her because he learned she had slept with Paul. Brock was stunned. But he loved her and decided to accept her weaknesses, just as she had accepted his. He told her that he and Marjorie would get a quick and secret divorce, and when he returned, he'd be ready to spend the rest of his life with her. Philip had other ideas. He wanted to test his son's loyalty to the "family," and he asked him to handle a situation similar to "that September night." Brock's blood ran cold. Philip explained that the Harper family was moving into Lombard territory, and he wanted Brock to rub them out. Brock convinced his father not to go that route, and in exchange, Philip insisted his son dump Emily. He informed Brock that Jason Benedict, who had been on the Lombards' backs for years, was prosecuting Paul's case. When Brock was served with a subpoena, Philip was sure Jason would use this opportunity to undermine his family's operation. Again, he demanded Brock drop Emily. When Brock told his father to get lost, Philip told one of his henchmen it was time to eliminate Emily and Ellie.

As the trial was about to begin, James's mother Greta Aldrin appeared in Oakdale. Jason Benedict argued that Paul killed James in a moment of passion.

Jessica argued that he was defending Emily. Margo's testimony was the most damaging—she mentioned how late they were in calling the police, and she read Paul's card to Emily. When Benedict asked Emily if her relationship with Paul was sexual, Emily hid the truth. Hal testified that he'd heard Paul say he wanted his father dead, and Barbara was reluctantly forced to testify to the same. After Emily completed her testimony, she steered clear of the trial, and Paul greatly missed her being there to support him. Brock told Paul he knew that Emily perjured herself on the stand, and he also knew all about the affair. Feeling totally betrayed, Paul admitted on the witness stand to having sex with Emily. Having heard about Brock's conversation with Paul, Emily rushed to the courtroom, but it was too late—Paul's revelation had everyone reeling. The jury didn't take long to reach its verdict— not guilty. Everyone was relieved except Emily, who was worried about going to jail for perjury. After the trial, Paul changed his last name to Ryan and announced he was quitting school to "find himself."

During this year a much-loved Oakdale couple, David and Ellen Stewart, were trying to come to terms with their changing relationship. David had been doing AIDS research in Zaire, and when he came home on one of his infrequent trips, Ellen felt as if he'd been gone for decades. She told him she couldn't live this way anymore—it was Africa or her. David asked if she'd consider joining him in Africa, but Ellen's home was in Oakdale. So they settled on Atlanta, where David could continue with his research, and Ellen could visit him on weekends.

On a happier note, Duncan continued to woo his lassie, and when she wouldn't say yes, he serenaded her at the Mona Lisa with "I Do, I Do" and took to reciting from *Romeo and Juliet* every chance he had. He even had "Duncan loves Shannon" written across the sky. One night he slipped an emerald engagement ring into her favorite drink, a stinger. The besotted man also wangled his way onto Judith Clayton's television show, where he urged viewers to plead his case to his stubborn, feisty lassie! When Shannon and Duncan got trapped in the turret room, Shannon finally said yes. As he held his terrified bride-to-be in his arms, and they swung from the turret window, the pipers below played "Comin' Through the Rye." Shannon and Duncan were married in his ancestor Margaret's castle in Scotland with Brian, Beatrice and Lisa in attendance.

Things were closing in on Brock as he considered turning state's evidence against his father, underworld figure Philip Lombard. Emily encouraged him to do what he felt was right. Then Emily met a man named Lucas Pryor who said he was interested in bringing business to Montgomery & Associates. Pryor worked for Philip and planned to kidnap Emily to use against Brock. The plan was foiled, and Tom put undercover cop Lloyd on the case. Pryor followed Emily to her apartment, unaware that Lloyd was already there. Pryor shot Lloyd with Brock's gun, but Lloyd quickly recovered and shot Pryor. A messenger later delivered Brock's gun to Ellie.

Brock was about to leave his hotel to pick up Emily when Caleb Snyder appeared and ordered him to stay away from his sister, Ellie. Later, Ellie found Brock dead at the hotel. Caleb was unconscious in the bedroom and later claimed someone had knocked him out. The fingerprints on the gun belonged to Ellie and Brock. Then Hal found a fortune in diamonds stashed in Caleb's pocket!

Emily accused Ellie of Brock's murder. Unfortunately, the messenger who had delivered Brock's gun to Ellie and could have cleared her was found dead in her office. Lucinda was champing at the bit to plaster the Lombard murder on the front page of the *City Times*. John declined to inform his wife that Lloyd's death had been faked, and that he was in a coma at Memorial.

While Philip was plotting Ellie's murder, Bruce Dreyfuss, the runaway who'd been staying at the Earl Mitchell Center under the name of Hey You, accused Philip of killing his entire family. Philip denied the charge, but the police wanted to talk to Bruce because his fingerprints were found on the door of Brock's suite. Bruce admitted he was there but swore he never entered the room. He did hear two men fighting, and then a gun went off. While hiding in a supply closet, he later saw Ellie enter the suite. That got Ellie off the hook, and Hal booked Caleb for murder. But it was all a ploy to lure Philip out into the open. Wearing a wire, Ellie told Philip she knew Caleb was being framed, and she had the keys to Brock's safe-deposit box, which she intended to turn over to the Crime Commission. Philip wondered why she hadn't removed her hat and realized she was wired. He called off the hit on Ellie—for now.

When Lloyd came out of his coma, he told the police Philip had ordered the hit on Brock. Then Lloyd died, leaving the police with no "real life" testimony to go on. Finally, Connie Lombard, Brock's distraught mother, broke down and gave them the information they needed. Philip swore he could refute every word. But it was too late. Connie had already surrendered the papers Philip took from Brock's suite the night he killed him.

Philip's henchmen closed in on Ellie, demanding the keys to the safe-deposit box. Kirk and the Luther's Corners sheriff appeared in the nick of time. A grateful Ellie impulsively slept with Kirk. She later dismissed Kirk as a one-night stand, but Kirk thought differently. Ellie was feeling tremendous guilt because she had Kirk while Iva was alone. When the Snyder family found out about Kirk and Ellie's relationship, they were up in arms. Even Caleb, her closest sibling, was ready to disown her. Kirk asked Ellie to move in with him, and she did, keeping the move a secret from Emma and Iva.

Lucinda was pleased with the Kirk/Ellie pairing, because it brought out the killer instincts in her star exec. Kirk bought Diana's yacht from Lisa and renamed the restaurant Ellie's. He also planned to turn one of the staterooms into a home for them. Caleb told his sister she was no better than a kept woman, and Iva warned Kirk that Ellie was just as selfish as he was. Ellie and Kirk launched a magazine supplement to the *City Times* called *Inside Oakdale*. They held an essay contest for the fledgling magazine on "Why I love Oakdale." Unbeknownst to Iva, Emma secretly submitted an essay on her lonely daughter's behalf, and Iva won first prize—a makeover, a new wardrobe and a cruise! At Iva's bon-voyage party, Jane, Lucinda's loyal secretary, went home with Ambrose Bingham.

On the ocean liner *Napoli*, Iva ran into Jason Benedict, the attorney who had prosecuted Paul Ryan in the Stenbeck murder trial, and they had a lovely time together. After she'd slept with him, she told him she was no longer haunted by her teenage rape. A radiant Iva returned to Oakdale, and people wondered what exactly happened on that cruise. Sadly, Jason broke up with Iva just as Kirk proposed to Ellie. To add insult to injury, Ellie asked her jilted sister if she would be her maid of honor.

Julie Wendall was having a clandestine affair with Tonio Reyes while she was still living with Andy.

Julie eventually moved into an apartment, with Tonio footing the bill. Once she made the move, Julie noticed that Tonio stopped telling her he loved her. After he read Julie's farewell letter, a distraught Andy had to fight the urge to drink. Bitter, he told her that no matter what Reyes had promised her, rumor had it she didn't have the job as signature model for Veronica Leathers. Julie soon found out the rumor was true. When she confronted Tonio, he told her she would be their "international" model. Julie was jealous of the time Tonio was spending with Blythe Nelson, a debutante from Philadelphia's Main Line who was to be station WOAK's new anchorwoman. When Blythe questioned Tonio about the striking redhead, he replied, "She's just a model."

Julie was beginning to feel like yesterday's garbage, and she didn't like it one bit! She'd noticed Caleb Snyder looking her way, and it was giving her ideas. To Tonio's surprise, she moved into Lisa Mitchell's penthouse and had set her sights on Caleb. Tonio vowed revenge.

Lily was back in town. This was a different, hardened Lily, and she astonished everyone by becoming an overnight success in the world of management consulting. Lily bought out Emily's shares in M&A and became a business rival to reckon with. Lucinda was shocked to find out her daughter's first big client was Jared Carpenter, Lily's wealthy maternal grandfather. She was also shocked when Lily tried to lure Kirk Anderson away to join her company, and she was livid that Kirk considered it. The FCC decided not to renew Lucinda's license to operate WOAK. Duncan and Tonio vied for ownership of the station, and Tonio won, leaving Duncan to console himself with a job as managing editor of the *Argus*.

Lucinda didn't know Lily had gotten dissatisfied Walsh employee Blake Stevens to give her Walsh company secrets. But business wasn't the only thing Lily was after. Having become bitter about marriage and love, Lily decided anyone was fair game. Frannie was appalled when Lily made a play for her beau, Sean Baxter, a recent hire at M&A who was trying to raise money to buy out Craig's partnership in the company. One night Lily arrived at Sean's apartment in a seductive mood and offered him the money he needed. Sean declined, and Lily left, but not before she was sure Frannie had seen her. When Sean and Frannie spent a few days at the Stewart cabin, Lily kept interrupting them with "emergency" business calls.

Frannie and Sean finally made love and were happy for a while. Then Sean got the disturbing news that his teenage sister, Courtney, had run away from boarding school and taken up residence in his New York apartment where his ex-girlfriend, Gail Kincaid, was still living. When Courtney finally arrived in Oakdale, she was unhappy to find her brother preoccupied with Frannie. Courtney endeared herself to Lily. Sean received a threatening letter from Gail—she wanted to slap him with a palimony suit. Gail came to Oakdale and set her sights on Tonio and his money. When the twosome confronted Sean in public, Sean punched Tonio, and Blythe Nelson, WOAK'S anchorwoman, got it on tape. Since Kim was out of town, Tonio suggested that Blythe do a special edition of "Patterns" on "Women Who Sacrifice for Ungrateful Men," and Gail would be the perfect guest. Needless to say, the show made Sean look very bad. Courtney was enraged, and Lucinda was horrified. Gail threatened to expose Sean's past with a woman named Donna. Sean frantically called Donna and told her Gail had copies of his letters to her. Lily offered to help Sean buy off Gail, but Frannie nixed the idea, and Gail increased the amount of damages she was seeking to $1 million. When Gail's suit came up for trial, Tonio was subpoenaed. In top form, Jessica Griffin established that Sean had never proposed to Gail, and Gail had never worked—in fact, she'd turned down job offers ever since she broke up with Sean. Tonio finally admitted he and Gail were lovers. Bitter for revenge, Gail told Frannie that Donna had a child by Sean and that Donna's husband thought the child was his.

Frannie's ex-boyfriend, Larry McDermott, came to Oakdale and took a staff position as a pediatrician at Memorial. Larry sought to rekindle what they'd had in Boston. When Sean saw them kissing, he hit Larry, and his temper frightened Frannie. Financier Gavin Kruger offered Sean a job in Zurich. Later, as Courtney and Frannie prepared to go to Zurich to spend Thanksgiving with Sean, Frannie received a letter from Sean asking her not to come—he had taken up with Kruger's personal assistant, Jade. Once again, Frannie was a loser in love.

Frannie's sister, Sabrina, returned to Oakdale, and Tonio, eager to earn some respect, decided she was his best bet. He told Sabrina not to believe everything she heard about him. Frannie warned her sister to stay away from Tonio. Fred Greer, Tonio's crooked lawyer, informed him Sabrina was loaded. When ex-fiancé Seth Snyder advised her to break up with Tonio, Sabrina told him where to go. Tonio commissioned Sabrina to paint his portrait. In preparation, she researched his Montegan history and was impressed by his heroic deeds. It wasn't long before they became lovers.

Before his death, Emily had lent Brock Lombard a considerable amount of money—money she now would never be able to recover. Since she'd sold her shares in M&A to Lily, Emily decided she had no choice but to return there as an employee. A furious Barbara told Lily that if she hired Emily, she'd withdraw her lucrative BRO account. Emily retaliated by threatening to tell Hal that Barbara knew about Adam's parentage before he did, and Lily overheard. Emily had had it with Barbara and decided to send Hal an anonymous note about Barbara and Adam. Emily didn't mail the note, but when Barbara terminated her contract with M&A, a vindictive Lily did. She later tried to intercept it, but Hal had already gotten it. To avoid incrimination, Lily retrieved it. Hal confronted Barbara and then stormed out. Barbara accused Emily of telling him, and Emily suspected Lily. Lily burned the letter.

Hal turned to Margo for advice, and she encouraged him to forgive Barbara. A grateful Hal kissed Margo and played with Adam, while Barbara watched through the window, drawing her own conclusions. She left Hal a letter saying she was leaving him, and then she disappeared. Not even Jessica Griffin knew where she had gone. Jess told Hal that Barbara left instructions for Paul to take over BRO. Paul promptly hired Barbara's nemesis Emily to

## Troubled Triangles

*They were sisters, and Iva (right) had him first. Iva had her share of problems, though, and Ellie (left) eventually got the man. Ellie felt guilty, but since Iva had ended the relationship, there was no reason for Ellie not to see Kirk. As for Iva, she blamed herself—if she'd been able to give Kirk what he wanted, he would have stayed with her.*

oversee financial matters.

Barbara was spotted in London and Rome. When she arrived in Edinburgh, she called former lover Brian McColl, who was having marital problems with Beatrice, to thank him for making the necessary arrangements. Through a fax Paul found on Jessica's desk, Hal tracked down Barbara, only to learn she was pregnant! Barbara and Hal worked out their differences and returned to Oakdale to await the birth of their first child. A curious Lucinda wondered when Barbara's due date was. Paul admitted to his mother that he and Emily were living together. Barbara didn't believe for one minute that Emily loved Paul, and she told Emily that if she hurt her son, she'd have her to deal with.

Cal brought his right-hand man, Linc Lafferty, from Waco to act as liaison between Cal's company and M&A. Linc's mother, Hannah, ran the local boarding house in Oakdale, but Linc moved in with Cal. Lily was taken with Linc and put herself on Cal's account so she could cozy up to him. Linc quickly moved into Lucinda's poolhouse. Then Holden returned to Oakdale on business for his father-in-law, Henry Lange, and confided to Lucinda that there were serious problems in his marriage to Angel. He and Lily began spending time together, supposedly as friends. To keep her away from Holden, Lucinda urged Linc to pursue Lily, but Linc told her he didn't play that kind of game. Holden escorted Lily to the AIDS ball and were both shocked when Angel and her father arrived. Angel told Holden they might not be in love, but they were still married. Holden wanted a divorce, and Angel replied that he'd get a divorce over her dead body, and that she'd drag his precious Lily's name through the mud! To keep her husband, Angel brought their adopted daughter, Noelle, from England. Lucinda offered Holden, who was no longer at Lange, a job running her London operation. Lily wasn't pleased.

Meanwhile, Holden's brother Caleb shocked the family by marrying Julie Wendall in Las Vegas. Julie, desperate that Caleb never know about her sleazy affair with Tonio, was uncomfortable in a farmhouse full of people. Emma set about teaching her how to cook—a skill Julie hadn't bothered to acquire. They never got past the fried chicken and Dutch potato salad, which remained Julie's specialty during her time on the Snyder farm. Emma encouraged Julie to call her mother in Seattle and tell her the good news about her marriage, but Julie's uninterested mom couldn't have cared less. When Cal offered to pay for a lawyer to help her get custody of her kids from ex-husband Frank, Julie said Pete and Jenny were a part of her past.

Angry at Julie for not showing up for a photo shoot in his bedroom, Tonio decided to burst Caleb's bubble and told him about their affair. When a crushed Caleb confronted her, Julie admitted it was true. She begged his forgiveness, and Caleb was so much in love that he gave in. Tonio wasn't the only man in Julie Wendall's past; she and Linc had had a steamy affair in Seattle. Then Frank showed up with Pete and Jenny in tow and told Julie it was her turn to play mother! Julie wanted no part of the children and offered to pay Frank's mother Helen to care for them. Frank retaliated by blackmailing Julie about Linc. Julie turned to Tonio for money to pay him off. When Tonio mentioned Julie's "financial problems" to Caleb, she covered by telling Caleb she had given Jessica a retainer to help fight for custody of her kids. An angry Caleb told Tonio off, and an angry Tonio stopped payment on Frank's check. When Frank tried to cash it and was refused, he high-tailed it to the farm and told Caleb that Julie was paying him to keep quiet about her affair with Linc. Caleb, who had tolerated Julie's past, wondered if he were just another stop on her Love Tour. Frank revealed he'd offered custody of Pete and Jenny to Julie, and she'd refused. A disgusted Caleb told Julie their marriage was over, and Julie took refuge in Lisa's penthouse.

Realizing Holden was committed to Angel, Lily asked Linc to help her get over him. They took Cal's jet to Texas on business—and pleasure. Before she left, Lily made one last call to Holden, telling him that since he had a child, he should put aside his feelings for her. When Lily tried to kiss Linc, she couldn't follow through, but when Holden called, and Linc answered, he told him Lily was in the shower, deliberately giving him the wrong impression. Holden headed to the Mona Lisa and drank himself into a stupor. Julie saw he was in no condition to drive and told him he could spend the night at the penthouse. A bleary-eyed Holden confused Julie with Lily. Vulnerable and lonely, they made love.

Emma told Caleb where Julie was staying. He was sickened to find her in bed with his brother, and he and Holden came to blows. Angel overheard Holden tell Emma he couldn't make his marriage work and was going to fly to Texas to be with Lily. She stopped him by telling him Noelle was sick.

Holden tried to explain to Lily what had happened with Julie. "I thought she was you," he said. Lily was heartsick. When Holden tried to patch things up with Caleb, he was no more successful than he'd been with Lily. He told Lily he still loved her and always would. But Lily said it was too late—what they had was in the past. Dejected, Holden decided to accept Lucinda's job offer in London. Meanwhile,

Julie, after threatening to break her contract with Tonio if he didn't leave her alone, left Oakdale for parts unknown.

Angel got word that Noelle was being taken back by her biological parents. Holden thought it was in her best interests, since their marriage was such a farce. He begged Lily to wait, and knowing she'd always love him, Lily agreed.

Holden thought Angel was in London, but she was hiding out at the Lange country house at Lake Geneva. She called her brother Barclay and asked him to tamper with Lily's car. Later, after Lily dropped Holden off at the farm, her brakes failed, and she crashed. Lily was shaken up but unhurt, and the mechanic told her the brake line could have been worn out from normal use. Angel then started to torture Lily by phone, calling her and hanging up and leaving strange messages on her machine. One night Lily was surprised by a masked man at her door. She fainted, and Holden found her unharmed. Later, at the Snyder pond, the masked man was lurking behind the trees. Angel found out her father was on his way to London, and she made plans to leave right away. Before she went, she told her therapist that if Holden tried to divorce her, she'd kill herself. Then she told Lucinda that Lily and Holden were seeing each other on the sly.

Wealthy industrialist Gavin Kruger was seeking representation in the Midwest, and Oakdale's business community was gearing up for his arrival. Kirk and Ellie were dispatched to Switzerland from Walsh to pitch their ideas, and over at M&A, Lily was hoping Emily would entice Kruger to sign with them. Everyone was shocked to learn that Shannon had a past with Kruger, and they all tried to use her as entrée. In Switzerland, Kruger sent Emily a single white rose, which Shannon said was his way of wooing a woman. Appalled, Lucinda ordered Kirk and Ellie home. Gavin arrived in Oakdale accompanied by his attractive personal assistant, Jade Sullivan. It wasn't long before Emily received another rose and an invitation to dine in Quebec City, courtesy of the Kruger company jet. Although Kirk was angry, Gavin took great delight in flirting openly with Ellie, and it wasn't long before she, too, received a white rose. Gavin approved Ellie's ad campaign for his account, and Lucinda lavished her with praise. As for Jade, she decided to seduce Linc.

A troubled Andy had gone to Chicago, where he spent his days in art galleries and his nights in seedy bars. Alone in his hotel room, Andy got a call from a mysterious girl he couldn't even remember meeting. Later she showed up in blurred images in some of his photos. John and Kim found Andy, and the news that Caleb and Julie had eloped didn't help his situation. They persuaded him to come home, but when they arrived at his hotel to collect him, they found their son passed out on the floor.

Back in Oakdale, Andy secretly stole liquor from friends' homes and boozed it up all around town. Duke hated to see his brother on this self-destructive path and dismantled his car engine so he wouldn't cause any damage. Andy retaliated by stealing Duke's van, Rosie. Lien was driving along the same highway to meet Duke when she saw the van coming toward her. The vehicles collided. Lien was brought to Memorial for emergency surgery to remove her spleen. The police found out who stole the van, and Andy was arrested and jailed. In an act of "tough love," John and Kim refused to post bail. When he realized he had nearly killed his stepniece, Andy hit bottom. Lien declined to press charges, but Jessica Griffin entered a guilty plea. Andy took full responsibility for his actions and was sentenced to a detox program and ordered to continue with AA. During a family therapy session, Andy was forced to face a grim reality when he asked his mother if she had ever loved John. Kim felt she had to be honest and told him no. Andy was crushed. When he returned from detox, Andy moved into John and Lucinda's poolhouse and began attending AA meetings with his sponsor, fellow recovering alcoholic Susan Stewart. Courtney Baxter identified herself as the mystery girl Andy met in Chicago while he was on his bender. She wanted to pick up where they left off, but a sober Andy wasn't interested.

To deal with Andy's alcoholism, Kim and John were attending Al-Anon meetings together, and Frannie noticed Bob was feeling left out. Bob seemed to be occupying his time worrying about Susan Stewart, who was taking an inordinate amount of prescription painkillers. Susan finally confessed that it was Lucinda who had caused the injury that led to her addiction. Bob decided to help her kick her habit, and he also decided to keep the secret from Kim. When she began to go through withdrawal and hallucinate, Susan turned to Bob. Kim wanted to know what kind of problem Susan had that required him to stay overnight in Susan's spare room. Keeping Susan's privacy a first priority, Bob sidestepped Kim's inquiries. Lucinda warned Kim that Susan was playing her husband like a fiddle. Bob told Kim he was beginning to feel like an outsider with her and John, and he confided to Tom that he sometimes felt as if Kim didn't need him anymore, but that Susan did. One night Kim arrived home with John and found Bob and Susan enjoying a cozy chat by the fire.

Bob was alarmed when he discovered empty pill samples in Susan's office. She had disappeared, and Bob found her at the Foxwood Lodge. Susan admitted she'd fallen in love with him. She told him she would only destroy his life, though, and refused to accept his pity. It wasn't pity Bob was feeling, and they shared a night of passion. Realizing she'd gone too far, Susan decided to resign from Memorial and leave town. She prepared a letter of resignation for John and wrote notes to Emily and Bob. In her note to Bob, she thanked him for helping her battle her addiction and promised to keep the night they shared a secret. As she was leaving, Bob showed up and stopped her. Meanwhile, the Hughes family couldn't understand why Bob had to spend the night with Susan at Foxwood Lodge to help her with a back problem. Bob confessed he'd turned to someone else out of loneliness. Kim refused to listen to Bob's plea for understanding, knowing that the woman who stole her husband's fidelity was the same one who'd made her life miserable when she was married to Dan. Bob told Susan that Kim had figured out the truth, and Susan offered to take the blame, but Bob wouldn't hear of it. Kim asked him to move out of their Yardley Place home. Susan paid Kim a visit, explaining that what happened was a moment of madness. Kim responded by throwing her out. Frannie was mortified to find out that her father had slept with Susan Stewart.

Kim told John what happened and broke down in his arms just as Bob returned home to discuss a reconciliation. Despite encouragement from Nancy and Margo, Kim didn't want to work things out. She eventually allowed him to come home, but after a sleepless night in the same bed, she asked him to move into the guest room. Kim remembered that she had had an affair with Bob while he was married to her sister,

## Issues: Right to Die

*Finding out his condition had worsened and he had encephalitis, Casey Peretti asked Margo to do something he could never ask his wife. He begged Margo not to let the doctors hook him up to a respirator—he wanted to die with dignity! Margo turned to prayer. Then she summoned up her courage and entered Casey's room, where, quivering with grief, she grabbed the plug to Casey's life support and ripped it from the wall!*

Jennifer, and she realized there was no easy way out.

Kim and Bob told Andy that their marriage was in trouble but didn't tell him why. Kim asked Bob if he kept Susan from leaving town because he still had feelings for her. Bob claimed he simply didn't want Susan to take all the blame for what had happened. Kim decided it was time to confront Susan, and the two women thrashed it out. "After being married to a saint for five years, Bob needed a real woman!" a defensive Susan shouted. She headed for the medical conference in Los Angeles that Bob was attending. Kim wasn't happy to know that Bob and Susan were in the same city; was history going to repeat itself? Bob told Susan he wanted to be her friend, while back in Oakdale, Kim had disturbing dreams about Bob and Susan being together. Later, Bob and Kim attended the AIDS ball, but contrary to tradition they were not the auctioneers. A clueless Ellen Stewart said that no one could replace Bob and Kim in the "perfect couple" department.

Finding it difficult to be "just friends" with Bob, Susan accepted an offer from the University of California, even though Bob had asked her not to make a decision until she talked to him. After Bob and Kim went to London to be with Sabrina, Susan prepared to leave Oakdale once and for all and asked Andy to tell his father she had gone. She was packing up her lab when she got a visit from Lucinda. While Lucinda was venting as only Lucinda could, Susan lost her footing and fell off a ladder, landing on broken glass. Susan injured her spine and was paralyzed from the waist down. Bob was still in London, and Susan didn't want him to know, but when he found out, he and Kim rushed home. Nancy wished he hadn't been told. Kim had agreed to marriage counseling, and after the first session she told Bob she had no intention of sharing him with Susan. Kim then saw Bob and Susan celebrating the return of feeling to her legs. Bob and Kim officially separated, and Susan decided to stay on staff at Memorial.

As Bob and Kim adjusted to living apart, they realized they missed each other very much. When the marriage counselor asked Bob what would happen if he had to choose between Kim and Susan, Bob couldn't decide. Later, he told Susan how much she meant to him, and Susan told Lyla that she thought she had a fair shot at winning him back. Meanwhile, Kim sympathized with John over his own problems with Lucinda and counseled him not to be too hasty about

divorce. Bob didn't like finding John at his house with Kim, and he confided to Frannie that he was afraid Dr. D. would become a fixture. It was going to be a long winter.

While the Hughes's marriage was falling apart, the Dixons were trying to patch things up. "Not so fast," said Lucinda. She wanted to be wooed. John brought her roses, and she invited him to stay the night. For now, they called a truce. Lucinda was still convinced that John was not Duke's father and since John never had the blood tests to prove it, she wanted concrete evidence to the contrary. John's former brother-in-law, Larry Wagner, arrived in town after having been paid by Lucinda to investigate Duke. He told Lucinda that Philip Lombard was Duke's father! Rosemary Kramer was seeing Philip at the same time she was seeing John. But Philip told Lucinda he had proof that John was Duke's father and would turn it over if she agreed to certain conditions. Lucinda lived up to her end of the bargain, and Lombard sent her a lavender box filled with Rosemary's letters. Every word confirmed Duke's status as a Dixon. In the meantime, Margo warned Duke that he could be Philip Lombard's son. Duke decided to visit Philip in jail, where he learned about the lavender box. John told Duke he didn't need medical proof; he knew in his heart that Duke was his son and that was all that mattered. To give Duke peace of mind, though, he finally agreed to a blood test. Lucinda wanted to tell John about the letters, but she couldn't bring herself to do it. Meanwhile, Kirk had read the contents of the lavender box and confronted Lucinda. She bought his silence by giving him Walsh stock. While waiting for the results of the blood test, John decided to speak to Philip Lombard. Lucinda nearly went into cardiac arrest! To keep the peace, she offered to join her husband in his plan to adopt his supposed son. After the papers were signed, Lucinda braced herself to tell John about Rosemary's letters. John finally got the test results that proved his paternity. Feeling that Lucinda did not live up to her end of the bargain, Philip gave John the delivery receipt for the lavender box. During the trial for the murder of his son, Brock, Philip was stabbed to death.

Just as Lucinda was about to burn the box, Ambrose told her John intended to file for divorce. When John sent Duke to the mansion to get his things, she refused to hand them over. Susan took great pleasure in Lucinda's misfortune, twisting the knife by pretending she was getting calls from John. Rejected, Lucinda thought back to her childhood when she was Mary Ellen Walters and how her selfish mother, Gloria, sent her to live with her father because Gloria's new husband, George, didn't want Mary Ellen around.

Tired of waiting for Lien to be "ready" for him, Duke met a Pony Girl at the Silver Dollar and took her home. Lien found out and confronted him. Duke insisted that his dalliance was meaningless. Lien was afraid one day Duke would write off his relationship with her as meaningless, too. Soon afterward, Lien had an unnerving flashback to her past in Vietnam. She remembered that while she and her mother were in a prison camp, some of the guards tried to rape her, and Lien's mother offered herself in order to save her daughter. Lien wasn't sure she'd ever get the heart-wrenching episode out of her mind. After working through her problems, Lien told Duke she had decided to go to Rutgers Law School after the new year. Not only was she ready for law school, she was ready for him as well, and the two finally made love.

Shortly after telling Lien about her first love, handsome Harry, and counseling her stepdaughter on the importance of safe sex, Margo was shocked to run into Harry at Memorial! He was using his full name of Darryl Harry Crawford, and he introduced Margo to his wheelchair-bound wife, Carolyn. Carolyn was the heiress to the DeWitt cereal fortune of Des Moines, and she was in town to get a second opinion regarding her paralysis. DeWitt was also in the market for a management consulting firm in Oakdale. Darryl and Carolyn bought a large mansion and settled down. Darryl confided to Margo that his wife's paralysis left him with no outlet for his passion.

Barbara Munson delivered a healthy baby girl and named her Jennifer Louise after her deceased mother. Lucinda paid a visit and dropped the news that Paul was taking Emily to Paris for her birthday. Barbara called Gavin Kruger and asked him to transfer Emily to Los Angeles. Paul asked Lily to overrule Kruger, but his was too big an account for Lily to rock the boat. Barbara told Gavin to make Emily's life in L.A. so fabulous that she'd never want to come back to Oakdale.

Darryl Crawford saw Barbara at the hospital after she'd delivered Jennifer and told her he thought that he was Jennifer's father. After Barbara had fled Oakdale, she met Darryl in Rome, and they shared a night of passion. Barbara asked Dr. Samuels to keep the fact that Jennifer was two weeks early under wraps, while in the hospital nursery, knowing he could never have a child with his wife, Darryl stared lovingly at Jennifer.

Suddenly Colin was Oakdale's hottest portrait painter. Tonio commissioned him, and Lucinda also expressed an interest. Duncan offered to pay Colin for any dirt he could pick up on Tonio. When Madeline's body showed up again, and Colin saw it, he fainted. Duncan returned to find the warehouse in a shambles and Colin gone. This had Lilith written all over it. A concerned Duncan contacted Sawyer in Montega and learned that Lilith had been in contact with Tonio. Then Shannon disappeared. Duncan found the white rose and thought she'd left town with Kruger. He later received a letter confirming his worst fears. Gavin arrived at Duncan's door. Gavin admitted he'd propositioned Shannon, but she flatly rejected him for Duncan. He added that he saw Tonio driving through the warehouse district with a woman. Suspecting it was Lilith, Duncan told Gavin she was dangerous and had a habit of announcing her arrival with African tribal masks. Julie told Duncan she had seen one in Tonio's office. Later, Lilith's fingerprints were found in the warehouse loft. Sure that she had Shannon, Duncan tracked her down in Africa. When he found her, Lilith told Duncan that Shannon was dead. Duncan demanded proof and Lilith gleefully produced Shannon's shrunken head! Duncan was horrified and ran for his life, avoiding the poisoned darts meant for him. Lilith was hit and fell to the ground in a lifeless heap. Duncan vowed to avenge Shannon's death, starting with Tonio.

Duncan's friend and lawyer, Jessica Griffin, was getting hot and heavy with unscrupulous business executive Blake Stevens. Jessica went home to the South Bronx to visit her mother Louise, her sister Fiona, her nephews Carl and Leon and her brother Lamar. She wanted to mend the rift between them. When Jess told them about Blake, Lamar was sure he was white and married, like Thornton Converse had been. Jess thought Lamar was angry because he blamed her for their father Popi leaving the family. He took her to see their estranged father. Popi asked Jess pointed questions about her ambition and how she'd alienated her family to get ahead. Back in Oakdale, Blake was fired from M&A for stealing some of Lily's and Sean's files for Tonio. Tonio turned him away, and Jess told Blake their romance was over. Blake left town, vowing to win back her trust and love someday.

In other Oakdale business news, Kirk was in New York for Walsh Enterprises and interviewed a rising young executive from Meridian named Connor Jamison. Now that Lily had lured Ellie to M&A, Kirk felt Connor would make an ideal replacement. Connor made a call and told the person on the other end that she had Kirk Anderson in her corner. Lucinda was impressed with Connor and invited her to stay at the mansion while she was getting settled. Connor made another mysterious phone call and confided to a friend that she was afraid Darryl Crawford had recognized her. Later she received a white rose from the infamous Gavin.

Dan McClosky had an angina attack, and John warned him he had better start taking it easy. Casey Peretti was not so lucky. He was losing his battle with Guillain-Barré syndrome and was confined to a wheelchair. Completely helpless, Casey had to be fed and bathed. His career in medicine over, Casey gave his surgical instruments to Duke. He then set up a trust for Katie and asked Margo and Tom if they would be her legal guardians. When Dan McClosky choked during a dinner party, Duke performed an emergency tracheotomy under Casey's guidance. The episode cheered up Casey enough to look into teaching at the local medical school, and he was thrilled when he was offered a position. Casey then began to have difficulty swallowing. His worst nightmare was confirmed when he found out he had a deadly brain virus and would soon slip into a coma.

Casey wanted to draw up a living will, but Jessica was out of town. He confided in Margo and asked her to keep the will a secret from Lyla. He wanted the will executed as quickly as possible. When Kirk and Ellie visited Casey, they brought him a tape recorder so he could make tapes for Katie. As he was explaining his condition one day to Margo, Casey unknowingly left the tape recorder on. The doctors ordered a respirator, and Casey begged Margo not to let them hook him up—he wanted to die with dignity. A gasping Casey told Margo what he needed her to do. Margo tried to reach Tom, but he was in Washington, D.C., and the living will wasn't finished yet. As Casey drifted in and out of consciousness, Margo turned to prayer. Left with no choice, Margo summoned up her courage and entered Casey's room. Her face tight with emotion and her chin quivering with grief, Margo grabbed the life-support plug and ripped it from the wall. Then she leaned over her stepfather and friend and kissed him goodbye. John encouraged Casey's parents, Joe and Maureen, and Lyla to honor Casey's last request to be taken off life support, not knowing that Margo had already done it. Lyla told John she could never do that. Then John got the news that Casey was dead. When Lyla entered her husband's room, she wondered why the respirator was unplugged. McClosky arrived to investigate Casey's death.

Lucinda set up a scholarship at the medical school in Casey's memory. Duke was especially broken up about Casey's death. "He was my best friend," Duke wept. Both Susan and Duke offered to testify on Margo's behalf. Craig came from Montega to help his mother through this difficult time. Believing she had nothing to hide, Margo answered the prosecutor's questions without Jessica there to represent her. The prosecutor asked Lyla if she condoned her daughter's act, and Lyla answered no. A grand jury was convened to see if there was enough evidence to indict Margo for first-degree murder. The night before the hearing, Joe and Duke found the tape recorder Casey had used to tape messages for Katie. Just as testimony was about to begin, Lyla and Joe listened to the tape and heard Casey explain to Margo what was going to happen once his system began to shut down. Maureen entered and was shocked to hear her son's voice asking Margo to disconnect the respirator. Lyla visited Casey's grave and told him she wished he had come to her with his request. Margo found her there and told her mother Casey loved her too much to put her in that position. Lyla told the grand jury she couldn't condone what her daughter had done, but after hearing her husband plead with Margo to let him die with dignity, she forgave Margo. The grand jury decided not to indict Margo. Everyone was jubilant except for Maureen, who had hoped Margo would pay for what she'd done for the rest of her life. Lyla told her daughter she would have done the same if she had been in Margo's position, and mother and daughter shared a tearful reconciliation. Lyla considered going back to school to get a master's degree in rehabilitative medicine. And so, the year ended on a sad but hopeful note.

# *1991-1996*

Now that he had a child to call his own, Hal bowed out of Adam's life. The tragic irony was that little Jennifer belonged not to Hal, but to Darryl Crawford. This fact only added fuel to the fire in Paul's disintegrating relationship with his mother. He was already furious that Emily broke their engagement because Barbara had Gavin transfer her to Los Angeles. After talking to Andy, however, Paul told Barbara he'd keep her secret, even though he'd never forgive her for short-circuiting his relationship with Emily. Barbara finally had an attack of conscience and told Hal. He was devastated. Hal asked her for a divorce and sent McClosky a letter of resignation. Barbara lied to her friends and family and told them Gavin was Jennifer's father.

Selfless Carolyn Crawford offered Darryl his freedom, but when he insisted on sticking by her, she encouraged him to go on a ski trip with Frannie. Alone with Darryl, Frannie tried hard to control her emotions, but it was clear that the attraction was mutual, and when they returned, Carolyn took note of their closeness. She decided to use a surrogate mother to have a child with Darryl. Frannie found a surrogate, Dana Lambert. The artificial insemination worked on the first try, and Dana moved into the Crawford home.

Arthur Claiborne, Carolyn's attorney, picked up on Darryl's infatuation with Frannie. Arthur accused Darryl of marrying Carolyn for her money. Of course, Arthur had his own designs on Carolyn, not to mention the DeWitt fortune. After Darryl learned that Carolyn had given Arthur a key and lent him $100,000, he beat up the sniveling swindler. Upset and confused, Frannie turned to Larry McDermott.

One night Carolyn was home alone. Darryl was visiting Tom and Margo, and Dana was out on a date. She heard strange noises and tried to call Darryl, but the line was busy because Darryl was trying to reach her. As Carolyn was dialing 911, someone cut the phone lines. When Dana's date didn't show up, she realized she'd been set up. Dana hurried home to find the place in a shambles and Carolyn dead. Important items from the safe were missing, including jewelry, a strongbox and Carolyn's journal. Dana had put some items in the safe for Carolyn but now claimed to have forgotten the combination.

Arthur's first order of business was to implicate Darryl in the crime. Arthur also insinuated that Darryl may have also done in Carolyn's father, Nate DeWitt. Darryl knew Arthur had a house key and accused him of turning off the security system. Privately, Darryl hoped the police would not find his dead wife's journal. Across town, someone was reading an entry in Carolyn's journal stating that she needed to find the strength to divorce her husband. This person called the police with the information—for a price. Carolyn had named Arthur executor of her will. However, she left the bulk of her estate to her husband and child, and $100,000 for Arthur to take care of his IOU. At the funeral, Arthur told Carolyn's uncle Charles and aunt Grace that Carolyn may have wanted a divorce because Darryl was involved with another woman. A man in a trench coat observed Darryl at the grave and later "guaranteed satisfaction" to Arthur on their agreement. Darryl got a call from a man with an accent who wanted to talk about the journal. Dan McClosky theorized that Darryl had suggested the surrogacy because he intended to kill Carolyn and thought the child might give him a better claim to the DeWitt fortune. At the same time, Det. Higgins found Carolyn's missing jewelry in Dana's drawer.

Torn between Darryl and Larry, Frannie went on vacation without telling either of them. Larry found out and followed her to Puerto Rico. They shared some warm moments that didn't include sex. When he learned that Larry had returned from seeing her in Puerto Rico, Darryl fueled his yacht and set sail. The lady did not protest when he proposed.

Dana told her ex-husband Billy Lambert that she was sorry she had agreed to go along with his plan, but he said it was too late for her to back out now. Margo learned that Frank Wendall, Julie's ex-husband, had sold someone the Crawfords' silver tea service. Sure enough, Frank showed up at Julie's Park Forest apartment with Carolyn's journal. While Julie was out, Frank got a call from someone who wanted to buy the journal. Later, the landlady discovered Frank's body, but the journal was gone. Det. Higgins found the key to the Crawford house on the body, and Darryl was sure this was sufficient evidence of Arthur's part in Carolyn's murder. Then Arthur called Frannie, and in a disguised voice warned her about her future husband.

Tongues wagged in Oakdale when Gavin Kruger hired Arthur to represent him on the riverfront property. Duncan wondered if Tom and Margo had questioned Gavin about Carolyn's death, but Tom claimed Gavin was nowhere near Oakdale on the night of the murder. Then Larry got a call from a man saying that Frannie was marrying a murderer. Meanwhile, the Oakdale police wanted to know what Frank Wendall's connection was to the Harper family and whether Arthur also worked for them. While Frannie and Darryl were seeing Tom about a prenuptial agreement, Billy was planning to kidnap Dana.

Larry got a call from a man with an accent, saying that Darryl had had many affairs in Europe before and after Carolyn's accident. Suspecting Darryl could be the father of Barbara's child, Larry told Barbara she had to tell Frannie before she married him. But the truth about Jennifer's parentage remained a secret. Frannie and Darryl were married by Darryl's father, who was a minister, in a beautiful ceremony in Bob and Kim's backyard.

Darryl and Frannie honeymooned in Sardinia, where they ran into Carolyn's first husband, Philippe Van Doren, and his current wife, Nicole. Philippe told Darryl that Arthur had aided Gavin's campaign to take over DeWitt. Darryl forwarded this information to Margo and then disappeared for the night. When Gavin invited Philippe to visit him in Oakdale, Barbara wasn't pleased—Philippe had seen her and Darryl together in Rome.

The Crawford mystery deepened. Arthur told Dana she could be in danger because she was carrying Darryl's baby and someone wanted the child's inheritance. Soon afterward, a bomb exploded in Dana's car. She was rushed to the hospital, where the doctors determined she and the baby would be fine. Darryl and Frannie flew home immediately. Meanwhile, Arthur encouraged Billy to stick around until the baby was born. While Darryl

Her affair with Bob a thing of the past, Susan became occupied with an unlikely suitor—young Larry McDermott. They met in the halls of Memorial, where he was a pediatrician, and she was doing research in adolescent medicine. Although she was initially concerned about the difference in their ages, it didn't take long for them to become involved.

and Frannie were visiting relatives in Des Moines, Billy told Dana to retrieve his address book, which he'd left at the Crawford's house. When she returned, he pulled out a gun and kidnapped her. Darryl paid the $2 million ransom and Dana was released. After giving the money to Arthur, Billy disappeared.

Hal informed Margo and Tom that he'd infiltrated the Harper family by working undercover as their chauffeur. When Hal voiced his suspicion that Anthony Harper was in cahoots with Arthur, Margo thought Arthur had killed Carolyn because she had discovered Arthur's duplicity in the attempt to take over DeWitt. In the meantime, a mysterious woman began "gaslighting" Dana by dressing up as Carolyn's ghost. Tom and Margo suspected Vicki Harper, wife of the Harper don, who bore a strong resemblance to Carolyn and had a past with Darryl. Darryl confronted Arthur and Vicki and told them he was on to them.

Gavin's assistant, Jade Sullivan, arrived in town and Gavin told her no one must know he was anywhere near Oakdale on the night Carolyn was murdered. Soon after, Carolyn's grave was desecrated with the message, "Find my journal, and you will know my murderer." Later, Philippe blackmailed Arthur into giving him part of Dana's ransom money by threatening to reveal Arthur's connection to Billy Lambert and the Harpers.

Barbara freaked when she got a blackmail note about her night with Darryl in Rome. She assumed it was from Philippe. Philippe received his own note signed "A," telling him to meet Arthur under the docks for the ransom money. Philippe's corpse was later found floating in the river. Arthur was immediately a suspect until the police determined that the note didn't match his typewriter. Arthur was now sure that Gavin had set him up and admitted that Philippe was trying to link him to Carolyn's murder. Surprisingly, Higgins traced the note to Philippe's own typewriter. Gavin entrusted Nicole with a locked briefcase containing "sensitive" material and instructed her to take it to an employee of his in Paris. Nicole was not seen again. Still undercover, Hal thought Arthur was on to him, and he told Tom that he had overheard Gavin identify Darryl as Jennifer's father.

Then Hal disappeared. Tom told Margo, who warned Darryl that if he didn't tell Frannie, Tom might do so for him. In the meantime, Dana delivered a baby girl, and Darryl named her Carolyn Dana Crawford.

Margo was busy gathering evidence in the murders of Carolyn and Philippe. She learned that Gavin had visited Philippe on the day he was murdered. Gavin admitted that he had gone to the hotel, but he overheard him arguing with Arthur and didn't go in. Meanwhile, Billy called Dana from Mexico City and advised her to tell the police it was Arthur who ordered the kidnapping. Dana followed through, and Arthur fled to Switzerland. Later, Darryl got a call reporting a break-in at his ski lodge in Switzerland. Carolyn's desk had been ransacked.

Hal resurfaced in Oakdale and found Barbara in Gavin Kruger's arms. When Gavin told Jade about his plans to take over DeWitt and Walsh, he added that Barbara would enhance his corporate image and would make the perfect wife. To help Barbara with the baby, Hal's sister, Claire, arrived in Oakdale with her spirited daughter, Tess. Tess took a liking to the Snyders' new stableboy Hutch, but slept with Paul because he had money. Paul caught on and told her where to go.

Gavin gradually revealed himself to be a bigot and a brute. He made a racist comment to Duncan about Jessica and then withdrew his business from Montgomery & Associates because Jessica was the firm's counsel. When Barbara confronted him, Gavin took offense and tormented her by admitting he knew that Darryl was Jennifer's father. Gavin vowed she could trust him with her secret. When Hal told Barbara he overheard Gavin say that Darryl was Jennifer's father, she didn't deny it. Gavin told Barbara he wanted to adopt Jennifer as soon as they were married, and they headed to the Dominican Republic so she could get a divorce from Hal.

Barbara wasn't the only one on the rocky road to romance. Her aunt Kim was afraid she could never trust Bob again. Kim started to enjoy the company of Jeffrey Talbot, co-owner of station WOAK with her and Cal. Finally, Bob got Kim to agree to a trial reconciliation. Lisa bought Kim a sexy nightgown, but their first night together was a disaster because Bob wasn't able to "perform." His therapist had a simple explanation: Susan.

Lucinda was determined to help Duncan prove that Tonio had funded his business with James Stenbeck's money. Then Colin Crawley called Sabrina and asked

her to see him in Toronto. Since Colin was a wanted felon, Sabrina contacted the police. When Tonio found out, he hired Richard Tyrell to dispose of Colin. Tonio then followed Sabrina to London, and after he got a look at her financial records, he proposed.

Jessica paid another visit home to the South Bronx, and there she found three unexpected visitors: Blake Stephens, Duncan and her father. Blake went to Toronto to meet with Richard Tyrell, but Tonio warned Tyrell that Blake may be working for Duncan. He ordered Tyrell to kill Blake, who then mysteriously disappeared.

Sabrina gave Tonio a million dollars to help him with his investment in the riverfront property, and Duncan accused him of murdering both Colin and Blake. Tonio got a call from Tyrell telling him that the money in the Swiss bank account had been frozen. Worried that his scams would be exposed, Tonio prepared to go to Montega. Since they were now engaged, Sabrina insisted on going with him. When Bob learned of their plans, he confronted Tonio and threatened to call the police. Desperate, Tonio shot him point-blank, then headed for the airport, where Sabrina was waiting. Bob underwent surgery and, in his delirium, called out for Susan as a hurt Kim watched. After he regained consciousness, Susan told him that Emily had overdosed on sleeping pills in L.A. As Bob consoled her, Kim walked in. Bob had decided, though, that he wanted to move back in with Kim. After some rough moments, Kim and Bob finally reconciled and happily renewed their wedding vows.

Susan soon became occupied with an unlikely suitor—young Larry McDermott. Susan learned she had a lump in her breast that required a biopsy, and Larry was very supportive. When Larry's father, L.J., came to town, Susan didn't want him to know she and Larry were dating. But L.J. took a liking to Susan. He thought they should "double date" and suggested that Susan fix Larry up with Emily.

In Montega, Sierra, who had not been killed by rebels as Lucinda had believed, told Sabrina that Tonio had shot Bob. When Sabrina confronted Tonio, he abducted her and took her into the jungle. Duncan and Sawyer searched the jungle in a helicopter. In a moment of passion, Sabrina and Tonio made love. Then she took his gun and hid it under a rock. As Sabrina and Tonio prepared to board their own helicopter, Sabrina told Tonio she wouldn't be going with him, but she shielded him from Duncan when Duncan tried to shoot him. Tonio was holding on to the rail of the helicopter when he lost his grip and fell into the waters below.

Because Tonio's body hadn't been found, the will was opened. Except for a stipend for Bianca, Tonio had left everything to Sabrina. Jessica was relieved that Duncan was alive but was upset that he had taken the law into his own hands. Jess had strong feelings for Duncan, but she knew she'd have to choose between him and her family. Jessica's brother Lamar accused her of using Duncan as her ticket to "Whitey Land." Her newly returned father, Ward, worried that she would be hurt, and her mother said she would disown her. Duncan didn't fare much better when he introduced Jessica to Beatrice. But the coup de grace was Lisa's reaction—in her world, interracial marriage didn't exist. Duncan was also hounded by a legal battle when Kira Johnson, a child at the Earl Mitchell Center, accused him of making sexual advances toward her. Duncan was arrested, but Kira eventually broke down and admitted she'd lied, and Duncan was exonerated.

During Duncan's trial, Jessica received a disturbing letter accusing her of denouncing her own race. Distressed, she told Duncan she was going to New York for the holidays. There she had a surprise visit from Blake Stephens, who was believed to have been murdered by Tonio. Lamar was delighted to see his sister with an African American, but his hopes were quickly dashed when he learned that Jessica and Duncan were engaged.

Love was also in the air when Kirk Anderson and Ellie Snyder tied the knot in a wacky ceremony at the yacht club, where the ship's captain married them. In the meantime, Lucinda and John flew to the Dominican Republic for a quickie divorce.

Emma told Cal she didn't think she could live in his world of big business and didn't see marriage in their future. At Christmastime, Cal turned his attentions to Lyla and stuffed all sorts of goodies for her and Katie under the tree. Lyla was just beginning to come out of her shell after Casey's untimely death. For her, one of the few bright spots was when Margo gave birth to a boy and named him Casey. By the time spring rolled around, Lyla and Cal were growing closer, but she still shied away from his affections, leaving the field open for Lucinda, who wasted no time in seducing the Texas millionaire. When Lyla angrily confronted Cal, he responded by proposing.

Sierra and Craig had their second child, a girl, Lucinda Marie. Susan wanted to use Cal's jet to go to Montega and see her new granddaughter. Lucinda got wind of the plan and arrived at the airport, bags packed. It didn't take her long to notice how cuddly Cal and Lyla had become—and no wonder, because Lyla had accepted Cal's proposal. Once again, Lucinda had lost in love, and she decided it was time to overhaul her life.

Meanwhile, Connor Jamison was moving into Lucinda's poolhouse and reporting her progress to her anonymous telephone friend. Darryl Crawford saw Connor and remembered meeting her before. Lucinda soon promoted Connor to sole executive on the DeWitt account. Connor was fast endearing herself to Lucinda, and Lucinda's reconciliation with Lily was putting a cramp in the ambitious young woman's plans. Kirk had his reasons for keeping Connor's secret, but Linc was beginning to tire of her enigmatic persona. Lucinda tried to contact Connor's brother, Evan, about a job, but Connor didn't want Evan in town. Lucinda hired him anyway. Curiously, when Darryl saw Evan, he called him Jamie. Kirk told Connor their plan was going better than

## Issues - Bulimia

Courtney and Andy were the picture-perfect couple, but Courtney suffered from low self-esteem and was overly conscious about her weight, so she stopped eating altogether. When she fainted and was rushed to the hospital, she was diagnosed with malnutrition. Forced to eat, Courtney began the vicious cycle of binging and purging. According to actress Haley Barr, "Courtney's most important relationship is with her boyfriend, Andy (Scott DeFreitas), himself a recovering alcoholic still obsessed with Julie Wendall and her out-of-wedlock baby. Courtney feels she's not beautiful enough or thin enough. She's trying to figure out how she can get Andy to love her." To help her overcome her eating disorder, Courtney worked with Dr. Michaels at Memorial and joined a support group of other college-age women suffering from this potentially fatal disorder.

expected, but she was getting closer to Lucinda and having second thoughts. Their plan was also interfering in her relationship with Linc.

It was time for Walsh Enterprises's annual stockholders meeting, and Lily was voting her shares by proxy. Kirk persuaded her to give the proxy to him. During the meeting, Lucinda announced Connor was the recipient of the award for top Walsh executive. In the meantime, Holden urged Lily to go to the meeting and vote. Back at the meeting, Connor dropped a bombshell by announcing that her grandfather was James E. Walsh, founder of the company and Lucinda's second husband. Connor owned much of the stock, but her father, James E. Walsh II, had run the company into the ground, allowing Lucinda to take it over. She had come to Oakdale to get the company back into the family. Evan, her brother, was James E. Walsh III. Connor asked the stockholders for their support. Connor had her shares, and Kirk had his and Lily's, giving them a strong voting block. Holden and Lily arrived too late to turn things around. Lucinda was off the board, Connor was named chairman and Kirk CEO. When Ellie learned what her husband of two weeks had done, she left him. Connor explained her reasons for the takeover to Linc and begged him for a second chance. Then she told Evan that their father had committed suicide after the company failed and that their mother didn't want Evan to know.

Lily blasted Kirk for his trickery. When Kirk tried to justify his actions to Ellie, she told him the only way she'd reconcile with him was if he reinstated Lucinda as CEO. However, Lucinda had her own master plan, and she presented a divide-and-conquer scheme to Evan: "Let's try ousting Kirk." Evan liked it. Furthermore, Lucinda was pleased to discover that Kirk and Ellie weren't legally married. Unbeknownst to the newlyweds, their ship's captain didn't have the authority to marry them on dry land! Wouldn't the stockholders just love to know that their CEO was living in sin?

Holden and Julie's one-night stand produced a child, Aaron. To protect her daughter Lily's marriage to Holden from being destroyed, Iva adopted the little boy. Iva's suitor, John Dixon, didn't know the identity of the boy and neither did Holden. It was a situation that would have far-reaching ramifications.

Lucinda soon formed a new company, WorldWide, and found a new right-hand woman in the wily, ambitious Marcy Breen, who had her eye on Linc. She wormed her way into Hannah Lafferty's heart, and Hannah put her up at the boarding house for free. But Evan knew her scheming ways, for they had had an affair in New York. He threatened to ruin her "good girl" reputation by telling Linc about her abortion. The clever Marcy drew Linc closer by implying that Connor had snared Darryl's commitment to Walsh with sex. When Linc confronted Connor, she told him Darryl had helped her when her father tried to commit suicide, but denied that they were lovers. Linc refused to believe her, and Connor told Marcy she'd made an enemy for life.

Because of his background, Linc desperately wanted a secure, honest relationship. Linc's father had left them, and Hannah had struggled to raise him alone. It was a jolt when Woody Hutchinson, Emma's new farmhand, turned out to be Linc's dad! Also on the farm, working as a stableboy, was Woody's son Hutch by a woman named Mary. Linc yelled at Woody for deserting him, and he was furious at his mother for not letting him know his father was in town. Hannah confessed that Melvin, now known as Woody, had cheated on her, and Hutch was living proof. Woody felt it was time to tell Hutch about his mother, Mary, whose early death ended Woody's plans to tell his son the truth about his birth. When Woody asked Hannah for a divorce, she said, "Never," and so they were still legally married. An angry Linc moved out of the boarding house, and Hannah had an attack of asphyxia, which she blamed on him.

Two troubled teenagers, Andy Dixon and Courtney Baxter, were growing closer to taking that fateful step. One night Courtney was preparing a romantic dinner for two when a very pregnant Julie rang the doorbell Never having gotten over his obsession with her, Andy took her under his wing and even began footing her medical bills. John was irritated that Andy would assume such responsibility for Little

Miss Seattle, while Courtney was so hurt and bewildered that she began to assume, wrongly, that the baby was his. Courtney began to enjoy Evan Walsh's attentions. To stop Lily and Holden from marrying, Lucinda offered Julie a huge sum of money to tell Holden that he was the father. But on the advice of Lucinda's adversary and Julie's mother confessor, Lisa, Julie threatened to tell Lily that Lucinda was trying to blackmail her. Lucinda backed off.

When Julie and Caleb's divorce became final, Andy told Lucinda he was the father, but Caleb told Holden the father was Ron Gillette, the head of Julie's modeling agency in New York. In her eighth month, Julie tripped over a phone cord and fell but managed to get herself to Park Forest Hospital, where Meg Landry saw her with Andy. Julie pleaded with Meg not to tell Holden or Caleb.

The situation with Julie had an adverse effect on Courtney, who was beginning to obsess about food and thought she was too fat. Meanwhile, Andy fantasized about him and Courtney adopting Julie's baby. Andy and Iva were at Julie's apartment when she went into labor, and together they delivered a baby boy. As Andy got ready to make his adoption pitch, Courtney returned his key and started seriously dating Evan. Iva managed to get Caleb and Holden's blood types and found out Holden was the father.

Julie told Andy she had lied about Ron Gillette's being the father, and Andy assured her it was OK. Determined to be a father if only in name, Andy signed the birth certificate. But Iva told John she had a "friend" named Diane Shea who had to give up a baby. To prove to Lucinda that Andy was the father, Iva showed her the birth certificate. Iva planned to name the baby Aaron. Lucinda wanted "honest" Iva to be caught and then rejected by both Lily and John. She instructed Ambrose to find the hospital records to prove that Holden was the father.

One day when she was with Evan, Courtney fainted, and Evan rushed her to the ER. John thought she was pregnant, but the problem proved to be intestinal, and he asked her if she'd been dieting excessively. A few weeks later at the yacht club, Courtney binged and then went to ladies' room to purge. She came running out in a panic, her throat gushing blood. She had popped a blood vessel in her esophagus, confirming John's suspicions that she was bulimic. After an intense discussion with Dr. Michaels, Courtney decided to enter group therapy to gain control over her eating disorder. Andy

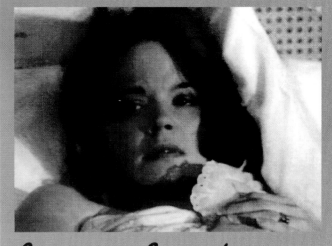

## Issues - Incest

Angel clung desperately to her marriage to Holden even though she realized he didn't love her. No one knew the real reason until it was revealed that she had been sexually abused by her father Henry Lange and needed Holden to protect her. Henry found Angel alone at their summer home and raped her. It later turned out that he was the father of her aborted child. An angry Caleb confronted him at gunpoint. His secret exposed, Henry took the gun and turned it on himself.

also decided to seek professional help to deal with his obsession with Aaron. When Iva named Lisa and John godparents, Andy was deeply disappointed. Lisa warned Iva that the closer she got to John, the more likely it was that he would learn Andy's name was on the birth certificate. Meanwhile, John suggested that for medical reasons, Iva should find out more about the father.

After Jessica delivered the surrender papers, Julie left for New York. Iva promised her she'd never tell Aaron who his biological parents were, but she did plan to tell him he was adopted. Andy finally leveled with Courtney and told her that Holden was Aaron's father, but if Holden or Lily found out, it would destroy their relationship. Lucinda vowed to go to New York and bribe Julie into telling the truth about Aaron.

Unaware that he had fathered Julie's baby, Holden was deeply involved in his wife Angel's dysfunctional family. Angel and Barclay were planning to embezzle money from their father Henry so that Angel could be financially independent. Henry was angry when Angel didn't come home for Christmas, and he went looking for her at their summer home at Lake Geneva. Angel was there thinking about her childhood and how her father would come into her room and her bed. Suddenly there he was, standing right in front of her! Angel panicked, and Henry raped her. By the time Barclay and Holden found her, Angel had overdosed on sleeping pills. Barclay told the doctors that the overdose was accidental. He then told Holden about Angel's sexual abuse. Holden took Angel to the farm and asked Iva, another rape victim, to persuade her to get counseling. When Henry Lange showed up at his office, an angry Holden told him he'd pay for what he'd done. Henry ordered his crony, Virgil, to wipe out Holden and make it look like an accident.

Virgil found Angel in the barn and tried to chloroform her, but Angel screamed, and Caleb came running. When Angel confessed her history to Caleb, he was shocked. She told him the baby she'd aborted with his help wasn't his; it was her father's, and Henry knew it. Caleb grabbed a gun and cornered Henry. Like a trapped animal, Henry wrested away the gun and turned it on himself. Angel's other brothers, Stephen and Jay, refused to believe that their father had raped their sister. To protect Angel, Caleb didn't tell Jessica why he and Henry were fighting, even though his silence meant he'd be charged with murder. When Angel found out that Henry had left everything except the business to her, she wanted nothing to do with the money. She ran to St. Mary's Convent to pray for guidance.

Acting D.A. Tom Hughes wanted to question Caleb about his involvement in the shooting of Henry Lange, but Caleb had fled to find Julie. Tom informed the Snyders that jumping bail was cause for arrest. Eventually Caleb was brought back to Oakdale. Ellie did her best to convince Caleb he'd rot in jail if he didn't tell Tom what was going on. But Caleb wouldn't listen, so Ellie told Tom herself. Stephen and Jay considered having Angel lobotomized to wipe out her memory. Holden found Angel at the convent and persuaded her to come home, while Caleb finally told Jessica about the incest. Barclay was in detox and couldn't testify, and Jess told Angel that if she didn't tell the court her father had impregnated her, the jury wouldn't believe Henry shot himself, and Caleb would go to jail. Angel's heart-wrenching testimony cleared Caleb. Because Angel had taken a giant step in putting the past behind her, Holden gently asked her for a divorce, and she agreed. Because of the ordeal, Angel and Caleb had grown close again, and they eventually became engaged.

With his divorce and Angel's ordeal behind them, Lily and Holden were at long last engaged. The star-crossed couple finally made love and planned to move into their new farmhouse. Sensing their intimacy, Lucinda made Gavin send Lily to Zurich on a phony emergency. Lucinda then cajoled Olivia Wycroft into hiring Julie to model Barbara Ryan's new fall line. Lucinda dropped another bombshell when she told Evan and Connor about Kirk's plot to unseat them and told Kirk about Holden's proposal to become chairman of WorldWide. Emma learned of both her son's and son-in-law's deceit, and Kirk refused to attend Lily and Holden's wedding. Lily denounced her mother. Lucinda told Iva if she didn't help her reconcile with Lily, she'd tell Holden he was Aaron's father.

The air was filled with tenderness and anticipation as the happy couple arrived at the Luther's Corners church. No one noticed the limo parked down the hill, but if one looked closely at the figure inside wrapped in fur, they might have recognized Julie Snyder. She heard Lily and Holden exchange their vows and saw Holden carrying Aaron. Julie drove away, defeated. After the honeymoon, Holden resigned from Walsh. It didn't take long for Lily and Lucinda to get into a fight over Holden. In a fit, Lucinda told her daughter to call her blessed Iva if she wanted to hear some lies. Shortly thereafter, John proposed to Iva. She said she needed time to think it over. Knowing she'd been lying to him about Aaron's parentage, she turned him down.

As 1991 drew to a close, an old chapter of Lisa Mitchell's life was reopened when she was reunited with her second ex-husband, John Eldridge, who informed her he had only a few months to live. When Eldridge fell into a coma, Lisa's former mother-in-law, Helen, told Lisa that if John didn't come out of it, she would have to re-examine the decision the three of them made long ago. Helen wanted Lisa to sign papers changing the divorce settlement, but Lisa refused. She confided in Grant Colman that she hoped Tom wouldn't discover the terms of her divorce. Lisa was frazzled when Tom said he was thinking of offering a position to Carl Eldridge, John's cousin, a prestigious attorney who had helped Helen keep tabs on Lisa all these years. Carl was now established in Oakdale and involved in a serious relationship with Monica Lawrence.

Finally, on a sad note, David Stewart died of a heart attack while doing AIDS research in Atlanta. Bob went to retrieve the body of his closest, dearest pal, who had defended him to Doug Cassen, stood by his side against Michael Shea and John Dixon and listened to his romantic problems over the course of many years.

It was a bittersweet year for Bob. He had won back his wife but had lost his best friend.

The complex mystery of Carolyn Crawford's murder had a profound effect on half-sisters Barbara and Frannie and gave ace cops Margo and Hal a golden opportunity to exercise their investigative acumen. In exchange for leniency, Margo persuaded Billy Lambert to testify against Arthur Claiborne in the Dana Lambert kidnapping case. But before she could get him back to Oakdale, Billy was shot by Anthony Harper's henchmen. The goons trailed Billy to Memorial Hospital and held Dana hostage on the hospital roof. Dana was saved by the police, and she admitted giving Carolyn Crawford's journal to Billy. Billy said that someone named George Stuart had offered a fortune for the journal. Arthur was imprisoned for kidnapping Dana, and he carried with him the secret that George Stuart was, in fact, Gavin Kruger! Hal was suspicious when he saw Gavin commiserating with Vicki Harper and warned Barbara to keep her distance from Gavin. Emily also told Barbara that several months ago, before he pulled his account from M&A, she and Gavin checked into a hotel under the name George Stuart. Touched by Emily's concern, Barbara apologized for coming between her and Paul. Barbara visited Paul in Zurich and told him Darryl was Jennifer's father. She continued to tell her other family members and acquaintances, however, that Gavin was the proud papa.

The question of Jennifer's paternity was the least of Gavin's worries. He noticed Barbara was no longer wearing his ring and realized she was only pretending to love him. Gavin also incurred serious financial losses from his South Korean division, prompting him to embezzle funds from the Earl Mitchell Center. Gavin set Sean Baxter up to be killed in an industrial explosion so the police couldn't question him about the trip he and Jade had taken to Hawaii. Sean survived but made sure to steer clear of Oakdale. Then one of Gavin's henchmen, Emile Seblon, murdered Nicole Van Doren after she phoned Darryl to tell him she was coming to Oakdale to clear up the Carolyn Crawford murder. Gavin soon paid an inmate to kill Arthur Claiborne, but Arthur lived to reveal that Gavin was George Stuart. Margo arrested Gavin for the murders of Carolyn Crawford and Philippe Van Doren. Shortly thereafter, Emile Seblon committed suicide. When the French police searched his safe-deposit box, they discovered Carolyn's journal as well as a letter confessing to murdering Frank Wendall and Philippe and Nicole on

Gavin's orders. Seblon's note also revealed that while he himself did not kill Carolyn, Gavin had arranged to have her "done away with." Gavin was convicted for the crimes. When Darryl came to visit him at the penitentiary, Gavin cruelly told him that Darryl, not Gavin, was Jennifer's father.

## On the Road

*With Cannon Mountain in Franconia, New Hampshire, substituting for the Swiss Alps, Frannie and Darryl's love story reached a terrifying climax in a tram 4,500 feet in the air. Frannie had just discovered letters that implicated Darryl in the death of his first wife Carolyn. Frannie justifiably felt that she would be the next of his wives to die. She hit him over the head with a poker and ran for the tram. When Darryl climbed into the tram, Frannie knew she was in trouble.*

As the mystery of Carolyn's murder grew, Frannie became more and more suspicious of Darryl. He was strangely evasive about their financial situation, and he had gotten several mysterious phone calls. Frannie went to the Crawford ski lodge in Zurich, and there she found Carolyn's letters about Darryl's affair with Connor and his possible involvement in the death of Carolyn's father Nate. Darryl caught up with Frannie and pleaded innocence, then tried to burn the letters. Frannie refused to believe him and ran. Darryl followed her into the ski tram and begged her for another chance. When they returned to Oakdale, Darryl finally admitted to that night in Rome with Barbara and told her Jennifer was his child. Frannie was shocked. Soon afterward, Frannie and Darryl came face-to-face with Carolyn's real killer. It was their creepy security guard, George Jessup, who had done the deed on Gavin's and Harper's orders. Jessup

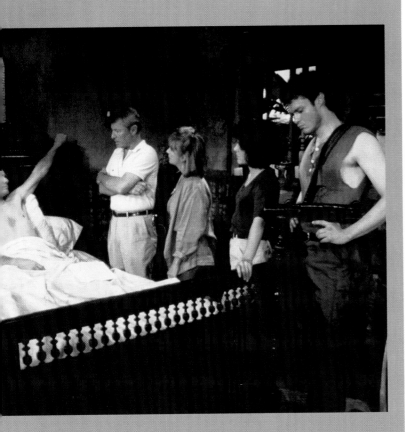

## Dastardly Deeds – Tonio Reyes

*He might not have been James Stenbeck, but he was bad to the bone. Believed to have plunged to the bottom of the sea, Tonio nevertheless survived and was cared for by his loyal Montegan followers. When he needed emergency surgery, Tonio abducted Susan and Bob at gunpoint and forced them to operate, then left them on a deserted island to die. Happily, the resourceful doctors were rescued and returned to Oakdale.*

ménage à trois between Carolyn, Gavin and Philippe. Carolyn was not the innocent, put-upon wife after all. The Hughes family was much relieved to be rid of the Crawfords.

Another agent of deception was Marcy Breen, who stunned Connor and everyone else in Oakdale by marrying Linc Lafferty after a brief courtship. Too devious for her own good, Marcy stole designs from Barbara's new BRO line. But then an ex-lover from New York seduced her and set her up to be discovered by Linc. Jade then gave proof to Lucinda that Marcy was also working for Gavin Kruger. Marcy ultimately blew out of Oakdale, pregnant with Linc's child.

Connor soon became enmeshed in the intriguing new situation involving Lisa and the Eldridge family. Lisa was strangely worried when Carl Eldridge agreed to work for Tom and when John Eldridge came out of his coma. Finally, Lisa poured out her heart to Nancy about a secret she had kept for many years. After Lisa married John Eldridge in Chicago, she carried on an affair with his brother Thomas. Lisa became pregnant and gave birth to a son Scott. Thomas claimed the child was his, even though John was actually the father. When Thomas was killed in an automobile accident, Helen and John persuaded Lisa to give up all claim to Scott in exchange for a large divorce settlement from John. John Eldridge died, leaving Lisa the estate Thomas had entrusted to him. In turn, Lisa added Scott to her will. Helen hoped Lisa could forge a relationship with Scott, an intelligent but floundering young man who was not making the most of his degrees in economics and law from Princeton and Yale. At first, Scott was antagonistic toward his estranged mother, while Lisa's other son, Tom, accused her of selling out her own flesh and blood for cash. To Tom's dismay, Margo befriended Scott and persuaded him to stay in Oakdale. Scott soon mellowed toward Lisa and moved into her penthouse. He started a relationship with Connor and landed a plum job as in-house attorney for his mother's arch-nemesis, Lucinda. By coincidence, Lucinda was kindling a business relationship with Kitty Fielding, Scott's old flame, who warned Connor that Scott had only one passion in life: money. After Connor betrayed Scott by giving privileged company information to Kirk, Scott turned to a new lover—Lucinda!

was trying to kill Frannie when Darryl charged at him. The two men tumbled out an attic window but both survived, and Jessup confessed to the authorities. Frannie, disgusted by both Barbara's and Darryl's actions, chose to join her sister Sabrina at her clinic in Montega, while Darryl returned to Des Moines with their daughter Carolyn Dana (Carrie) Crawford.

As for Hal, Anthony Harper finally deduced that his "chauffeur" was a cop and shot him. The authorities managed to nab both Harper and his wife, Vicki, who was a member of the notorious Cerrone crime family. Hal was presumed dead, but Tom knew he was alive and under government protection. Tom was reluctantly forced to keep this information from Margo and Barbara, who was pregnant with Hal's child. Ironically, before he was shot, Hal had discovered a negative of a

Life was equally complex for the Snyders. Iva officially adopted Aaron just as Lily and Holden learned they were expecting a child. John continued to press Iva to marry him, and she intended for Aaron's parentage to remain a secret. Then Greer hit her up for $10,000 to keep his mouth shut. Iva finally leveled with John, who eventually forgave her. Emma, on the other hand, did not. John privately admitted to Margo that Holden was Aaron's father and was furious at Andy for putting his name on the birth certificate. Lily suffered a miscarriage, and later Holden overheard Iva, John and Lucinda discuss the fact that he and Julie had conceived Aaron. Holden rushed to New York and confronted Julie, who told him how many people in Oakdale already knew the truth. Holden stormed out of Julie's apartment and onto the mean streets of New York, where he was mugged and left for dead.

Lily was worried about Holden, and Lucinda dispatched her detectives to find her missing son-in-law. They located Holden's car and jewelry and traced him to a New York hospital, where he was suffering from permanent memory loss. Playing God as usual, Lucinda decided that Lily would be better off without a husband who did not remember her. Holden underwent intensive rehabilitation under the care of Dr. Marsha McKay. Holden soon found himself attracted to Marsha. When the Snyders finally located Holden, it was a wrenching reunion, for everyone was a mere stranger to him. Holden returned to Oakdale with Marsha. Lucinda, Iva and Julie finally admitted to Lily that Holden and Julie were Aaron's biological parents. Julie told Lily that Lucinda had located Holden before anyone else and had kept it quiet for months. Lily swore she would never forgive Lucinda and Iva. However, she did forgive Holden and told him she was ready for a fresh start. Instead, Holden asked Lily for a divorce. Devastated, Lily left Oakdale for Switzerland and Rome.

Other lives were altered forever in the fallout of the Aaron situation. John and Iva decided not to marry but were both supportive of Andy as he successfully turned his attention back to Courtney Baxter, who was now in a relationship with Evan Walsh. Evan was not pleased to see Andy and Courtney together. To make matters worse, his overbearing mother, Edwina Walsh, arrived in Oakdale. Evan was Edwina's favorite, and she prodded him incessantly about his love life and career. He soon found a release for his tensions—a one-night stand with Emily. Courtney eventually discovered the indiscretion and broke off their relationship. Evan left Walsh to work with Emily at M&A. Courtney grew closer to Andy, but before she committed herself to him, she got Evan to

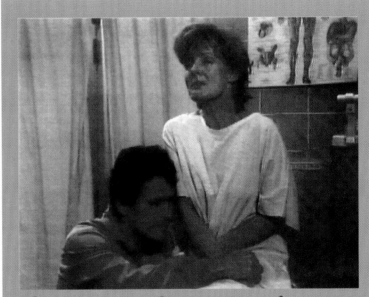

## *Issues - Rape and the HIV virus*

*Their lives seemed perfect—too perfect. Back from an idyllic Cape Cod vacation, Margo went to the liquor store to buy some wine, only to be caught in the middle of a robbery. The simple shopping trip ended in terror when Margo was grabbed by the thugs and raped. As if dealing with the rape weren't traumatic enough, Margo had to face the possibility that she had contracted HIV. After a long six months, she tested negative for the virus.*

agree to an HIV test. Much to Courtney's relief, the test was negative. Andy and Courtney were married at Christmastime in Bob and Kim's living room.

Oakdale celebrated two other marriages in 1992. Susan had given Larry back his ring and gone to the clinic in Montega to think. Bob was also there assisting Frannie. Suddenly Tonio, who had survived his fall into the sea, appeared with a gun. They were saved by Larry, who had come to Montega worried about Susan. Larry and Susan said, "I do" right then and there. Not so fortunate, however, were newlyweds Duncan McKechnie and Jessica Griffin. Duncan was now editor of the *Argus*, and Jessica was now a member of the Hughes law firm. Sadly, their wedding was not attended by Jessica's parents or Duncan's Scotland-based family, Beatrice and Brian, all of whom disapproved of the union. However, Jessica's brother Lamar had come around, and he attended along with their sister Fiona. After the wedding, Lamar stayed in Oakdale and went to work for Duncan. Duncan and Jessica decided to move into Tom and Margo's neighborhood, where they were welcomed openly and warmly.

Tom and Margo would need the support of friends like Duncan and Jessica during the next rocky chapter in their lives. Having just returned from a wonderful Cape Cod vacation with the boys, Margo went out to buy a bottle of Tom's favorite red wine and was caught in the middle of a liquor store holdup. To get their license plate, Margo pursued the gunmen into a back alley, where they grabbed her. One of them dragged her into a truck and raped her. At first Margo suppressed the trauma and poured her energy into catching the rapist, Elroy Nevins, and his partner, Fickett. With Tom's unwavering and tender support, Margo finally worked through her unjustified feelings of guilt and shame. They later learned that Nevins tested positive for HIV. To their relief, though, Margo tested negative on her first antigen exam, but it would be a long wait for the second and third. Margo befriended one of Nevins's other victims, Dawn Wheeler, who tested positive for HIV.

Margo still found time to listen to her mother Lyla's woes about her love life. Lyla had rented a room to Simone Bordeau, a Navajo girl who was attending Oakdale University. Simone's sister, Leslie, was trying to block Cal from claiming sacred tribal land to drill for oil. The dispute was headed for court. Appalled by what she perceived as Cal's insensitivity and lack of morals, she put their wedding plans on hold. Cal then grew friendly with Connor.

Life became considerably less staid for Cal's former ladyfriend, Emma Snyder. Her oldest son, Seth, sent his editor, Ned Simon, to interview Emma as a prospective romance novelist. Ned's current author, writing under the pseudonym of "Amber D'Amour," was retiring, and Ned wanted Emma to write the next D'Amour romance.

Emma was immediately attracted to the rugged, quietly charming Ned. Protective Seth told Emma that Ned had a wife, Valerie, and a daughter, Debbie. Ned said his sole reason for remaining with Valerie was to provide a stable home environment for Debbie, who was on medication for a chemical imbalance in the brain. Shortly thereafter, Ned learned that Debbie had tried to jump off a building. With Emma's permission, Ned brought the girl to stay on the farm, where she was quick to notice Hutch.

At this point, though, Hutch had more than his share of young ladies in his life. He was still involved with Tess but was taken with Rosanna, a new girl who had arrived at the Earl Mitchell Center, who was as fiercely proud and independent as she was secretive. She spent time on the Snyder farm, where she endeared herself to Emma. When Hutch admitted to Tess that he had feelings for Rosanna, Tess vindictively swiped $200 from Fashions Ltd. and pinned the theft on Rosanna. The police arrested her but later released her when Barbara discovered that Tess had set her up. Rosanna then caught the eye of Evan Walsh, who was shocked to discover that she was not as down-and-out as she seemed. Rosanna was the daughter of Alexander Cabot, a megamillionaire automobile magnate from Grosse Pointe, Michigan. Alex pressed Rosanna to return to Michigan, but Rosanna told her father that she had found herself on Emma's farm, where she'd discovered the simple values she'd been searching for ever since her mother died.

The Snyder farm was also abuzz with news of the deteriorating marriage of Ellie and Kirk. Ellie was surprised to find out that she was pregnant and then learned the baby was malformed. After some private soul-searching, Ellie realized that her career came first, and she had an abortion. Kirk was livid but suggested they have another child. That was not what Ellie wanted, so she took a job with Meridian in New York. Kirk turned to Connor.

Emily finally thought she'd found true love with Royce Keller, a dynamic, award-winning architect from San Francisco who was working on a project with Lucinda. But Royce was vague about his connection to a charming young woman named Neal Alcott, who was also working for Lucinda. Lisa was trying to fix Neal up with her son Scott. One night, while they were making love, Emily was baffled when Royce cried out, "Cynthia." Royce denied knowing anyone by that name. Later, though, he was heard talking to a Cynthia on the phone...

**1993**

The most prominent event in 1993 was the story behind Oakdale newcomers Royce Keller and Neal Alcott. They were keeping the secret that they were Lucinda's estranged half-brother and half-sister! Their shrewish mother, Gloria, had given birth to Lucinda prior to marrying their alcoholic father. George. Lucinda did not know their true identities because Gloria had dumped her on her father's doorstep when she was very young. The victim of Gloria's abuse and George's neglect, Royce harbored a deep resentment toward Lucinda for deserting the family. Royce and Neal thought they had a bright future in Oakdale—Royce was seeing Emily, and Neal was being courted by Scott. Then Michael Alcott, Neal's ex-husband, appeared and tried to blackmail Royce about his true identity. Royce hired him to work on the construction site for the new WorldWide Tower, but that contract wasn't enough for Michael. Royce and his loyal butler, Graham, swore they would kill Michael before Royce paid him a cent. Later, Michael was blinded by a bright light while he was on a scaffold and fell to his death.

Neal finally revealed to Scott that she was Lucinda's half-sister. Scott reacted explosively and accused her of lying about her whereabouts when Michael was killed, a crime for which he was also a suspect. Then Scott fled Oakdale, and Neal was murdered. Distraught, Royce shocked Lucinda by admitting that he and Neal were her long-lost siblings. But this was only the beginning of the skeletons in Royce Keller's closet. As he pledged his undying love to Emily, he began coming on to Julie, claiming that she reminded him of a redhead from his past. In truth, though, this redhead was still very much a part of his life. Her name was Cynthia Linders, and she was wearing Royce's engagement ring at the same time he proposed to Emily.

Royce's inexplicable demons rose to the surface as his sex with Emily grew increasingly rougher, bruising her. Pizza delivery girl Lexi Funk described to the police the man who bumped into her near the scene of the crime, and the police sketch resembled Royce. Royce was arrested for Neal's murder, and Jessica represented him. Royce was not the only suspect. Scott seemed a likely culprit until it was proven that someone had seen him near the crime scene after the likely time of the murder. Lisa went to Europe to search for her son, to no avail. Graham, Royce's butler, had been a murder suspect in his native England, a fact Lucinda gleefully

exposed in the *City Times*. Then Cynthia testified that she and Royce had carried on an affair for 18 years and that she had seen Neal on the night of the murder. She added that Neal vehemently opposed her involvement in Royce's life. Then Royce took the stand. As Tom fired questions at him, Royce suddenly announced that his name was Roger and that he had murdered Neal! Royce was a victim of multiple-

**On the Road - Amalfi, Italy**

*How far would you go to find love? "As The World Turns" journeyed overseas to Italy and the town of Amalfi, site of medieval churches and breathtaking ocean views, to tell the love story of Emily and Royce. Emily had been in Rome on business when she decided to take a side trip to Amalfi, and Royce surprised her there. The couple embarked on a romantic holiday with little knowledge of the problems they would face upon their return.*

personality disorder. A third personality, a little boy named Dooley, surfaced and said that he saw Roger shove Neal and that she had hit her head on the mantel. Tom withdrew the charges against Royce, and both Neal's and Michael's deaths were ruled as accidents. Royce obtained psychological help to "fuse" his personalities and emerged strong enough to persuade Emily to marry him. But after a visit from a calculating Susan, Royce realized that although he loved Emily, he was not the same man he was when he had proposed to her. He left a stunned and shaken Emily at the altar.

Another Walsh learned that he had convoluted origins. Edwina informed Evan that her intended, Alexander Cabot, was his father. This bombshell put the brakes on Evan's blossoming relationship with Alex's feisty daughter, Rosanna, for it now appeared that they were brother and sister. Evan had Larry McDermott run a DNA test. The results proved that Alex was not the

## Teenage Triangles

*Debbie Simon (right) was painfully insecure, and she wanted Hutch. Debbie plotted and planned and used all sorts of underhanded tricks to catch him, but Hutch couldn't get Rosanna (left) out of his mind. Realizing this, the unstable Debbie promptly slept with Hutch's hostile half-brother, Linc. It was a major mistake.*

father, and Evan hotly confronted his mother. Edwina said she wanted to keep him from marrying Rosanna, whom Edwina hated for running away from her "society" roots. Rosanna told Edwina off but agreed to keep her future stepmother's harebrained scheme a secret from her father. Edwina and Alex were married, and Edwina entered the life she'd always wanted, among the elite of Grosse Pointe society.

Both Evan and Hutch had feelings for Rosanna, and Debbie Simon fervently hoped she would choose Evan. To Debbie, Hutch was the man of her dreams, even though he wanted to be "just friends." The insecure Debbie's emotional state worsened when her father, Ned, divorced her mother to pursue Emma Snyder. Debbie made Hutch think that Rosanna and Evan were having an affair. Hutch's jealousy angered Rosanna, and she began spending more time with Evan. Debbie moved in on Hutch. When Hutch couldn't get Rosanna out of

his system, Debbie had an affair with Hutch's bitter half-brother, Linc. Rosanna soon lost her virginity to Evan.

Woody was shocked to see Emma selling apples to the nominal owner of Aunt Mary's Baking Company. Aunt Mary was, in fact, the mother Hutch believed was dead! Hutch didn't know this, but both Evan and Linc found out. Meanwhile, Connor made one more attempt to reconcile with Linc. She went to his hotel room wearing a sexy teddy under her trench coat, only to find him in bed with Debbie. Connor told Linc that it was over for good. Linc threw Debbie out. Debbie told Hutch that she'd slept with his half-brother. Linc was packed and ready to leave town when Hutch confronted him. Linc not only confirmed what Debbie said, but he cruelly broke the news to Hutch that Aunt Mary was his biological mother.

Linc had turned from a simple, trusting soul into a selfish heel. He was coldly ambitious in his recent position at the newly merged Walsh-Montgomery Company, which was run by Emily and Linc's ex-lover Connor, who was now seeing Cal. When his bosses lambasted him for his deplorable attitude, Fred Greer persuaded Linc to sue Walsh-Montgomery for harassment. But before that plan could come to fruition, Hannah Lafferty discovered her son's body on the floor of his hotel room! The gun was traced to Cal, who had good reason to kill him because of Connor. Cal had satisfied Lyla by eventually settling with the Navajos in their land deal, but Lyla had decided that she needed a new start and left Oakdale on a singing tour. Connor soon found herself pregnant with Cal's child, right before she was arrested for Linc's murder. But the real killer was Ned Simon. He'd been out to avenge the mental breakdown of his daughter after her affair with Linc. While Debbie languished in a hospital, Ned tried to deal with his guilt.

As Lucinda wrestled with her childhood demons, Lily was traveling around the world. Her travels took her to the beautiful Italian coast and the picturesque town of Amalfi. Holden followed her there and found Lily in a cafe singing the plaintive ballad "I Can't Make You Love Me." Lily had obtained the divorce Holden had said he wanted. She returned to Oakdale and legally disavowed her adoption to Lucinda because of the information she had withheld when she found Holden in a New York hospital. As an added shock, Lily revealed that she had married handsome, charming Damian Grimaldi, Emily's business associate in Malta. Together they operated a yacht club by day and a floating gambling casino by night. It was called the Falcon Club, and

Lily was the featured chanteuse. As charming as Damian was, he was also quite the chauvinist, and he made no secret of his jealousy over Holden.

Holden was desperately trying to regain his lost memory. He spent one night with his therapist, Marsha McKay, but she wisely put off his declarations of love and returned to New York so that Holden could rebuild his life on his own. The brothers were soon at it again, fighting over Julie, when Caleb blurted out that Holden was Aaron's father. Disgusted that his family had lied to him, Holden sought refuge with Janice Maxwell, Kim's ambitious assistant at WOAK. One night, Holden had a dream in which he was standing on a hill during a thunderstorm and calling out Lily's name. Realizing that the dream was a memory flash, Holden went to Lily and asked her to help him recover his past. To the dismay of both Damian and Janice, Holden began to have more memory flashes, and they were all of Lily. He begged her to return to him, but Lily insisted that she was still committed to Damian. Lily had been determined to wipe the slate clean after she left Oakdale. Connor and Kirk were the beneficiaries of Lily's Walsh shares, and before he disappeared, she had sold Scott her stock in WorldWide.

Walsh and WorldWide were engaged in a fierce competition for the lucrative Kingsley-Malta account, half of which belonged to Damian. The Kingsley part belonged to Bertram Kingsley, an English friend of Duncan's who had been mysteriously kidnapped and murdered. As part of Lily's vendetta against Lucinda, Damian gave the Kingsley-Malta account to Walsh and arranged for the merger of Walsh and M&A into a company known as Walsh-Montgomery. Connor and Emily would be equal partners and run the corporation. Lucinda turned around and bought back the *City Times* from Walsh-Montgomery, using a phantom company name. And Kirk, the quintessential corporate weasel, deserted Connor and joined WorldWide. He was now actively flirting with "Aunt" Mary, whose baking business he brought into the WorldWide fold. All of this corporate gamesmanship was fun for Lucinda, yet it was small consolation for the losses in her personal life. Lily had rejected her, Neal was dead, and Royce was struggling to regain some semblance of normal life. Lucinda had one hope left: her "other" sibling, Royce's twin, but although she had her detective Mr. Grey on the case, there was no guarantee that she would find him.

With the help of psychiatrist Lynn Michaels, Lucinda was able to come to terms with her mother's

A shattered Lily thought she'd done what Holden wanted when she got the divorce he asked for. Then she met dashing Damian Grimaldi in Rome. He called her "my wounded bird" and helped heal her pain. They were married in Malta, and when they returned to Oakdale, Lily and Damian operated the Falcon Club—a yacht club by day and a floating casino by night.

rejection of her. She took up with John again for a while, but he soon went back to Iva, with whom he now shared a son, Matthew John, affectionately known as M.J. Iva came to realize that M.J. was the reason John wanted to marry her. Because of his memory loss, Holden felt no loyalty to his sister, and he decided to sue her for custody of Aaron. In a courageous move, Iva handed Aaron over to Holden.

Iva had grown tired of John's domineering ways. She soon met up again with Jason Benedict. They were married on the Snyder farm and moved to Washington, D.C. John decided not to sue Iva for custody of M.J. He had been diagnosed with colon cancer, and his future seemed fragile. The only person John confided in was Bob, his former adversary, whom he had finally come to trust, at least as a doctor. Bob urged John to share the burden with his loved ones, but John adamantly refused. Both of his grown offspring, Margo and Andy, had enough to deal with. Andy was now a freelancer, and he and Courtney often lacked the resources to pay their bills. Then Courtney won a scholarship to attend Oxford University in England. When Andy flew in for a surprise visit, the two dined with Patricia Kingsley, Bertram's widow. After dinner, Andy was injured in an explosion rigged by a mysterious man named Hans that was meant to kill Patricia. Andy recovered, and Duncan

## Dueling Divas

*Damian's cousin, the urbane Eduardo, arrived in Oakdale and divas Lucinda and Lisa took note. The feeling was mutual. When Lily and Damian threw a Venetian ball at the yacht club to benefit affordable housing in Oakdale, neither Lisa nor Lucinda was aware that Eduardo was escorting them both. He was constantly switching masks and capes until the ladies found him out.*

flew to England to investigate. He traced Hans to a gatehouse in Montega. Hans rigged the gatehouse with explosives just as Duncan and Sabrina arrived. The building exploded, but Duncan and Sabrina escaped unharmed. A body found in the rubble turned out to belong to another Montegan criminal named Santiago. Duncan realized Hans might still be alive.

On the home front, Duncan and Jessica were blessed with a baby girl. They named her Bonnie Louise, Bonnie because she was Duncan's bonnie lassie, and Louise for Jessica's estranged mother. This happy event brought out the best in everyone, including Lisa, who had previously opposed their marriage. Lisa was named godmother. Jessica's family finally accepted the relationship, and they attended Bonnie Louise's christening and welcomed their granddaughter into the family. Lamar left the *Argus* and went to work for Damian at the Falcon Club. Duncan warned him to watch out for Damian, who he suspected was involved in the attempt on Patricia's life.

Supercop Hal Munson was released from government protection and happily reunited with Barbara. He was thrilled that she was pregnant with their child. Barbara gave birth to a boy, William Ryan (Will) Munson, and remarried Hal. Hal helped her manage Barbara Ryan Originals, and he soon put his detective skills to work. Barbara had entered into a business alliance with Franco Visconti, who made yet another play for her behind his wife Angela's back. Hal noticed

that Franco's employee, Gregory, was playing peculiar games with the Visconti bags that were arriving from Italy. It was discovered that they were smuggling jewels on Kingsley-Malta ships. Hal went to Rome to question Renata Minardi, executive assistant to the late Bertram Kingsley. Renata claimed not to know the whereabouts of Kingsley's missing appointment book. When Hal mentioned the possible animosity between Kingsley and Damian's powerful family, Renata warned him to stay away from the subject or "people would get hurt." Franco was interested to learn that Hal had met with Renata.

Damian's cousin and beloved father figure, Eduardo Grimaldi, arrived in Oakdale. Damian and Eduardo's private conversations indicated that they knew something about Renata and that they had shady dealings all over the globe. By all outward appearances, however, Eduardo was charming and delightful, and he paid particular attention to Oakdale's warring, wealthy adversaries—Lisa and Lucinda. Lisa had been without a love interest since the death of Earl Mitchell, and Eduardo's joie de vivre and European charm reminded her of him. Lisa was ready for love.

## Issues – Interracial Marriage

*There had been much objection to the marriage of Jessica and Duncan, and her parents and his daughter refused to attend the wedding. But the birth of their little girl, Bonnie Louise, went a long way toward cementing family relationships. Jessica's parents, Ward and Louise, made a surprise appearance at the christening, and the once prejudiced Lisa was named godparent along with Jessica's brother Lamar.*

It was a great relief when Margo's final HIV tests turned up negative following her brutal rape at the hands of Elroy Nevins. However, Nevins escaped from prison and broke into Tom and Margo's home bent on revenge. Tom confronted Nevins with Margo's service revolver. When Nevins reached for his gun, Tom shot the rapist not once, but twice, and snuffed out his sorry life. The grand jury acquitted him after he testified that he was only protecting his family. The Hugheses then took in Dawn Wheeler, another of Nevins's victims. Bob treated her free of charge when her insurance company dropped her because she'd tested positive for AIDS. Dawn soon set up housekeeping in the Hugheses' garage apartment, and Tom had no idea that this vulnerable young lady was developing strong feelings for him.

At the same time, the family had to cope with the realization that Dan McClosky, Nancy's beloved new husband and Margo's devoted boss, had Alzheimer's disease. True to form, Nancy was proud and stubborn when her family offered their support. Penny and Anton visited briefly to rally around Nancy, as did Donald and Mary.

Bob and Kim's marriage was stronger than ever. Bob lent a medical hand to the suffering residents of Bosnia, while Kim's main concern was the antics at WOAK. Co-owner Jeffrey Talbot turned out to be a compulsive gambler who frequented Damian's Falcon Club. When Jeffrey got into debt up to his eyeballs, he gave his share of the station to Damian as collateral. Another questionable employee was Janice Maxwell, who shared Damian's hopes of separating Lily and Holden forever. Kim tried to be a mother figure to this confused young lady and gave her a ticket to Akron, Ohio, to visit her family. But when Janice reached the airport, she changed her destination to New York City, where someone was sending her love poems.

Ellen was shocked when Emily donated an egg to Susan for in vitro fertilization. Susan and Larry were thrilled when they learned they were expecting a baby girl. And Emily soon found herself with a new admirer, Craig Montgomery, who had returned to Oakdale during a rough patch in his marriage.

Finally, the romantic merry-go-round of the Snyder siblings came full circle. Caleb and Julie announced their engagement and planned to remarry once he agreed to curb his jealous streak. And Angel, now completely over Holden, married her soulmate, Seth, and they left Oakdale for New York.

## 1 9 9 4

The charming, mysterious Grimaldi family provided most of the Oakdale intrigue in 1994 as the shocking truths behind the powerful Kingsley-Malta corporation began to unfold. Lily was made painfully aware of Damian's violent streak when he beat Holden senseless in a jealous rage. After Holden recovered, he and Lily made love in the bell tower, where they'd spent so much time in the past, and they made plans to be together. Their plans were mercilessly cut short when Hans, the terrorist who had tried to murder Patricia Kingsley, kidnapped Lily. Stashing her away in a cabin cruiser, Hans called a frightened Damian and demanded $850,000. Despite Eduardo's urging not to notify the police, Damian summoned Tom, and Hal rejoined the police force to help with the case.

To elude the authorities, Hans moved Lily to an abandoned clock factory, where he constructed a bomb. He then forced Lily to record a message to Damian. In

*Dastardly Deeds –*
*Hans*

*Seeking revenge on Kingsley-Malta, Hans kidnapped Lily, stashed her in an abandoned clock factory and constructed a bomb. Holden rushed to the scene, only to be taken hostage as well. When Damian arrived with the ransom money, Hans taunted him by saying that Lily and Holden were lovers. Damian lunged for him and was shot. The Oakdale police arrived seconds before the factory was blown to bits. Lily, Damian and Holden were saved, but Hans escaped to Iran.*

One day, when Jessica was in Chicago taking part in a demonstration, Duncan got a call from the police saying that his wife had been arrested. Duncan rushed to help his wife—but it wasn't Jess, it was Shannon, back from the dead!

the background, a llama could be heard. When Tom and Hal listened to Lily's message, little Adam heard the animal's noise and said, "lamb." Holden remembered there was a petting farm near the clock factory. He rushed to the scene, only to have Hans grab him and tie him up next to Lily. Damian left the ransom money at the designated spot and followed Hans, but the terrorist saw him. When Hans sadistically intimated that Lily and Holden were lovers, Damian lunged, and Hans shot him. Hal and an FBI agent saved the captives only seconds before the factory exploded. Hans escaped and was later traced to Iran. Lily told Hal that Hans had used the code word "Rigoletto."

As Damian recovered from his wound, Damian's indomitable mother, Orlena, came to Oakdale. Sierra returned from Montega to lend Lily moral support. Once Damian was well enough to travel, he and Lily went to Malta to elude Hans. One night when Lily was giving her recovering husband a sponge bath, passions reignited and their marriage began to improve. Damian called Eduardo to Malta and confronted him about a disquieting coincidence. Some time before, he'd heard Eduardo mention the sum of $850,000, which was the same amount Hans had demanded in ransom. Eduardo insisted it was related not to Hans, but to a proposed company acquisition. Damian wasn't so sure.

Holden was hopping the globe in search of answers to the Kingsley-Malta capers. When Renata was uncooperative, Holden went to Patricia, who informed him that Renata had once been Damian's mistress. She also said that a few days before Bertram was killed, he was heard arguing with Damian. Sharing Patricia's conviction that Hans was working for the Grimaldi family, Holden met with Lily in Malta and confronted her with this suspicion. Lily reacted angrily and told him to go back to Oakdale. Later, on a dimly lit street, a statue mysteriously fell on Holden's head. When he recovered, he learned that Lily and Damian were back in Oakdale. Meanwhile, Eduardo and Hans were communicating by phone.

The three tormented lovers were back in Oakdale just in time for Caleb and Julie's wedding. At the reception, Holden challenged Lily on her staunch belief in Damian, then admitted to Cal that he and Lily had made love. Holden persuaded Marina, a Kingsley-Malta secretary and friend of Renata's, to go through Bertram Kingsley's files. Cesare, Eduardo's right-hand man, caught her in the act, drugged her and sent her off a bridge in her car to drown. Frightened, Renata cooperated with Holden. Together they rushed to the Falcon Club, where Lily and Damian were renewing their vows, and interrupted the ceremony. Renata showed Lily the last entry in Bertram Kingsley's datebook, which read, "Meet Patricia, Cafe Rigoletto." Renata claimed that Damian told her to lure Bertram to the cafe by saying that Patricia wanted to meet him there. Damian replied that he had done it only because he needed to meet with Bertram about business. Lily's doubts about Damian resurfaced, and she went to stay with her grandfather, Cal.

Orlena accused Lily of wanting Holden and threatened to expose Eduardo's affair with none other than Patricia. Eduardo warned Orlena that he could easily expose some of her own secrets as well. The Kingsley mystery finally came to a head in Rome when Lily, Holden and Damian flew there separately to investigate. Holden and Damian agreed to join forces to help solve Marina's murder. Lily sneaked into the Kingsley-Malta file room and overheard Cesare. Noting that his voice sounded remarkably like Damian's, Lily realized that it was he, not Damian, whom Patricia heard arguing with Bertram. Damian trailed Cesare to a warehouse and trapped him. Just as Lily and Holden arrived, Cesare admitted to killing Bertram, and a violent fight broke out. Eduardo arrived in the nick of time and shot Cesare dead in his tracks. The senior Grimaldi wanted Cesare out of the way before he could reveal any more indiscretions.

Back in Oakdale, Lily and Damian decided to try to make a go of their marriage when they found out they were expecting a child. To Orlena's dismay, Damian moved the Kingsley-Malta headquarters to Oakdale and bought Lily a new mansion called Fairwinds. As Damian and Orlena pampered and dominated Lily during her pregnancy, Lily turned to Lucinda, and the two tried to patch up their strained relationship. Lily found herself once again pining for Holden, but Holden's number one priority was being a good father to Aaron. One day at Aaron's play group, he met a single mother, Tracey, who had a hearing-impaired son, R.J. Tracey remembered Holden from high school, a period in his life of which Holden still had no memory. Tracey reunited Holden with another mutual high school chum, Jef Hamlin. Holden and Aaron spent a lot of time with their new acquaintances, and Holden bonded with R.J. after he saved the boy from a Christmas tree fire. Soon Holden and Tracey realized they had feelings for each other.

After the Rome encounter, Eduardo came out looking spotless to everyone but Duncan. Duncan had other things to deal with, however. One day when Jessica was in Chicago taking part in a demonstration, Duncan got a call saying that his wife had been arrested and was being held at O'Hare Airport. Duncan rushed to her aid and did indeed find a wife, but it wasn't Jess— it was Shannon, back from the dead! He brought Shannon back to Oakdale, where she said that she had escaped the murderous Lilith in the African jungle. Jess was hurt and angry to discover that her marriage to Duncan wasn't legal and that Duncan seemed torn between the two of them. Duncan went so far as to spend an entire night by Shannon's side while she was recovering from a strange African fever. In her delirium, Shannon kept calling out the name "Devere." Duncan decided to remain faithful to Jessica, and Shannon was distraught.

## Issues: In Vitro Fertilization

*Susan's husband, Larry, swore he didn't want children but then changed his mind. Susan's daughter, Emily, generously offered one of her eggs, and little Alison was born. Emily and Susan had a difficult relationship and the question of "Whose baby is it?" was often raised.*

Lisa, however, was delighted to see Shannon again. The two adventurous women took off for Mexico after Lisa spotted Scott in a magazine photo. After some madcap adventures with Mexican criminals, a government agent revealed that Scott was implicated in the theft of a valuable Mayan statue called the Sundancer. Lisa returned to Oakdale at Tom's urging, and Duncan flew to his lassie's side to help her search for Scott. When Duncan asked her what had really happened in Africa, Shannon tearfully explained that she had been imprisoned with a man named Devere, who was later killed. But Devere was very much alive and looking for Shannon in Oakdale. Duncan and Shannon made love before they returned to Oakdale and decided to live together at the castle. Shannon was overjoyed to see Devere. Devere had befriended Jessica during her separation from Duncan. He also knew something about Shannon, which he told Duncan: Shannon had been pregnant with Duncan's child during her imprisonment. She gave birth to a boy, who died shortly after. Shannon had blocked out the painful memory, and Devere advised Duncan that it would be too traumatic for her to remember. Duncan disagreed and consulted psychiatrist Lynn Michaels, who said that Shannon might be suffering from post-traumatic stress disorder. Duncan married Shannon in front of a justice of the peace in Indiana and then gently told her the tragic story of the son they had lost. The memories came flooding back, and Shannon wept in her Scotsman's arms. The two were now closer than ever.

As Lisa frantically sought clues to Scott's whereabouts, she was consoled by the company of Eduardo. But her old adversary, Lucinda, also had eyes for the charming foreigner and hired him at WorldWide while Damian assumed the reins at Kingsley-Malta. Eduardo enjoyed being fought over but eventually realized he had feelings for Lisa. The two became engaged, and a rebuffed Lucinda fired him. Tom still had his suspicions about Eduardo's involvement in the Bertram Kingsley affair but was relieved when Eduardo came to him without Lisa's knowledge and signed a prenuptial agreement. Eduardo discovered scruples he never knew he had.

Scruples were an issue for another attractive lady who remembered Eduardo from her dubious travels. She was Samantha Markham, the long-lost sister of Lucinda and Royce. Lucinda's crackerjack detective, Mr. Grey, had found her. Sierra had insisted on staying in Montega with their children, and Craig was easily smitten with the beautiful Sam. Lucinda was also briefly charmed by Eliot Markham, Samantha's urbane adoptive father. But like every newcomer to Oakdale, there was far more to Sam than met the eye. She was not really Eliot's adoptive daughter, but a con artist and partner in his phony art-trading schemes. Lucinda and Craig caught on when they found her copying Lucinda's treasured Pissarro. Eliot escaped, and Samantha was legally in the clear because no wrongdoing could be proved.

After a brief affair with Emily, Craig was reunited with Sierra in Montega. Emily was living in Larry and Susan's carriage house, and as she tried to get over Royce, she found herself enjoying the attentions of her handsome young stepfather Larry whenever she ran around the house in a sexy teddy. Emily saw Andy's contact sheets from the wedding that never was, and Andy innocently mentioned that he had seen Susan visiting Royce that day. Emily asked Royce, who admitted that Susan had expressed a deep concern about their marriage and had prompted him to reevaluate whether he was ready to marry Emily. Stunned, Emily confronted Susan, telling her that Larry was attracted to her, and that she, not Susan, had a right to the baby Susan was carrying, because it was Emily's egg. Susan angrily wrote her daughter off, and she and Larry celebrated the birth of their daughter, Alison. Susan gradually mellowed toward Emily until she realized Larry was letting Emily get closer to Alison than what was appropriate under the circumstances. Larry then accepted Bob's offer to become temporary chief of staff at Memorial, and his autocratic new attitude showed that he was tired of being pushed around. Royce, meanwhile, accepted a new project in Singapore and left Oakdale to pick up the pieces of his life.

Emily's business partner, Connor, had an eventful year as well. She had miscarried her and Cal's baby but won a surprise inheritance from the late, unlamented Linc Lafferty. Connor was cleared of killing Linc after Ned Simon died of a cerebral hemorrhage and left behind a letter confessing to the crime. During Connor's absence, Emily had tried to take over her position at Walsh-Montgomery until Cal warned her he would yank his StrickCo account if she persisted. Cal and Connor then became engaged, leaving Kirk disappointed. Normally a self-serving shark, Kirk showed his loyalty to Connor when he foiled her own brother, Evan, in an attempt to dupe her in a business deal. But Connor explained to Kirk that they would never be more than friends. Evan's ruthlessness so angered Rosanna that she found herself enjoying the company of the hunky young mechanic who had repaired her car. His name was Mike Kasnoff, and he was as unaffected and down to earth as Evan was to the manner born. A jealous Evan found out that Mike was a parolee in the wake of a minor break-in. Evan arranged for Mike's parole officer, the vindictive Doug Schaff, to use unreasonable strong-arm tactics with his charge. Schaff was later brought under scrutiny for his actions.

Then a skeleton was revealed in the Cabot family closet. Rosanna's aunt, Lee Tenney, told her that her husband, Ray, had been married before—to Rosanna's late mother and Lee's sister, Sheila Washburne Cabot. When Sheila met the wealthy Alex, she saw him as her ticket out of the downtrodden town of Musselshell and left behind her husband, Ray, and a baby girl named Carly. For years Rosanna had assumed that Carly was her cousin when in fact, they were half-sisters. No one knew Carly's whereabouts, because she'd run away from Musselshell seven years before. While Rosanna wrestled with this revelation, Evan instigated a new plot. Mindful that Alex did not want a grease monkey for his daughter, Evan convinced Alex to offer Mike a plum job as a Cabot race car driver. The catch was that Mike would have to give up Rosanna. Naturally, Mike chose the girl over the gig.

When Rosanna went to Musselshell in search of her roots, Mike followed, and they made love for the first time out on the Montana ridge. Mike told Rosanna about Alex's double-edged offer, and Rosanna told her father off. Evan then began charming an older woman— Barbara Ryan! Barbara and Hal's marriage had begun to deteriorate when Hal resumed the dangerous life of a detective. Barbara needed him beside her more than ever when someone began sending her threatening notes consisting of letters cut out of magazines. Then Gregory,

Franco Visconti's slippery employee, discovered a scrap from one of Barbara's magazines with a letter cut out of it. Barbara was sending herself the notes in an effort to get Hal's attention. Meanwhile, Hal had learned that Gregory was using BRO as a front for Franco's smuggling operations. Gregory rigged an elevator with the intention to kill Hal, but Barbara got on instead and was injured when the elevator crashed. Hal quit the force to be by her side. Later, Barbara saw diamonds spill out of Gregory's briefcase. Gregory was about to kill Barbara when Hal arrived. The two men struggled and fell through a skylight, and Gregory was killed. By now, Margo suspected that Barbara had been sending the threatening notes to herself, but Hal refused to believe it until he saw a glue stick drop from Barbara's purse. Their marriage a sham, Barbara and Hal separated. Feeling the heat, Franco's secret boss had him pull their smuggling operation out of Oakdale. The secret boss was none other than the ubiquitous Eduardo.

At Caleb and Julie's wedding, Cal surprised them by bringing Julie's children, Pete and Jenny. They had been staying in Seattle with Helen Wendall, Julie's ex-mother-in-law. After the wedding, Helen took Jenny back and dumped the rebellious teenage Pete on the newlyweds. Pete quickly took up with the nubile Dani Andropoulos, Ellen's great-granddaughter, who was staying with her in Oakdale. Meanwhile, Julie's modeling career began to fizzle when she wouldn't "put out" for Ron Gillette. She became so desperate that when she came upon a briefcase filled with cash—$850,000—she kept it. Unbeknownst to Julie, this was the ransom money which Damian had given to Hans, and which Hans had buried pending his return. Caleb was angry to see his wife on a spending spree and wondered where all the money was coming from. Then Pete found what was left of the stash and swiped it.

Fed up by Andy's preoccupation with becoming a sensationalistic tabloid photographer, Courtney left Oakdale to rejoin her brother, Sean, in Switzerland. Kim was not pleased when Andy began to date the grasping Janice Maxwell, especially after Janice tried to poison Kim so that she could host "Patterns." John was a difficult patient when he was forced to reveal that he had colon cancer, and he had a brief involvement with his equally strong-willed doctor, Bethany Rose. In the meantime, Dan's Alzheimer's disease grew worse. AIDS-infected Dawn Wheeler's condition also deteriorated, and she wondered what would happen to her son Jeremy after her inevitable death.

## 1995

The schemes of the Grimaldis finally came to light in 1995, placing Tom, Margo and other major players in the middle of a heart-wrenching family conflict. Lisa and Eduardo's marriage was threatened before they even had a chance to honeymoon, as Hans arrived in Oakdale and waved a letter in front of Eduardo. He threatened to use the letter against him because Eduardo didn't pay him what he promised. They shot each other as Lisa looked on in horror. Both men were rushed to Memorial, where Lisa implored John to treat Eduardo right away. Seeing that Eduardo's life was not in immediate danger, John treated Hans first, but Hans expired. Meanwhile, Orlena visited Eduardo in his ER cubicle and he showed her the letter. A determined Orlena increased the drug flow of

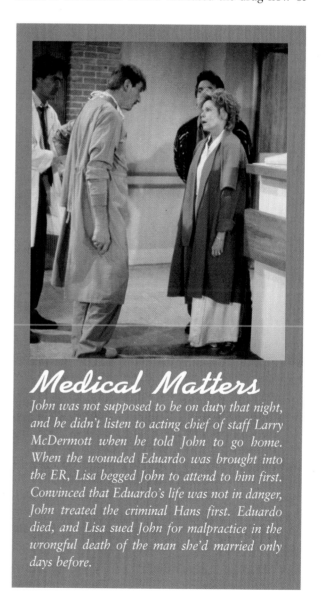

## Medical Matters

*John was not supposed to be on duty that night, and he didn't listen to acting chief of staff Larry McDermott when he told John to go home. When the wounded Eduardo was brought into the ER, Lisa begged John to attend to him first. Convinced that Eduardo's life was not in danger, John treated the criminal Hans first. Eduardo died, and Lisa sued John for malpractice in the wrongful death of the man she'd married only days before.*

After Lily gave birth to a son, Luciano Eduardo, affectionately called Luke, she made plans to separate from her husband, who'd grown cold and distant. Unfortunately, Damian overheard her plans. He drugged her and spirited her away to Malta, where he and his scheming mother, Orlena (Claire Bloom), plotted to keep Lily in a disoriented state.

his IV drip and then vanished with the letter. The next person to enter Eduardo's room found him dead.

The repercussions of Eduardo's death were far-reaching. Lisa found hollow comfort in a campaign to destroy John, whom she blamed for her husband's death. So vehement was Lisa's smear campaign that when she ran a blistering story about John in the *Argus*, Duncan quit in disgust. Larry moved to have John dismissed from the hospital, and John retaliated by bad-mouthing Larry to a hospital in Texas that was about to offer Larry a lucrative position. Susan disagreed with Larry and supported John, as did Kim, Margo and Lucinda. Then Lisa slapped him with a $2 million malpractice suit. Unfortunately, John had let his malpractice insurance lapse after the insurance company had raised his premium because of his colon cancer. Then John's world really began to close in on him. An ambitious resident named Tony Cook tried to extort money from Orlena, threatening that he would reveal her presence in Eduardo's room the night he died. Orlena killed him. Jessica represented John, and Lisa's hired gun was Rick Hamlin, whose son, Jef, was involved with Emily. Marriages faltered as Kim resented Bob's inordinate sup-

port of his ex-wife Lisa against her ex-husband John. Tom fought to stay neutral as Margo sided with John against his parents, and Susan saw a nasty side of Larry as he stepped up his vendetta against John. Once the court ruled in Lisa's favor, however, Bob told Lisa he resented her having placed Tom in the middle of this conflict and was beginning to regret having supported her.

Eduardo's death so deeply affected Damian that he became cold and distant to Lily. He wondered if the child she was carrying was his or Holden's. It was Holden who helped Lily deliver a baby boy when she went into labor on the Snyder farm. But when newborn Luciano (Luke) Eduardo needed a transfusion, it was not Holden's blood that was compatible, but Damian's. Holden moved to Maryland with Aaron to enter a special program to help him recover his memory, and his girlfriend Tracey moved to Chicago with her son R.J. When Damian overheard an unhappy Lily making plans for a legal separation, which included custody of Luke, he drugged her and whisked her away to Malta, where Orlena was waiting. Orlena agonized over the letter she had stolen from a dying Eduardo. The letter had revealed that she was not Damian's mother after all. Orlena was actually Damian's nanny, and she had "gaslighted" his real mother, Bettina, to get Damian the same way she was "gaslighting" Lily to get Luke.

Not one to sit back, Lucinda flew to Malta and managed to keep Lily away from the Grimaldis. Lily insisted that she was being drugged. Lucinda didn't know what to believe but was bound and determined to protect her daughter. One night, out on the docks, Lily was accosted by a sailor and was saved by a young man named Mark. Lily pleaded with Mark to help her escape from the Grimaldis. Mark worked for Damian, and he was loath to believe her story until he overheard Orlena psychotically ranting at Lily. Mark helped Lily steal Luke from the Grimaldi mansion and escape to the States. Orlena tried to stop them, only to fall off a cliff and suffer major injuries. Damian vowed to make Lily pay. When Lily reached Oakdale, the two fought bitterly over custody of Luke. Orlena, now recovered, came from Malta and falsely accused Lily of pushing her off the cliff. To Lily's surprise, Mark arrived and testified on her behalf. Lily was still having drug-related hallucinations and, putting the safety of her child first, admitted she could not vouch for her own state of mind. The judge awarded Damian temporary custody of Luke.

The situation grew downright grotesque. Orlena's mute female servant, Smythe, saw her putting poison on Lily's envelopes. An unsuspecting Damian licked one of the envelopes, began hallucinating and tumbled over a railing. Orlena hid the comatose Damian while Mark nosed around and discovered Damian's bloody shirt. Just as John and Tom began to suspect that Orlena killed Eduardo, Damian came to and vented his rage at Orlena. When Lily arrived, Orlena locked them in the basement and held on to little Luke. Mark arrived at Fairwinds and gave Smythe a pen and paper. He was puzzled when she wrote, "Where's my baby?" Finally, John and Lucinda arrived with a gun. Trapped, Orlena took a swan dive off the roof and was rushed to Memorial, where she asked to see Lisa. Orlena murmured something to Lisa about Eduardo, saying that "he would win that night." Larry had accepted a post in Chicago, so Bob returned as chief of staff and agreed to help John prove that Orlena had killed Eduardo. Lisa apologized to John for ruining his life and did not follow through on collecting the $2 million she had been awarded. In a bizarre twist, Smythe regained her ability to speak and revealed that she was Bettina, Damian's real mother! Damian made sure Bettina was cared for at a psychiatric facility and then sent her back to England.

To everyone's surprise, Mark turned out to be the brother of Mike Kasnoff. Rosanna and Mike had planned a trip to Florida, where Mike was going to race his car "Ludie Bell," but his sleazy parole officer, Doug Schaff, refused to let him out of the state. Schaff changed his mind, however, when Rosanna and Mike discovered he was a frequent "john" at a local brothel. Mike came in second in the race, then was shocked to see Rosanna talking to a girl named Missy. Missy was the ex-girlfriend who had set him up to do the robbery that landed him in trouble. She and Rosanna were laughing, and

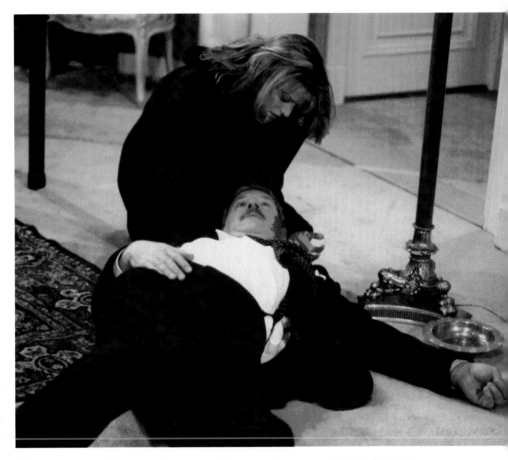

After an angry Mike confronted millionaire Alexander Cabot for breaking up him and Rosanna, Rosanna found her father bleeding on the floor. Mike was arrested for the murder until heart failure was ruled as the cause of death. Rosanna blamed him anyway and barred him from the funeral.

Mike mistakenly thought they were laughing at him. He stormed off, and a heartbroken Rosanna returned to Oakdale alone. Meanwhile, Alex paid Missy off and thanked her for hastening the end of Rosanna and Mike's relationship. Evan disapproved of the way Alex had manipulated Rosanna, so he told her the truth. When Mike bitterly confronted Alex, Alex had a heart attack and died! Rosanna blamed Mike for her father's death. Then Schaff nailed Mike for going across the state

Carly moved in on her sister's ex-beau and picked up Mike in a bar. Not knowing Carly was Rosanna's sister, a lonely, unhappy Mike took her to bed. Ironically, an unsuspecting Rosanna showed up the next day and told Mike she wanted him back. The triangle grew hotter when Rosanna threw Carly a birthday bash and introduced her to a shocked Mike as her sister. Later Rosanna generously gave Carly $30,000 from their mother's trust fund, but that wasn't enough for Carly. She was livid upon finding out that Mike and Rosanna were back together, and she threatened to reveal her tryst with Mike. Mike got Carly to admit something he had suspected for some time: that Carly already knew she was Rosanna's sister prior to Alex's funeral, and had plotted to hop onto the Cabot gravy train. Without revealing Carly's identity, Mike admitted to Rosanna that he'd slept with someone during their time apart, but they became engaged anyway. Undaunted, Carly let it slip out—just as Rosanna was getting ready to walk down the aisle—that she'd slept with her betrothed. Mike and Rosanna never said, "I do."

Fellow schemers Kirk Anderson and Samantha Markham found they had a lot in common and set out to con Lucinda. Kirk would marry into the family and take over the business, and Sam would inherit the money. Then Sam's ex-fiancé showed up begging her for another chance. It was none other than Scott Eldridge, Lisa's missing son. Tom begrudgingly cut a deal for Scott to pay a fine and do community service in exchange for pleading guilty to stealing the Mayan statue. When Kirk spotted Scott kissing Sam, she admitted that they had a past.

Lucinda threw her sister and her chief executive shark a lovely wedding on her lawn, but unbeknownst to her, the minister was a fake. She sent the "happy couple" on a honeymoon cruise. The "honeymooners" soon realized that they were in love for real. Then Kirk fell overboard during a storm. He was presumed dead, but in fact he had washed ashore on the island of Gozo and was on his way back to Oakdale. Thinking Kirk was dead, Sam was drawn closer to Scott. When he was beaten up by thugs, Scott admitted that he was in debt and pleaded with Sam to run away with him. Sam was wavering when Tom and Margo arrested her on suspicion of participating in a forgery scam. They believed she

When Nikki Graves arrived in town, she turned the boathouse into her "pad" and began to follow Hal. It was soon discovered that she was the daughter Hal never knew he had. It didn't take Hal long to become the overprotective father, especially when he found her anywhere near Jeremy Wheeler.

line without permission. With Rosanna and Cal's help, Mike exposed Schaff's proclivity for ladies of the evening and was given a parole officer who truly cared about his well-being.

Rosanna was happy when Carly Tenney, the cousin she had learned was her half-sister, showed up at Alex's funeral. Rosanna told this willowy blonde about their true kinship, and Carly accompanied Rosanna back to Oakdale. Outwardly, Carly was sweet and grateful to Rosanna. In actuality, she was a social climber. She seethed quietly when Rosanna inherited the bulk of Alex's estate and humbly gave most of it to charities, friends and other relatives. Carly looked to Evan as a potential meal ticket, but he was busy sharing Barbara's bed before leaving Oakdale to sail around the world. So had pushed Kirk overboard to get the insurance money. Lucinda bailed her out. Scott then became pals with Carly, who shared his love of the good life. One night, two goons abducted Carly. The men demanded $50,000 in ransom money, and Scott shrewdly scammed the wealthy Rosanna by claiming they'd asked for $150,000. The men released Carly, who learned of Scott's scheme and demanded he give her the difference. Scott refused and set his sights on the attractive and wealthy Rosanna now that she had split with Mike. When Kirk returned from the briny deep, he reconciled with Sam and they made a pact to be honest and above-board from now on. The happy couple were married for real on Christmas Eve at Fairwinds. Soon afterward, Kirk formed a secret alliance with an unscrupulous Kingsley-Malta figure, Umberto Malzone.

At year's end, Caleb and Julie reconciled and moved to Seattle with Pete. Sadly, Dawn Wheeler died of AIDS, and Tom and Margo agreed to raise her son Jeremy as their own. Dani Andropoulos was interested in Jeremy. But Jeremy was intrigued by a young runaway named Nikki, who mysteriously began to follow Hal. Margo discovered that her mother was Lynda Graves, Hal's ex-wife. Nikki revealed that she was the daughter Hal never knew he had. Hal took her in and was soon playing the overprotective father, voicing his disapproval when Nikki and Jeremy "made out." At the same time, Hal and Barbara edged toward a reconciliation.

Duncan and Shannon learned that their latest marriage was not legal and began anew by leaving Oakdale separately. Shannon had written a book about her experiences in Africa and went on tour. Ever the adventurer, Duncan journeyed to Bosnia. Kim foiled Janice in her further attempts to sabotage and poison her, and the disturbed young woman was carted off to jail and then to a sanatorium. Emily Stewart had a whirlwind courtship with Jef Hamlin but bared her fangs when Susan planned to join Larry in Chicago. Determined to keep Susan from leaving with Alison, Emily called the hospital where Susan planned to get a job and told them Susan was an alcoholic. And Andy was ready to leave Oakdale for wider horizons when he was offered a position as a photographer for a magazine in Paris.

Happily some things in Oakdale never change. It's Christmas, and the Hugheses have gathered at Tom and Margo's for their annual Christmas Eve celebration. As always, they start the holiday with a toast: "To the Hugheses, their loved ones and their friends and to every home that is fortunate enough to have a family in it."

## A S F O R 1 9 9 6 . . .

There will be good times...

And bad...

You know what they say: **Life begins at 40!**

They were the core family of "As The World Turns" when the show debuted in 1956, and they retain that position today, 40 years later. When Chris and Nancy Hughes decided to settle in Oakdale, Illinois, he was a country lawyer, and she was the schoolteacher who put him through law school. They had four children: Penny, Don, Susan and Bob. Tragically, Susan had drowned in an accident two years earlier. A classic '50s wife, Nancy gave up teaching to devote herself to her family, and sometimes, as her children would attest, she meddled in their lives a little too much. The Hughes family is steeped in tradition and strong family bonds. They still raise the flag every Fourth of July at the annual Hughes barbecue and toast to "health, freedom, family and this wonderful country." The perfect example of an extended family, Nancy and Chris welcomed "Pa" Hughes into their home after he was forced to sell the family farm, and Nancy took care of her grandson Tom when Bob and Lisa were going through their difficult divorce. As recently as 1995, Bob and Kim welcomed Nancy and her second husband Dan into their garage apartment so they could be nearby for family comfort and care. When the independent Nancy resisted, Tom told her she had only herself to blame. "You're the one who taught us that family sticks together—we're certainly not going to walk away now." The Hugheses always have room in their home and their hearts for the people they love.

In the early '60s, actor Don MacLaughlin (Chris Hughes) sketched his "As The World Turns" family on the back of a script. Pictured here are (from back to front) Chris, Donald, "Pa," Dr. Bob, Nancy and Penny.

FAMILY PORTRAIT

A typical day in the Hughes household began with breakfast, coffee and conversation at Nancy's kitchen table.

After dinner, Nancy always brought Chris his coffee and paper in the living room. The Hugheses favorite evenings were spent in the serenity of their home with family close by.

In the early '60s, feisty Lisa Miller joined the family, having charmed Bob, then a young medical student, into marriage. When Lisa became pregnant, Nancy took them in. Chris was hard put to understand what his often critical wife saw in this spoiled girl who frequently took advantage of their hospitality. But Nancy loved her daughter-in-law's spirit, and although it has been many years since Lisa and Bob divorced, Lisa is still considered family, and the two remain great friends.

Now living in Arizona, the eldest Hughes son, Donald (back row right), often returns home for family occasions.

In 1985, Bob Hughes married Kim Andropoulos. It was the fifth marriage for both, and it was truly a match made in heaven. Nancy and Chris returned to Oakdale from Arizona for the wedding and decided to remain.

In 1986, the Hughes family posed for this family portrait. Kim's son Andy (bottom right) was now an official part of the family.

In the early '90s, the Hugheses posed for this family portrait. Carrying on the family tradition, Bob and Kim's son Christopher (front center) was named for his late grandfather, the beloved Christopher Hughes.

The Hughes women combine great beauty and great strength. Here (left to right), as 1995 draws to a close, Margo, Nancy, Kim and Barbara prepare for the annual Hughes Christmas celebration.

# THE LOWELLS
# AND THE STEWARTS

The Lowell family had more status than the Hugheses, but they weren't immune from problems. The head of the family, Judge James T. Lowell—affectionately known as "the Judge"—had a sterling reputation as head of the prestigious law firm Lowell, Barnes & Lowell. The Judge's son, Jim, was also a member of the firm. As the daughter of Jim and Claire Lowell, Ellen Stewart provides a binding tie to one of Oakdale's founding families. Her great-granddaughter, Betsy's daughter Dani, is a sixth-generation Lowell.

Judge Lowell (far right) and "Pa" Hughes might have been from different worlds, but these two elder statesmen were great pals. Judge Lowell was the only person in Oakdale who called "Pa" Hughes by his first name, "Will."

The Lowells and Hugheses were bound together by business, as Chris Hughes and Jim Lowell both practiced law at Lowell, Barnes & Lowell. Jim had a scandalous affair with Chris's sister, the high-living Edie Hughes. The romance greatly troubled both families and eventually led to the break-up of Jim and Claire Lowell's proper but loveless marriage.

A major force in bringing the families together, Penny Hughes's and Ellen Stewart's friendship would last a lifetime.

Ellen was forced to give up her illegitimate son "Jimmy," later known as Dan, for adoption. After a bitter custody battle, which she lost, Ellen eventually married David Stewart, Dan's adoptive father. Together they raised Dan and Paul, the son from David's first marriage, and had two daughters of their own, Annie and Dee.

Claire married physician Doug Cassen, who proved to be a good husband and a caring and reliable father to the teenage Ellen. However, Claire remained very close to her father-in-law, the Judge, and for many years they all lived under one roof.

What started out as a marriage of convenience for David and Ellen Stewart ended in a love story that lasted until David's death in 1991.

After Kim married Dan, she became a mother in every way to his daughter Betsy, a product of an affair with Liz Talbot, who died soon after the two were wed.

Dan Stewart (above right) followed in his stepfather's footsteps and became a doctor. Dan married the ambitious Susan Burke, but he fell in love with Kim Dixon, and the two eventually married. An alcoholic, Susan started to drink, left town briefly and then returned. She was always considered a Stewart, although the alliance was and still is an uneasy one. Susan's relationship with David Stewart was interesting, as they were both research doctors, often working side-by-side in the lab.

The Stewart family multiplied by leaps and bounds in the early '80s when Annie Stewart and her husband Dr. Jeff Ward welcomed quadruplets into the world.

Three generations of Stewart women live in Oakdale— (from left) Susan, Ellen and Emily—a doctor, a grand-mother and a hard-hitting businesswoman.

# THE SNYDERS

It is no coincidence that the Snyder family appeared in the vicinity of Oakdale around 1986, soon after Douglas Marland took over the reigns as head writer of "As The World Turns." Marland grew up on a farm at the end of a lane known as Snyder Road, and he wanted to bring the show back to the grass roots that he believed were at the heart of American culture. Like Marland's mother, Emma Snyder was a single parent whose husband died prematurely of a heart attack, leaving her to raise her brood of children on the land that had once belonged to her parents. They didn't all stay on the farm, but they all came back to celebrate weddings and births, for a good talk and a shoulder to cry on, and without fail they gathered to cut the Hubbard squash for Thanksgiving dinner. Holden was on the farm, and working for Lucinda as a stable-boy, when we first met the Snyders. He would fall in love with spoiled Lily Walsh, but that's another story. Soon after, adopted daughter Iva arrived. She'd been away for a long time, but she felt it was time to come home. She was followed by tempestuous, boy-crazy Meg, the youngest Snyder, who was very close to Holden. Middle children Ellie and Caleb needed the farm to heal and rebuild. Eldest son Seth, who had assumed the role of head of the house and surrogate father when Emma's husband Harvey died, soon followed. A writer, Seth was very close to Douglas Marland's heart.

Emma (center) and her brood—(counter-clockwise) Ellie, Seth, Holden, Caleb, Iva and Meg—enjoy a family reunion.

Emma tried hard to teach daughter-in-law Julie how to cook, but they never got past the fried chicken and the Dutch potato salad. Luckily for Julie, they were Caleb's favorites.

Everything of importance in the Snyder home revolved around the kitchen table, and there was usually a family member or two or three to give Emma needed helping hands. Above, Caleb brings in the groceries while Emma bakes one of her famous apple pies.

Snyder family and friends gather to cut the traditional Hubbard squash and celebrate Thanksgiving. The squash is so thick it can be cut only with a saw!

Life was tough on the farm, and that made the Snyders grittier than most of the people they came in contact with. Their "gritty" side didn't keep them from getting involved. Soon after he returned to the farm, Seth Snyder and Frannie Hughes fell in love and planned to marry, until his head was turned by Frannie's long-lost, lookalike sister, Sabrina.

The Snyder parlor was the scene of many joyous weddings. This was the second time around for Julie and Caleb, who married impulsively in Las Vegas and then divorced. This time they were determined to do it right.

Often thought of as the spinster in the family, Iva (below) had an unhappy love affair with John Dixon, which produced a son, M.J. But she finally found happiness with Jason Benedict, and after they were married on the farm, they moved to Washington, D.C., where Jason was set to take over as head of the prestigious Crime Commission.

She had had an affair with Caleb, and a brief, unhappy marriage to Holden, but Angel Lange (above center) finally found her soulmate when she married the eldest Snyder, Seth. After the wedding they moved to New York so Seth could pursue his writing.

It was not a happy day when Caleb (below), now a cop, was forced to arrest his mother for unwittingly passing counterfeit money. To Caleb's horror, the money was traced to Julie and her teenage son, Pete. They had found a briefcase filled with ransom money related to Hans and Lily's kidnapping and decided to keep it for themselves.

One drunken night, when Holden (above) was pining for Lily, and Julie and Caleb had had a fight, Holden and Julie found themselves together and shared a lonely night. Nine months later, Aaron was born. Iva tried to protect her daughter, Lily, soon to marry Holden, and she adopted Aaron. But when the truth came out, it tore the family apart. Eventually, Holden was given custody of his son and had his own struggles with being a single dad.

# THE WALSHES

Lucinda Walsh is a fighter and a survivor. As Mary Ellen Walters, she was sent away when her selfish mother Gloria married an oaf named George. Today she heads a business empire as well as a family and resides in a mansion. The Walshes—more of a catch-all family than a classic family, held together by Lucinda's fierce loyalty—are: eldest daughter Sierra, adopted daughter Lily, a half brother and sister and Bianca, a Montegan orphan who lived briefly at the mansion.

The Walsh women are strong women. While Lucinda ran her business, her daughter Sierra ran the country of Montega, and Lily held hearth and home together while being tortured by a crazed mother-in-law who wanted Lily's baby for herself.

When teenage Lily fell in love with Holden Snyder, Lucinda's sullen, sultry stableboy, Lucinda did everything in her power to come between them until the day they married—and even after. Lucinda's interference provoked Lily to disavow her adoption from the mother who had raised her.

Lucinda with daughters Sierra (left) and Lily. Lucinda was forced to abandon Sierra as a baby when she left wealthy Montegan Jacobo Esteban, her first husband. Years later, with Montega in the throes of revolution, Lucinda sent Craig Montgomery to rescue her daughter, waiting perhaps too long to tell her she was her mother.

Lucinda was less than pleased when Sierra and Craig fell in love and planned to marry. Craig was one of Lucinda's up-and-coming junior executives, and the two had shared a night of passion.

"The other side of the family." Connor Walsh came to town calling herself Connor Jamison and wormed her way into Lucinda's home and heart. Soon, as a junior executive at Walsh, she schemed to take over the company and bring it back into the family—hers. She succeeded, and her brother Evan and their mother Edwina (left) were constant thorns in Lucinda's side. Not to be outdone, Lucinda formed another company, WorldWide, and made it an even bigger success than Walsh was.

Lucinda and John's combined family included (from left) John's son Andy, Lucinda's adopted daughters Bianca and Lily, and Duke, John's son from a long-ago affair.

Lucinda knew John Dixon from his days as an intern in Chicago, but he had no memory of her. The two quickly became sparring partners and adversaries until the day John marched into her home to tell her off about one of her schemes. They fell into the hot tub, made love and later married in Las Vegas. It would not be a marriage made in heaven.

Lucinda didn't know her half brother and sister until they came to Oakdale, angry that this wealthy woman had never tried to find them. She didn't even know that Neal was her sister until Neal was accidentally killed by her brother Royce, who was suffering from a multiple-personality disorder. Lucinda was devastated that Neal died before she knew that they were sisters. Neal was a talented artist, and in her honor Lucinda dedicated a gallery at the new Riverwalk Mall, opening it with an exhibition of Neal's work.

A talented architect, Royce (above) left for Japan soon after he was cleared of Neal's murder, but not before he met his "sister" Sam, a con artist who claimed to be his twin.

Sam (near left) fell in love with Craig, who was estranged from Sierra and back working for Lucinda. When Sierra returned from Montega for a visit, Sam was not a happy participant in the welcome-home toast.

After Craig and Sierra reconciled, Sam fell in love with Lucinda's chief executive "shark," Kirk Anderson (left). It was a strange twist of fate to be welcoming Kirk into the family, as he was part of the original scheme to oust Lucinda from Walsh—but Lucinda valued family.

Lily, her husband Damian, Lucinda, the minister and Kirk await the bride at Sam and Kirk's Christmas Eve wedding at Fairwinds, Lily and Damian's home...and so the Walsh family welcomed another member into the fold.

# Young Love, First Love

## PENNY AND JEFF

They were the first soap super-couple before the phrase was even coined, and their romance propelled "As The World Turns" into the number-one spot. Penny was a rebellious teenager when she met Jeff Baker. He was handsome and spoiled, and he dreamed of writing music, but his aggressive mother Grace wanted him in the family business. Penny had never had an easy relationship with her own mother either, and, tired of their parents' interference, the young people eloped while they were still in high school. Their angry families insisted that the marriage be annulled, but Penny and Jeff remained very much in love and continued to see each other in secret.

When Jeff agreed to settle down and join the family firm, he and Penny received their parents' blessing and were married in a beautiful church ceremony on Christmas Eve 1958, with family and friends in attendance. Viewers all around the country dressed up in their Sunday chiffon to watch the ceremony on TV.

Unfortunately, Penny and Jeff's happiness was short-lived. Penny had a miscarriage, and when Jeff found out his mother was using him as a puppet in the business, he went to New Orleans, got a job playing piano in a bar and increasingly turned to drink. Jeff returned to Oakdale just in time to stop Penny from divorcing him on the grounds of abandonment, and the two finally settled down to a happy married life. Jeff composed several hit songs, one of which, "Penny," was dedicated to his wife. He also realized another dream when he bought a successful recording company. His life was back on track, and so was Penny's. But tragedy struck one rainy night when their car swerved off the road. Penny survived but was suffering from amnesia. Jeff was killed instantly. Penny would marry two more times before settling down in England with race car driver Anton Cunningham. Jeff was her first love, though, and he will always hold a place in her heart.

# B E T S Y
# A N D
# S T E V E

Betsy and Steve were a fairy-tale couple who captured the audience's imagination from the moment they met.

Dark, handsome Steve Andropoulos met sweet, innocent Betsy Stewart when his brother Nick was courting her stepmother, Kim. Steve and Nick did not get along, and Nick, who eventually married Kim, was determined to do everything in his power to keep his disreputable brother away from his naive stepdaughter. Steve knew, though, that she brought out the best in him, so against all odds these two opposites fell deeply in love. The discovery of their love led to Nick's fatal heart attack, and on his deathbed he made Betsy promise that she'd stay away from Steve. After Nick's death, a guilt-ridden Betsy married ambitious, conniving Craig Montgomery (upper right) while Steve stood outside the church, tears streaming down his face. But the marriage was doomed from the start.

Unable to consummate the marriage due to Craig's impotence and realizing that she had made a terrible mistake in marrying him, Betsy went to

the medieval mountaintop village of Ronda, Spain, to think. Steve followed her. Actor Frank Runyeon (Steve) composed the song that accompanied the search for the woman he loved:

*"I hear you, I touch you, In the silence, In the endless sky. And I need you to be here again...Warm by my side."*

Once they found each other, Steve and Betsy (right) made love for the first time.

Back in Oakdale, Craig did everything in his power to keep the lovers apart. Although they finally consummated their marriage, Craig withheld the fact that he was sterile, letting Betsy believe that the child she had conceived was his.

Steve became a fugitive from the law after being wrongly accused of stealing a valuable coin from Whit McColl's collection (Craig had set him up). Hot on the trail of the stolen coin, Steve boarded a cruise ship with Betsy, who wanted to help Steve clear his name. Steve and Betsy rekindled their romance, but their getaway was foiled when Craig decided to surprise his wife and join her on the ship.

Spoiled Diana McColl had her eye on Steve and tried hard to make him forget Betsy, while Craig did everything in his power, including faking paralysis, to keep his wife.

After learning that Betsy's divorce from Craig was final, Steve and Betsy finally wed. On May 31, 1984, they exchanged crowns and vows in a traditional Greek ceremony. Twenty million viewers watched as these young lovers said, "I do," and their theme song, "Nobody Loves Me Like You Do," became a national hit.

# LILY AND HOLDEN

Star-crossed lovers straight out of Shakespeare, Lily Walsh and Holden Snyder met as teenagers when Holden jumped out from behind the stable door and into Lily's life. Actress Martha Byrne, who plays Lily, puts it this way. "It was like, whoa....You knew something intense was going to happen."

It was the first time in Lily's life that she could trust someone. She felt comfortable and safe with Holden, especially during the dark days when she found out she was adopted. She fled to Wyoming, and Holden followed her there, but her trust was broken when she found out that Holden knew about the adoption all along and had chosen not to tell her.

Lily returned to Oakdale and into the waiting arms of childhood friend and confidant Dusty Donovan (above), and they moved in together.

Deeply hurt by Lily's rejection, Holden turned to Emily (bottom right), then pregnant with James Stenbeck's child, and married her on the rebound. They moved into a condo that overlooked Dusty and Lily's carriage house.

When Dusty left, Lily turned to Holden's brother Caleb. The union propelled Holden, now divorced from Emily, into the arms of Angel Snyder, Caleb's former love.

Devastated and vulnerable, Lily eloped with con artist Derek Mason (above). Unbeknownst to Lily, Derek and his father Niles were plotting to kill her for her millions, but Derek had a change of heart at the last minute and died trying to save Lily from the explosion that was meant for her.

Lily returned to Oakdale hardened by her experience, determined to become a businesswoman and rival the success of her (adopted) mother Lucinda. However, it didn't take long for Holden and Lily to find each other again—the pull between them was too great to ignore. The night before their wedding, Holden and Lily went up to the bell tower to be alone.

**LILY:**

Holden, do you realize what's happening tomorrow? We're getting married.

**HOLDEN:**

It won't make me love you any more. I couldn't.

**LILY:**

Do you think there are any two people in the world who love each other as much as we do?

**HOLDEN:**

No...impossible. Do you remember the first time I told you we'd always be a part of each other?

**LILY:**

Of course I do. It was in the hayloft when your mother was in Kansas. You said we were meant to spend our lives together.

**HOLDEN:**

I meant it. We are...We have to, because we're a part of each other.

Lily (Heather Rattray below) and Holden married in a traditional ceremony at the Luther's Corners church in the fall of 1991. But at the heart of this union lay a secret that had the potential to destroy their future and their lives. The child Holden carries in this wedding portrait was supposedly his nephew Aaron. In reality, the child was the product of a drunken one-night stand between Holden and Caleb's then-wife Julie, and not even Holden knew the truth!

Lily and Holden were happy for a time, but soon after, Holden discovered the truth about Aaron. While in New York seeking answers from Julie Snyder, Holden was mugged and suffered head injuries. Months later, when he was found, Holden had no memory of Lily and their love. He didn't want to hurt her and thought they should get divorced. The pain was more than Lily could bear, and she fled to Europe.

It was New Year's Eve in Rome when Paul Ryan introduced a sad and lonely Lily to the dashing Damian Grimaldi, heir to the multimillion-dollar conglomerate Kingsley-Malta. He called her his "wounded bird" and nursed her broken heart back to health. The two were married in Damian's native Malta.

Then the Grimaldis came to Oakdale, bought the Yacht Club and opened a casino.

Holden had begun to have memory flashes of Lily and fell in love with her again, all because of what he heard they'd shared. Lily tried to help him regain his memory and they made love, but she recommitted to her husband. As fate would have it, only Holden was present when she went into labor in the Snyder kitchen, and he helped deliver another man's child.

Now Damian is gone, having died tragically in a plane crash, and Lily is the mother of a little boy, Luke. Who knows what the future will bring?

According to actress Martha Byrne (Lily), Holden was the great love of Lily's life. If they found each other again, "it would be a forever kind of thing."

**LILY:**
We used to sit on the floor, enjoy the fire, but...if you'd like a chair—

**HOLDEN:**
The floor'll be fine. (He spots the carved cat on the hearth. Picks it up. Sees Lily misty-eyed)

**LILY:**
That was the first present you ever gave me...you carved it yourself.

**HOLDEN:**
Really?

**LILY:**
I had this kitten I tried to keep in the stable when you worked there because my mother was allergic. She used to sneeze like crazy every time she came into the stables, so you carved this one for me. I kept it by my bed at Lucinda's for years. I've taken it with me wherever I've lived since. It was one of the first things we moved in here.

**HOLDEN:**
I worked in your mother's stables?

**LILY:**
That's how we met. I'll always remember the day Dusty and I were walking to the stables, and suddenly you jumped from out of nowhere and introduced yourself as the new stableboy.

**HOLDEN:**
Who's Dusty?

**LILY:**
Someone I was close to at the time. He lives in England now. But anyway, that's how we first met. Would you like to hear more?

**HOLDEN:**
Sure, if it's not too painful to talk about.

**LILY:**
It's not, because they're the happiest memories of my life.

They met at Sparky's Garage, and the sparks sure flew! Rosanna was having trouble with her Cabot Mountaineer. Mike was the mechanic, and he took his sweet time fixing it. They didn't like each other, or so they thought.

# R O S A N N A
# A N D
# M I K E

She was the heiress to the Cabot Motor fortune, even before her father died and left her $600 million. He was an ex-con (framed by a former girl-friend) and was as tender as he was intense.

In an effort to deny their underlying attraction to each other, Rosanna and Mike fought like cats and dogs. But after he kissed her at the Snyder pond, things would never be the same.

When Rosanna headed for Musselshell to find her roots, Mike followed, and the two made love for the first time.

It was a sweet, wonderful moment, one they would hold in their hearts for many months to come. Shawn Christian (Mike) says, "For Mike, it was his first time out of the state. He was like a wild child looking for adventure. He was watching Rosanna the whole time, watching her radiate joy, and even with all the problems they had, she saw the goodness in his character. She was a fighter."

Mike had a dream of being a race car driver, and Rosanna helped him realize it when they hit the race-car circuit in Florida, behind the wheel of his treasured "Ludie Bell." Mike finished in first place.

Then came Carly, Rosanna's long-lost half-sister. Carly appeared at Alexander Cabot's funeral, all sweetness and light. Hungry for family, Rosanna welcomed her with open arms.

One drunken night, after Rosanna had rejected him, Mike met a lonely Carly by chance at Yo's, the local bar. He didn't know she was Rosanna's sister, and she claimed she had no idea he was the man Rosanna loved and hoped to marry. He took her to his apartment above the garage and they made passionate love. Mike recognized a part of himself in Carly—a part he didn't like.

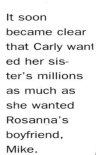

On their first trip to Florida, Mike proposed to Rosanna with a ring from a Cracker Jack box, and that meant more to her than any diamond. Their love for each other was so overpowering they weren't even thinking about things like where or how they were going to live. "They were two kids with unbridled passion, not a care in the world and no responsibilities, just crazy in love," says Shawn Christian (Mike).

It soon became clear that Carly wanted her sister's millions as much as she wanted Rosanna's boyfriend, Mike.

Mike admitted to having a one-night stand but never told Rosanna with whom, and their wedding plans proceeded full speed ahead.

Marrying Mike symbolized for Rosanna the beginning of her own family, and she cherished the feeling. Yvonne Perry (Rosanna) sees them "in a little cabin in the woods. She would have an art studio upstairs with lots of windows. And there would be a couple of kids around. Mike would be a wonderful father." Sadly, Rosanna learned of Mike's indiscretion on her wedding day, and they ultimately never said their vows.

As for what could break up this couple, Yvonne Perry (Rosanna) says, "She makes him socially acceptable, and he brings vibrancy to her life. It's a union that could work." Shawn Christian (Mike) adds "You might be able to physically break them up, but I don't know how you're going to take away the experiences and the love that they feel for each other."

On New Year's Eve, Oakdale's younger set gathered at Yo's to welcome in 1996. Mike was there with Carly. Rosanna was there with Scott. Just before midnight they found each other.

**MIKE:**
I miss you...I miss you so much, Ro. I—God, I can't stand it. I never loved anybody—I didn't know I could love this hard. It's—I can't let go! I wander around, goin' through the motions, bein' halfway normal one day, gettin' into trouble the next, numb from the heart up, 'cause I...lost you, threw us away...

**ROSANNA:**
Mike, don't...

**MIKE:**
No, let me say it all! See, I beat up on myself 'cause it's right! Nobody to blame but me! OK! But when I try to move past it, no way...I go to sleep. I dream about you. I wake up, I reach for you...

**ROSANNA:**
Oh, Mike...don't...

**MIKE:**
Put my face in the pillow for the smell of your hair, but it's fadin', and I can't stand that! Every day you're further and further away...every day it hurts more, not less...

**ROSANNA:**
Yes... yes...all the time.

**MIKE:**
Here you are, and all I can think about is how much I want to hold you, and I can't. When McKnight was singing our song, I was dancin' with you—in my mind, y'know? We were alone, and I could remember what you felt like in my arms. I tried to remember what it was like to bury my face in your neck and your hair and breathe you inside me and...I did! For a split second, I was home. Then, the song was over and I woke up, more alone than I've ever been in my life...so I got out of there. Please...say something...anything...

**ROSANNA:**
God help me...I...miss you, too.

*This is a love story to be continued...*

## Lisa In Love

**M**ore than anything else, Lisa Miller Hughes Eldridge Shea Colman McColl Mitchell Grimaldi loves being in love! She might be many other things—businesswoman, mother, mentor and friend—but she's an incurable romantic who has married seven times in her quest for the ultimate mate, and she's not averse to trying it again.

(Left) Lisa today, and in the early '60s (above).

### HUSBAND #1: BOB HUGHES

She was a feisty college coed from Rockford, Illinois, and he was a first-year med student. It was the first love for both, but what pretty Lisa Miller wanted most of all was to be a doctor's wife, and she persuaded young Bob Hughes (above) to elope. Nancy and Chris were stunned when they found out and wanted the marriage annulled, but Lisa was already pregnant, so the newlyweds moved into the family home. Lisa soon grew bored with being a wife and mother. Leaving son Tommy in Nancy's care, she returned to college and drifted into an affair with wealthy shoe tycoon Bruce Elliot. The affair convinced Lisa that she wanted out of her marriage, and, as usual, she got her way. Lisa was in love with Bruce, but Bruce wasn't the marrying kind. Lisa begged Bob to take her back, but Bob had been truly hurt by her infidelity. It would be a long time before Bob married again, and it seemed that every time he got involved with a woman, Lisa would come back into his life. Sometimes it looked as if they would get back together, but they never did.

According to Don Hastings, who has played Bob Hughes for some 35 years, "There were times when she came back, and I consoled her, and she mistook it for love." As for their relationship, he says, "I've always been kind of wise to her, and I think he's someone she can let her facade down with because she trusts him. The marriage didn't work out, but there is a valid friendship." And, of course, there is their son Tom.

### HUSBAND #2: JOHN ELDRIDGE

Lisa ran off to Chicago, leaving Tom behind. She settled down in the Windy City, where she wed and then divorced wealthy John Eldridge (played by Nicolas Coster, who also played Eduardo Grimaldi, husband #7). Lisa returned to Oakdale with a hefty divorce settlement and was ready to enter Oakdale society in the style she'd always dreamed of. She turned to society doctor, Michael Shea, mentor to Dr. John Dixon, and he became…

### HUSBAND #3: MICHAEL SHEA

When Lisa met Michael Shea, he was married to Ellen Stewart's mother, Claire, whom he was using for her money and her social position. Undeniably attracted to Lisa, Shea allowed her to lure him into an affair. All was going smoothly until Lisa discovered that she was pregnant with his child. Lisa begged him to marry her, but Michael liked his life the way it was, and he refused. When Claire learned the truth, she divorced him. After Lisa gave birth to a son, Chuckie, Michael became attached to the boy and finally asked Lisa to marry him, but she turned him down, still smarting from his previous rejection. The devious doctor then blackmailed Lisa into marriage

after Tom, who had returned from Vietnam with a drug problem, was caught stealing drugs from Shea's office. According to Eileen Fulton, it was a terrible marriage but a "luscious story line" because as "the woman scorned," Lisa got him back by prancing around the house in sexy negligees and then denying him sex. "It was great fun!" Eileen recalls. Michael got what many people in Oakdale thought he deserved when he was murdered by a jilted lover from his past.

Lisa was soon enjoying lobster, caviar and champagne with millionaire Simon Gilbey, but the affair was short-lived. Another unsuccessful attempt to woo Bob back led to a fling with his older brother Don. When Chuckie was killed in a car crash, a disheartened Lisa turned to a new project, running the Wade Book Shop. That is, until husband #4, Grant Colman, came to town.

### HUSBAND #4: GRANT COLMAN

Grant Colman came to town to join the Hughes law firm, and he became smitten with Lisa. After he heroically rescued her from a stalker, Grant proposed. He was handsome and successful, and she happily accepted. But Grant had neglected to tell her that he was already married to a clingy woman who had no intention of giving him up. Joyce Colman came to town and did everything in her power to interfere with the romance between Lisa and Grant. She finally gave Grant the divorce he so dearly wanted, and he and Lisa made plans to marry. On their wedding day, Joyce presented the happy couple with the unwelcome news that she and Grant had a son named Teddy, who was living in Laramie, Wyoming. Grant decided to cancel the honeymoon and investigate Joyce's wild claim. The bride was not amused! Much to everyone's surprise, Joyce's story turned out to be true. But Joyce wasn't the only threat to the Colman marriage: Women were always fighting over Grant, and Lisa was very jealous. Eileen Fulton (Lisa) says, "Grant didn't see it. He was just so handsome, he couldn't stand it. He didn't realize these women were just falling all over him. He just thought Lisa was overreacting, so the more he said, 'This is not happening,' the angrier she got, because she didn't know that he really didn't see it. It made for great friction." According to actor James Douglas (Grant Colman), "It was a very painful moment when he gave her back the keys. It was agonizing for them both, because they loved each other, but he knew she didn't trust him." Out of their difficult parting a trust and friendship grew, and Lisa and Grant remain great friends and confidants to this day.

After divorcing Grant, Lisa decided that she wanted to be independent for a while, and she threw herself into a new project. She and

One of James Douglas's favorite moments was when, as husband #4, he gave Lisa away to husband #6. Here he dances with her at her wedding to Eduardo Grimaldi, husband #7.

Barbara Stenbeck opened a boutique together and called it Fashions, Ltd.

### HUSBAND #5: WHIT MCCOLL

This relationship often resembled more of a power struggle than a marriage. Lisa had always craved security and stability, and Whit's money and social position returned her to the center of Oakdale society. Whit had a secret wife as well—Charlene L'Amour. He had married her during a drunken stupor in Las Vegas and had forgotten all about her. Charlene ended up living at the McColl mansion under the guise of pretending to be Whit's sister, and miraculously everyone got along! While Lisa was off on another buying trip, Lucinda Walsh came to town and tried to wrest the McColl empire away from Whit. Housekeeper Dorothy Connors, who had been secretly in love with Whit for years, took advantage of his low spirits and heavy drinking in the hope that he would give in to her desires. Lisa returned from her trip to find Whit dead on the library floor! Lisa blamed Lucinda, but the culprit turned out to be spurned housekeeper Dorothy Connors.

### HUSBAND #6 EARL MITCHELL

Earl Mitchell was the dashing uncle of Shannon O'Hara, new in town and involved in diamond smuggling. Nobody, including Lisa, knew that Earl was an Interpol agent sent to check out the drug ring run by the infamous Falcon

Lisa went off to Paris on an extended buying trip and returned with husband #5, publishing magnate Whit McColl.

(James Stenbeck). Eileen Fulton says of Earl, "He was romantic and exciting, and I think he supplied all the romance that Lisa had always been looking for." But their road to love was a rocky one. Lisa went through menopause and was sure that he wouldn't find her attractive, and Earl would disappear on missions Lisa knew nothing about. When Earl announced his departure from Oakdale, Lisa was sure that all was lost, but he returned on Christmas Eve just as Lisa was getting ready to take down her tree...and he proposed.

### HUSBAND #7 EDUARDO GRIMALDI

Eduardo had a dark side, and Lisa's family, especially Tom, did not approve of the relationship. Eileen Fulton says, "Lisa has never doubted anything in her life." She was sure that he was right for her and hoped that Eduardo would be her lucky charm.

With two of her ex-husbands, Bob and Grant, in attendance, Lisa

It was 1987 when Lisa married Earl Mitchell, husband #6, and they were very happy. But due to Earl's dangerous line of work, their happiness was short-lived. On the trail of the Falcon, Earl lost his life, and Lisa nearly died as well. In his honor, Lisa and Earl's niece, Shannon, established the Earl Mitchell Center for runaway children. Lisa had loved Earl deeply, and after his death she remained single longer than she ever had before.

Miller Hughes Eldridge Shea Colman McColl Mitchell became Lisa Grimaldi in a stylish ceremony aboard the *Valleta*, Damian's yacht. Once more, Lisa's happiness would not last long. Before they could even plan their honeymoon, terrorist Hans, believing Eduardo had short-changed him for the dirty deeds he'd done for Kingsley-Malta, arrived at the newlyweds' penthouse and shot Eduardo in the shoulder, severely injuring him. Eduardo summoned Orlena Grimaldi to his side to discuss a family secret. It was a mistake that would prove fatal. Distraught, Lisa sued attending physician John Dixon for malpractice.

He was a Maltese aristocrat and the cousin of Lily's husband Damian. A charming international adventurer, Eduardo reminded Lisa immediately of Earl.

## Lisa on her favorite husbands...

**HUSBAND #1:**
**BOB HUGHES**

He was her first love and the feelings still remain. "I wish she would go after Bob. I truly do."

**HUSBAND #4:**
**GRANT COLMAN**

"I love James Douglas, and I loved working with him. She'll always love Grant. She feels comfortable with him, brotherly."

**HUSBAND #6:**
**EARL MITCHELL**

Eileen Fulton was thrilled when she found out that husband #6, Earl Mitchell, was going to be played by Farley Granger: "I have had a crush on him since high school!" Eileen dressed for the occasion like a proper diva—black dress, pearls and all. "When I got up from my chair, I almost strangled him with my necklace, and I thought, my God, I've killed my leading man, and I haven't even worked with him yet! I've loved him to death!"

**HUSBAND #7,**
**EDUARDO**
**GRIMALDI**

"Eduardo was all romance. He was a combination of everything. He was romantic, and she didn't know him well enough to know any of the bad things."

## Lisa's favorite husbands on Lisa / Eileen...

**HUSBAND #1: (DON HASTINGS)**
**BOB HUGHES**

"Eileen is a hoot to work with. Bob has an attachment to the woman who was one of his first loves as a kid. If it weren't for his pride, there were times when he might have gone back to her."

**HUSBAND #4: (JAMES DOUGLAS)**
**GRANT COLMAN**

"Eileen has created a character who can be both nasty and lovable. Lisa is a trouper with amazing, phenomenal energy, and she managed to marry all those husbands! I miss Lisa's aura, her energy. I loved the love scenes, and I loved the fights! She is a true daytime diva. People love to hate Lisa. She's a survivor! Only babies, dogs and Eileen Fulton can steal a scene."

**HUSBANDS #2 AND #7: (NICOLAS COSTER)**
**JOHN ELDRIDGE/**
**EDUARDO**
**GRIMALDI**

"Lisa has the best qualities of Eileen. She's a southern lady —she has gentility and humor and spunk! However, Eileen is not as conniving as her character. She's a delightful, intelligent woman of enormous talent."

As for the other two men in her life, sons Tom (with Bob Hughes) and Scott (with John Eldridge), Lisa's relationships with them are as complex and complicated as any or all of the relationships with her exes. As Eileen Fulton says, she'll "do something redeeming, and then she's got to do something else awful again." But one thing's for sure, adds Fulton, "She's gotta have fun."

# *Married Love*

## TOM AND MARGO

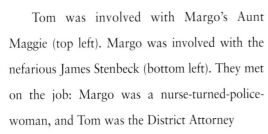

I**s there life after marriage? Meet Tom and Margo Hughes. He was Bob Hughes's straitlaced, principled son. She was John Dixon's feisty daughter who liked to live on the edge.**

Tom was involved with Margo's Aunt Maggie (top left). Margo was involved with the nefarious James Stenbeck (bottom left). They met on the job: Margo was a nurse-turned-police-woman, and Tom was the District Attorney

Strong, impetuous, independent and funny, Margo was ruled by her passions, and she both frightened and excited the upstanding Tom. He was the realist, she the romantic. Together they shared an intelligent humor and made snappy repartee their trademark. It was and continues to be an interesting match.

Over the years, three distinctive acting couples have put their stamp on Tom and Margo.

They were rafting down a river, hot on the trail of a dwarf known as Mr. Big, the infamous head of a drug ring. During their adventure they fell in love, and by the time they nabbed Mr. Big, they were engaged to be married. Twelve years later they are still husband and wife.

Tom and Margo, 1996 (Ellen Dolan and Scott Holmes).

True to form, this off-the-wall couple did not opt for the traditional ceremony. Without any warning, they called their friends and family to the local park and told them to come quickly, that it was an emergency! The minister arrived in an ice cream truck. The mother of the bride was in a housecoat and curlers, and the bride and groom made their grand entrance on a motorcycle!

Actress Margaret Colin (Margo) and actor Justin Deas (Tom) tied the knot in real life.

## HILLARY BAILEY SMITH
## AND GREGG MARX

They were not without their problems. Headstrong policewoman Margo suffered a miscarriage on the job, and the stress nearly tore the marriage apart. Then a false claim by Barbara that a drunken Tom had slept with her in New York drove Margo into the arms of partner Hal Munson with whom she had a baby (upper right with current Tom, Scott Holmes). Gregg Marx (Tom) feels that the relationship "is really about two people who belong together in the best possible way. From day one Hillary brought out the best in me as an actor, as I think Margo brought out the best in Tom as a character, as a person. In a certain way, it was like art imitating life imitating art." Hillary Bailey-Smith says she was lucky. "Although Margo is more gutsy then I am and far more career-oriented, it was a relief to be playing one of the more intelligent women on television."

Just as Hillary Bailey-Smith had to take over the role from the popular Margaret Colin, Ellen Dolan had to do the same with the popular Hillary Bailey-Smith. Today Ellen Dolan and Scott Holmes (the longest running of the 13 Toms) have made the parts very much their own. Ellen describes her Margo as "opinionated, independent and loyal, and she often leaps before she looks. It's built into the character that she makes mistakes and that's what makes her so human." According to Scott Holmes, "Tom's the nicest guy on TV."

What the actors and writers are trying to show is a "real" family of the '90s. Both parents work, they have their differences, they yell at each other, and they send out for pizza, with the kids underfoot and the phone ringing. Scott Holmes says, "He's wonderfully romantic and feels very passionate about his wife." Ellen Dolan describes the relationship this way: "It's like a physics thing. Margo is always bringing a sort of adventure or spark to Tom's life, while Tom is the grounding force in her life."

ELLEN DOLAN AND SCOTT HOLMES (WITH "ADAM" AND "CASEY"

# BOB AND KIM

She was Kim Reynolds, a beautiful widow. He was Bob Hughes, and he was married to her sister, Jennifer. When she saw Bob, it was love at first sight, but it would take them 14 years and four marriages each before they would say "I do."

Actress Kathryn Hays (Kim) explains, "Kim could not control herself, even though he was married to her sister. She just took one look at him and fell in love." Kathryn feels there's a certain kind of love that exists between two people to the point where "you have no choice but to let it take its course. Kim just plain loved Bob so much."

By the time Jennifer died in a car crash, leaving Bob to care for their infant daughter Frannie, Kim had finally gotten her divorce from John and fallen in love with Dan Stewart.

They have withstood adversity in the form of deranged kidnappers (Douglas Cummings) and crazy baby sitters (Laura Simmons). Today Kim's and Bob's trust in each other is complete, and their marriage is a model everyone in Oakdale can aspire to.

# ON THE ROAD TO EACH OTHER

Bob married beautiful Miranda Marlowe, who had once participated in an organized crime ring.

In 1977 Kim married Dan, and they were happy together until he died suddenly and tragically of a blood disorder. Kathryn Hays says that "Dan was a strong, sweet, solid love, a step toward Bob." But she and Bob were not about to wed...not yet.

Meanwhile, Kim was swept off her feet by handsome Greek restaurateur Nick Andropoulos. Both marriages were drastic mistakes. Nick wanted Kim to remain at home and be the "perfect" little wife, whereas Kim, always active in business, wanted a hand in managing the restaurant.

Nick died of a heart attack, and Miranda ran off with another man. Through it all, Bob and Kim remained caring friends and confidants. She wanted to remain friends because it was safe. Kim went up to her cabin to think, and Bob followed. Bob proposed, and, knowing that he was the love of her life, Kim said yes.

In April of 1985 Kim and Bob were finally wed in a sunrise ceremony at the Oakdale Botanical Gardens. Kathryn Hays believes that "strong affection is the basis of a strong marriage." Kim and Bob had shared a loving friendship for more than a decade, and now they were husband and wife. Appropriately, they chose as their song, "Friends in Love."

The wedding party consisted of member's of both the Hughes and Stewart families.

The Hugheses stable marriage was seriously threatened only once. Kim was preoccupied with her son Andy's drinking problem, and John, the boy's father, was a constant presence in the house. Feeling neglected, Bob turned to Kim's nemesis, sultry Susan Stewart.

A very needy Susan was battling an addiction to pain-killers, and what started as a kindness on Bob's part turned into a brief affair.

Kim and Bob's mutual love for each other and their son Christopher brought them back together. Today their marriage is on solid ground.

Kim and Bob surely remain the moral center of Oakdale. They proudly carry on the tradition of raising the flag at the Hugheses annual Fourth of July barbecue and explaining the meaning of freedom and living in America to their young son.

# NANCY AND CHRIS

## "Until Death Do Us Part"

Nancy was the quintessential '50s housewife when "As The World Turns" premiered in 1956. She would never hire a maid, and her kitchen remained the center of her home.

Chris was an upstanding citizen and partner in the law firm headed by another patriarch of Oakdale, Judge Lowell.

They were college sweethearts. Nancy had been a schoolteacher, but once she became a wife and mother, she considered it her job to nurture her family and keep things running smoothly in the home. They survived the tragic death of a daughter and raised three children—Penny, Don and Bob. Their marriage was a classic example of what can happen when two people love each other with the proper kindness and respect.

They had one of the few marriages in the world of soaps that seemed to endure. She knew his idiosyncrasies, and he knew hers, and this man and her children were the fabric of her life.

In 1986 Chris and Nancy Hughes celebrated their 50th wedding anniversary, a first for a soap couple, and they set an example for us all. Sadly, actor Don MacLaughlin (Chris) died soon after. This much-loved actor and character is greatly missed by his family and friends and everyone whose life he touched in Oakdale, U.S.A., and on the set of "As The World Turns."

# NANCY AND DAN

## Life Goes On

Nancy Hughes had enjoyed a rich and fulfilling marriage and had reservations about marrying again. But Nancy said yes to Lt. Dan McClosky over the initial objections of her son Bob and Dan's daughter Bernice. They were married in the fall of 1988 in the Hugheses backyard, and their union proved that you can love at any age. At his grandmother's request, Tom sang "Time After Time." It would become Dan and Nancy's song.

Today their love is being put to the test as they deal with the early stages of Dan's Alzheimer's disease. But Nancy Hughes McClosky is a strong woman, and she loves her husband very much. As Helen Wagner says, "She's certainly not going to give way and break up. That's not her style. She's been through too much with all her children to do anything like that."

Life does indeed go on.

# Notable Nuptials

**I**rna Phillips, creator of "As The World Turns," put her own special spin on the traditional wedding vows: "All our lives are serial stories, and the marriage ceremony outlines the plot for us at the altar: 'For better, for worse, for richer, for poorer, in sickness and in health'...this is a blueprint of every woman's life. Each day brings a new installment in our private soap opera, and no matter how bad yesterday was, who can resist tuning in tomorrow to find out what will happen next?"

"I do."

Whether it is in a castle or a barn, in the Hugheses backyard, on a yacht or in a church, a wedding in Oakdale is a glorious event.

## THE STEWARTS GIVE A DAUGHTER'S HAND IN MARRIAGE

### ANNIE STEWART AND BRAD HOLLISTER (1980)

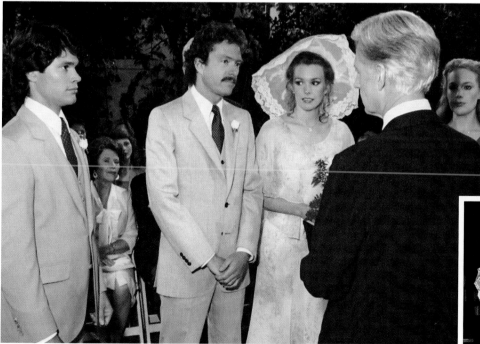

A proud David Stewart walked his daughter, Annie, down the aisle when she married Brad Hollister on the Stewarts' patio.

This was the second marriage for Annie, who had been previously married to Beau Spencer, and it was the second time she had married a man her sister Dee (standing to the bride's left) had been in love with. Eric Hollister (standing to the groom's right), Brad's brother, was best man. The marriage unraveled when Annie discovered Brad had feelings for her sister after all.

# OTHER NOTABLE NUPTIALS

**MARCY THOMPSON AND LORD STEWART MARKAM CUSHING (1985)**
Waif Marcy Thompson wed her Prince Charming when she married Lord Stewart Markam Cushing, a Stewart grandson, in the ruins of a castle. Torchlights glowed, candles burned, and the scent of flowers filled the air. It was a fairy-tale wedding! The couple moved to England, where we presume they are living happily ever after.

**MAGGIE CRAWFORD AND FRANK ANDROPOULOS (1984)**
It was another case of two sisters being in love with the same man, but Maggie Crawford won the heart of Frank Andropoulos as sister Lyla (standing behind the bride) looked longingly on. Steve Andropoulos, Frank's cousin, served as best man when the couple said, "I do" on Christmas Eve.

**CONNOR WALSH AND CAL STRICKLYN (1994)**
Connor Walsh and Cal Stricklyn chose a barn for their impromptu wedding. The guests donned cowboy hats, and the bride wore her red boots. Connor's snobbish mother, Edwina (standing to Connor's left), was horrified, but everyone else had a grand old time!

### ANDY DIXON AND COURTNEY BAXTER (1993)

Young Andy Dixon and Courtney Baxter chose the Hugheses' living room for their Christmastime wedding. Many family members thought they were too young to handle the responsibilities of marriage. Sadly, this time the grown-ups turned out to be right. They were married for barely a year before they parted ways.

### LYLA MONTGOMERY AND CASEY PERETTI (1987)

It was a touching May-September romance when Lyla Montgomery and young Dr. Casey Peretti fell in love. Just before the birth of their daughter Kate, Casey was diagnosed with Guillain-Barré syndrome. He put up a valiant fight, but in the end he asked Lyla's daughter Margo to pull the plug. Lyla left Oakdale with Kate to pursue a singing career and took with her all the cherished memories of this special man and the brief time they had spent together.

### ELLIE SNYDER AND KIRK ANDERSON (1991)

Ellie Snyder and Kirk Anderson were married in a wacky, offbeat wedding at the Yacht Club. Kirk asked his friend, ship's captain Giddeon "Windy" Wyndom, to officiate. They later found out that a ship's captain isn't authorized to tie the knot on dry land, so they had to make it official at a Justice of the Peace. This time around, the bride was allergic to the flowers, although she still managed to say, "I do." Unfortunately, the marriage didn't last.

### JESSICA GRIFFIN AND DUNCAN MCKECHNIE (1992)

The obstacles to Jessica Griffin and Duncan McKechnie's union were many. Both families strongly objected to their interracial marriage, and good friends like Lisa had prejudices that were hard to shake. With the love and support of true friends, Duncan and Jessica were finally married. The couple were happy for a while and managed to beat the odds until Duncan's former wife, Shannon, who had been presumed dead, returned to Oakdale and tore the marriage apart.

# Upstairs / Downstairs

### THELMA DAILEY AND GRAHAM HAWKINS (1995)

The effervescent Thelma Dailey was Lucinda's secretary, and she'd had many loves, the latest of which was Graham Hawkins. Graham was Lucinda's brother Royce's loyal butler and had moved with him to Oakdale. It was an unusual match, but it worked.

## SOME OAKDALE COUPLES WHO CHOSE TO WED ON FOREIGN SHORES

### JOHN DIXON AND ARIEL ALDRIN (1982)

John Dixon married Ariel Aldrin on the island of Jamaica. Ariel was a fortune hunter and thought she was marrying a wealthy doctor. She promptly went out and bought a mansion. John was sinking deeper into debt when Ariel found out that her engagement ring was a fake. This marriage didn't stand a chance.

### SHANNON O'HARA AND DUNCAN MCKECHNIE (1989)

Duncan McKechnie wed Irish lass Shannon in an ancestral castle in his native Scotland. They shared many an adventure together. But Duncan's jealous ex-wife, the dreaded Lilith, appeared in Oakdale, kidnapped Shannon, and sent her shrunken head to Duncan as proof that she was dead, or so he thought…

### SUSAN STEWART AND LARRY MCDERMOTT (1992)

Susan Stewart was reticent about getting involved in a relationship with a younger man, but in another May-September pairing, she let fellow doctor Larry McDermott sweep her off her feet. With the scent of exotic flowers filling the air and a lone guitar player strumming a soft Spanish ballad, Larry and Susan said their vows and married in Montega. They had a daughter, Alison, by in-vitro fertilization (with daughter Emily's egg). Larry was too ambitious to pass up a prestigious post at Boston General. They tried a long-distance marriage for a while, but it was work rather than the age difference that eventually drove this couple apart.

# " I  D O N ' T "

**Not every love story has a happy ending...**

## JAMES STENBECK AND KAREN HAINES (1983)

James Stenbeck was blackmailed into marriage by Karen Haines after she discovered the truth of his heritage. At the ceremony, when the Justice of the Peace said, "You may kiss the bride," James replied, "No, I don't want to kiss the bride." Things never got much better after that. In an effort to get his son Paul away from Barbara, James and Karen (below with Paul) followed Barbara and Gunnar to Spain and forced a confrontation. In an odd twist of fate, Karen later married Stenbeck's nemesis, John Dixon.

## BARBARA RYAN AND JAMES STENBECK (1981)

Barbara Ryan had James Stenbeck's son when she was an art student in New York and was dazzled by the dashing Swedish prince. She was at the altar, all set to marry Tom Hughes, when James suddenly walked back into her life. She married James instead. James was an aristocrat, and aristocrats make their own rules. As such, he saw nothing wrong with having both a mistress (Margo) and a wife (both above). Actor Anthony Herrera (James) says, "I have a Ferrari and a Bentley and a mistress and a wife— same difference." Married life with James was torture for Barbara in more ways than one. There was no way this marriage could work, and he would become her nemesis for life.

## EMILY STEWART AND ROYCE KELLER (1993)

It was a rocky road to romance for Emily Stewart and international architect Royce Keller (top right). He was Lucinda's long-lost half-brother, and Emily and Lucinda couldn't lay eyes on each other without getting into a cat fight. In protest, Lucinda wore dark glasses to the wedding. Matters got muddled when Royce's multiple personalities began to emerge. When it came time to say, "I do," Royce realized he was a different person from the one who'd asked Emily to marry him, and he decided he could not make the commitment because of who he was.

## ROSANNA CABOT AND MIKE KASNOFF (1995)

Mike Kasnoff and Rosanna Cabot made it to the church but not to the altar. On cue, twisted sister Carly (below right) revealed that she'd slept with Mike. Shocked, Rosanna fled the church and crashed her car. She continues to struggle with her unresolved feelings for the man she almost married.

# THE SECOND TIME AROUND...

**S**ome stories have a happy ending...or so we hope.

## DAVID AND ELLEN STEWART (1966 AND 1982)

Ellen and David Stewart had a romance that lasted a lifetime, but it was not without its problems. They met because he was the adoptive father of her illegitimate son. A bitter custody fight led to respect, love and marriage. But in 1973, following the trauma of their daughter Dee's marital rape at the hands of John Dixon, David suffered amnesia and disappeared. He was found in a nearby town under a different name and was preparing to marry a woman named Cynthia Haines, who had helped him through this difficult time. David had no memory of Ellen and their love, and it was a long road back for this solid Oakdale couple. In 1982, with their daughter Dee (standing to Ellen's right) and family and friends in attendance, David and Ellen said, "I do" again and remained happily married until David's untimely death.

## BARBARA RYAN AND HAL MUNSON (1989)

He liked beer, she preferred champagne. It was an unusual match when fashion designer Barbara Ryan married detective Hal Munson in an elegant ceremony at the Lakewood Towers. It was her third and his second. What they didn't know at the time was that Margo was carrying Hal's child and hiding out in Greece, where the newlyweds were planning to honeymoon.

## BARBARA RYAN AND HAL MUNSON (1993)

The revelation of the son Hal had with Margo sent Barbara to Europe. Hal went underground to work for crime lord Anthony Harper, and for many months Barbara believed he'd been murdered by the Mob. When Hal reappeared, the two remarried on Hal's sister Claire's front porch in Alva, Kentucky.

## KIRK ANDERSON AND SAMANTHA MARKHAM (1995)

Kirk Anderson "married" Samantha Markham in Lucinda's backyard with Kirk's children from his first marriage, Stephen and Linda Ann, in attendance. What the guests didn't know was that the minister was a fake, and the marriage was a con, designed to bring Kirk into the family and the business and Sam into her half-sister's millions. On their "honeymoon" cruise, though, something unexpected happened—they fell in love. Then a storm blew in, and Kirk was lost at sea.

## KIRK ANDERSON AND SAMANTHA MARKHAM (1995)

When Kirk returned from the briny deep, the happy couple said, "I do" for real at a Christmas Eve wedding hosted by the Grimaldis at their Fairwinds home.

# Dastardly Deeds

**I**rna Phillips, the creator of "As The World Turns" said she never wrote villains or heroes, but people who "behaved badly" in some situations and "well in others." Oakdale has surely had its share of "villains," but two who stand out are John Dixon and James Stenbeck. Their styles were very different, but they managed to cause much turmoil and trouble for the citizens of Oakdale.

John was briefly married to James Stenbeck's sister, "Shop Till You Drop" Ariel Aldrin. The union of the two schemers did not last. Other Dixon wives included Dee Stewart, Karen Stenbeck and Lucinda Walsh.

## JOHN DIXON

Larry Bryggman, the actor who brings John Dixon so vividly to life, says, "I don't think you play a villain...you play a *person*." According to Bryggman, John was "a very ambitious fellow who came from the wrong side of the tracks," whose driving passion was to "better himself. He was willing to fight for what he wanted and felt that he was entitled to play any kind of game that it took; the end justified the means."

Before John came to Oakdale, he had an affair with Lyla Montgomery (pictured here), and Margo is their daughter. Social climber Dixon offered to marry beautiful, rich widow Kim Reynolds when she was carrying Bob Hughes's child. After she lost the baby, he blackmailed her into staying in the loveless marriage.

When he first came to town, John went into practice with Dr. Michael Shea, and it is said that Shea helped to create the monster that John became. Bryggman says, "John is a good doctor, he's always been a good doctor" who takes great pride in his work. It was a dark day when longtime nemesis Lisa Grimaldi sued Dixon for malpractice in the wrongful death of her husband Eduardo.

# JAMES STENBECK

John's arch-rival, James Stenbeck, was even more devious. The war began when James had an affair with John's daughter Margo. Time and time again, the two men tried to kill each other. First, James blinded John in a car accident and later tortured him with a dagger. Then, in the ultimate act of revenge, John staged his own death, hoping to send James to jail as a murderer. But he returned when his ex-wife Dee was falsely accused of the crime.

According to Anthony Herrera, who played him so brilliantly, James Stenbeck "entered Oakdale a glorious hero of the Swedish aristocracy who was working for the U.N." On his first Fourth of July in Oakdale, he was welcomed into the community by none other than Chris Hughes. According to Herrera, Stenbeck "was not a villain...he was a good guy...he was an aristocrat... he was upper class." His attitude was "What do I care about your silly laws and mores?...People like Stenbeck buy and sell countries.

He wants something, he takes it. I never played him evil—mean, tough, vengeful, yes, but never evil." Like his nemesis, John Dixon, James always felt totally justified in whatever he did.

James did not grieve when John was presumed dead, but when he returned, and they confronted each other outside the courtroom, the look on James's face when he saw John was worth the wait.

When the dashing James Stenbeck and the beautiful Barbara Ryan spotted each other across a crowded room, sparks flew, and their love story began. But they did not live happily ever after. He didn't know she was pregnant when he broke off with her and returned to Sweden to marry a woman of his family's choosing. When his wife died, he returned to Oakdale to claim Barbara as his own—no matter that she was about to marry Tom Hughes. Did he love her? In the course of their marriage, he tried to drive her crazy, committed her to a sanitorium, trapped her in a bullring with a raging bull and came back from the dead several times to taunt her. As Herrera put it: "He loved her, but she got a little out of hand."

As it turned out, James was not the true Stenbeck heir. Herrera admits, "It might have thrown him on some levels, but emotionally and psychologically, he was still a Stenbeck." Nanny Greta Aldrin had switched her son James with the true Stenbeck heir, Gunnar St. Clair. When the two men met, the forces of good and evil clashed. James fought Gunnar to the death in Spain and tried to push him out of an airplane window. But Gunnar prevailed. The Stenbeck fortune became his, as did the fair Barbara.

One fateful day in 1989 at a heliport in New York City, Paul saw his father shoot his mother's friend Hank Eliot in cold blood. Paul turned his back on his father for good, and James vanished. Not one to go down in defeat, James returned. To his shock and horror, he discovered love letters written from Paul to James's ex-mistress Emily Stewart. James attacked Emily, and in the fray that followed it was Paul's turn to shoot. He killed his father to save Emily. It was a grizzly yet fitting end for this evil man. When asked by a journalist what it was he didn't like about James Stenbeck, however, Herrera replied, "What's there not to like?"

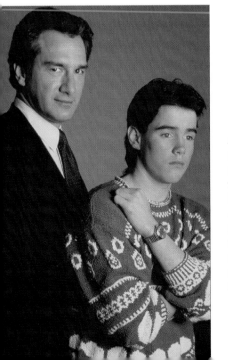

As for his relationship with his son Paul, James tried to convince Paul that he should want the things only his father could give him, mainly power and wealth. James was very good at mind games, and for years Paul idealized his father. Everyone tried to convince the boy that James was evil incarnate, but Paul couldn't quite believe it.

# *Happy Anniversary*

## CAST PICTURES THROUGH THE YEARS...

*Neil Wade*    *Bob Hughes*    *Doug Cassen*    *Claire Cassen*    *James Lowell*

*David Stewart*    *Ellen Cole*

*...ry Miller*    *Penny Wade*    *Lisa Hughes*      *Chris Hughes*

*Nancy Hughes*

*Alma Miller*    *Pa Hughes*    *Tom Hughes*

COMPLIMENTS OF CHEE...

In the early 1960s when the show was live, for 25 cents and two box tops of Cheer detergent, you could receive this picture of the cast.

On April 2, 1966, "As The World Turns" turned ten years old. Helen Wagner (Nancy Hughes, center), Don Hastings (Dr. Bob Hughes, looking over Helen's shoulder), and Eileen Fulton (Lisa, standing to Helen's right), still reside in Oakdale, where they continue to give advice (Nancy), tend to patients (Dr. Bob) and seek out romance (Lisa).

**246**    AS THE WORLD TURNS

In 1981, "As The World Turns" celebrated a quarter century on the air!

In 1983, the cast of "As The World Turns" gathered for this group picture. The hot love story that year involved Betsy Montgomery (Meg Ryan, front row, second from left), who was married to Craig Montgomery (Scott Bryce, sitting to her right). But Betsy was deeply in love with Steve Andropoulos (Frank Runyeon, standing behind them). Betsy thought the baby she was holding was Craig's, but Craig was sterile, and little Dani was really Steve's. Today Dani is an active member of Oakdale's teenage set.

In the spring of 1986, "As The World Turns" turned 30, and it was a landmark year! Not only was it the show's anniversary, but Chris and Nancy Hughes (Don MacLaughlin and Helen Wagner, center), one of Oakdale's most beloved couples, celebrated 50 years of wedded bliss.

The date was April 17, 1991, and cast and crew assembled for the taping of the 9,000th episode of "As The World Turns!"

The grande dames of Oakdale used the occasion to have their own special reunion. From left to right: Rosemary Prinz (Penny Hughes), Helen Wagner (Nancy Hughes) and Ruth Warrick (Edith Hughes) were all members of the original cast. Eileen Fulton (Lisa) and Patricia Bruder (Ellen Stewart) joined in 1960.

In honor of the show's 35th anniversary, everyone responsible for keeping "As The World Turns" turning day after day was invited to celebrate in style at New York's famed Rainbow Room.

On April 20, 1995, "As The World Turns" reached a milestone with the taping of its 10,000th episode. Helen Wagner (Nancy Hughes, sitting far right), opened that episode with the same line she spoke on the first show back in 1956: "Good morning, dear." Chris Hughes had died, though, and Nancy was greeting her second husband, Lt. Dan ("Mac") McClosky (Dan Frazer, center). They are joined by longtime cast members Patricia Bruder, Don Hastings and Kathryn Hays.

(Below) The cast of "As The World Turns" in 1996. Happy Anniversary!

Eileen Fulton

Kathryn Hays

Scott Holmes

### EILEEN FULTON (LISA GRIMALDI)

It's family, it's great love, it's great deceit, it's great longing. You can see it and feel it. From the roots come these truths, why these people do what they do. It's that powerful. It's like life, but bigger, and that's why we're so believable. The Hughes family is really my family. And Nancy is really like my mother in a way, though she's younger than my mother; she's the older sister.

### KATHRYN HAYS (KIM HUGHES)

I've always thought what was special about this show was that we maintained the main family unit. And whatever else has happened on the show, those family bonds have been maintained, and I think that's encouraging. I think there is a very strong desire, young and old, to have some touch of those qualities in your life.

### SCOTT HOLMES (TOM HUGHES)

Hands down, it's the only show out there that shows the extended family and really deals with it. You know when all this stuff has happened out there in the world, you go to your family, because your family loves you, they forgive you for everything. I think it's charming that my grandmother's still here with a new husband and all that. It's so warm, and I love it. Everybody's always together.

### MARIE MASTERS
### (SUSAN STEWART MCDERMOTT)

I think there's a lot of things that make the show stand out, especially the fact that nobody tells family stories better than 'As The World Turns.' I know people think all the soaps have to be about perfect bodies, perfect hair and everyone being gorgeous. We've got all that. But we also have fabulous actors, directors and writers and a very vivid production. Our show is much more human and based in reality. It deals with issues in a very in-depth way. As an all-around viewing experience, it's just more satisfying. It's meat and potatoes. It's more human.

## COLLEEN ZENK PINTER (BARBARA RYAN)

The Hugheses are the only family Barbara's ever loved. I'm an orphan. My parents are both dead, so Bob really is my dad. And Kim has always been my mother figure, which is why over the years when she's had to berate me for whatever nasty things I had done...it was always so difficult. It's like talking to my mom. The Hugheses are Barbara's family.

## PAUL LAMMERS (DIRECTOR)

I think first of all the acting, the quality of the acting on this show, is very special. The other shows don't compare. And this show has an awful lot of legacy with Irna. The core is still here with Helen Wagner and Don Hastings and Patricia Bruder. That's the nice thing about it, the continuity of so many of these characters.

## SCOTT BRYCE (CRAIG MONTGOMERY)

I would have to say what a phenomenal collection of talent there is on this show. There's a core group of people who are just always there, who have been there since the beginning and keep the backbone and the history. And that's its strength. When the show deals its own deck to history, it can't lose. Because that's what the medium is. It's about people, not plot devices—It's about what did you do to me today? Do I love that person? Do I still love that person even though I divorced her ten years ago? Those histories count. The fans remember who loved who, who hated who, who hurt who, who lost who...the stuff that makes us human. And that's what the medium is.

## BROOKE ALEXANDER (SAMANTHA ANDERSON)

Just trying to hold on to family values and issues is hard to sell in this day and age because of what else is going on. They represent that part of human beings that I think we as a group have to be careful of losing. The show's always striven for integrity. You see a lot of projects sell out for the obvious, for the superficial, and I'm really proud to be a part of a group that really believes in that integrity.

Colleen Zenk Pinter

Scott Bryce

Brooke Alexander

# A FOND GOODBYE

A few short months after Nancy and Chris Hughes celebrated their 50th wedding anniversary on the air, the world stopped turning for Don MacLaughlin, the actor who had created the memorable part of Chris.

His obituary in *Variety* read: "A face we'll never forget." He was Chris Hughes, patriarch of the Hughes family, and he was Don MacLaughlin, father, friend and congenial gentleman with a sense of humor that put everyone at ease. According to Helen Wagner, who shared Don's "onscreen" life for 30 years, "It was a gentle humor where everybody could join in." After all, as Don would say, "There are enough problems in Oakdale." His friends and colleagues at "As The World Turns" remember him fondly and well.

Helen thought of Don MacLaughlin as her "second husband." Indeed, her 1955 wedding photo with husband Bob Willey (left), was used in the opening credits of the show, with the face of her television husband, Don MacLaughlin, superimposed onto Willey's body to create Chris and Nancy's wedding picture. Helen says, "Don and I were as close to being married as possible for two people who were already married. I spent more time with Don during the first 25 years of the show than I did with Bob, and it was a most happy relationship in every possible way." Helen recalls the painful day when they taped Chris's death on the show. "We had always been the happiest kind of show, but that day everybody was at everybody's throats. Nothing you did was right. When we played his death and got Chris buried, the show settled down. It was a most remarkable psychological reaction. We had lived it...so to lose him again was more then anybody could stand. That's how important he was to the show."

# Behind the Scenes: Then and Now

**THEN:** In the early 1960s, when the show was live, actress Helen Wagner studied her script in "Nancy's kitchen," a favorite meeting place and set during the early days.

**NOW:** More than 30 years later, another Hughes set is readied for taping: Kathryn Hays and Don Hastings, as Kim and Bob Hughes, prepare to celebrate Christmas Eve at Tom and Margo's, while technicians and crew prepare the scene.

# A Day in the Life of "As The World Turns"

## EPISODE #10, 155

**TAPE:** WEDNESDAY, NOVEMBER 29, 1995          **AIR:** FRIDAY, DECEMBER 22, 1995

## A TOUR BEHIND THE SCENES

Actors Ellen Dolan, Joanna Rhinehart, Larry Bryggman and Scott DeFreitas have coffee and share a brief moment of relaxation before their long taping day begins.

From 7:00 A.M. to 9:30 A.M., director Maria Wagner takes Kathryn Hays, Colleen Zenk Pinter, Don Hastings, Larry Bryggman, Dan Frazer, Helen Wagner, Scott DeFreitas, Ellen Dolan, Joanna Rhinehart and John Dauer through the "dry run." This is the initial meeting between the director and the actors and is the cast's only rehearsal out of the studio. According to Maria, the dry run is when everyone gets to "moan and groan" and iron out the problems and kinks. "That's where the collaboration really begins...in rehearsal."

Stars Eileen Fulton, Dan Frazer and Helen Wagner in rehearsal.

With director Maria Wagner, longtime adversaries Bob Hughes (Don Hastings) and John Dixon (Larry Bryggman) rehearse their latest encounter.

Director Maria Wagner's preparation starts well before the day of shooting, simply called the "day of," when she receives her assigned script and breaks it down scene by scene for props, hair, makeup and so forth. Specifics get ironed out in weekly production meetings with the department heads. Major events like a fire or a plane crash might take up only one line in a script—"The plane explodes!"—but there's a lot more to the scene than that. After the meeting, she does her camera blocking, which can take anywhere from two days to every waking hour! For Maria, the "day of" is the fun part.

Director Maria Wagner talks Scott DeFreitas (Andy) and Ellen Dolan (Margo) through a moving brother-sister scene that will be a part of the Christmas Eve show.

Deborah Paulmann gets Elizabeth Hubbard (Lucinda) ready for her sister Samantha's Christmas Eve wedding.

Makeup artist Deborah Paulmann puts the finishing touches on Kelley Menighan.

Hairstylist Lillian Cvecich readies Eileen Fulton (Lisa) for another Christmas Eve celebration.

A veteran of 35 years on "As The World Turns," Eileen Fulton has turned her tiny dressing room into a charming mix of pictures and chintz.

# LAST STOP BEFORE THE SET: WARDROBE

Costume designer Toni-Leslie James came to "As The World Turns" from Broadway, where she won several Tony nominations, most notably for the hit show *Jelly's Last Jam*. She's a lady with flair, and the show reflects her talent. In preparation for the day's shoot, Toni reads the scripts two days in advance and makes up computerized cards for each actor and scene to help her organize wardrobe changes.

Outfits are accessorized several days in advance, and each actor has his or her own jewelry drawer. Here Toni and associate costume designer Victoria Wortz choose just the right necklace.

The day-to-day activity on a daytime soap can be very intense. Toni-Leslie James works with an associate, a wardrobe supervisor and four dressers. There's always a dresser on the set to deal with last-minute rips and repairs. Toni tries to give each day a special "look"—of course, an Oakdale day can go on for two or three "real" days. When new characters come on board, Toni learns their history. Then she scopes out the clothing stores and does a general pick, matching their wardrobe to their personalities. "As The World Turns" has accounts at Barneys, Saks and Bergdorf Goodman, and Toni intends to branch out to the Soho boutiques. Toni shops till she drops with a new actor to get the proper clothes to suit the character. Old and outdated clothes are sold in rummage sales or donated to charity.

Each actor has his or her own locker of clothes from which Toni does her "pick for the day."

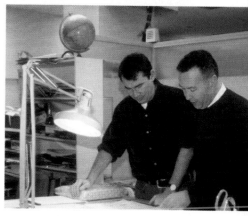

While things are buzzing down on the set, up in their offices in the CBS Broadcast Center, production designer William Mickley and art director Christopher Clarens design the homes, offices, stables, bedrooms, bathrooms (Lucinda has one complete with whirlpool and sauna!), planes and pools of Oakdale's many residents.

Every set must be "dressed," and set decorators Dennis Donnegan, Catherine McKenney and David Blankenship have a lot to choose from in the well-stocked prop room.

The first order of business on the set is the "reading of the cart." Here, head properties man Michael Gillen, head electrician John Brunton, director Maria Wagner, set decorator Dennis Donnegan, producer Vivian Gundaker, prop man Stephen Lee, stage manager Meryl Augenbraun Jaffe and wardrobe assistant Lyle Jones make sure that all the props ordered for the day's shoot are present, accounted for and in working order.

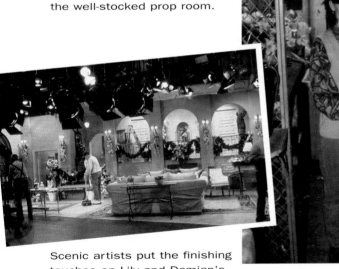

Scenic artists put the finishing touches on Lily and Damian's Fairwinds living room in preparation for the wedding of Samantha and Kirk.

In-house florist Tess Casey prepares Samantha's bridal bouquet. Sam was touched that Kirk remembered she wanted an amaryllis in her bouquet.

Lighting designer Stephen Reid lights the set for the wedding with the help of stagehand Al Blair.

It's 9:30 A.M. and "Here comes the groom." At the camera-blocking rehearsal, director Maria Wagner shows Tom Wiggin (Kirk) how to walk down the aisle.

Associate director (A.D.) Michael Kerner (far right) checks out the positions of the evening's hosts, Lily Grimaldi (Martha Byrne) and Damian Grimaldi (Paolo Seganti). According to Maria, her A.D is her "right hand." He often runs the edit sessions, interpreting her notes.

In the control room during dress rehearsal, associate director Michael Kerner readies the shot, director Maria Wagner calls the shot, and production assistant Tracey Hanley records the times. A note session follows.

Technical directors Nancy Stevenson and Alexander Ciecieski, at the board in the control room, operate the keys that change the camera shots in response to the director's calls during taping.

The happy couple: Kirk (Tom Wiggin) and Sam (Brooke Alexander) say, "I do."

From doorbells to telephone rings, from car crashes to explosions and thunderstorms, Sid Bean in sound effects is responsible for all of these background effects.

Audio assistant Gregory Cordonne and music director Donovan Sylvest cue the music for the walk down the aisle.

(Above) While the morning session gets ready to "wrap," video and sound editors Robert Mackler and Steven Shatkin prepare an episode, taped two weeks ago, for air. With them is Joel Aronowitz, the A.D. for that episode.

(Right) From his office, producer David Domedion, who is producing the next day's show, checks the studio feed for "pick-up" scenes.

From her office at the CBS Broadcast Center, music supervisor Jill Diamond scores future episodes of "As The World Turns." Her job is a far cry from the days when the organist sat behind a curtain in the studio and played along as the action unfolded live on the set. All the music for the show is original. Several "As The World Turns" love songs, such as "Nobody Loves Me Like You Do," Steve and Betsy's theme, and "Every Beat of My Heart," Mike and Rosanna's love theme, have become popular hits. Because she needs to fill at least 30 to 40 minutes of music a day, the hardest thing for Jill is to keep it fresh. She considers music an accessory: "You're just a color—you don't want to interfere with a scene; you're an enhancer."

Casting director Vince Liebhart stands proudly in front of head shots of the show's cast.

If a new character is created or a recast needed, the first thing Vince does is come up with a "breakdown"—a description of the character, including his or her age, qualities and look. He sends the information to a breakdown service and soon receives a stream of pictures and résumés. He pares these down to his "ideal list" and starts calling people in to audition. Callbacks and screen tests follow, and the executive producer, the network executives and the head writers join in making the final decision.

Sometimes a recurring role goes to contract, as was the case with Hal Munson, and sometimes a day player becomes permanent, like the dastardly Dr. John Dixon.

In casting a role, sometimes an actor seems to jump off the screen, like Shawn Christian's Mike Kasnoff. Vince doesn't think that soaps require a special style of acting—to him, "acting is acting."

Production assistants Alexandra Verner Roalsvig, Brett Hellman and Kristen Bradley meet with assistant to the producer Jef-Spenser Hira in the production office.

Jef is responsible for the production schedule. After reading the script, he breaks it down scene by scene for characters and sets, determines a page count and a scene count for each set and decides in what studio the sets will play. Jef tries to give the shooting day as much continuity as possible, but with births, deaths, illnesses, vacations and untoward happenings, the schedule often resembles a giant jigsaw puzzle! However, there are no understudies in soap opera, and the show must go on five days a week.

Assistant casting director Tom Alberg (left) is responsible for casting extras and everyone with "under five" lines. There's much more to being an extra than people think. Hospital people have a certain look, as do the customers at the neighborhood bar, Yo's, not to mention the upscale diners at the Mona Lisa and the Falcon Club, who must provide their own wardrobes. An emergency-room worker has to appear confident and be able to run with a gurney, while a Yacht Club extra has to look good in a bikini.

It's 3:30 P.M. The afternoon dry run is finished, and it's back to the set for camera blocking and dress rehearsal. In this scene, Emily (Kelley Menighan) has abducted the groom (Tom Wiggin) and taken him for a wild ride—only the car isn't moving. Instead, off to the side, the stage manager calls out, "Tree wavers, car rockers, audio person, cameras ready, actors ready, cue action!" And away they go, or so it seems.

Up in the production office, Helen Wagner reads her fan mail.

Leela Pitenis is the associate producer in charge of continuity, and she must make sure that everything that's in the script did indeed happen in the past and tracks with what's happening now. If somebody in Act II said, "I'm out of here. I'm going to the farm," that person should be shown later on the farm, not on a different set, as happened when Emma was at the farm and at Rosanna's bridal shower at the same time. Then there's the question of who's related to whom—sometimes it seems as if everyone in Oakdale is related to everyone else in town! Believe it or not, Leela has most of this in her head. Leela also runs weekly production meetings and is the last one to see the script before it goes to the typist.

John Dixon (Larry Bryggman) and Bob Hughes (Don Hastings) try to iron out a legal problem with the help of lawyer Jessica Griffin (Joanna Rhinehart).

Stage manager Meryl Augenbraun Jaffe, producer Vivian Gundaker and stage manager Nancy Barron check their notes for the afternoon's taping.

Vivian produces two shows a week, and her goal is to ensure that the day goes as smoothly as possible. If the show is long, it will need cuts; if it's short, it will need to be stretched out with extra material; and if there are flashbacks, tapes will need to be pulled. Because "As The World Turns" is a character-driven show, Vivian feels strongly about protecting the vision of the head writers. On the day of taping, Vivian may pull the actors aside to discuss a particularly emotional or difficult scene. Other things to consider include special effects. If there's a fire or a car crash, stunt doubles that are "body matches" might be needed, flame bars have to be rigged, and safety on the set must be ensured.

The most important part of her job is to "anticipate disaster and be on top of the game." When the director starts blocking the scenes, Vivian stays on the set so that she can get an idea of how the show is going. She then watches the dress rehearsal from the control room. After dress, the director gives notes, and it's time to tape. For Vivian, emotion takes precedence over technical problems, unless, of course, the technical problem is a glaring one. She also listens to the music score in the control room to make sure it supports the scene. Things move fast on the show, and there's no time to waffle over decisions. Every element of the show is crucial, and Vivian feels that the staff works brilliantly together: "It starts with an idea in the producer's head, and by the time it reaches the air, it has everyone's fingerprints on it, including the director and the actors. This is ultimately a group effort."

After a false start—the guests were there, but the hosts weren't—the Hugheses' Christmas celebration is ready to roll. But before calling out " 5, 4, 3, 2, 1...action!" the stage manager is heard telling the cast, "Don't drink the punch, because we don't want to wash the glasses!"

According to assistant to the producer Jef-Spenser Hira, "In a perfect world, 'World Turns' usually stops turning between 7:30 and 8:00 P.M." However, when you're doing anything out of the ordinary—which is often—"things could go on all night, and have," says director Maria Wagner. At the end of a long workday, she often thinks, "I can't believe I did that in a day. We pulled it off...and it feels great!" But whatever time this particular "world" goes to bed, it has to be up and ready to go at 7:00 A.M. sharp the next day.

Larry Bryggman

Eileen Fulton

### LARRY BRYGGMAN (JOHN DIXON)

I remember a lot of things that went wrong and accidents that happened: Doors not opening and chairs breaking; people walking into the studio and making noise when they shouldn't be and muffed lines. All those things seem funny now, but when they happened, they were just death!

### LEONARD VALENTA (DIRECTOR)

There was this constant fear that something would go out of control on the air, and you couldn't fix it. Well, at least once on that show, that happened to me. The scene opened with Nancy coming onto the porch to get the newspaper, then going back into the kitchen and expressing concern to Donald that Bob was flying home from someplace or other in fog. Since it was supposed to be foggy, the script called for just a little bit of fog outside the kitchen set. If we wanted a low mist, we'd have dry ice boiling in water on the ground, whereas for a high mist we would put the boiling water on a pedestal. The effects department provided so much fog that it seeped under the doorway and under all of Nancy's appliances, right into the kitchen set!

### EILEEN FULTON (LISA GRIMALDI)

It was during the famous 'phantom fetus' storyline. Lisa was entertaining her friend Liz Talbot, and her line was, 'I'm pregnant, and I don't know how it happened,' and Liz was supposed to look like…she's pregnant and she doesn't know how it happened?  At that moment organist Charlie Paul flipped the page, and the last page stuck, and he thought, *That's the end of show*, and he went right into the closing theme song. The stage manager had given me a cue, and the organ went off, and I thought, *Well, I guess we went over time, and we're off the air*. And I started to reach in and pull out that pillow and say, 'See, I'm not really pregnant!' And something froze me…something said don't say anything…you better go ahead and do the scene. It's a good thing, because it would have gone coast to coast, my pulling out that pillow and saying, 'I'm not pregnant.' That would have been the end of that storyline!

## DON HASTINGS (BOB HUGHES)

There are so many 'live' stories...having a bed collapse with Michael Ebart, who played Chuck Ryan, and winding up in each other's arms, lying on the floor. We got up, put the bed back together and finished the scene. One day, one of our directors told me my back was going to be to the camera because 'you never forget your lines' (the TelePrompTer was on the camera). Well, I forgot every line in the scene! In the original Hughes kitchen, there was a hutch with china in it. We taped in Grand Central Terminal, and there was a train that left at 1:55 almost every day. And a lot of times the china would rattle, and we used to say, 'Everything's on time today!'

Don Hastings

## MARIE MASTERS (SUSAN STEWART)

I would get so nervous that I actually would have fantasies about leaving the studio, leaving town, leaving the country. There it would be—ten seconds before countdown, and our director would do this thing: 'All right everybody, tense up, eight million people will be watching you, and 8, 7, 6, 5, 4...' I remember walking into a scene and being introduced to someone and forgetting my name. I couldn't remember who I was!

Marie Masters

## ROSEMARY PRINZ (PENNY HUGHES)

In the late '50s nice women stayed home, and they knew everything about the kitchen. Of course, this was not a kitchen that worked! In one scene, it was late at night, and Don MacLaughlin (my father) and I came down to have this very serious talk, and I had to open the refrigerator and get something out; milk, because we never drank anything except milk! In between dress and air, somebody brilliantly said, 'We have to dress the refrigerator, because she opens the door.' So I opened the door, and everything fell out! Smash! Jelly jars! Bottles! And there's nothing to clean it up with, so it was clear that this was not a functional kitchen. Besides, we had to get out of the scene. Thank God for Don. I just said, 'I can't deal with this now, Dad. I'm just gonna leave it. I'll do it in ten minutes.' And we went right on with the scene. My favorite live story has to do with my on-screen husband Mike Lipton (Neal Wade). He was going blind and blaming me for everything. I don't know what I did wrong, but I did something. And I turn back in the archway of the bookshop, and he said something absolutely scathing to me, and the curtain fell right on his head!

Yvonne Perry

Bill Fichtner

### YVONNE PERRY (ROSANNA CABOT)

Yvonne first auditioned for a part on "All My Children," which she didn't get. When the call came from "Guiding Light" to audition for Eleni, Yvonne dyed her hair, darkened her eyebrows and did a Greek accent, but she didn't get that part either. Casting director Betty Rea liked what she saw, however, and cast Yvonne in a small recurring role that was whittled down to two days' work. But as Yvonne says, "I had this little thing on my résumé when Rosanna came along." She auditioned for the role of Tess but didn't even get to read. Rosanna was her lucky charm. She auditioned, screen-tested and was booked the next day. "It was exciting."

### BILL FICHTNER (ROD LANDRY/JOSH SNYDER)

Vince Liebhart, the casting director, said 'I don't really have anything for you to read right now, because there's really nothing you're right for. We do have this part of Lily's father. You're much too young for it, but why don't you read this scene, and I'll get to know you a little bit.' Then he said, 'Why don't you come back and meet with Phyllis Kasha.' Phyllis worked with Vince at the time. So I came back and met her and read the scene. And she said, 'That's very good; you're young for this, but maybe you should come back and meet Cal (Robert Calhoun),' who was the executive producer at the time. Well, I met Cal, and he said, 'That was really wonderful; you're young for this.' And then I got a call to come in and test for it. It was me and three other guys, and they all looked older than I did. Martha Byrne watched the test and said, 'Oh, I think that's my dad!' And that's how it worked out.

### MARTHA BYRNE (LILY GRIMALDI)

Martha had auditioned for the role of Lily, but they wanted more of a tomboy type, and the part went to Lucy Deakins. Martha remembers, "I hadn't worked for about three months on anything, and I was getting very depressed. I said to my mom, 'I've really had it. I've just had it. I really need a break.' There was one audition I was going for, a movie called *The Boy Who Could Fly*. My agent said that they had cast a girl who's on a soap opera, Lucy Deakins, and the soap opera wouldn't let her do it. So they're scrambling for someone, and you have to go. So I went. I remember the producer saying in the background, 'Oh Lucy, Lucy, why can't you be here for me?' I'm thinking, *God, I'm 15 years old. I stink that bad?* I'm sure I did a fine job, but it didn't matter because he wanted her. So I flew back to New York and found out that I didn't get it. And I was so upset, I decided to quit. I'd auditioned for 'As The World Turns' eight months before, and I didn't get it. Lucy got it. Now Lucy had gotten the part in the movie. Then Lucy quit the show and went to do the movie, and they called me. I didn't even have to audition for them or anything!"

### ROSEMARY PRINZ (PENNY HUGHES)

They'd seen every ingenue in New York, and I'm sure I was like the third dredging up of whoever was left...so I went over to the office, and even though they'd seen everybody in New York, there were about 30 girls. It was an hysterical scene with Aunt Edie (Ruth Warrick) in which Penny told Edie that she knew her mom wished that it were Penny who had died instead of Susan, her sister, in that swimming accident. The scene was extremely emotional. By the time they got to me, I guess they'd asked maybe two or three girls to stay. I was sort of toward the end. I went in, and Ruth Warrick was there. It was a radio studio. Ted Corday and Irna Phillips were the only people I remember. They were in this glass booth, and I was standing at a mike like I was doing a radio show. So I kicked off my shoes and proceeded to do this emotional scene and scream and cry, and cry and cry and cry. And they said, 'Thank you. Would you wait outside?' And I waited outside, and there were about three other girls by then, and they go in first, and I went in last. And I kicked off my shoes, and I proceeded to cry just as much as I had cried on the first take, and they said, 'Thank you so much. Would you wait outside, please?' And I waited outside, and I noticed that I was the only one waiting outside. The other three girls weren't there. After about five minutes, Ted Corday came out and said, 'I hate to do this to you, but would you mind reading again?' And I went inside, kicked off my shoes and cried even more than I cried on the first two takes. When I got through, there was this long silence, and they said, 'Wait here.' Then they came out and said, "You're Penny!"

Martha Byrne

Parker Posey

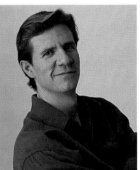

Tom Wiggin

### PARKER POSEY (TESS SHELBY)

It was like Alice in Wonderland's worst nightmare. I get on the set, and I'm like projecting my lines, and Ben Hendrickson said, 'See those mikes?' And I look up, and there's this big microphone. He said, 'You can talk just like this' (whispers). Then he patted me on the shoulder, just like Daddy. One of my first scenes was with Colleen Zenk Pinter. We walked through it earlier in rehearsal...just blocking. Now Hal is leaving, and when we had to shoot it, I'll never forget it. She turned around, and she was in tears. I had no idea she would be crying in that scene!

### TOM WIGGIN (KIRK ANDERSON)

I hadn't done daytime for five years, and I had forgotten about just how to memorize the lines. The night before, I was looking over the script, and around midnight I realized I didn't know any of my lines. So I forced myself to learn them. I was exhausted. I was wound up. And there was a divided camp...the network people weren't sure about me. The second day, I had six scenes with Liz Hubbard. So I hit the set, and I've got 20-25 pages of dialogue, and it's all business stuff. I have to be a business whiz. And I'm just such a wreck that I get these canker sores on my tongue. I get a bottle of Anbesol, and all I can do is keep dumping the Anbesol on my tongue to numb the pain. So all I could basically do for characterization for Kirk was stand and deliver, sort of talk in this really kind of hard, straight way and just be very concise, not move my lips too much. And wouldn't you know, people thought, *That's an interesting choice for the role!*

### MING-NA WEN (LIEN HUGHES)

At the time it was Scott Holmes and Hillary Bailey Smith playing Tom and Margo, and it was my very first day working on the set, and I'm kind of nervous, and there was Scott. He really made me feel comfortable because, in my first scene, when I rang the doorbell, and he opened the door and saw me for the first time, he went, 'Did you remember the extra duck sauce?' And it just made me feel so at home because they were joking all the time. I would be like, 'Excuse me...I'm trying to concentrate here. It's my first day, okay?' It really broke the ice and made it an easy two years.

# FAVORITE STORY LINE

### EILEEN FULTON (LISA GRIMALDI)

I love what we've done recently. This past year…the whole thing with Eduardo, the wedding, the murder. I have absolutely loved every bit of it! I have loved turning everybody inside out and having my son be so awful again.

Eileen Fulton

### SCOTT HOLMES (TOM HUGHES)

I loved the whole rape/HIV story. It was played out in real time and gave us an opportunity to show how much Tom and Margo love each other. Because so many people that we've worked with have died of AIDS, there was something that really connected us to this story. There was a lot of support for this story line.

Scott Holmes

### ELIZABETH HUBBARD (LUCINDA WALSH)

The search for Sierra (Lucinda's daughter) was real and meaningful. Lucinda had a purpose. The famous hot tub scene with John Dixon was my idea, and Larry says it was his. Maybe it was both of our psyches. The idea was, her towel drops, and then they're married. I mean, he's my doctor! So I said no, and we talked about it and decided as long as we don't get killed.…So we checked with wardrobe to see if they minded if we got his clothes wet, and I had a robe on, and he pulled me in the tub, and we're in this primordial mood. Why are we here, and what are we doing? That was our favorite scene.

Elizabeth Hubbard

### GREGG MARX (EX-TOM HUGHES)

The story that was the most involving, and the one that I think brought out some of my best work, was when Tom and Margo lost the baby. It affected me very gravely. And that's kind of a gift for an actor, if you can get there just because it was written well or because something in you responds to the material or the situation. It was a very wrenching, powerful experience in a lot of ways.

Martha Byrne

### MARTHA BYRNE (LILY GRIMALDI)

There were so many with Jon Hensley (Holden). The bell tower was definitely one of them.…His sensitivity came out, and he just let himself go. It was a great moment. And so many in the stables.…Lily was just 16, and he was always lurking, catching her off guard. And when I found out I was adopted, and he followed me to Wyoming. That was a ball! It was just the two of us. We had our own set, we always worked in the afternoon. It was like we had our own little world.

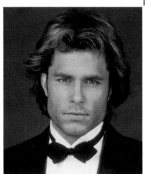

Scott Bryce

Yvonne Perry

Shawn Christian

### SCOTT BRYCE (CRAIG MONTGOMERY)

As an actor, I've been in bed with some of the most beautiful women in the world. And one of my favorites was a Craig nightmare. I was in bed with Lucinda, and I rolled over, and Sierra was there with us! And that was Craig's nightmare. I thought...*I don't think that would be a nightmare!*

### YVONNE PERRY (ROSANNA CABOT)

I love the Montana stuff when Mike followed me. It was the first time that I was ever given that amount of story line, and the excitement that I had as an actress equaled the excitement that I felt on camera with the Mike and Rosanna story. They were just discovering each other. It was the blooming of a relationship.

### SHAWN CHRISTIAN (MIKE KASNOFF)

There was so much innocence [in the Montana story line]. It was just two kids trying to find each other. For Mike it was his first time out of the state, and he was like a wild child looking for adventure. He was just looking, watching this Rosanna character the whole time...watching her radiate joy. Even with all the problems he had, he loved that. He got excited, he had a feisty girl, and she just saw the goodness in his character, hanging in there. She was a fighter.

# *The People Behind*
# *"As The World Turns"*

**O**n April 2, 1956, Procter & Gamble put the soap in soap opera when the company launched television's first half-hour daytime serial—"As The World Turns"

Bob Short

**I**n 1983, Bob Short won the N.A.T.A.S. Trustees Award for his achievements in daytime programming. He is pictured above after the ceremonies with Agnes Nixon, who wrote with the legendary Irna Phillips when "As The World Turns" first went on the air.

Bob Short became manager of daytime programs for Procter & Gamble in 1956, the year "As The World Turns" was launched. Initially, there was much controversy over launching a half-hour serial in the afternoon, because nothing had succeeded in that time period. People said women wouldn't watch TV in the afternoon because they wanted to go shopping instead! In spite of the nay-sayers, "As The World Turns"

took off almost immediately. According to Short, "It's a classic example of how, if you put on a good show and leave it alone, and give the audience a chance to find it...they'll seek it out, and with any luck you'll develop a franchise...and, of course, that's what happened."

Ed Trach

**E**d Trach came to Procter & Gamble from the halls of Yale Drama School. Hired by Bob Short, he worked closely with Irna Phillips, eventually taking over Short's position.

During Trach's stay, "As The World Turns" held the record as the longest-running number-one show in daytime history. In his eyes, what made the show unique was that "it was the most character oriented of the serials, the most family oriented...and it had the biggest heart in terms of

character relationships. Other shows might take more liberties and be more adventurous, but on 'As The World Turns,' when we had a story meeting, it was often a discussion of the psychology of human behavior. The motivation of why people did what they did and felt what they felt."

Kenneth L. Fitts

**A**s the mantle had been passed from Bob Short to Ed Trach, it also was passed from Trach to Kenneth L. Fitts, Procter & Gamble's current executive in charge of production. Before taking over Trach's position, Fitts was a supervising producer for Procter & Gamble and has a long association with "As The World Turns."

Fitts feels strongly about the importance of listening to what the audience thinks and feels. If audience response to a character is negative, chances are the character will quickly be written off. P & G's main goal has always been entertainment first and on "As The World Turns," stories about relationships. Fitts believes that "we present a positive message of how relationships can grow and deepen, and that is the essence of soap opera."

# FROM LIVE TO TAPE: JOE WILLMORE

In the "live days," "As The World Turns" was shot in one piece from beginning to end. When it

Joe Willmore

went to tape, it was done film style, which means scenes would be shot out of continuity. So executive producer Joe Willmore took a deep breath and insisted that they "keep day for day." In other words, whatever he shot on a Monday had to air on a Monday, and whatever he shot on a Friday had to air on a Friday. He would shoot out of order only on the condition that he had completed that show by the end of the day.

Live or tape, the bottom line for Willmore was always character-

## LAURENCE CASO, PRODUCER, 1988–1995

He was with the show for seven years. During that period Laurence Caso (above with Helen Wagner) produced 1,800 episodes and dealt with many things, not the least of which was the untimely death in 1993 of legendary head writer Douglas Marland. Caso characterizes his years on "As The World Turns" as when much of the show was "retrieved and recaptured." The return of Nancy and Chris, the re-emergence and renewal of the Hughes family and the introduction of the Snyders all helped to restore the core of the show. Caso believes that what sets the tone of the show is the core of people who have been there for many years: Helen Wagner and Don Hastings, Larry Bryggman, Kathy Hays, Marie Masters and Patsy Bruder. They set a tremendous example. "They often do a scene in one take. They're always on time. They're always prepared. They're always in character," he points out. Caso looks upon soap operas as one of the uniquely American art forms—this country created it.

motivated story. "If it's not believable, and it's motivated out of character, that's when they're going to turn you off. If it comes out of character, and it's well done, then you're going to see your numbers go up."

Willmore's proudest moment as executive producer came on the eve of the show's 20th anniversary in April of 1976. The serial had dipped

to sixth place in the ratings, but it was beginning to regain prominence with the Bob/Jennifer/Kim/John story. Willmore waited until he received the ratings to leave for the celebration party, and when he arrived, he took the microphone and told everyone that "As The World Turns" had resumed its rightful place and was number one again!

# INTO THE FUTURE WITH EXECUTIVE PRODUCER JOHN VALENTE

John Valente

Since executive producer John Valente took the helm in 1995, the show's ratings have improved significantly. As the show approaches its 40th anniversary, he wants it to be perceived as 40 years young. He intends to maximize on the history and tradition of the show, but not be bound by it, maintain the family structure and basic integrity and open it up to newer characters as well. He believes the daytime audience wants a deeper connection to the characters and an involvement in their lives. He wants them to wish they had a guy like Mike or Damian. Valente thinks that the need for fantasy is greater than it's ever been: "Our lives are under assault. Our sensibilities are attacked from dawn till dusk. If we can present an entertaining alternative where there's a little escapism, a little romantic fantasy, why not?"

Valente is thrilled to be at the helm of "As The World Turns" as the show celebrates its 40th anniversary. "It's a very special time to be a part of the show, because we're going to be a part of television history—and American cultural history. It's not just television....This is American culture."

## THE WRITTEN WORD

There have been many gifted head writers of "As The World Turns," and they are:

Irna Phillips—mid-1950s to late 1960s, early 1970s

Kathryn Babecki—late 1960s

Joel Kane & Ralph Ellis—early 1970s

Winifred Wolfe—early 1970s

Katherine L. Phillips—early 1970s

Robert Soderberg & Edith Sommer—mid- to late 1970s

Ralph Ellis & Eugenie Hunt—late 1970s

Douglas Marland—late 1970s, mid-1980s to early 1990s

Bridget & Jerome Dobson—early 1980s

Paul Roberts—early 1980s

K.C. Collier—early 1980s

Carolyn Franz & John Saffron—early 1980s

Tom King & Millee Taggart—early 1980s

Richard Culliton—mid-1980s, mid-1990s

Susan Bedsow Horgan & Cynthia Benjamin—mid-1980s

Juliet Packer & Richard Backus—mid-1990s

Stephen Black & Henry Stern—mid-1990s

The show also counts Agnes Nixon and Bill Bell among its talented roster of dialogue writers during the "early days."

At 8:45 every morning, Irna Phillips would sit down at a worn-out card table and go to work. She never used a typewriter; rather, she acted out her dialogue for her secretary of many years, Rose Cooperman, who knew by the tone of her voice which character she was playing.

Irna was a plain and sickly child who spent her days creating rooms out of cartons for characters who were happier than she. In 1930, Irna wrote what was to become the first ongoing radio serial, "Painted Dreams." Painted dreams were Irna's dreams. The lead, Mother Monahan, had one daughter, Irene, who was very beautiful, had lots of men in her life and a closet full of gowns. By 1943, Irna had five serials going at the same time.

Irna felt she shared the same essential hopes and fears of the average housewife. "All of us are rich or poor, famous or infamous," she said, "faced with fear and failure and indifference, ill health and unrequited love, petty men and thankless chil-

dren and the quirks of fate that can change anyone's life in an instant."

There isn't a soap opera today, with the possible exception of "General Hospital," that doesn't bear Irna Phillips's stamp. She created the entire roster of P&G soaps, which includes "As The World Turns," "The Guiding Light" and "Another World." Agnes Nixon, who created "All My Children," "One Life to Live" and, with Douglas Marland, "Loving" (since renamed "The City"), was her protégée as was Bill Bell of "The Young and the Restless" and "The Bold and the Beautiful" fame. Ted Corday, one of the first directors of "As The World Turns," went on to create "Days of Our Lives."

Irna stayed with "As The World Turns" for many years. Ed Trach, who worked closely with her, says, "Irna's strength was in human interaction and the way she shaped and loved the characters she developed. She was unique." It is a testament to her genius and talent that the Hughes family has welcomed a fourth generation into the world of daytime television.

Honest storytelling was of great importance to Douglas Marland, and he would say it again and again. It doesn't have to be flamboyant, it can be something as simple as the eternal triangle, but it doesn't come from contrivance, it comes from character. Doug took a great deal of pride in issue-oriented storytelling—he introduced the first gay character on a soap and the right-to-die story line, and he got rid of some of the taboos such as incest. He saw issue-oriented stories, though, as secondary to the task of entertainment.

According to Laurie Caso, "Douglas had a tremendous fascination for people, and he had such compassion. And the blend of the two set him on interesting adventures. He loved a puzzle, and in his storytelling that's basically what he did. He set out a maze for himself and his characters, and he had an incredible instinct for what was dramatic."

During his tenure on "As The World Turns," he went far in restoring it to its roots by bringing back core family members such as Nancy and Chris Hughes and Susan Stewart.

Doug knew that soaps were about people, relationships and romance, and therein lay their greatest strength. Laurie Caso never worried when an actress came to him and said, "I'm pregnant," because Doug was a master at using the unexpected. Hillary Bailey Smith's pregnancy led to the "Adam" story, a tale of illegitimate birth and adoption that is still sending reverberations through Oakdale and will for years to come.

Doug's strong family roots originated on a farm on Snyder Road in upstate New York where he grew up and where his family, like the Snyder family, which he created on "As The World Turns," sawed and served the Hubbard squash every Thanksgiving. Doug was very close to his family and spoke to his mother Bea every day. On the night before his death, when he won the *Soap Opera Digest* Editor's Award for Excellence and Outstanding Social Issue Story Line, the first person he called was his mother.

In terms of sheer output, Doug Marland was one of the most prolific head writers in soap opera history.

His challenge was to keep the characters true. He looked for the emotional truth, the conflict from within. Loyalty, family roots, dignity and lack of prejudice—he carried these traits with him in and out of the stories he weaved, and that was his genius.

Doug Marland considered "As The World Turns" the high point of his career.

## THE MAKING OF A SCRIPT

John Kuntz

"According to script editor John Kuntz, "If you have story, the show goes. If you don't have story, it doesn't. It's just that simple."

The story starts in the mind of the head writer, who turns his or her vision into a long-term document, projecting what's going to happen for the next six months and beyond. It's the head writer who provides the "what if?" The head writer sits down every week with the breakdown writers and lays out the story for the week, working toward a big Friday climax. It's up to them to provide the guts and emotional beats of each scene. After the breakdowns are edited, they are sent to script writers to "dialogue." They provide the colors and emotions that the actors then turn into a show.

## LUCY JOHNSON

Lucy Johnson, senior vice president of daytime programming and special projects at CBS, has been a fan of "As The World Turns" almost from the beginning. A friend of the family was a cameraman assigned to the show. The show was done live in a tiny little studio, and she would go there to watch it. "To this day it was one of the most exciting things I remember," she says. CBS is entering its precedent-setting eighth year as the number-one network in daytime. "It's about continuity, entertainment, history, quality and touching the audience emotionally. On 'As The World Turns' we're probably into our fourth generation of viewers. The people we all grew up with—Bob, Lisa, Nancy—are still there, so there's a sense of comfort and continuity. Having the luxury and privilege of actors who are still portraying original characters is so rare—I don't think there's any other show that you can say this about. In that sense, I think this show on our schedule has a particular signature, and it's so beautifully reflected in each generation of CBS viewers who are watching. Its heart and soul, its integrity, has not been tampered with. Yes, we love the romance, and yes, we love the mystery, but part of the fantasy is that Grandma is still in the kitchen, and relatives and loved ones are where we left them." In terms of the future, CBS intends to "take the best ingredients that have kept the show in its prominence for the last 40 years and maintain them with love and care, so that the stories of the struggles, hopes and dreams are identifiable and translate into exciting, compelling, must-tune-in-tomorrow entertainment!"

# Star Turns on "World Turns"

Numerous celebrities have passed through Oakdale. Before his "Waltons" fame, Richard Thomas played one of the 13 Toms. Acclaimed director Mark Rydell (*On Golden Pond*) played Jeff Baker, Penny Hughes's first love. James Earl Jones briefly joined the staff of Memorial Hospital as Dr. Jerry Turner, and in 1977 Kathleen Turner made a brief appearance as a court stenographer. In the early 1970s Swoosie Kurtz played a character known as Ellie Bradley, and Martin Sheen was in Oakdale early in his career. Funnyman Eddie Murphy was a stunt double, and in 1985 Joey Buttafuoco played a thug. And for many years, former child star Freddie Bartholomew was the show's dearly loved and much respected executive producer.

## RISING STARS

In 1983, Marisa Tomei (below with Christian LeBlanc) played homeless waif Marcy Thompson. Casting Director Betty Rea says, "It was a lucky stroke, her coming in. She was very young... something like 19...and, boy, was she ever talented!" Before her time in Oakdale was up, Marcy had lived out a Cinderella fantasy and married a British lord. Tomei went on to win the Oscar® for Best Supporting Actress for her work in *My Cousin Vinny*.

Meg Ryan (above) was a journalism student at New York University when she joined "As The World Turns" in 1982 "just to pay for school," she recalled. Ryan had never had an acting lesson and wasn't looking to make it her career, but viewers instantly warmed to her effervescence and her spunk. Ryan has become a major movie star.

Steven Weber (with Julianne Moore below) joined the cast of "As The World Turns" in 1985 as Kevin Gibson, Frannie Hughes's Yalie boyfriend. Weber admits to having some difficulty learning his lines at first, and he was just getting the hang of it, when, in his words, "I took some lead for my woman" and left the show. Moore switched to movies and now counts Hugh Grant and Sly Stallone among her costars. Weber went on to Broadway and a part in Tom Stoppard's *The Real Thing*, played young John F. Kennedy in the TV miniseries "The Kennedys of Massachusetts" and then soared to TV fame on "Wings."

Kevin took the bullet for Frannie after her then-boyfriend, deranged Doug Cummings (John Wesley Shipp, right), abducted her. Shipp won an Emmy for his portrayal. He remembers, "There was a very sweet and dear thing that Kathy Hays [Kim Hughes] said to me as we were going into this tortured story line. We were on the bed, and the character

Dana Delany joined the cast of "As The World Turns" in 1981 as Hayley Wilson. Hayley met and fell in love with Eric Hollister (Peter Reckell above), and before they both left Oakdale, the two were wed. Delany went on to movie fame and to starring in TV's "China Beach," while Reckell put his undeniable stamp on heartthrob Bo Brady from "Days Of Our Lives."

Casting director Vince Liebhart met Julianne Moore at a party. "Julianne auditioned for three or four roles before I could figure out where she was going to fit in, but I knew it was going to be somewhere."

was just coming apart, and he was crying. I was going through a lot of stress. Kathy took me aside, and she said, 'You know, honey, you're going to have to take care of yourself through this part or you're liable to get sick.' I've never forgotten that, and subsequently, when i've played other characters, I've often felt her hand on my shoulder and heard those same words." For Shipp, his work on "As The World Turns" was a turning point in his early career. He went on to win another Emmy for his work on "Santa Barbara" and has had recurring roles on the TV hits "N.Y.P.D. Blue" and "Sisters." In 1990 he starred in his own series, "The Flash."

Ming-Na Wen, seen below with Andy Kavovit (Paul) and Scott DeFreitas (Andy), was appearing in an off-Broadway showcase when she was seen by a producer from "As The World Turns." Casting director Vince Liebhart had said, "If you happen to come across an Asian actress, let me know, because I'm casting the role of Lien Hughes." Wen remembers the audition well. "I had just gotten out of college, so I was 21, and Andy Kavovit (Paul) was just 16. You know how when you get out of college, you just think you're so mature? I remember thinking, *Oh, my God! I've gotta kiss a 16 year old.*

Craig Montgomery (Scott Bryce) is seen below with sometime mentor, sometime lover and current mother-in-law Lucinda Walsh (Elizabeth Hubbard). Four members of the Bryce family have spent time in Oakdale, but as Craig Montgomery, actor Scott Bryce has had the longest run. Dad Ed Bryce played Dr. Philip Deming, father of Tom Hughes's first wife Carol. Bryce's mother played a retired Vegas stripper named Bunny, and brother Philip was the pilot of Lucinda Walsh's plane. Soon after he arrived on the "As The World Turns" set, Bryce was called to the executive producer's office and asked, "How would you like to be a villain?" He replied, "I thought that was what you hired me for." And so the evil Craig was born. As Bryce explains, his character "was always a car accident waiting to happen, and then love redeemed him." Bryce has shuttled back and forth between Oakdale and Hollywood. He's appeared on the TV series "Murphy Brown," "Golden Girls" and "L.A. Law" and in the movie *Up Close and Personal.*

It was April Fools' Day, 1991, and casting director Vince Liebhart was down to the wire on casting Tess Shelby. According to Vince, "She (Parker Posey above) walked in here with a cigarette and read for me. I brought her in to read for Laurie Caso [the executive producer]. She walked into his office, put her feet up and said, 'So what are we going to do?' She had a lot of nerve, and the accent was perfect." When she found out they wanted her for three years, her first reaction was, "You've got to be kidding. I can't do anything for three years. I haven't struggled, I haven't waited tables, I don't even know what it's really like to starve!" That was Monday. On Tuesday she went to Saks for wardrobe, and on Wednesday she was on the set. Posey's family was delighted. "It's my grandmother's favorite soap," she said. Since she left Oakdale, Posey has made a big splash on the independent film scene, getting rave reviews for her portrayal of the title character in *Party Girl.*

*I'm robbing the cradle!"* Wen was one of the first Asian contract players on a soap. When she left "As The World Turns," Wen went on to star in the *The Joy Luck Club*, a movie that has a special place in her heart. She also appeared on the popular TV series "ER" and is a regular on the sitcom "The Single Guy." In 1997, her voice will be heard as the lead character in Disney's animated feature, *The Legend of Mulan.*

# AND SOME THAT GOT AWAY...

In 1984, Courteney Cox of "Friends" fame auditioned for Frannie and lost out to Julianne Moore. She did, however, get to do a short scene in the country club with Marcy Thompson (Marisa Tomei). That same year, movie star Hugh Grant tried out for the part of Marcy's Prince Charming, Lord Stewart Cushing, but Ross Kettle got the part instead.

## GUEST STARS

Stars who graced Oakdale with their presence for a short while and then moved on...

In 1981, glamorous Zsa Zsa Gabor (upper right) made her soap opera debut in the role of Lydia Marlowe, sister of mysterious Miranda Marlowe (Elaine Princi). Of her experience on the soap, Gabor had this to say: "Darling, I never have worked so hard and fast in all my life. I just hope I looked OK."

In 1982, when Ellen Stewart (Patricia Bruder) moved into her new apartment, she made a new friend in next-door neighbor Suz Becker (Betsy Palmer). Suz offered moral support by introducing Ellen to two of her most vibrant and flamboyant friends, Corinne (Pearl Bailey, left) and Rosanne (Edie Adams, third from left). Ms. Bailey was a noted jazz singer and a highly popular star of stage and screen. Ms. Adams came to prominence costarring with her late husband, zany comedian Ernie Kovacs and went on to forge her own successful career.

In 1981, Dr. Joyce Brothers stopped in Oakdale on a lecture tour, and her old friend Dr. Bob Hughes (Don Hastings) asked her to visit Memorial Hospital to counsel some young victims of PCP-laced marijuana.

Robert Horton, star of the long-running TV series "Wagon Train," arrived in Oakdale in 1982 as wealthy publishing giant Whit McColl, Lisa's fifth husband.

Elegant matinee idol Farley Granger (above) played Lisa's sixth husband, dashing Interpol agent Earl Mitchell, and Lisa loved him dearly. Earl's dangerous work led to his untimely death at the hands of James Stenbeck.

In 1984, zany comedienne Phyllis Diller made her daytime debut as the Fairy Godmother in Marcy Thompson's Cinderella fantasy, and she proved to be the perfect choice.

"The Man from U.N.C.L.E.," actor Robert Vaughn (below), joined the cast of "As The World Turns" in 1995 as sharp-shooting, high-powered attorney Rick Hamlin. Hamlin came to town as Hal Munson's divorce attorney and stayed on to represent Lisa in her malpractice suit against John Dixon.

In 1983, Imogene Coca appeared at the Oakdale police station as Alice Hammond, an elderly mugging victim. Ms. Coca described her experience on the soap this way: "I'm going through a trying period....I play a woman living on Social Security who got mugged and is living in an apartment that is about to be torn down. It's fun."

Another "Man from U.N.C.L.E" star, David McCallum (near left) with Frank Runyeon and Scott Bryce, joined "As The World Turns" in 1983 as Maurice Vermeil, a coin collector with questionable underworld ties.

# FASHIONS LTD.

In 1984 and 1985, Lisa and Barbara, co-owners of Oakdale's fancy fashion emporium, Fashions Ltd., ran a series of lunchtime fashion shows featuring the likes of Albert Capraro, famous for outfitting such luminaries as Barbara Walters, Jane Fonda and Diana Ross. Internationally known designer Oleg Cassini also brought his designs to town and was a major hit.

Nicole Miller (above center), known for her splashy ties and upbeat designs, was right on time for her appointment at Fashions Ltd. with co-owners Lisa and Barbara, but Barbara's husband Hal mistook Nicole for a tardy seamstress and chewed her out for being late. Barbara was mortified!

Jermaine Jackson took time out from the Jacksons' 1984 Victory Tour to come to Oakdale with his then backup singer Whitney Houston as part of the "Cinderella Fantasy" story. Marcy Thompson was the lucky winner, and she was duly serenaded by Jackson and Houston (below) with their versions of "Take Good Care of My Heart" and "Nobody Loves Me Like You Do," the love song that was written for Betsy and Steve.

In the early 1970s, when Kim Reynolds followed Bob Hughes to Florida, he found her singing in the hotel lounge. Entertainer Bobby Short (pictured above center with executive producer Joe Willmore and a casting director for "As The World Turns") was on hand to back her up.

In 1985, Doug Cummings opened Caroline's, a chic restaurant named for his late wife, which quickly became a favorite with the cream of Oakdale society.

Singing superstar Tony Bennett (below) was on hand for the opening, and he serenaded his rapt audience with "Why Do People Fall In Love?" and that old standby, "Someone to Watch over Me."

In 1992, when Rosanna Cabot was dating Hutch Hutchinson, Lee Greenwood and Rita Coolidge (above) appeared at the popular teen hangout, the Cellar, to sing Rosanna and Hutch's love song, "Heart Don't Fail Me Now."

In 1986, Caroline's became the Mona Lisa. The restaurant was Lisa's latest venture, and she opened it in style with Melba Moore at the microphone.

In 1991, Johnny Mathis and Patti Austin appeared at the Mona Lisa where they sang Jessica and Duncan's love theme, "You Brought Me Love."

By 1995, Rosanna had moved on to be with Mike Kasnoff, and the new hangout in town was a bar called Yo's. It was New Year's Eve, and Mike and Rosanna were having problems when Brian McKnight (below) arrived and ushered in the new year with his version of their song, "Heart Don't Fail Me Now."

# Fanfare

"As The World Turns" has had its share of famous fans—author Stephen King and pianist Van Cliburn, who could always tell when the organist was on vacation because the background music wasn't nearly as good. Fred Astaire, Bobby Short, Andy Warhol and hockey star Ron Greschner all watched religiously, as did Roy Rogers, Dale Evans and famed historian Shelby Foote. With its emphasis on family values, "As The World Turns" has been the favorite of several administrations. In *Backstairs at the White House*, it is revealed that Mamie Eisenhower, who defined the '50s, as did "As The World Turns," was an avid fan, and everything stopped at the White House between 1:30 and 2:00 P.M. so that she and the president could watch the show. Betty Ford, Lillian Carter and Barbara Bush were also frequent viewers. The show was a special favorite of legendary actress Bette Davis, who once said that she "deplores the term soap opera because it invites derision." She preferred to call them "daytime dramas." And how did she become a fan? "My mother was watching them since they began!"

Children remember that their grandmothers and mothers never said, "I'm going to watch the show" or "I'm going to watch 'As The World Turns.'" Instead, they said, "I'm going to watch my story." Four generations of the family of the show's number one fan, Frances Nonemacher, have watched four generations of the Hughes family live their daily lives. "I've watched religiously since the first scene in the kitchen when Nancy poured Chris a cup of coffee and said, 'Good morning, dear,' and that little couple captured my heart"...and kept it. Estelle Davis, the fan club's coordinator, says it's not unusual for her to get three fan letters from the same house, each from a different generation. Actress Helen Wagner (Nancy Hughes) adds that people often come up to her and say, "I've grown up with the Hughes family as much as my own."

## FAN TALES

Many of the actors on the show were fans first. Ellen Dolan says, "When I was a little kid we had a second TV downstairs, and my mom would be down there doing laundry and watching the show. When we had the 35th anniversary party, they had a bank of monitors showing the old shows in black and white. I remember running around the party having a great time, then stopping dead in my tracks and watching, because it took me back to when I was three, four and five years old, and I thought, *God! I do that!... and it's been there my whole life!*"

My mother and me.

When someone writes a fan letter, there are usually three things he or she wishes for: that the person he or she is writing to receives it, that the person will read it and, last but not least, that the fan will get a response and know that the letter made a difference. Fan letters *do* make a difference. Even if a letter is negative, it shows that people are involved and interested, and for actors it's a gauge of how they're doing.

When Grandpa Hughes (Santos Ortega) celebrated his 70th birthday on the show, he received more than 175,000 greeting cards and salutations, as well as many handsome gifts. Ortega said that "people write to tell me I remind them of their own grandfather, or they write, 'I wish I had a grandfather like you.'"

This is clearly a show that's been passed down from generation to generation. One fan wrote, "I've been watching 'ATWT' for 15 years now. I first began watching with my mother when I was ten. I am now 25, and it is still my favorite show." Helen Wagner (Nancy Hughes) sums it up this way: "The fans are getting older, and the fans are getting younger." However, fan encounters can go from the sublime to the other extreme.

Eileen Fulton (Lisa) had to hire a live-in bodyguard after she received death threats from "World" watchers who thought she was behind a miscarriage suffered by her TV daughter-in-law, Margo. Angry fans remembered a clause written in Eileen's early contracts that prevented her from becoming a grandmother on the show. As Eileen and her character grew older, the clause was dropped, something the fans were obviously unaware of. When Lisa first arrived in Oakdale, remembers Eileen, "Most of the mail was negative—'Grow up! Don't be so selfish!' My father was a minister, and people would approach my mother after church and say, 'Margaret, did you see what your daughter did? How

could she?' When I was first on the show, I was standing in front of Lord & Taylor's, and this is the first time anybody recognized me. She came up to me, a lovely looking woman dressed in a Chanel suit, and she said, 'Are you Lisa?' And I said, 'That's the part I'm playing.' I'm getting ready to give her an autograph, and she whacked me!"

Larry Bryggman (John Dixon) has been attacked on the streets of Manhattan, whereas his rival Don Hastings (Bob Hughes) gets heaps of praise for his gentle bedside manner and letters from fans asking if he's really a doctor.

When actor Anthony Herrera (James Stenbeck) was touring with a play in his native Mississippi, ardent fan Leslie Criss was in the audience. "The show's been a TV staple in my family since I could peer through the bars of my playpen. We've always hated James Stenbeck. We cheered when death claimed him—all three times." But Leslie was thrilled to meet the actor. Leslie says, "I never won a beauty pageant and chances are no Pulitzer prizes will ever come my way. But to my grandmother, I've already had my greatest accomplish-

ment: I've met James Stenbeck!"

On a more serious note, cast members Ellen Dolan and Anthony Herrera expressed how moved they were when former White House Press Secretary James Brady and his wife Sarah visited the set. Mrs. Brady was thrilled to meet her favorite soap actors, and they were thrilled to meet her. But what made it so memorable for everyone involved was when she told them how much she looked forward to that hour a day of watching "As The World Turns," because it offered her a brief respite from the difficulties she has had to deal with since her husband was tragically shot.

Another high point came when the show's then executive producer, Laurence Caso, received a letter from New York Representative Susan Molinari, who had just introduced the Sexual Assault Prevention Act of 1993 into the U.S. House of Representatives. She wrote, "Thank you for addressing the issue of AIDS and women—it is one of the most underreported, underaddressed problems in our society. Your program will go a long way toward preventing more needless tragedies."

Helen Wagner and Don MacLaughlin with the average amount of fan mail they received in their heyday. Helen once got a letter addressed to Mrs. Chris Hughes, New York City—and the postal carrier knew just where to find her! Most of her mail is complimentary, like "You make me glad my daughter's name is Nancy," but there are disapproving ones as well. One of Helen's favorites is a letter that was written with a fountain pen on lined tablet paper in great fury, because every punctuation mark poked right through the paper! It read: "Dear Nancy, You do one of the dirtiest, filthiest things on TV. You put your cup towel over your shoulder. I wish you'd stop it and stop Penny from doing it too! Signed, Four Clean People from Trenton."

When Kim Hughes (Kathryn Hays) was in love with Nick Andropoulos, she followed him to Greece, where they made love before they got married. According to Hays, "The fans went absolutely berserk!" They thought this was totally unacceptable behavior for Kim! Helen Wagner believes that "one of the things 40 years has to offer is the loyalty of the fans." That's why the fan mail often reads like this: "My mother has watched this show since its inception, and I have been a fan since the late '50s. In fact, I was pregnant with my oldest son at the same time Lisa was pregnant with Tom on the show (however, Tom has certainly aged faster!)." And then there is the fan in a wheelchair who signed her letter, "See you in Oakdale on Monday, my friend." That says it all.

Martha Byrne

Elizabeth Hubbard

Allyson Rice-Taylor

Don Hastings

### ROSEMARY PRINZ (PENNY HUGHES)

Part of the original cast, Rosemary Prinz has had fan mail that ran the gamut from truckloads of gifts when Penny Hughes married Jeff Baker to an envelope with a little dead fish in it that read, "Penny you stink. You stink like fish!"

### MARTHA BYRNE (LILY GRIMALDI)

I got a letter once. The woman captured everything about me that I was trying to portray as a character and as a person. It was great. I was so touched. The viewers are very smart and mostly very nice. On my 16th birthday I got so many presents! So many stuffed animals! People are very generous, and I try to use it in a positive way.

### ELIZABETH HUBBARD (LUCINDA WALSH)

Ladies would come up to me and say, "I learned so much." I think what they mean is they're taking a chance. People say they're gonna go for it. Lucinda's that kind of a role model, even though she has been quite crazy and unhappy and has caused her share of misery.

### ALLYSON RICE-TAYLOR (CONNOR WALSH STRICKLYN)

Finding out that all these people actually watch soaps... whose mothers and grandmothers watched it. It's very interesting. I've had a lot of professional people write because they've identified with the characters. One of the most difficult times was when they were doing the bulimic recurrence, because I got letters from young women who were bulimic, who had never told anyone about it — and that was their cry for help. I felt a real responsibility to not just send an autographed photo. And I wrote back to these women. It was like, I will help with this information, and here's what you're doing to your body. I've done a lot of research on it, so I know quite a bit about it, and I just sort of spelled that out. These are places that you can call, and you need to call because you can die from this if you don't get help. You can't save everybody—I don't feel that it's really my job—but I did feel the responsibility of writing back and encouraging the help. When you're in someone's living room every day of every week of every year, you can't overlook the effect that it has, or that it could have, on somebody... It's a gift to be able to have that kind of impact on people.

### DON HASTINGS (BOB HUGHES)

A veteran of 35 years on the show, Hastings has gotten his share of angry mail, especially when Bob was married to Kim and having an affair with Susan Stewart. One that he remembers well, read: "You ingrate. You jerk. Kathryn Hays has carried you for years, and you do this to her!" Hastings says, "Much of the mail I get is from overseas, which is kind of fun. I had a guy recognize me in the elevator at Saks. He was German. He said, 'Dr. Bob?' I said, 'Yes.' He said, 'I see you in Germany.' I said, 'Well I'm a little younger there!' He said, 'Yes, you are!'" The show is several years behind over there.

Brooke Alexander

### BROOKE ALEXANDER (SAMANTHA ANDERSON)

I did this play recently in New York. There was a girl who drove up from Maryland with her father. She was probably 16, and she said she was one of my biggest fans. They drove all the way up for the weekend to see me in the play! She even sent me a birthday card. A lot of people have said, 'You know, I grew up watching the show with my mom.' To realize that I'm part of tradition, I'm part of family—It's really wonderful to be able to touch people's lives and make them feel something.

Benjamin Hendrickson

### BENJAMIN HENDRICKSON (DETECTIVE HAL MUNSON)

I was down in Virginia for an autograph session, and I asked this fan what she did. She said she was a chicken farmer. And I said, 'If I wasn't doing the soap, I think I'd be a chicken farmer, too.' Just off the top, I said, 'That's like the next thing on my list.' And she came back with a box and said, 'Here. When you want to be a chicken farmer, you can start with Betsy!' Betsy was one of her prized hens. So, for my work on 'As The World Turns' I've gotten ten years of employment and a live chicken! And that's the truth.

Ashley Williams

### ASHLEY WILLIAMS (DANI ANDROPOULOS)

I've been getting some weird letters. A lot of people, they give me advice. 'Don't you listen to your aunt Emily! She doesn't know anything!' One person wrote me this whole letter, it was so cool. 'You go, girl. You tell her off!' It was written in like huge letters, and they were obviously all excited about it. The letters can run the gamut, like some people say, 'What do you see in Jeremy?' Other people are like, 'Oh, my God—he's gorgeous!' But I think it's pretty funny, 'cause I don't have a say in it.

Jordana Brewster

### JORDANA BREWSTER (NIKKI GRAVES)

I like the letters from teenagers that tell me that they understand what it's like, because then I know that it's working, that they can relate to Nikki. I like that...the best thing to hear in a letter is when they say, 'Oh, I was flipping through the channels, and I just had to stop, and I got hooked on the show.' I love that! It's like the ultimate compliment...that's cool.

# And the Winner Is...

I t's called an Emmy, it looks great on a shelf, and it's a professional and personal triumph to receive one. But more than anything else, this prestigious award, given each year by the Academy of Television Arts and Sciences for excellence in daytime drama, means that your peers have recognized your work. To the winners and to all the nominees, a hearty congratulations!

© N.A.T.A.S.

**AWARD YEAR
1983–1984**

**OUTSTANDING ACTOR
IN A DAYTIME
DRAMA SERIES:
LARRY BRYGGMAN**

Emmy Award winner Larry Bryggman gets a congratulatory kiss (above). A consummate New York stage actor, Bryggman was hired back in 1968 for a three-day stint on "As The World Turns." One of the characters had had a heart attack, and Bryggman (as Dr. John Denton, later changed to Dixon) was the cardiologist in charge of monitoring her heart. Every now and then David Stewart and Bob Hughes would poke their heads into the room and ask how the patient was doing. Bryggman's first line on the show was "80 over 20," and for the next three days he sat in front of that machine spouting numbers. He must have made a strong impression on the show's creator, Irna Phillips, however, because she asked him to stay on for three weeks, which turned into a year. Today, Bryggman can still be found in Oakdale playing the devious, curmudgeonly Dr. Dixon, whom viewers love to hate.

**OUTSTANDING SUPPORTING
ACTOR IN A DAYTIME
DRAMA SERIES:
JUSTIN DEAS**

One of the 13 actors who have played Tom, Justin Deas put his own spin on this straitlaced character. Deas was cast by

Betty Rea, who was at that time casting director for both "As The World Turns" and "Guiding Light." He had auditioned for a part on "Guiding Light" and, according to Betty, "They thought he was wonderful, but they didn't think he was right for what they were looking for, and we'd been looking for a young man for 'As The World Turns' forever and ever." She took Dea's audition tape over to the show's executive producer, Fred Bartholomew, and asked him to take a look. "He said, 'Dear heart, I'm so busy at the moment,'" Betty recalls. "I said, 'Please, just take ten minutes.' So he watched it, and then he said, 'That's what we've been looking for.' Of course we'd been looking for the exact opposite, but I said, 'Just like that?' and he said, 'Yes.'"

AWARD YEAR 1984–1985

## OUTSTANDING JUVENILE/ YOUNG MALE IN A DAYTIME DRAMA SERIES: BRIAN BLOOM

August 1, 1985, is a day Oakdale's then teenage heartthrob, Brian Bloom (Dusty Donovan), will never forget. Not only did his character, Dusty, awaken from a coma, but at the age of 15 Bloom (below) won his first

major award for his portrayal of the sensitive young man. His Emmy acceptance speech started with "Wow!"

AWARD YEAR 1985–1986

## OUTSTANDING SUPPORTING ACTOR IN A DAYTIME DRAMA SERIES: JOHN WESLEY SHIPP

John Wesley Shipp was a good guy on "Guiding Light," but his eight-month stint as tragic villain Douglas Cummings on "As The World Turns" got him his first Emmy. He remembers that Ed Trach, Procter & Gamble's executive in charge of production, paid him and Doug Marland, the head writer who created the story line, the nicest compliment about his devious character. "He said, 'If anyone had told me that a character would come on to this show and start terrorizing the characters I have watched and loved for so many years, and that I would feel sympathy for the guy who was doing this, I would have said that's an impossible feat.'"

## OUTSTANDING LIGHTING DIRECTION FOR A DAYTIME DRAMA SERIES: FRANK OLSEN, JEN YOUTT, HAL ANDERSON, LINCOLN JOHN STULIK

AWARD YEAR 1986–1987

## OUTSTANDING DAYTIME DRAMA SERIES: ROBERT CALHOUN, EXECUTIVE PRODUCER. MICHAEL D. LAIBSON, BONNIE BOGARD, CHRISTINE BANAS, PRODUCERS.

## OUTSTANDING LEAD ACTOR IN A DAYTIME DRAMA SERIES: LARRY BRYGGMAN

## OUTSTANDING SUPPORTING ACTOR IN A DAYTIME DRAMA SERIES: GREGG MARX

Another Tom took home the Emmy for his portrayal of a

core member of one of Oakdale's most visible families. Gregg Marx had already left the show for his native California when he learned he had won the award, and he flew back to New York for the ceremonies. According to Marx, "It was like, What? There must be some mistake! Me? And it was really a nice thing to have happen, especially for work that had meant something to me. It was very gratifying."

## OUTSTANDING INGENUE IN A DAYTIME DRAMA SERIES: MARTHA BYRNE

Martha Byrne (above) was a mere 17 and blessed with a story line that included two of the most gorgeous leading men in daytime, Brian Bloom (Dusty Donovan) and Jon Hensley (Holden Snyder), when she won the Emmy for Outstanding Ingenue. At the time, Byrne (Lily) was involved in a story that dealt with a young girl trying to come to terms with her father's suicide. Byrne says, "I

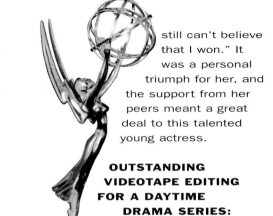
© N.A.T.A.S.

still can't believe that I won." It was a personal triumph for her, and the support from her peers meant a great deal to this talented young actress.

**OUTSTANDING VIDEOTAPE EDITING FOR A DAYTIME DRAMA SERIES: JOSEPH A. MASTROBERTI, STEVEN SHATKIN**

AWARD YEAR 1987–1988

**OUTSTANDING INGENUE IN A DAYTIME DRAMA SERIES: JULIANNE MOORE**

After a brief tenure on "Edge of Night," Julianne Moore came to "As The World Turns" and took over the role of Bob Hughes's daughter, Frannie. She also created the role of Frannie's half-sister Sabrina, playing them both simultaneously.

AWARD YEAR 1989–1990

**OUTSTANDING JUVENILE MALE IN A DAYTIME DRAMA SERIES: ANDREW KAVOVIT**

(Below) He might look young, but as Paul Stenbeck, son of

evil villain James Stenbeck and fashion maven Barbara Ryan, he had to grow up fast! Andrew Kavovit's sensitive portrayal of a young man's first love (which happened to be with his father's ex-mistress and mother's nemesis, Emily Stewart) earned him much praise.

**OUTSTANDING ART DIRECTION/SET DIRECTION/ SCENIC DESIGN: LAWRENCE ICING, ART DIRECTOR; ELMON WEBB, SCENIC DESIGNER; HOLMES EASLEY, DAVID HARNISH, PAUL W. HICKEY, SET DECORATORS**

AWARD YEAR 1990–1991

**OUTSTANDING DAYTIME DRAMA SERIES: LAURENCE CASO, EXECUTIVE PRODUCER; KENNETH L. FITTS, SUPERVISING PRODUCER; CHRISTINE S. BANAS, DAVID DOMEDION, PRODUCERS; LISA ANNE WILSON, COORDINATING PRODUCER**

AWARD YEAR 1992–1993

**OUTSTANDING DIRECTING TEAM IN A DAYTIME DRAMA SERIES: PAUL LAMMERS, MARIA WAGNER, DAN HAMILTON, CHARLES C. DYER, LARRY CARPENTER, DIRECTORS; JOEL ARONOWITZ, MICHAEL KERNER, ASSOCIATE DIRECTORS**

**OUTSTANDING ACHIEVEMENT IN GRAPHICS AND TITLE DESIGN: JIM CASTLE, CAROL JOHNSEN, TITLE DESIGNERS; BRUCE BRYANT, PAULA CONN, GRAPHIC ARTISTS**

# SOAPY AWARDS

**B**efore they became the *Soap Opera Digest* Awards, they were known as the Soapys, and they are particularly rewarding to the recipients because they reflect the fans' favorites!

### FAVORITE JUVENILE ACTRESS: SUZANNE DAVIDSON

She was young Betsy Stewart when the show was still filmed live, and she had a lot to deal with. Betsy thought her uncle Paul was her real father, and when she found out Dan was her father, she went through a difficult period of adjustment. What she wanted more than anything else was to get Kim and Dan together, and she ultimately succeeded. After Dan's death, Betsy and stepmother Kim remained very close.

### SPECIAL AWARD FOR OUTSTANDING ACHIEVEMENT IN THE WORLD OF DAYTIME DRAMA: EILEEN FULTON

A favorite with fans, Eileen Fulton (right) deservedly won her Soapy for her portrayal of the spunky, wily and always irrepressible Lisa.

**G**iven annually, these awards are voted on by the fans and reflect the viewers' favorite drama, leading man and woman, villain, villainess, ingenue and hunk. They have been broadened to include super couples, story lines, weddings and death scenes.

## THE SOAP OPERA DIGEST AWARDS

### AWARD YEAR 1992–1993
### GOVERNORS' LIFETIME ACHIEVEMENT AWARD: DOUGLAS MARLAND

Douglas Marland (right) was a weaver of stories, a master of his craft. This Lifetime Achievement Award, signifying the acceptance and acknowledgment of the fans, meant more than words could express to this legendary daytime writer. It was, without a doubt, one of the highlights of his distinguished career. One week later, Doug Marland died prematurely, but he left his mark on the show that he loved and on the genre known as daytime drama.

## OUTSTANDING SUPPORTING ACTRESS:
### ELLEN DOLAN

It was a harrowing year for Det. Margo Hughes (Ellen Dolan above). Back from a glorious vacation in Cape Cod, she was caught in a liquor store holdup and brutally raped. Soon afterward, it was discovered that the rapist was HIV positive. For Dolan, the rape and its aftermath, and how it affected her marriage and her outlook on life, was a deeply felt and rewarding story.

AWARD YEAR 1992–1993
## OUTSTANDING FEMALE NEWCOMER:
### YVONNE PERRY

When she arrived in Oakdale, Rosanna Cabot (Yvonne Perry, right) was running away from a life in Grosse Pointe that had lost its meaning after her mother died. Then her father died and left her $600 million, and

she met Mike Kasnoff. Her life was never the same. Perry's touching performance in this star-crossed love story captured the imagination of the viewers.

## OUTSTANDING SOCIAL ISSUE STORY LINE:
### MARGO'S RAPE

Doug Marland didn't believe in "issue" stories: he believed in entertainment. Margo Hughes was strong, and so was her marriage when she was forced to live through the ordeal of a rape and possible HIV infection. Everything was carefully researched and presented. The story, played out in real time, emphasized Margo's growth as a character and the strength of her marriage to Tom. It was daytime drama at its best.

AWARD YEAR 1995
## OUTSTANDING FEMALE NEWCOMER:
### BROOKE ALEXANDER

Brooke Alexander (right) came to "As The World Turns" as Samantha, a con artist who posed as Lucinda Walsh's sister only to find out they really were sisters. According to Alexander, "It was a great honor just to be nominated. Of course I was ecstatic. It's always nice to be

acknowledged, and the fans have been wonderful." It was her first job in daytime. "What I saw in the first year, what I learned almost immediately, was the level of professionalism and just good hard work that goes into what our jobs are."

# OTHER NOTABLE HONORS

## AWARD YEAR 1990
### GLAAD (GAY AND LESBIAN ALLIANCE AGAINST DEFAMATION): THE HANK ELIOT STORY

This story introduced daytime to its first male homosexual character and developed into a story of the other characters' reactions.

## AWARD YEAR–1991

On the occasion of the show's 35th anniversary, "As The World Turns" was given a certificate of appreciation by the Mayor of New York, David Dinkins, "for this television show that has been produced in our city for 35 years and enjoyed by people throughout America, on the occasion of the taping of its 9,000th broadcast." That year the show also received a citation from the governor of New York, Mario Cuomo, stating that "since its debut on April 2, 1956, 'As The World Turns' has entertained countless millions of television viewers with its time-honored blend of characters and situations.... 'As The World Turns' can be proud of its contributions in making New York a world-class production center."

## AWARD YEAR 1993
### NANCY J. REYNOLDS AWARD SPONSORED BY THE CENTER FOR POPULATION OPTIONS (CPO) MEDIA PROJECT: MARGO'S RAPE STORY AND SUBSEQUENT HIV SCARE.

The meaning of the story line hit home for actress Ellen Dolan (Margo Hughes) when she spoke at a UCLA symposium focusing on media response to women with AIDS. After her speech, Dolan was approached by a young college student. "She told me she had never watched 'As The World Turns' before, but she said Margo's story had happened to her." The young woman had tested positive for HIV and months later a follow-up test came out negative. "This story could have been presented as a mere fact sheet, a little pamphlet of information on HIV," Dolan points out. "Instead, we took it to a more personal level. We made it clear that we are people just like you...and this can happen to you." She believes "family strength was the key to this story line's success."

## AWARD YEAR 1993–1994

"As The World Turns" is known for its strong acting ensemble.

In 1994 casting director Vince Liebhart was the recipient of the Casting Society of America's coveted Artious Award. Artious is Greek for "perfectly fitted" and is given for outstanding achievement in casting. Like the Emmys it is a peer award, voted on by the membership.

## AWARD YEAR 1993
### BRICK SOAP OPERA OF THE YEAR

According to then executive producer Laurie Caso, "The Bricklayer Association of America says they actually monitor all the soaps over a specified period of time. They saw that we had, quantitatively and qualitatively, the most and the best use of brick in our sets. So they called us up and said, 'We're going to give you an award. Can we come to the studio?' And they showed up with this brick!" How many other soaps can claim this honor?

# "As The World Turns"

## CAST LIST

| CHARACTER | ACTOR | DATE | CHARACTER | ACTOR | DATE |
|---|---|---|---|---|---|
| Bill Abbott | Patrick O'Neal | Early 60s | Marilyn Best | Randie Jean Davis | 1981 |
| Karen Adams | Doe Lang | 1968–70 | Dr. Henry Bickford | Charles White | 1979 |
| Dr. Roger Adams | Mark McConnell | 1983 | Mr. Big | Brent Collins | 1982 |
| Michael Alcott | Richard Beakins | 1993 | Ambrose Bingham | Dick Latessa | 1993 |
| Neal Keller Alcott | Mary Kay Adams | 1992–93 | Ambrose Bingham | William LeMessena | 1985–92 |
| Ariel Aldrin (Dixon Donovan) | Judith Blazer | 1982–85 | Antoine Bisset | Jean LeClerc | 1983 |
| Greta Aldrin | Rosemary Murphy | 1989 | Meg Blaine | Teri Keane | Early 60s |
| Greta Aldrin | Joan Copeland | 1983 | Blondie | Dorothy Bryce | 1986 |
| Kirk Anderson | Tom Wiggin | 1988–Present | Rev. George Booth | Philip Sterling | Mid–Late 70s |
| Nels Andersson Einar | Perry Scott | 1980–84 | Simone Bordeau | Kimberly Norris | 1992–93 |
| Logan Andrews | Don Chastain | 1987 | Leslie Bordeau | Kim Snyder | 1992–93 |
| Nick Andropoulos | Michael Forest | 1980–82 | Kent Bradford | Ernest Townsend | 1984 |
| Steve Andropoulos | Frank Runyeon | 1980–86 | Ellie Bradley | Swoosie Kurtz | 1971 |
| Frank Andropoulos | Jacques Perreault | 1983–85 | Mrs. Bradley | Elspeth Eric | 1971 |
| Dani Andropoulos | Ashley Williams | 1994–Present | Rose Brando | Ethel Everett | Late 60s |
| Dani Andropoulos | Kristanna Loken | 1994 | Marcy Breen (Lafferty) | Jill Powell | 1991–92; 1994 |
| Dani Andropoulos | Colleen Broomall | 1984–88 | Marcy Breen | Kathleen McNenny | 1991 |
| Angela | Vanessa Bell | 1983 | Franny Brennan | Toni Darnay | 1963–65 |
| Joe Bailey | Don Billet | 1988 | Ed Brewster | Donald Barton | 1985 |
| Jeff Baker | Mark Rydell | 1956–62 | Elaine Brody | Joan Lovejoy | Late 60s |
| Dick Baker | Court Benson | Early 60s | Ralph Brown | Staats Cotsworth | Late 60s |
| Dick Baker | Carl LowLate | 50s–Early 60s | Ralph Brown | Hugh Franklin | Late 60s |
| Grace Baker | Muriel Williams | Early 60s | Buddy | Loren Dean | 1989 |
| Grace Baker | Grace Matthews | Early 60s | Mr. Bundy | John McGovern | Mid 60s |
| Grace Baker | Frances Reid | Late 50s–Early 60s | Julia Burke | Fran Carlon | 1968–75 |
| Grace Baker | Selena Royle | Late 50s | Dr. Fred Burke | William Van Sleet | Late 60s |
| Taylor Baldwin | Maggie Baird | 1987 | Dr. Fred Burke | James Karen | Mid–Late 60s |
| Phil Banner | Douglass Parkhirst | Early 60s | Susan Burke (Stewart McDermott) | Marie Masters | 1968–79; 1986–Present |
| Natalie Bannon (Triandos) | Janet Zarish | 1981 | | | |
| Natalie Bannon (Hughes) | Judith Chapman | 1975–78 | Susan Burke (Stewart) | Judith Barcroft | 1978 |
| Lenore Barclay (Anderson) | Breon Gorman | 1988 | Susan Burke | Leslie Perkins | 1968 |
| Meg Barnes | Gail Strickland | Early 70s | Susan Burke | Jada Rowland | 1967–68 |
| Hank Barton | Gary Sandy | 1970 | Susan Burke | Diana Walker | 1967 |
| Hank Barton | Paul Falzone | Late 60s | Susan Burke | Connie Scott | 1966–67 |
| Hank Barton | Peter Burnell | Late 60s | Grace Burton | Eugenia Rawls | Early 70s |
| Mr. Barton | Barnard Hughes | Late 60s–1970 | Peter Burton | Christopher Hastings | Early 70s |
| Dr. Bruce Baxter | Ben Hayes | 1972–73 | Dr. Matt Butler | Robin Thomas | 1981–82 |
| Dr. Bruce Baxter | Steve Harmon | 1972 | Rosanna Cabot | Yvonne Perry | 1992–Present |
| Sean Baxter | Mark Lewis | 1992 | Sheila Cabot | Leslie Lyles | 1992 |
| Sean Baxter | Burke Moses | 1989–91 | Alexander Cabot | Paul Hecht | 1992–95 |
| Courtney Baxter (Dixon) | Hayley Barr | 1990–94 | Lauren Cabot | Lauren Bailey | 1995 |
| Suz Becker | Betsy Palmer | 1981 | Peter Cabot | Chuck Santoro | 1995 |
| Dr. Bellows | P. Jay Sidney | 1967 | Lt. Kevin Callaghan | Ron McLarty | 1984 |
| Dr. Bellows | Brock Peters | 1966 | Dr. Doug Campbell | Denis Romer | 1979 |
| Jason Benedict | Jonathan Hogan | 1989–94 | Marsha Campbell | Cynthia Bostick | 1979 |
| Wendy Bennett | Leigh Lassen | Late 60s | | | |

| CHARACTER | ACTOR | DATE |
|---|---|---|
| Brian Campbell | Jason Kimmel | 1979 |
| Mary Hopkins Campbell | Lisby Larson | 1993 |
| Jarred Carpenter | Lou Bedford | 1988 |
| Jarred Carpenter | Warren Frost | 1988 |
| Elizabeth Carpenter (Cromwell) | Katherine Kane | 1988 |
| Virgil Cartwright | Steve Deighan | 1990–91 |
| Dr. Doug Cassen | Nat Polen | 1956–67 |
| Cesare | Matt Servitto | 1994 |
| Tad Channing | Larry Pine | 1986 |
| Tad Channing | Andrew Potter | 1986 |
| Linda Chase | Margo McKenna | 1981 |
| Michael Christopher | Harris Yulin | 1984–85 |
| Jane Clark | Lois Smith | Early 70s |
| Ben Clark | Mark Gordon | Early 70s |
| Arthur Clayborne | Bill Tatum | 1991–92 |
| Judith Clayton | Jill Larson | 1987 |
| Dr. Tim Cole | William Redfield | 1958 |
| Louise Cole | Mary K. Wells | 1958 |
| Claudia Colfax | Mary McDonnell | 1980 |
| Ray Colfax | Tom Everett | 1980 |
| Grant Colman | James Douglas | 1974–81, 1988 |
| Grant Colman | Konrad Matthaei | 1973–74 |
| Joyce Colman (Hughes) | Barbara Rodell | 1973–81 |
| Marion Connelly, R.N. | Clarice Blackburn | 1976–78 |
| Jay Connors | Breck Jamison | 1984–86 |
| Dorothy Connors | Nancy Pinkerton Peabody | 1984–85 |
| Thornton Converse | Dan Hamilton | 1988 |
| Valerie Reynolds Conway(Keith) | Judith McConnell | 1976–79 |
| Nick Conway | Douglas Travis | 1978 |
| Dr. Tony Cook | Jeffrey Donovan | 1994–95 |
| Matt Cooper | Edward Grover | Early 70s |
| Harriet Corbman | Sloane Shelton | 1985–91 |
| Tina Cornell | Rebecca Holden | 1978 |
| Nick Costello | Rick Giolito | 1986–88 |
| Maggie Crawford (Andropoulos) | Mary Linda Rapeleye | 1981–85 |
| Darryl Crawford | Rex Smith | 1990–92 |
| Carolyn Crawford | Leslie Denniston | 1990–91 |
| Carrie Crawford | Felicia Cambi | 1991–92 |
| Colin Crowley | Christopher Cousins | 1990–91 |
| Colin Crowley | Jeffrey Hayenga | 1988 |
| Colin Crowley | Howard McGillin | 1987 |
| Douglas Cummings | John Wesley Shipp | 1985–86 |
| Pat Cunningham | Jean Mowry | Late 50s |
| Anton Cunningham | Patrick Horgan | 1987 |
| Lord Stewart Cushing | Ross Kettle | 1985 |
| Thelma Dailey | Jenny O'Hara | 1991 |
| Heather Dalton | Tonya Pinkins | 1984–86 |
| Lionel Dalton | Earle Hyman | 1985 |
| Lionel Dalton | Jim Moody | 1984 |
| Denise Darcy | Marie Marshall | 1986; 1988 |
| Marsha Davidson | Elizabeth Lawrence | Mid 70s |
| George Davidson | Lawrence Weber | Mid 70s |
| Spence Davies | Robert Tyler | 1988 |
| Jack Davis | Martin Sheen | Mid 60s–Early 70s |

| CHARACTER | ACTOR | DATE |
|---|---|---|
| Meredith Delaney | Wendy Benson | 1992 |
| Dr. Philip Deming | Ed Bryce | Early 70s |
| Carol Deming (Hughes Stallings Andropoulos Frazier) | | |
| | Rita McLaughlin Walter | 1970–81 |
| Jack Devere | Darnell Williams | 1994–95 |
| Evelyn DeWitt (Lewis) | Ellen Tobie | 1991 |
| Charles DeWitt | Forrest Compton | 1991 |
| John Dixon | Larry Bryggman | 1969–Present |
| Andrew Dixon | Scott DeFreitas | 1985–95 |
| Andrew Dixon | Sean Anthony | 1983–84 |
| Andrew Dixon | Alfie Smith | 1982 |
| Andrew Dixon | Robert Dwyer | 1980 |
| Andrew Dixon | Jason Ferguson | 1976–79 |
| M.J. Dixon | Leonard Manning | 1993–94 |
| Jeff Dolan | Ryan Reid | 1989 |
| Tracey Donely | Sarah Knowlton | 1994–95 |
| R.J. Donely | Dane Leach | 1994–95 |
| Burke Donovan | David Forsythe | 1983 |
| Dustin Donovan | Brian Bloom | 1983–88 |
| Mitchell Dru | Geoffrey Lumb | Late 50s–Early 60s |
| Stan Eastman | Joel Stedman | Early 70s |
| Marty Egan | Don Scardino | Early 70s |
| Dave Egan | Ken Garito | 1994 |
| John Eldridge | Michael Levin | 1991–92 |
| John Eldridge | Nicolas Coster | 1966 |
| Scott Eldridge | Doug Wert | 1995–Present |
| Scott Eldridge | Christopher Cass | 1993 |
| Scott Eldridge | Joe Breen | 1992–93 |
| Helen Eldridge | Anne Shropshire | 1991 |
| Carl Eldridge | Richard Backus | 1991–92 |
| Thomas Eldridge | Mark Deakins | 1992 |
| Hank Eliot | Brian Stracher | 1988–89 |
| Bruce Elliot | James Pritchett | 1962 |
| Linda Elliot | Bonnie Toman | Early 60s |
| Linda Elliot | Beverly Owen | Early 60s |
| Dr. Russ Elliot | Richard Backus | 1984–85 |
| Mary Ellison (Hughes) | Kelly Wood | 1975–80 |
| Brian Ellison | Robert Hover | 1975 |
| Teddy Ellison | Timothy Hill | 1979–80 |
| Teddy Ellison | Vincent Capalupo | 1979 |
| Teddy Ellison | Tommy Baudo | 1979 |
| Teddy Ellison | Joseph Christopher | Late 70s |
| Teddy Ellison | Jason Matzner | Mid 70s |
| Emma | Alice Yourman | Late 60s |
| Emmett | John DeVries | 1983–84 |
| Judy English | Sibyl Collier | Mid 60s |
| Sierra Esteban (Reyes Montgomery) | | |
| | Finn Carter | 1985–88 |
| Kathy Evans | Catherine Kellner | 1987–88 |
| Richard Fairchild III | Norman Snow | 1983 |
| Beau Farrell | Neil Maffin | 1988–89 |
| Dr. Steve Farrell | Phil Peters | 1978 |
| Joe Fernando | Michael Lombard | Early 70s |
| Dr. Field | Jonathan Frid | Mid 60s |

| CHARACTER | ACTOR | DATE |
|---|---|---|
| Dr. Field | Sheppard Strudwick | Mid 60s |
| Kitty Fielding | Margaret Klenck | 1992 |
| Dr. Fisher | James Ray | Late 60s |
| Adelaide Fitzgibbon | Susan Brown | 1988 |
| Dr. Ben Forrest | David Bailey | 1983 |
| Stacey Forrest | Danielle DuClos | 1983 |
| Tucker Foster | Eddie Earl Hatch | 1982–85 |
| Lincoln Foster | Ron Foster | 1982 |
| Roy Franklin | Count Stovall | 1985–89 |
| Nella Franklin | Kasi Lemmons | 1986–89 |
| Nella Franklin | Victoria Rowell | 1988 |
| Nella Franklin | Tiffani Caesar | 1985–86 |
| Leonard Franklin | Mel Winkler | 1986 |
| Sarah Franklin | Novella Nelson | 1986 |
| Rev. Norman Frazier | Norman Walter | 1985 |
| Freda | Peg Small | 1991 |
| Dr. George Frey | George Petrie | Late 50s–Early 60s |
| Connie Fuller | Wendy Girard | 1979 |
| Sara Fuller | Gloria DeHaven | 1966–67 |
| Lexi Funk | Annie Meisels | 1993–94 |
| Emerson Gallagher | John Cunningham | 1992 |
| Mark Galloway | Anthony Herrera | 1974–75 |
| Mark Galloway | Stephen Bolster | 1974 |
| Norman Garrison | Michael Minor | 1975 |
| Simon Gibley | Jerry Lacy | 1971 |
| Kevin Gibson | Steven Weber | 1985–86 |
| Ron Gillette | Malcolm Gets | 1994 |
| Ron Gillette | Tony Carlin | 1991–94 |
| Sally Graham | Kathleen Cody | Late 60s |
| Marian Graham (Burton) | Laurie Heineman | 1973 |
| Nikki Graves | Jordana Brewster | 1995–Present |
| Lynda Graves | Priscilla Lopez | 1995 |
| Melinda Gray (Spencer) | Ariane Munker | 1978–80 |
| Fred Greer | William Bogart | 1989–94 |
| Mr. Grey | Robert Kasel | 1992–95 |
| Cora Griffin | Barbara Hayes | Mid 60s |
| Jessica Griffin (McKechnie) | Joanna Rhinehart | 1995–Present |
| Jessica Griffin (McKechnie) | Tamara Tunie | 1987–95 |
| Ward Griffin | Arthur French | 1990 |
| Ward Griffin | Carl Gordon | 1990 |
| Louise Griffin | Billie Allen | 1990 |
| Lamar Griffin | Chris Walker | 1995 |
| Lamar Griffin | Michael Genet | 1990–95 |
| Lamar Griffin | Vince Williams | 1988 |
| Fiona Griffin | Iona Morris | 1988 |
| Damian Grimaldi | Paolo Seganti | 1993–96 |
| Eduardo Grimaldi | Nicolas Coster | 1993–95 |
| Orlena Grimaldi | Lynn Milgrim | 1995 |
| Orlena Grimaldi | Claire Bloom | 1994–95 |
| Luke Grimaldi | Spencer Goodnow | 1995 |
| Bennet Hadley | Doug Higgins | 1979 |
| Alice Hammond | Imogene Coca | 1983 |
| Cynthia Haines | Linda Dano | 1981–82 |
| Karen Haines (Stenbeck Dixon) | Kathy McNeil | 1981–84 |

| CHARACTER | ACTOR | DATE |
|---|---|---|
| Meredith Halliday | Nina Hart | 1970–71 |
| Jerry Halpern | Harry Spillman | 1985–86 |
| Jef Hamlin | Christopher Fuller | 1994–95 |
| Rick Hamlin | Robert Vaughn | 1995 |
| Juliette Hanovan | Tracy Kolis | 1984 |
| Hans | Gerrit Vooren | 1993–95 |
| Bill Harper | Wayne Maugans | 1991 |
| Bill Harper | John Dossett | 1989–90 |
| Vicki Harper | Donna Mitchell | 1991–92 |
| Anthony Harper | Michael Hammond | 1991–92 |
| Glenn Harrington | Richard Burgi | 1988–89 |
| Mark Harrington | Christopher Durham | 1989 |
| Felix Harrison | Kevin Ramsey | 1991 |
| Jack Haskell | David Cryer | 1985 |
| Graham Hawkins | Nick Ullett | 1992 |
| Sam Hayden | Michael Hayden | 1993 |
| Harry Haywood | David Froman | 1981 |
| Steve Hennessy | Robert Mackey | 1992–93 |
| Steve Hennessy | James Carroll | 1992 |
| Hey You/Bruce Dreyfuss | Jean Wolfman | 1989–90 |
| Joel Higgins | Damian Leake | 1991–95 |
| Sylvia Hill (Suker) | Millette Alexander | 1964–66 |
| Avril Hobson | Norman Parker | 1986 |
| Stan Holden (Harper) | W.T. Martin | 1981–83 |
| Pat Holland (Dixon), R.N. | Melinda Peterson | 1967–77 |
| Brad Hollister | Peter Brouwer | 1980–81 |
| Eric Hollister | Peter Reckell | 1980–82 |
| Ann Holmes | Augusta Dabney | 1966–67 |
| Bill Holmes | William Prince | 1966–67 |
| Amanda Holmes | Deborah S. Soloman | 1966–70 |
| Ginny Hopkins | Robin Groves | Late 70s |
| Dr. Howard | Joe Sirola | Early 60s |
| Dr. Len Howell | Robert Elston | 1981 |
| Arthur Howell | Chip Zien | 1995 |
| Det. Hoyt | James Secrest | 1987 |
| John Hughes | Walter Burke | Early 60s |
| John Hughes | Laurence Hugo | Late 50s |
| Chris Hughes | Don MacLaughlin | 1956–86 |
| Nancy Hughes (McClosky) | Helen Wagner | 1956–Present |
| Dr. Bob Hughes | Don Hastings | 1960–Present |
| Bob Hughes | Ronnie Welch | 1958–60 |
| Bob Hughes | Bobby Alford | 1956–58 |
| Penny Hughes (Baker Wade McGuire Cunningham) | Rosemary Prinz | 1956–68; 1985; 1986–87 |
| Penny Hughes | Phoebe Dorin | 1971 |
| Donald Hughes | Conrad Fowkes | 1978–81 |
| Donald Hughes | Martin West | 1977–78 |
| Donald Hughes | Peter Brandon | 1966–72 |
| Donald Hughes | James Noble | 1962 |
| Donald Hughes | Richard Holland | 1956–62 |
| Donald Hughes | Hal Studer | 1956 |
| Will (Grandpa) Hughes | Santos Ortega | 1956–76 |
| Will (Grandpa) Hughes | William Lee | 1956 |

| CHARACTER | ACTOR | DATE | CHARACTER | ACTOR | DATE |
|---|---|---|---|---|---|
| Edith Hughes (Frey) | Ruth Warrick | 1956–60 | Royce Keller | Terry Lester | 1992–94 |
| Tom Hughes | Scott Holmes | 1987–Present | Gloria Walters Keller | Elizabeth Hubbard | 1993 |
| Tom Hughes | Gregg Marx | 1984–87 | Chip Kelly | James Carroll | 1979 |
| Tom Hughes | Jason Kincaid | 1984 | Matt Kelly | John Tripp | 1979 |
| Tom Hughes | Justin Deas | 1981–84 | Gail Kincaid | Stephanie Roth | 1990 |
| Tom Hughes | Tom Tammi | 1979–80 | Patricia Kingsley | Rebecca Holden | 1993–94 |
| Tom Hughes | C. David Colson | 1973–78 | Andrea Korackas | Patricia Mauceri | 1980–81 |
| Tom Hughes | Peter Galman | 1969–74 | Sophia Korackas | Robin Leary | 1981–82 |
| Tom Hughes | Peter Link | 1969 | Madame Koster | Marilyn Raphael | 1982 |
| Tom Hughes | Paul O'Keefe | 1967–68 | Marie Kovac | Mady Kaplan | 1985 |
| Tom Hughes | Richard Thomas | 1966–67 | Ian "Duke" Kramer (Dixon) | Michael Louden | 1989–91 |
| Tom Hughes | Frankie Michaels | 1964–66 | Joe Kravitz | Abe Vigoda | 1985 |
| Tom Hughes | Jerry Schaffer | 1963 | Gavin Kruger | Mark Tymchyshyn | 1990–92 |
| Tom Hughes | James Madden | 1963 | Gavin Kruger | Joris Stuyck | 1990 |
| Amy Lin Hughes | Una Kim | 1986–87 | Linc Lafferty | Lonnie McCullough | 1993 |
| Amy Lin Hughes | Irene Yaah–Ling Sun | 1973–74 | Linc Lafferty | James Wlcek | 1990–92 |
| Frannie Hughes (Crawford) | Mary Ellen Stuart | 1989–92 | Hannah Lafferty | Lee Bryant | 1991–94 |
| Frannie Hughes | Julianne Moore | 1985–88 | Dana Lambert | Louise Roberts | 1991–92 |
| Frannie Hughes | Terri VandenBosch | 1983–84 | Billy Lambert | Michael Lord | 1991–92 |
| Frannie Hughes | Helene Udy | 1983 | Rod Landry/ Josh Snyder (Landry) | | |
| Frannie Hughes | Tracy O'Neil | 1980 | | William Fichtner | 1987–89 |
| Frannie Hughes | Maura Gilligan | 1975–79 | Ed Lang | Jay Barney | Mid 60s |
| Frannie Hughes | Kelly Campbell | 1973 | Angel Lange (Snyder Snyder) | Alice Haining | 1988–94 |
| Sabrina Hughes | Claire Beckman | 1990–92 | Henry Lange | James Rebhorn | 1988–91 |
| Sabrina Hughes (Fullerton) | Julianne Moore | 1986–88 | Barclay Lange | John Ottavino | 1988–91 |
| Christopher Hughes | Christian Seifert | 1992–Present | Stephen Lange | Ray Virta | 1991 |
| Christopher Hughes | Eren Ross Cannata | 1990–91 | Jay Lange | James Harlow | 1991 |
| Christopher Hughes | Adam Hirshan | 1987–90 | Dr. Howard Lansing | Charles Cioffi | 1986 |
| Lien Hughes | Ming–Na Wen | 1988–91 | Monica Lawrence (Eldridge) | Juliet Pritner | 1992 |
| Adam Hughes | Harry Zittel | 1996–Present | Monica Lawrence | Julianne Lowery | 1986–88 |
| Adam Hughes | Michael Zderko | 1989–95 | Corrine Lawrence | Patricia Gage | 1986–87 |
| Adam Hughes | Phillip Webster Smith IV | 1988–89 | Mark Lewis | Biff Warren | 1978 |
| Casey Hughes | Cruise Russo | 1991–Present | Cynthia Linders | Linda Cook | 1992–93 |
| Brianne Hunt | Jordan Baker | 1991 | Brock Lombard | Gregory Beecroft | 1989–90 |
| Lucy Hunter | Linda Cook | 1981 | Marjorie Lombard | Mary Ann Urbano | 1989–90 |
| Alexander "Hutch" Hutchinson | Judson Mills | 1991–93 | Philip Lombard | David Cryer | 1989–90 |
| Woody Hutchinson | Dan Ziskie | 1991–93 | Connie Lombard | Barbara Caruso | 1989–90 |
| Mary Jackson | Abby Lewis | Early–Mid 60s | Lonnie | Matthew Cowles | 1983 |
| Fred Jackson | Joseph Boland | Early 60s | Dr. Eric Lonsberry | Douglas Marland | Early 70s |
| Al James | Donald Madden | Late 50s | Jim Lowell | Les Damon | 1956–57 |
| Mr. Jason | Joe Silver | Late 50s | Claire Lowell (Cassen) | Barbara Berjer | 1965–71 |
| Dr. Bill Jenkins | John Swearingen | Early 70s | Claire Lowell | Joan Allison | 1964–65 |
| Bessie Jennings | Bibi Osterwald | Mid–Late 60s | Claire Lowell | Nancy Wickwire | 1960–64 |
| George Jessup | Stephen Beach | 1992 | Claire Lowell | Gertrude Warner | 1960 |
| Jester | Terrence Mann | 1987 | Claire Lowell | Anne Burr | 1956–59 |
| Joe | Joseph Julian | Early60s | Judge James Lowell | William Johnstone | 1956–79 |
| Kira Johnson | Lauryn Hill | 1991 | Ellen Lowell (Stewart) | Patricia Bruder | 1960–Present |
| Katherine Johnson | Kim Staunton | 1991 | Ellen Lowell | Wendy Drew | 1956–60 |
| Samantha Jones | Juanita Mahone | 1983 | Jane MacDonald (Bingham) | Ann Mitchell | 1985 |
| Peter Kane Arlen | Dean Snyder | Late 60s–Early 70s | Mike Malloy | Rudolph Willrich | 1983 |
| Mike Kasnoff | Shawn Christian | 1994–Present | Wayne Manning | Marcus Lovett | 1992 |
| Mark Kasnoff | Alexander Walters | 1995–Present | Ruth Mansfield | Ann Flood | 1992–93 |
| Laurie Keaton | Laurel Delmar | Mid–Late 70s | Laura March | Georgann Johnson | Early 60s |
| Dr. Alex Keith | Jon Cypher | 1977–79 | Tony Marino | Carmine Stipo | Early 70s |

| CHARACTER | ACTOR | DATE |
|---|---|---|
| Maria Marino | Jill Harmon | Early 70s |
| Samantha Markham (Anderson) | Brooke Alexander | 1994–Present |
| Eliot Markham | Philip Bosco | 1994 |
| Miranda Marlowe (Hughes) | Elaine Princi | 1981–82 |
| Lydia Marlowe | Zsa Zsa Gabor | 1981 |
| Bilan Marlowe | Kathleen Rowe McAllen | 1982 |
| Karen Martell | Dee Hoyt | 1992 |
| Dick Martin | Edward Kremmer | 1966–70; 1975–1978 |
| Dick Martin | Joe Maross | 1966 |
| Otto Martin | Allen Nourse | 1966–68 |
| Derek Mason | Thomas Gibson | 1989–90 |
| Niles Mason | Charles Keating | 1989–90 |
| Trish Mason | Sherry Ramsey | 1989–90 |
| Matthew | Paul Bartel | 1986–95 |
| Cliff Matson | Jay Acovone | 1982 |
| Dr. Henry Matthews | David Brand | 1990–91 |
| Dr. Wally Matthews | Charles Siebert | Early–Mid 70s |
| Janice Maxwell | Holly Cate | 1993–95 |
| Lt. Dan McClosky | Dan Frazer | 1984–Present |
| Whit McColl | Robert Horton | 1982–84 |
| Brian McColl | Mark Pinter | 1984–87 |
| Brian McColl | Frank Telfer | 1982–84 |
| Brian McColl | Robert Burton | 1982 |
| Kirk McColl | Christian J. LeBlanc | 1983–85 |
| Diana McColl | Kim Ulrich | 1983–85 |
| Charmane L'Amour McColl | Lee Meredith | 1983–84 |
| Larry McDermott | Ed Fry | 1990–95 |
| L.J. McDermott | Robert Hogan | 1991 |
| Alison McDermott | Amy Princine | 1994–Present |
| Ian McFarland | Peter Simon | 1979–80 |
| Roy McGuire | Konrad Matthaei | 1966–68 |
| Sandy McGuire (Garrison Thompson) | Barbara Rucker | 1975–79 |
| Sandy McGuire | Ronnie Carrol | 1975 |
| Sandy McGuire (Hughes) | Jill Andre | 1968 |
| Sandy McGuire (Hughes) | Dagne Crane | 1966–71 |
| Jimmy McGuire | Michael Cody | Mid–Late 60s |
| Dr. Marsha McKay | Justine Miceli | 1992–93 |
| Duncan McKechnie | Michael Swan | 1986–95 |
| Beatrice McKechnie (McColl) | Ashley Crow | 1986–87 |
| Lilith McKechnie | Sara Botsford | 1988;90 |
| Bonnie Louise McKechnie | Carolyn Aimetti | 1993–Present |
| Nurse Meade | Lori March | Early 60s |
| Dr. Meadows | John Boruff | Late 50s–Mid 60s |
| Anne Meadows | Barbara Joyce | Late 50s–Early 60s |
| Dr. Lynn Michaels | Courtney Simon | 1985-Present |
| Lois Middleton | Diane Franklin | 1979 |
| Lisa Miller (Hughes Eldridge Shea Colman McColl Mitchell Grimaldi) | Eileen Fulton | 1960–Present |
| Lisa Miller (McColl) | Betsy Von Furstenberg | 1983–84 |
| Lisa Miller | Pamela King | 1964 |
| Alma Miller | Dorothy Blackburn | 1978 |
| Alma Miller | Ethel Remey | 1963–77 |
| Alma Miller | Joanna Roos | Late 50s |
| Henry Miller | Luis van Route | Late 50s–Early 60s |
| Renata Minardi | Elizabeth Satre | 1993–94 |
| Mary Mitchell | Joan Anderson | 1963–65 |
| Ralph Mitchell | Keith Charles | 1977–Present |
| Sally Mitchell | Delphi Harrington | Late 70s |
| Earl Mitchell | Farley Granger | 1986–87 |
| Dr. Henry | Moller John Seitz | 1982 |
| Lyla Montgomery (Peretti), R.N. | Anne Sward | 1981-94 |
| Lyla Montgomery, R.N. | Velekka Gray | 1980 |
| Margo Montgomery (Hughes) | Ellen Dolan | 1990–93; 94–Present |
| Margo Montgomery (Hughes) | Glynnis O'Connor | 1993–94 |
| Margo Montgomery (Hughes) | Hillary Bailey Smith | 1983–90 |
| Margo Montgomery (Hughes) | Margaret Colin | 1981–83 |
| Cricket Montgomery (Ross) | Lisa Loring | 1981–83 |
| Bart Montgomery | Jim Raymond | Early–Mid 80s |
| Craig Montgomery | Scott Bryce | 1982–87; 90–94 |
| Bryant Montgomery | Jamie Kenyon | 1986 |
| Lorrie Moore | Nandrea–Lin Courts | 1988–89 |
| Hal Munson | Benjamin Hendrickson | 1985–Present |
| Harold Munson | Barton Heyman | 1989 |
| Claire Munson (Shelby) | Kirtan Coan | 1989 |
| Jennifer Munson | Alexandra Herzog | 1995 |
| Jennifer Munson | Brianne Sassone | 1993–94 |
| Jennifer Munson | Sara Garney | 1990–93 |
| Will Munson | John Pink | 1993–Present |
| Nicole | Magda Wawrzyniak | 1991–92 |
| Blythe Nelson | Shelly Conger | 1990 |
| Elroy Nevins | Cliff Weissman | 1992–93 |
| Jim Norman | James Broderick | 1962 |
| Nurse Claire | Karen Fineman | 1995 |
| Shannon O'Hara (McKechnie) | Margaret Reed | 1985–90; 94–95 |
| Mary Pat O'Neil | Barbara Garrick | 1987 |
| Mr. Parsons | William Prince | Early 70s |
| Mrs. Parsons | Augusta Dabney | Early 70s |
| Dr. Casey Peretti | Bill Shanks | 1986–90 |
| Kate Peretti Cori | Ann Hansen | 1989–94 |
| Joe Peretti | Frank Biancamano | 1987–90 |
| Maureen Peretti | Luce Ennis | 1987–90 |
| Karen Peters | Leslie Denniston | 1978 |
| Miss Peterson | Margaret Hamilton | 1971 |
| Miss Peterson | Nancy Andrews | 1971 |
| Hester Pierce | Ann Stanchfield | 1979 |
| Charles Pierson | Ben George | 1987–88 |
| Tom Pope | Charles Baxter | Late 50s–Early 60s |
| Tom Pope | Hal Hamilton | Late 50s |
| Luke Porter | Ted Agress | Mid 70s |
| Margaret Porter | Kathleen Noone | Mid 70s |
| Rick Putnam | Tony Cummings | 1985 |
| Peter Quinn | George Petrie | 1964–74 |
| Rachel | Tracey Douglas | 1995-Present |
| Rachel | Lisa Gay Hamilton | 1995 |

| CHARACTER | ACTOR | DATE |
|---|---|---|
| Cal Randolph | Luke Reilly | 1984–85 |
| Peggy Reagan | Lisa Cameron | Early 70s |
| Chris Reagan | Ingrid Helmke | Early 70s |
| Reenie | Amy Ryan | 1990 |
| Rennie | Welker White | 1989 |
| Tonio Reyes | Peter Boynton | 1986–91 |
| Mr. Renyolds | Herb Nelson | Late 60s |
| Kim Sullivan Reynolds (Dixon Stewart Andropoulos Hughes) | Kathryn Hays | 1972–Present |
| Kim Sullivan Reynolds (Dixon) | Patty McCormack | 1975–76 |
| Carol Rice | Gloria Hoye | Early 60s |
| Ed Rice | John McMartin | Early 60s |
| Edna Rice | Helen Shields | Early 60s |
| Mr. Rice | Judson Laire | Early 60s |
| Tina Richards | Toni Bull Bua | 1975 |
| Ed Richardson | Frank Thomas Jr. | Early 60s |
| Hank Robinson | Kipp Whitman | Late 70s |
| Joan Rogers | Joan Copeland | 1966–67 |
| Ted Rogers | Clifford Carpenter | 1966–67 |
| Candace Rogers | Anne Lange | 1992 |
| Dr. Bethany Rose | Tovah Feldshuh | 1994 |
| Ernie Ross | Marshall Watson | 1982–83 |
| Dr. Chuck Ryan | Don Chastain | Early 60s |
| Dr. Chuck Ryan | Michael Ebert | Early 60s |
| Dr. Chuck Ryan | Bob Kaliban | Early 60s |
| Jennifer Sullivan Ryan (Hughes) | Gillian Spencer | 1972–75 |
| Jennifer Sullivan Ryan (Hughes) | Geraldine Court | 1971–72 |
| Dr. Rick Ryan | Gary Hudson | 1978 |
| Dr. Rick Ryan | Con Roche | 1972–73; 86 |
| Barbara Ryan (Stenbeck Stenbeck Munson) | Colleen Zenk Pinter | 1978–Present |
| Barbara Ryan | Donna Wandrey | 1971–72 |
| Barbara Ryan | Barbara Stanger | Early 70s |
| Barbara Ryan | Judi Rolin | Early 70s |
| Dr. Audrey Samuels | Maggie Burke | 1986–Present |
| Helen Saunders | Lisa Howard | Early 60s |
| Lt. Gary Savage | Lloyd Allen | 1981–82 |
| Sawyer | Barry Cullison | 1989–91 |
| Doug Schaff | Terry Eno | 1994 |
| Doug Schaff | Adam LeFeure | 1994 |
| Dr. Michael Shea | Roy Shuman | 1968–70 |
| Dr. Michael Shea | Jay Lanin | 1966–68 |
| Chuck Shea | David Perkins | Mid 70s |
| Chuck Shea | Shane Nickerson | Early 70s |
| Chuck Shea | Johnny Breen | Early 70s |
| Chuck Shea | Willie Rook | Early 70s |
| Chuck Shea | Roger Morgan | Early 70s |
| Chuck Shea | Pip Sarser | Early 70s |
| Chuck Shea | Keith Pomeroy | Early 70s |
| Tess Shelby | Parker Posey | 1991–92 |
| Laura Simmons | Carolyn Clark | 1988 |
| Simon | Roderick Cook | 1984 |
| Ned Simon | Frank Converse | 1992–94 |
| Debbie Simon | Sharon Case | 1992–93 |
| Valerie Simon | Sigrunn Omark | 1992–94 |
| Ike Slattery | William Hickey | 1983 |
| Jerry Smith | Haywood Nelson | Early 70s |
| Smythe (Bettina Grimaldi) | Annette Miller | 1995 |
| Dr. Snyder | Ed Prentiss | Mid 50s |
| Holden Snyder | Jon Hensley | 1985–89; 90–95 |
| Emma Snyder | Kathleen Widdoes | 1985–Present |
| Iva Snyder (Benedict) | Lisa Brown | 1985–94 |
| Meg Snyder (Reyes Landry) | Jennifer Ashe | 1986–89 |
| Seth Snyder | Steve Basset | 1986–88; 91–94 |
| Caleb Snyder | Graham Winton | 1992–95 |
| Caleb Snyder | Michael David Morrison | 1988–92 |
| Ellie Snyder (Anderson) | Renee Props | 1988–92 |
| Aaron Snyder | Mason Boccardo | 1991–95 |
| Raymond Speer | Donald May | 1984 |
| Julie Spencer | Lynne Rogers | Early 60s |
| Julie Spencer | Lisa Howard | Late 50s |
| Beau Spencer | Wayne Hudgins | 1977–79 |
| Jane Spencer | Georgann Johnson | 1977–79 |
| Dr. David Spiros | Munson Hicks | 1993 |
| Spree | Dana Kaminski | 1985 |
| Jay Stallings | Dennis Conney | 1973–80 |
| Gil Stallings | Edward Grover | Early 70s |
| Amy Stallings | Claire Doyle | Early 80s |
| Bert Stanton | Peter Donat | Late 50s |
| Mr. Steiner | Dan Frazer | Late 60s |
| Mrs. Steiner | Margaret Hayes | Late 60s |
| Mother Steiner | Dorit Kelton | Late 60s |
| James Stenbeck | Anthony Herrera | 1980–83; 86–87; 89 |
| Gunnar St. Clare Stenbeck | Hugo Napier | 1982–85 |
| Paul Stenbeck (Ryan) | Andrew Kavovit | 1986–91 |
| Paul Stenbeck | Damion Scheller | 1986 |
| Paul Stenbeck | C.B. Barnes | 1985–86 |
| Paul Stenbeck | Eldin Ratliss | Mid 80's |
| Paul Stenbeck | Danny Pintauro | 1983–84 |
| Dr. Jerry Stevens | Roy Poole | 1964–65 |
| Dr. Jerry Stevens | Stephen Elliot | Early 60s |
| Blake Stevens | Peter Francis James | 1989–90 |
| Dr. David Stewart | Henderson Forsythe | 1960–90 |
| Dr. David Stewart | Ernest Graves | Early 60s |
| Betty Stewart | Patricia Benoit | 1960–62 |
| Paul Stewart | Dean Santoro | 1970–71 |
| Paul Stewart | Marco St. John | 1969–70 |
| Paul Stewart | Garson DeBramenio | 1969 |
| Paul Stewart | Michael Hawkins | 1968 |
| Paul Stewart | Steven Mines | 1966–68 |
| Paul Stewart | Edmund Gaynes | 1964–67 |
| Paul Stewart | Alan Howard | 1962–64 |
| Dan Stewart | John Colenback | 1966–73; 76–79 |
| Dan Stewart | John Reilly | 1974–76 |
| Dan Stewart | Jeffrey Rowland | 1966 |
| Dan Stewart | Doug Chapin | 1964 |

| CHARACTER | ACTOR | DATE |
|---|---|---|
| Dan Stewart | Paul O'Keefe | 1962–63 |
| Carol Ann (Annie) Stewart (Ward) | Mary Lynn Blanks | 1982–84 |
| Carol Ann (Annie) Stewart | Randall Edwards | 1982 |
| Carol Ann (Annie) Stewart (Hollister) | | |
| | Julie Ridley | 1980–82 |
| Carol Ann (Annie) Stewart (Spencer) | | |
| | Martina Deignan | 1976–79 |
| Carol Ann (Annie) Stewart | Shelly Spurlock | 1973–74 |
| Carol Ann (Annie) Stewart | Ariane Munker | 1972–73 |
| Carol Ann (Annie) Stewart | Barbara Jean Ehrhardt | 1970–71 |
| Carol Ann (Annie) Stewart | Jean Mazza | 1969–70 |
| Dawn (Dee) Stewart (Dixon) | Vicky Dawson | 1982–83 |
| Dawn (Dee) Stewart (Dixon) | Jacqueline Schultz | 1979–82 |
| Dawn (Dee) Stewart | Heather Cunningham | 1980 |
| Dawn (Dee) Stewart | Marcia McClain | 1976–78 |
| Dawn (Dee) Stewart | Glynnis O'Connor | 1973 |
| Dawn (Dee) Stewart | Jean Mazza | 1972–73 |
| Dawn (Dee) Stewart | Simone Schachter | 1971 |
| Betsy Stewart (Andropoulos) | Jordan Baker | 1994 |
| Betsy Stewart (Andropoulos) | Lindsay Frost | 1984–88 |
| Betsy Stewart (Montgomery Andropoulos) | | |
| | Meg Ryan | 1982–84 |
| Betsy Stewart | Lisa Denton | 1981–82 |
| Betsy Stewart | Suzanne Davidson | 1972–80 |
| Betsy Stewart | Patricia McGuiness | 1971 |
| Betsy Stewart | Maurine Trainor | Early 70s |
| Betsy Stewart | Tiberia Mitri | Early 70s |
| Emily Stewart | Kelley Menighan | 1992–Present |
| Emily Stewart (Snyder) | Melanie Smith | 1987–90 |
| Emily Stewart | Colleen McDermott | 1986–87 |
| Emmy Stewart | Marisa Morell | 1979 |
| Emmy Stewart | Jenny Harris | 1975–79 |
| Emmy Stewart | Pat Reynolds | Mid 70s |
| Emmy Stewart | Janine Sagan | Mid 70s |
| Dr. Zachary Stone | Leon Russom | 1983–84 |
| Dr. Jim Strasfield | Geoffrey Horne | Mid–Late 70s |
| Cal Stricklyn | Patrick Tovatt | 1988–Present |
| Capt. Aaron Striker | Mark Gordon | 1983 |
| Dr. Al Suker | Michael Ingram | 1964–66 |
| Martha Suker | Ann Hegira | 1964 |
| Helene Suker | Jerrianne Raphael | 1964 |
| Cody Sullivan | Beau Gravitte | Early 80s |
| Jade Sullivan | Laura Baler | 1990–92 |
| Dr. Sussman | John Rothman | 1992 |
| Otis Sutton | Charles Brown | 1987 |
| Charles Svenstrom | Roy K. Stevens | Early 80s |
| Elizabeth Talbot (Stewart) | Judith McGilligan | 1972–73 |
| Elizabeth Talbot (Stewart) | Jane House | 1969–72 |
| Ronnie Talbot | Curt Dawson | 1973 |
| Ronnie Talbot | Peter Stuart | 1970 |
| Mrs. Talbot | Eleanor Wilson | Late 60s |
| Marsha Talbot | Giulia Pagano | 1985–86 |
| Jeffrey Talbot | Sam Stoneburner | 1993 |
| Gary Tanner | Brian Brownlee | Early 70s |
| Inez Tariche | Barbara Gonzalez | 1992 |

| CHARACTER | ACTOR | DATE |
|---|---|---|
| Richard Taylor | Michael Finn | Early 70s |
| Richard Taylor | Arthur Marcus | Early 70s |
| Beverly Taylor | Wendy Edmead | 1984–85 |
| Lee Tenney | Lizbeth McKay | 1994 |
| Ray Tenney | Peter McRobbie | 1996 |
| Ray Tenney | Thomas Kopache | 1994 |
| Carly Tenney | Maura West | 1995–Present |
| Miss Thompson | Jacqueline Brookes | Early 70s |
| Kevin Thompson | Max Brown | 1978 |
| Kevin Thompson | Michael Nader | 1976–78 |
| Marcy Thompson (Cushing) | Marisa Tomei | 1983–85 |
| Peggy Thompson | Cheryl Gianni | 1984–85 |
| Dr. Larry Travis | Gary Lahti | 1981 |
| Ari Triandos | Richard Council | 1981 |
| Janice Turner (Hughes) | Virginia Dwyer | 1962 |
| Janice Turner (Hughes) | Joyce Van Patten | 1956–57 |
| Thelma Turner | Leona Powers | Mid 50s–Early 60s |
| Dr. Jerry Turner | James Earl Jones | 1966 |
| Miss Tyler | Betty Garde | Late 60s |
| Philippe Van Doren | Simon Jutras | 1991 |
| Gregory Varner | Mark Kevin Lewis | 1993–94 |
| Maurice Vermeil | David McCallum | 1983 |
| Walter Vested | Joel Stedman | Late 70s |
| Franco Visconti | Ronald Guttman | 1987 |
| Angela Visconti | Lilliana Komorowska | 1987 |
| Dr. Neil Wade | Michael Lipton | 1962–67 |
| Judith Wade (Stevens) | Connie Lembecke | 1964–67 |
| Pamela Wagner | Robin Morse | 1987–89 |
| George Waldron | Robert Fitzsimmons | Late 60s |
| Lucinda Walsh (Dixon) | Elizabeth Hubbard | 1984–Present |
| Lily Walsh (Mason Snyder Grimaldi) | | |
| | Martha Byrne | 1985–90; 93–Present |
| Lily Walsh (Snyder) | Heather Rattray | 1990–92 |
| Lily Walsh | Lucy Deakins | 1984–85 |
| Bianca Marquez Walsh | Karina Arroyave | 1989–94 |
| Bianca Marquez Walsh | Christine Langer | 1991 |
| Connor Jamison Walsh (Stricklyn) | | |
| | Allyson Rice-Taylor | 1990–Present |
| James Evan Walsh III | Greg Watkins | 1991–95 |
| Edwina Walsh (Cabot) | Rita Lloyd | 1992–95 |
| Dr. Jeff Ward | Robert Lipton | 1978–84 |
| Lowell Ward | David Goldman | 1983–84 |
| Gregory Ward | Joshua Goldman | 1983–84 |
| Nancy Ward | Arianna Goldman | 1983–84 |
| Maria Ward | Rachel Goldman | 1983–84 |
| Ken Wayne | Jered Holmes | 1985–86 |
| Rose Welinski | Lilia Skala | 1985 |
| Sparky Wells | Ray Aranha | 1994 |
| Julie Wendall (Snyder Snyder) | Susan Marie Snyder | 1989–95 |
| Frank Wendall | Keith Douglas Pruitt | 1990–91 |
| Pete Wendall | Jason Biggs | 1994–95 |
| Helen Wendall | Elizabeth Franz | 1994–95 |
| Grace Westcott (Andrews) | Kelly Bishop | 1987 |
| Dawn Wheeler | Alexandra Neil | 1993–95 |

| CHARACTER | ACTOR | DATE | CHARACTER | ACTOR | DATE |
|---|---|---|---|---|---|
| Dawn Wheeler | Lisa Emory | 1992–93 | Hayley Wilson (Hollister) | Dana Delany | 1981 |
| Jeremy Wheeler | John Dauer | 1995 | Connie Wilson | Debbie McLeod | 1981 |
| Jerry Wheeler | Sam Rovin | 1993–94 | Martha Wilson | Anna Minot | 1966–70 |
| Debbie Whipple | Kimetha Laurie | 1962 | Sheila Winston | Martha Lambert | 1979 |
| Debbie Whipple | June Harding | 1962 | Dana Woodward (McFarland) | Deborah Hobart | 1979 |
| Alice Whipple | Leslie Charleson | 1966 | Olivia Wycroft | Cynthia Dozier | 1989 |
| Alice Whipple | Jean McClintock | 1962 | Dr. Brad Wyndham | Jack Gwaltney | 1993–95 |
| Rex Whitmore | Bernie McInerney | 1985 | Dr. Sam Yee | Aki Aleong | 1981 |
| Lance Whittaker | Cain Devore | 1987 | Mary Yee | Kitty Mei–Mei Chen | 1981 |
| Greg Williams | Robert Readick | Late 50s–Early 60s | Norma Young | Dolores Sutton | Early 60s |
| Carl Wilson | Martin Rudy | 1966–71 | | | |

# "As The World Turns"

*Executive Producer:* John Valente

*Producers:* David Domedion, Vivian Gundaker

*Associate Producer:* Leela Pitenis

*Head Writers:* Stephen Black, Henry Stern

*Writers:* Don Chastain, Christina Covino, Stephen Demorest, Patti Dizenzo, Susan Kirshenbaum, John Kuntz, Mimi Leahy, Louise Shaffer, Addie Walsh, Lorin Wertheimer

*Directors:* Maria Wagner, Dan Hamilton, Charles C. Dyer, Larry Carpenter, Paul Lammers

*Production Designer:* William Mickley

*Costume Designer:* Toni-Leslie James

*Associate Directors:* Joel Aronowitz, Michael Kerner

*Assistant to the Producers:* Jef-Spenser Hira

*Production Assistants:* Tracey Hanley, Fritz Brekeller

*Stage Managers:* Jennifer W. Blood, Nancy I. Barron, Meryl Augenbraun Jaffe

*Casting Director:* Vince Liebhart, C.S.A.

*Assistant Casting Director:* Tom Alberg

*Art Director:* Christopher Clarens

*Associate Costume Designer:* Veronica Worts

*Production Coordinators:* Alexandra Verner Roalsvig, Brett Hellman, Kristen Bradley, Kimberly Pierce

*Assistant to the Writers:* Hallie Leland Leighton

*Technical Directors:* Nancy J. Stevenson, Alexander Ciecierski

*Audio:* Hal Schur, Philip Cecchini

*Lighting Designers:* Stephen Reid, Nick Varacalli

*Video:* John Kokinis

*Videotape Editors/Sound Mixers:* Steve Shatkin, Bob Mackler

*Camera:* David B. Hersh, John Hannel, Claus Stuhlweissenburg, Steve Scalcione, Dan Flaherty

*Audio Assistants:* Gregory Cordone, John Spagnola

*Sound Effects:* Sidney Bean

*Wardrobe:* Pat Smouse, Mary Jestice, Gregg Simmons, Lyle Jones

*Music Supervisor:* Jill Diamond

*Music Directors:* Robert Bard, Donovan Sylvest, Gary Deinstadt

*Set Decorators:* Dennis Donegan, Catherine McKenney, David Blankenship

*Makeup:* Deborah Sperber Paulmann, Marilyn Peoples

*Hairstylists:* Lillian Cvecich, Frank Vazquez

*Special Effects:* Bob Taylor

*Theme Music Composer:* Barry DeVorzon

*Production Supervisors:* Richard Reyes-Guerra, Vincent Verrico

*Production Manager:* Sid Sirulnick

*Main Title Design:* Castle/Bryant/Johnsen

*Executive in Charge of Production:* Kenneth L. Fitts

# PHOTO CREDITS

All photographs and video images are copyright © CBS, Inc. and are provided courtesy of CBS, Inc. Photographer credits, as available, are as follows:

Title page: E.J. Carr
7: Victoria Arlak
12: Irv Haberman
13: Emil Romano
14: Irv Haberman
15: Emil Romano
16: top left/bottom, Irv Haberman
top right, Emil Romano
17: Emil Romano
18: top, Emil Romano
19: bottom left, Bill Warnecke
right, Emil Romano
20: left, Emil Romano
21: left, Emil Romano
22: bottom, Bill Warnecke
23: Emil Romano
24: Emil Romano
27: Lennie Lautenberger
28: Bill Warnecke
35: Bill Warnecke
39: Emil Romano
42: Emil Romano
43: Irv Haberman
46: top, Irv Haberman
48: Irv Haberman
52: Helen Wagner Private Collection
57: Bob Deutsch
60: Emil Romano
70: Ira Lewis
74: Helen Wagner Private Collection
75: Ira Lewis
77: Bob Greene
98: Courtesy *Soap Opera Digest*
115: E.J. Carr
131: Don Hastings Private Collection
137: Robin Platzer/Twin Images
148: Robin Platzer/Twin Images
158: Craig Blankenhorn
160: James Levin
166: Nora Feller
179: E.J. Carr
181: E.J. Carr
182: E.J. Carr
185: Dennis Welsh
186: E.J. Carr
190: E.J. Carr
192: top, Robin Platzer/Twin Images
bottom, Victoria Arlak
194: E.J. Carr
197: Victoria Arlak
198: Victoria Arlak
199: Victoria Arlak
200: E.J. Carr
201: E.J. Carr

202: Helen Wagner Private Collection
203: bottom left, Irv Haberman
bottom right, Helen Wagner Private Collection
204: top right, Helen Wagner Private Collection
center, Robin Platzer/Twin Images
bottom, E.J. Carr
205: top, Irv Haberman
206: top, Irv Haberman
207: top, Irv Haberman
bottom right, Victoria Arlak
208: Victoria Arlak
209: top left and right and middle, E.J. Carr
bottom right, Victoria Arlak
210: Victoria Arlak
211: top right, Nora Feller
212: top left, Mike Fuller
top right, Victoria Arlak
bottom left, James Levin
bottom right, Nora Feller
213: top, Barry Morgenstein
left, Victoria Arlak
right, E.J. Carr
214: top, Victoria Arlak
bottom, E.J. Carr
215: left, Bill Warnecke
216: left, courtesy *Soap Opera Digest*
217: top left, Raeanne Rubenstein
218: top right, Nora Feller
220: top right and bottom left, Victoria Arlak
bottom right, E.J. Carr
221: top left and right, E. J. Carr
bottom, Victoria Arlak
222: top left and bottom right, E.J. Carr
bottom left and top right, Victoria Arlak
223: Victoria Arlak
224: Victoria Arlak
225: left, Victoria Arlak
right, Irv Haberman
227: bottom left, E.J. Carr
228: bottom, Victoria Arlak
229: Victoria Arlak
230: bottom, E.J. Carr
232: top left, Gregg Marx Private Collection
bottom, E.J. Carr
234: top left, Irv Haberman
bottom right, Mike Fuller
235: top left, Craig Blankenhorn
top right and bottom, Victoria Arlak
236: top left, Helen Wagner Private Collection
bottom right, E.J. Carr
238: bottom right, Victoria Arlak
239: top left, Victoria Arlak
middle, E.J. Carr
240: top left, Victoria Arlak
right, Robin Platzer/Twin Images
241: top and bottom right, Victoria Arlak
242: bottom middle and right, Victoria Arlak

243: bottom right, E.J. Carr
244: top right, Dominique Silberstein
245: bottom, Nora Feller
right, Anthony Herrera Private Collection
246: Helen Wagner Private Collection
247: Helen Wagner Private Collection
248: bottom, Helen Wagner Private Collection
249: top, E.J. Carr
left middle, Victoria Arlak
bottom, Danny Sanchez
250: E.J. Carr
251: Pinter and Alexander, E.J. Carr
252: top and bottom right, Helen Wagner Private Collection
253: top, Helen Wagner Private Collection
bottom, E.J. Carr
254-265: E.J. Carr
263: top right, Leela Pitenis Private Collection
266, 267, 268: top, E.J. Carr
269, 270: bottom, E. J. Carr
271: E. J. Carr
272: middle and bottom, Victoria Arlak
273: left, Bob Short Private Collection
middle, courtesy Procter & Gamble
right, E.J. Carr
274: left, Joe Willmore Private Collection
right, Laurence Caso Private Collection
275: E.J. Carr
276: Courtesy Procter & Gamble
277: left, E.J. Carr
279: top left, Ira Lewis
280: top left, E.J. Carr
middle, Nora Feller
right, Victoria Arlak
281: bottom left, Ira Lewis
282: bottom left, Raeanne Rubenstein
middle, E.J. Carr
283: top left, Joe Willmore Private Collection
top and bottom right, Victoria Arlak
284: Laurence Caso Private Collection
285: Emil Romano
286: Helen Wagner Private Collection
287: Byrne/Hubbard/Hastings, E.J. Carr
Rice-Taylor, Danny Sanchez
288: Alexander/Hendrickson, E.J. Carr
Williams/Brewster, Danny Sanchez
289: Emmy © The National Academy of Television Arts and Sciences
290: right, Martha Byrne Private Collection
291: bottom, Courtesy N.A.T.A.S.
292: courtesy *Soap Opera Digest*
293: top right, Sean Hahn
bottom, Yvonne Perry Private Collection
294: E.J. Carr

Front cover: Hubbard/Byrne, Robert Milazzo
All other photos, E.J. Carr
Back cover: Danny Sanchez
Author photo: Jim Mackiewicz